IMMIGRATION, INTEGRATION AND THE LAW

What does it mean to integrate or to be integrated? The European Union is based on the objective of the ever closer union of the peoples of Europe which is to be achieved by the integration of our economies. This book examines what it means to take the concept of integration from its setting in economic policy and apply to individuals, inevitably non EU citizens, as a way of categorising them with legal implications. The research is crisp and incisive and a pleasure to read. This book extends our understanding of the relationship of people belonging and law in Europe.

Elspeth Guild, Queen Mary, University of London, UK
and Radboud University Nijmegen, the Netherlands

Clíodhna Murphy's book is a well written exposé of a very complex matter. She manages to make theoretical and legal approaches to integration, as well as connections between law, integration and social realities digestible for the reader while covering the international, European, as well as national level in her analysis. Additionally, she does not shy away from developing and applying her own definition of integration in order to underpin her 'human-rights based paradigm of integration' – something not easily done by other authors.

Moritz Jesse, Leiden University, the Netherlands

The relationship between integration, law and policy remains a contested one at national, European and international arenas. Critical questions related to identity, diversity and mobility are increasingly intertwined with law in the normative realms of migration and citizenship. This nexus however poses a number of human rights and liberty challenges to the European Union and its Member States. This book provides an excellent analysis of the issues and tensions emerging from the relationship between integration and law from the perspective of states' international and European law obligations.

Sergio Carrera, Centre for European Policy Studies, Belgium

Murphy's incisive and engaging analysis of the concept of integration addresses a gap in current legal scholarship in human rights and migration law. Combining an analysis of EU, Council of Europe and UN human rights standards, this book brings together some of the most pressing legal and policy debates in the field of migration law. This text will quickly become an indispensable reference point for legal practitioners and policy makers working in the rapidly evolving field of integration.

Siobhán Mullally, University College Cork, Ireland

Law and Migration

Series Editor
Satvinder S. Juss, King's College London, UK

Migration and its subsets of refugee and asylum policy are rising up the policy agenda at national and international level. Current controversies underline the need for rational and informed debate of this widely misrepresented and little understood area.

Law and Migration contributes to this debate by establishing a monograph series to encourage discussion and help to inform policy in this area. The series provides a forum for leading new research principally from the Law and Legal Studies area but also from related social sciences. The series is broad in scope, covering a wide range of subjects and perspectives.

Other titles in this series:

Migrants and the Courts
A Century of Trial and Error?
Geoffrey Care
978-1-4094-5196-9

Regulating Marriage Migration into the UK
A Stranger in the Home
Helena Wray
978-1-4094-0338-8

Chinese Immigration Law
Guofu Liu
978-1-4094-0940-3

The Control of People Smuggling and Trafficking in the EU
Experiences from the UK and Italy
Matilde Ventrella
978-0-7546-7466-5

Gender and Migration in 21st Century Europe
Edited by Helen Stalford, Samantha Currie and Samantha Velluti
978-0-7546-7450-4

Immigration, Integration and the Law

The Intersection of Domestic, EU and International Legal Regimes

CLÍODHNA MURPHY
Dublin City University, Ireland

Routledge
Taylor & Francis Group
LONDON AND NEW YORK

First published 2013 by Ashgate Publishing

2 Park Square, Milton Park, Abingdon, Oxon OX14 4RN
711 Third Avenue, New York, NY 10017, USA

Routledge is an imprint of the Taylor & Francis Group, an informa business

First issued in paperback 2016

British Library Cataloguing in Publication Data
A catalogue record for this book is available from the British Library

The Library of Congress has cataloged the printed edition as follows:
Murphy, Clíodhna.
Immigration, integration, and the law : the intersection of domestic, EU and international legal regimes / By Clíodhna Murphy.
p. cm. -- (Law and migration)
Includes bibliographical references and index.
ISBN 978-1-4094-6251-4 (hardback)
1. Emigration and immigration law--European Union countries.
2. Immigrants--Cultural assimilation--European Union countries. 3. Social integration--European Union countries. I. Title.
KJE6044.M87 2013
342.2408'2--dc23

2013020864

ISBN 978-1-4094-6251-4 (hbk)
ISBN 978-1-138-26720-6 (pbk)

Contents

Acknowledgements

Chapter 4 is partly based on Clíodhna Murphy, 'Towards a Human Rights-Based Paradigm of Integration? The Contribution of International Law, European Human Rights Law Review' (2013) 2 *European Human Rights Law Review*. This article is reproduced, in part, with kind permission from Thomson Reuters.

Chapter 5 is a modified version of Clíodhna Murphy, 'The Concept of Integration in the Jurisprudence of the European Court of Human Rights' in *European Journal of Migration and Law*, ISSN 1388-364X, volume 12.1 (2010), pp. 23–43. This article is reprinted with kind permission from Brill.

I would like to express my deep gratitude to the many colleagues who have provided advice and assistance to me in the preparation of this book, in particular, Dr Oran Doyle, Dr Des Ryan and Dr David Fennelly, who provided invaluable comments on draft chapters. I am also particularly grateful to Professor Hilary Biehler for her encouragement throughout my time at Trinity, and for her supervision of my MLitt thesis.

Dr Eva Ersbøll (Danish Centre of Human Rights) and Dr Neville Cox (Trinity College Dublin) examined my doctoral thesis, on which this book is based, and provided welcome pointers on how it could be adapted for publication.

Most of all, I would like to thank my doctoral supervisor Dr Rosemary Byrne for her patience, her insightful comments and suggestions, her contagious enthusiasm and, above all, her constant efforts and help over the last number of years.

And, of course, I wish to thank my family, especially Shane, for all the support they have given me throughout.

List of Abbreviations

CCPR	Human Rights Committee
CEAS	Common European Asylum System
CEDAW	Convention on the Elimination of All Forms of Discrimination Against Women
CERD Committee	Committee on the Elimination of Racial Discrimination
CESCR	Committee on Economic, Social and Cultural Rights
CJEU	Court of Justice of the EU (formerly the European Court of Justice)
CMW	International Convention on the Protection of All Migrant Workers and Members of Their Families
CRC	UN Convention on the Rights of the Child
ECHR	European Convention on Human Rights
ECN	European Convention on Nationality
ECtHR	European Court of Human Rights
EU	European Union
FRD	Family Reunification Directive
ICCPR	International Covenant on Civil and Political Rights
ICERD	International Convention on the Elimination of All Forms of Racial Discrimination
ICESCR	International Covenant on Economic, Social and Cultural Rights
LTRD	Long-Term Residents Directive
MIPEX	Migrant Integration Policy Index
NGO	Non-governmental organisation
TCN	Third-country national
TEU	Treaty on European Union
TFEU	Treaty on the Functioning of the European Union
UDHR	Universal Declaration of Human Rights
UK	United Kingdom

UN	United Nations
UNHCR	The Office of the United Nations High Commissioner for Refugees
US	United States

Chapter 1
Introduction

Immigration, Integration and Law in Europe

The integration of migrants has, in recent years, emerged as a key policy area in EU Member States, as well as receiving considerable attention at the EU level, within the Council of Europe and in the work of the United Nations (UN) human rights treaty monitoring bodies. Integration is a contested concept, with some commentators arguing that the idea of integration is predicated on a rejection of diversity by migrant receiving societies.[1] The rise of 'integration' has coincided with the 'crises of multiculturalism' across Europe,[2] and the concept is frequently associated with cultural assimilation and discrimination. This frame of analysis has become increasingly relevant in the context of the increasing use of integration tests, as a mandatory condition for entry to the state or access to social welfare, residency and citizenship rights, by European states.[3] At the same time, however, competing narratives of integration centred on holistic, two-way paradigms continue to emerge from NGOs, international organizations and academics.[4] The meaning, scope and implications of integration thus remain controversial.

Despite these developments, relatively little attention has been paid to the interpretation and development of integration through law. Integration, as a social dynamic, is often viewed by policymakers, legislators and courts as a non-justiciable social concept falling outside the legal sphere. This perspective is encapsulated in the remarks of Chief Justice Keane in his judgment in the Irish Supreme Court in *AO and DL v Minister for Justice, Equality and Law Reform*,[5] in which he considered the desirability of a tolerant and pluralist society in the shadow of the

---

1 Elspeth Guild, *The Legal Elements of European Identity: EU Citizenship and Migration Law* (Kluwer Law International, 2004), p. 234.

2 See Alana Lentin and Gavan Titley, *The Crises of Multiculturalism* (Zed Books, 2011).

3 See Anja Wiesbrock, 'Discrimination Instead of Integration? Integration Requirements for Immigrants in Denmark and Germany', in Elspeth Guild, Sergio Carrera and Kees Groenendijk (eds), *Illiberal Liberal States: Immigration, Citizenship and Integration in the EU* (Ashgate, 2009).

4 Rosa Da Costa, 'Rights of Refugees in the Context of Integration: Legal Standards and Recommendations', UNHCR Legal and Protection Policy Research Series (UNHCR, June 2006); Alistair Ager and Alison Strang, 'Understanding Integration: A Conceptual Framework' (2008) 21(2) *JRS* 166.

5 [2003] 1 IR 1.

respective roles of the Parliament, executive and judiciary in immigration matters. He gave this opinion, in a passage which is worth quoting in full:

> Many would wish to see the development in Ireland of a tolerant and pluralist society capable of accommodating immigrants from diverse ethnic and cultural backgrounds, because that is a desirable objective in itself … At the same time, the legislature and executive cannot be expected to disregard the problems which an increased volume of immigration inevitably creates, because of the strains it places on the infrastructure of social services and, human nature being what it is, the difficulty of integrating people from very different ethnic and cultural backgrounds into the fabric of Irish society. The resolution of these complex political, social and economic issues which, it need hardly be said, are not in any sense unique to Ireland, is entirely a matter for the [Parliament] and the executive. The function of the courts is to ensure that the constitutional and legal rights of all the persons affected by the legislation in question are protected and vindicated.[6]

This book argues for a broader understanding of the relationship between integration and law. While the theme of integration fuses emotive social issues such as identity, belonging and social cohesion, it also raises essential legal issues which must be dealt with within the confines of domestic, EU and international law. It will be shown that these include, for example, family unity, access to the education system, the place of religion in the public sphere and the citizenship regime.

There is a small but growing body of legal scholarship addressing the development of a framework for integration at the EU level and the use of integration measures, conditions and programmes by countries across Europe.[7] Much of the existing literature analyses the interaction of integration and law solely in terms of the use of integration as a mandatory element of immigration and citizenship law, rather than looking at the wider connections between integration and law. This book aims to fill these gaps in the literature by providing a broad-based study of the interaction between law and integration. It examines the nexus between integration and law, exploring the legal dimensions of the concept of integration

6 Ibid., at 26.

7 See, for example, Saskia Bonjour, 'Between Integration Provision and Selection Mechanism. Party Politics, Judicial Constraints, and the Making of French and Dutch Policies of Civic Integration Abroad' (2010) 12(3) *EJML* 299; Ricky Van Oers, Eva Ersboll and Dora Kostakopoulou (eds), *A Re-Definition of Belonging? Language and Integration Tests in Europe* (Martinus Nijhoff Publishers, 2010); Sergio Carrera, *In Search of the Perfect Citizen? The Intersection between Integration, Immigration and Nationality in the EU* (Martinus Nijhoff, 2009); Elspeth Guild, Sergio Carrera and Kees Groenendijk (eds), *Illiberal Liberal States: Immigration, Citizenship and Integration in the EU* (Ashgate, 2009); Kerstin Rosenow, 'The Europeanisation of Integration Policies' (2009) 47(1) *International Migration* 133.

in a European and international context. In order to do this, it examines the legal and policy framework for the integration of migrants that is being constructed in selected EU Member States (Ireland, the United Kingdom and France) and critically discusses the multiple paradigms of integration that are influencing the development of these frameworks. In addition, by analysing the approaches of the UN (human rights), Council of Europe and EU systems in detail, the book will consider the actual and potential impact of these systems on national law and policy on integration.

It will be seen that the interactions between integration and law are more far-reaching than express references to integration in immigration and citizenship law. Despite the fragmented, disparate and often incoherent nature of the legal dimensions of integration identified in the course of the book, a central role for law in interpreting the meaning of the indeterminate concept of integration is identified. This study advocates a broad understanding of the nexus between integration and law, which recognizes the complexity of the concept of integration and the extent of law's influence on the integration process, taking into account the obligations of states in international and European law. The book identifies an evolving paradigm of integration as the progressive realization of equality, emerging from the universal treaty regime, which provides a real alternative to the way in which integration is being conceptualized at the national level as a mandatory process and a tool of immigration control. This model of integration as the progressive realization of equality is replicated in the EU context in the case of EU migrants. This paradigm forms the basis for a number of concrete suggestions for the development of holistic and human-rights based integration frameworks in EU Member States.

Core Questions

The central questions which are addressed by the book are as follows:

- How is the concept of integration developed through the adoption and interpretation of legal norms impacting on migrants?
- How are legal frameworks for the integration of migrants being constructed in EU Member States?
- What paradigms of integration are influencing the development of these legal frameworks, and what factors influence the implementation of these paradigms?
- How have the universal treaty regimes, the Council of Europe and the EU approached integration, and what is the actual and potential impact of the EU and international legal frameworks on integration in national law and policy?
- Is there coherence within and between the international, EU and national frameworks, and how do these frameworks inter-relate?

The book is structured in three parts. The first part addresses the meaning of integration and the nature of its relationship with law. The second analyses the legal foundations of integration at the international and regional (Council of Europe and EU) levels. The third part examines two discrete areas of law with strong links to integration as a means to consider the relationship between integration and law in the domestic setting. This structure is intended to ensure that the analysis captures the interaction of the three legal spheres relevant to this book: international, EU and national law. In this way, the significance of the international and EU law dimensions of the interaction between integration and law is highlighted. Finally, the conclusions draw together the central themes permeating the chapters, and underline the contribution of the book to a broad understanding of integration and law. As mentioned already, the conclusions also set out a number of recommendations for the development of holistic, human-rights based approaches to integration in EU Member States.

France, the UK and Ireland have been selected as the primary national examples for examination and analysis. The French case study has been at the centre of many studies specifically focussed on integration, due to France's long engagement with the concept and express reference to integration and assimilation in immigration and citizenship law.[8] In contrast, critiques of laws and policies connected to migration and 'race relations' in the UK have not generally referred to 'integration' as such, but the evolution of state responses to multiculturalism has been the subject of much comment there.[9] In addition, relatively recent moves to enshrine language and integration tests in immigration and citizenship tests in the UK have led to a discussion of the ethical and political dilemmas involved in integration.[10] The Irish example is not discussed at all in the existing body of work on integration and law. Ireland provides an example of a country which has experienced intense migratory change within the last decade and has only very recently started to publicly discuss issues relating to diversity and migration. The recent nature of the discourse on 'diversity' is surprising given Ireland's well-known history of religious and sectarian division. These three jurisdictions have

8 See, for example, Friedrich Heckmann and Dominique Schnapper (eds), *The Integration of Immigrants in European Societies – National Differences and Trends of Convergence* (Lucius and Lucius, 2003), p. 14; Saskia Bonjour, note 7; Kees Groenendijk 'Pre-departure Integration Strategies in the European Union: Integration or Immigration Policy?' 13 (2011) *EJML* 1.

9 See, for example, Arun Kundnani, *The End of Tolerance: Racism in 21st Century Britain* (Pluto Press, 2007); Derek McGhee, *The End of Multiculturalism: Terrorism, Integration and Human Rights* (Open University Press, 2008); Yasmin Alibhai-Brown, *After Multiculturalism* (Foreign Policy Centre, 2000).

10 See, for example, Bernard Ryan, 'The Integration Agenda in British Migration Law', in Elspeth Guild, Sergio Carrera and Kees Groenendijk (eds), *Illiberal Liberal States: Immigration, Citizenship and Integration in the EU* (Ashgate, 2009), p. 277; Bernard Ryan 'Integration Requirements: A New Model in Migration Law' (2008) 22(4) *Journal of Immigration Asylum and Nationality Law*.

had varied experiences of migration, citizenship and issues related to identity and integration and thus provide an interesting spectrum of approaches to integration.

Outline of the Book

Part I: Conceptual Foundations of Integration

Part I considers the conceptual basis of integration and is thus concerned with setting out some of the background relevant to the remainder of the book. Chapter 2 discusses some of the difficulties with 'integration' as a concept, but concludes that, despite these difficulties, integration is a significant and useful topic of study. It outlines a working definition of integration, based on an analysis of the Irish, Council of Europe, EU and UNHCR definitions of integration and a consideration of various integration 'models'. A number of models of integration which are commonly used to describe the basis of integration policy in different states, including Britain and France, are identified and explained, and the limitations of these models noted. A central part of this book involves questioning the usefulness of such models, and determining whether any national integration framework can be said to be based on a coherent 'model'. Some 'wider perspectives' on integration are also identified which will be used to frame the analysis in Part III. These include the links between integration and national identity; social inclusion and equality; and the management of diverse societies generally. Finally, a working definition of integration for the purposes of the rest of the book is outlined. This working definition is broad-based and emphasizes the functional and wider elements of the integration process.

Chapter 3 outlines the interactions that take place between integration and law in a number of practical settings such as citizenship, family reunification and the legal regulation of the expression of cultural and religious identity in the public sphere. It also examines the specific way in which immigration law and integration have been linked in many European countries in the form of integration requirements for entry, residence and family reunification. A key idea underlying the chapter is that this frame of analysis is not sufficiently broad to capture the complex interaction between integration and law. This chapter also suggests that legal approaches to integration are shaped by a number of factors, including a number of interacting legal frameworks (international, EU and national law), and are also inextricably linked to national identity and the 'public philosophy' of the state in question.

Part II: Legal Foundations of Integration

Part II is concerned with identifying the legal structures within which integration fits. The discussion of integration is posited within a framework of multiple legal orders: international, EU and national norms are all relevant. Chapters 4 and 5 examine the approach to integration taken in international refugee and human rights law, including under the European Convention on Human Rights (ECHR). First, the connections between international refugee law and integration are analysed. The role and value of international human rights law in addressing integration issues is then explored. The chapter examines the concluding observations on State Reports of the monitoring committees for the core UN human rights treaties, as well as the jurisprudence of the European Court of Human Rights, to determine whether there has been any normative development of the concept of integration by these international bodies. The analysis illustrates that, while international norms do not provide a comprehensive framework for integration, they impact on national integration frameworks in a number of concrete ways (which are set out in the chapters). In addition, it is argued that the normative development of integration by the UN treaty monitoring committees provides a valuable resource for the interpretation of the concept of integration in a way which avoids the problems of national public philosophy-influenced integration policy and practice, and could help to re-orientate national integration policy and practice towards a more human rights-based approach.

Chapter 6 explores the concept of integration contained in EU law and policy by looking at specific integration policy, concepts of integration contained in EU immigration and asylum law and the approach taken to the integration of EU citizen migrants. It highlights the importance of the EU approach to integration from an Irish perspective, but also points out the limits of EU action in the context of integration. The chapter illustrates that EU law encompasses numerous conceptions of integration, depending principally on the status of the individual as a citizen of the EU or a third-country national (TCN). It concludes that the EU soft law framework on the integration of TCNs is not strong enough to counterbalance the deficiencies and the problems encountered in national integration policy and practice. Moreover, the inclusive concept of integration contained in the policy documentation is in any event usurped in the legally binding immigration measures, in which the use of integration as a mandatory norm in immigration law is endorsed. In contrast, in relation to EU migrants, EU law has altered the relationship between EU citizens living and working in EU Member States other than their own, such that the idea of integration has become almost superfluous in the context of EU migrant citizens. EU law and policy on integration thus lacks coherence and enshrines multiple concepts of integration.

Part III: Functional and Wider Perspectives on Integration and Law: Domestic Legal Regimes

Part III examines a number of areas of domestic law of particular importance to integration, comparing it to the law in other jurisdictions and in light of international law. These include first of all what are described as 'functional' aspects of integration: providing a legal status and core services such as education, welfare and health services linked to that status; and secondly, aspects of integration with 'wider' connections to the broader themes of national identity, responses to diversity in society and social policy. While the themes to be examined are broken into two chapters, the themes and chapters naturally overlap and intersect, as will be clear from the analysis.

Chapter 7 considers access to citizenship in the selected EU jurisdictions in terms of both the rules relating to birthright citizenship and the law of naturalization. Citizenship is a fundamental integration issue which draws together some of the themes referred to in Part I. First, the chapter looks at some of the recent experiences and debates in Ireland, the UK and France in the area of birthright citizenship, and traces the trend in each country towards restricting access to birthright citizenship for those born in the territory of the state to non-citizen parents (*jus soli*). The next part of the chapter concentrates on access to nationality through naturalization. Access to citizenship in Ireland is contrasted to law and practice in the UK and France, which impose integration and/or language conditions in the naturalization process. Overall, it will be seen that legal access to citizenship, which is becoming increasingly restrictive in most European countries, contrasts with the importance placed on citizenship attainment in academic literature on integration. Finally, the chapter assesses the idea of integration testing in citizenship law in light of the international law of citizenship.

Chapter 8 examines the place of religion in Irish public life though an analysis of the law relating to religion and the education system, in addition to the legal regulation of the use of religious symbols in public spaces (particularly focussing on schools). First, the chapter considers some of the legal issues raised by the denominational nature of the education system at primary and secondary level. It seeks to apply the existing legal framework relating to religion and education to the new issues raised by increased religious and cultural diversity in Ireland. This is an area which has spawned significant jurisprudence in other jurisdictions and under the rubric of the ECHR. This case law will be used to inform the analysis. Secondly, the issue of religious symbols in state education and other public space will be looked at. This has emerged as a divisive and controversial integration issue in many countries with a long tradition of immigration, particularly in the UK and in France, where the wearing of Islamic dress in public schools has been the subject of extensive legal debate.

The concluding chapter draws out a number of conclusions from the common threads running through the chapters. The first of these is that integration is largely indeterminate, with a significant role for law in determining the meaning of integration. The incoherence and contradictions contained in domestic, international, and EU legal frameworks for integration are the second main conclusion. Finally, the complex intersection between the frameworks of international, EU, and national law, and the impact which this has on the shape of integration at the national level is a key finding of the book. Building on these conclusions, the book suggests two main ways in which a human rights-based approach to integration can be promoted. First, the importance of the use of a broad-based definition of integration which takes into account both its functional and wider dimensions is emphasized. Secondly, the development of a conceptual framework which recognizes and utilizes the extent of the interaction between integration and law, moving beyond the conceptualization of integration as a mandatory element of immigration law, is advocated. On this basis, a number of basic recommendations for the development of holistic and human rights-based integration policy in EU Member States are outlined.

Terminology

While the terminology used in this book is generally defined in the body of the text itself, a small number of terms require some clarification. The terms 'migrants' and 'immigrants' will be used interchangeably to describe persons who enter or reside in the territory of a state which is not that of their nationality. This encompasses – *inter alia* – voluntary migrants in search of better opportunities, family migrants, refugees and beneficiaries of other forms of international protection. The term 'third-country national' as applied in EU law means any person who is not a citizen of a Member State. The terms 'EU migrant' and 'EU citizen migrant' are both used to refer to EU citizens who exercise their right to free movement to enter or reside in another EU Member State.

Finally, the working definition of 'integration' used for the purposes of the book, the identification of which is one of the core strands of the analysis, is set out in Chapter 2. The definition is as follows:

> Integration is an on-going, multidimensional, two-way process between, on the one hand, migrants and, on the other hand, existing members of the receiving society along with the receiving state itself. This process involves a series of interlinked spheres, which, for the purposes of this book, will be characterized as forming part of "functional" or "wider" perspectives on integration. "Functional" aspects of integration include first of all protecting fundamental rights and secondly providing a legal status which acts as a gateway to the core policy areas of housing, health, education, social welfare and family reunification. "Wider" aspects of integration connect to these functional themes but place integration in its broader thematic context. These are aspects of integration with wider connections to the broader themes of national identity, responses to diversity in society, social policy and equality – most importantly, approaches to citizenship and the place of culture and religion in public space.

PART I
Conceptual Foundations of Integration

Chapter 2
The Concept of Integration

Introduction

> Integration is a chaotic concept: a word used by many but understood differently by most.[1]

The difficulty in defining integration is a pervasive problem encountered by lawyers and sociologists attempting to explore the concept, with these definitional difficulties hindering clarity of debate and the formulation of coherent policies.[2] This chapter will investigate different understandings of the concept of integration in order to develop a conceptual framework for the analysis of the relationship between integration and law. As a starting point, the philosophical and ethical difficulties surrounding the idea of 'integration' are discussed. A number of integration models which are often used to describe the responses of states to difference and diversity will then be identified and the continued usefulness of these models questioned. Multiculturalism and assimilation are the two classical opposing 'models', which have often been identified with the UK and France.

The approaches taken by the Council of Europe, UNHCR, and the EU, as well as Irish policymakers, to defining integration will then be compared in order to gain a sense of the scope of the meaning of integration. It is argued that the definitions examined broadly converge around the idea of integration as a two-way, multi-faceted and gradual process. Finally, the value of situating integration in its broader context (in particular given the circularity and incoherence which often pervades debates on the meaning of integration) will be underlined, by looking at some of the wider debates and social themes of which integration forms a part. This analysis of the variety of possible conceptualizations of integration and its broader dimensions is synthesized to develop a working definition of integration, which will be used to frame the rest of the book.

1 Vaughan Robinson, 'Defining and measuring successful refugee integration', in ECRE, *Proceedings of ECRE International conference on Integration of Refugees in Europe* (ECRE, 1998).

2 Alistair Ager and Alison Strang, 'Understanding Integration: A Conceptual Framework' (2008) 21(2) *JRS* 166.

The Philosophical Foundations of Integration: Difficulties with Integration as a Value

It cannot be taken for granted that integration is, of itself, a moral imperative. If migrants are guaranteed an effective protection of their civil and other rights including, most pressingly, the right to equality, then arguably there should be no need to 'integrate' them into society. Provided that human rights are respected, what social good does integration serve? The question of integration as a value in itself has been the subject of debate. In the UK, research commissioned by the Home Office revealed that the term is often considered problematic for a number of reasons. The 2004 report based on this research recorded that some members of the NGO and community sector, in particular, did not like the connotations of the term and would not choose to use it.[3] NGO representatives commented that integration seemed to represent a kind of medicine that newcomers should take in order to 'fit in', rather than a process which ensured that they had rights and access to services they needed. The way in which the verb can be used to suggest that people would 'be integrated' through various 'integration programmes' was felt to undermine positive concepts of empowerment, choice, growth and development.[4] These findings reflect concerns raised elsewhere that 'integration ... can too easily imply a largely one-sided process in which newcomers adapt themselves to the structures of life and dominant culture of their host society',[5] with the result that the concept of integration has 'been suspected of a homogenizing bend'.[6]

Integration can be seen as based on the fiction that migrants are to be integrated into an already functioning, consensual, organic whole.[7] Favell makes this argument as follows:

> (The) happy, idealized language of integration ... is ... an under-theorised, elite re-production of a long-lost idea of political community; papering over inequality, conflict and power relations with a therapeutical, top-down discourse of multicultural unity. Moreover, it offers hope and the glimpse of a legitimate, universal social order which *works*, in the form of a knowingly counterfactual national public philosophy, falsely projecting a normative ideal as the teleological factor of present social dynamics.[8]

3 Ibid., p. 114.

4 Ibid.

5 T. Alexander Aleinikoff and Douglas Klusmeyer (eds), *From Migrants to Citizens: Membership in a Changing World* (Carnegie, 2000), p. 20 (Introduction).

6 Rosemarie Sackmann, 'Collective Identities and Social Integration', in Rosemarie Sackmann, Bernhard Peters, Thomas Faist (eds), *Identity and Integration: Migrants in Western Europe* (Ashgate, 2003), p. 1.

7 Steven Loyal, 'Getting our heads around reality of multiculturalism', *Irish Times*, 22 August 2007.

8 See Adrian Favell, 'To belong or not to belong: the postnational question', in

In this respect, integration policies could be interpreted as representing a rejection of diversity in the host society by the state concerned. According to Guild, '(t)he idea of integration in itself presupposes that diversity is a bad thing',[9] while Castles and Miller note that 'integration policies are often simply a slower and gentler form of assimilation'.[10] While these viewpoints are insightful, they are based on a narrow view of the meaning of integration. This narrow view fails to reflect the complex nature of the concept and does not acknowledge the real dilemmas faced by states in this area of policy. However, these arguments lead to what is perhaps a more nuanced point, captured in Weiler's observation that 'concern for cultural, linguistic and ethnic integration of aliens may send a signal which accentuates both the otherness of the alien and an intolerance of the dominant culture towards such otherness'.[11] Viewed in this way, even well-meaning attempts to include immigrants in the fabric of the host society can be seen as contributing to the marginalization and 'other'-izing of migrant communities. Selecting immigrants as targets for 'integration' could enhance their difference and hinder their chances of integration in practice. As will be seen in the coming chapters, the potentially negative effects of the use of the concept of 'integration' are evident in the proliferation of integration 'tests' in Western Europe which seek to 'unravel people's attitudes, political beliefs and political sensibilities'.[12] This 'bogus integrationism'[13] has been linked to new stigmatizing discourses, developed in the last decade in particular, which Arun Kundnani (among others) has argued form part of a broader trend towards 'interpreting any signs of cultural difference (expressed by Muslim communities in particular) as acts of Anti-Western aggression and meeting such difference with a series of state measures aimed at assimilation'.[14] Unfortunately, then, the politics of integration are inextricably linked to the 'crises of multiculturalism'.[15] Counteracting the narratives of civic integration which have 'taken root' in Europe over the last decade is one of the

Andrew Geddes and Adrian Favell (eds), *The Politics of Belonging: Migrants and Minorities in Contemporary Europe* (Ashgate, 1999), p. 214.

9 Elspeth Guild, *The Legal Elements of European Identity: EU Citizenship and Migration Law* (Kluwer Law International, 2004), p. 234.

10 Stephen Castles and Mark Miller, *The Age of Migration* (3rd edn, Palgrave Macmillan, 2003), p. 250.

11 Joseph Weiler, 'Thou shalt not oppress a stranger: On the Judicial Protection of the Human Rights of Non-EC nationals' 3 *European Journal of International Law* (1992) 65, p. 67.

12 Dora Kostakopoulou, 'The Anatomy of Civic Integration' (2010) 73(6) *Modern Law Review* 933, p. 934.

13 Arun Kundnani, *The End of Tolerance: Racism in 21st century Britain* (Pluto Press, 2007), p. 7.

14 Ibid.

15 Alana Lentin and Gavan Titley, *The Crises of Multiculturalism* (Zed Books, 2011).

reasons why delineating an appropriate meaning for the term 'integration' is so important.[16]

Despite the difficulties associated with the concept of integration, this 'treacherous'[17] concept is increasingly prevalent in the public sphere: it will be seen in the course of this book that the term is used by international refugee and human rights bodies such as UNHCR, UN human rights treaty bodies, the Council of Europe and European Court of Human Rights, as well in the law and policy of the EU, and there is a growing corpus of academic and governmental literature on the topic, all of which is indicative of a general acceptance of the usefulness of the concept by advocates and protectors of migrants' rights, among others. These organizations have seemingly accepted that integration serves some useful purpose and a 'social good'. Contemporary formulations of integration thus add something extra to basic human rights guarantees, by emphasizing the 'dynamic process' necessary to transform these rights into a social reality.[18] Moreover, there is no alternative categorization or term which would appear to be a useful or less controversial substitute for the concept of integration. Thus, while the problems and controversies associated with the subjective meanings and theoretical bases of the term 'integration' must be acknowledged, the usefulness of the concept of integration depends less on the connotations of the word itself than on developing an appropriate working definition upon which to base the analysis. With this in mind, the purpose of this book is to present a way to develop a 'human rights-based' paradigm of integration, which would frame the process of integration as a process involving the realization of true equality for migrants.

Theoretical Models of Integration

Aside from the debate over the correct meaning or definition of the concept of integration, certain national examples are taken as illustrating various models of integration or civic incorporation.[19] The models usually referred to are the exclusionary model, multiculturalism and assimilation. The use of these models has been criticized and their descriptive value questioned. They are somewhat crude and fail to reflect the complex reality of community relations in each of the

---

16 Dora Kostakopoulou, 'The Anatomy of Civic Integration', note 12, pp. 933–934.

17 Michael Banton, 'National Integration in France and Britain' (2001) 27(1) *Journal of Ethnic and Migration Studies* 151, p. 152.

18 Hathaway makes this point in context of international refugee law. James Hathaway, *The Rights of Refugees Under International Law* (Cambridge University Press, 2005), p. 978.

19 For an over view of this comparative analysis as well as a look at its limitations, see Herman Kurthen and Barbara Schmitter Heisler, 'Immigrant Integration: Comparative Evidence from The United States and Germany' (2009) 32(1) *Ethnic and Racial Studies* 139.

countries discussed.[20] In fact, in most countries, elements of each model coexist in different policy areas.[21] It has also been argued that the differences between the various models are 'more apparent than real'.[22] It has been suggested that other types of classification may be more suitable for capturing the nature of immigration incorporation. Richard Alba, for example, argues that boundary concepts such as bright and blurred boundaries between immigrant and host populations provide a productive basis for comparisons between the populations.[23] An alternative means of comparative analysis has also been employed by UNHCR, which has identified practical trends in European countries as broadly reflecting either a 'mainstreaming' or a 'targeted' approach to integration.

Nevertheless, while the descriptive value of these models may be limited, '(b)y liberating us from the tyranny of details ..., the models enable us to perceive the grand contours of real-life contrast'.[24] The models provide a conceptual framework for the comparative analysis of various diverse issues relating to integration.[25] This is of particular value in the context of integration, where the concept is itself hotly contested and the conceptual framework is thus difficult to pin down. Furthermore, the models discussed below provide a useful general guide to the differing philosophies which underpin integration policies[26] and indeed they are frequently referred to in academic literature on integration. For these reasons, it is proposed to briefly describe three of the most important of the theoretical models: the exclusionary, multicultural and assimilation models.[27] In respect of the

20 See, for example, Sergio Carrera, *A Typology of Different Integration Programmes in the EU* (CHALLENGE Liberty and Security Briefing Paper, DG Internal Policies of the Union, Directorate C – Citizens' Rights and Constitutional Affairs, 4 December 2005), p. 4; Christian Joppke and Ewa Morawska, 'Integrating Immigrants in Liberal Nation-States: Policies and Practices', in Christian Joppke and Ewa Morawska (eds), *Toward Assimilation and Citizenship: Immigrants in Liberal Nation-States* (Palgrave Macmillan, 2003) 1, pp. 6–7.

21 Stephen Castles and Mark Miller, note 10, p. 250.

22 Piaras MacEinrí, 'Integration Models and Choices', in Bryan Fanning (ed.), *Immigration and Social Change in the Republic of Ireland* (Manchester University Press, 2007) 214, p. 216. See also Christian Joppke, 'Beyond National Models: Civic Integration Policies for Immigrants in Western Europe' (2007) 30(1) *West European Politics* 22.

23 Richard Alba, note 60.

24 Mirjan Damaska, 'Evidentiary Barriers to Conviction and Two Models of Criminal Procedure: A Comparative Study' (1972–1973) 121 *U. Pa. L. Rev.* 507, p. 577.

25 Ibid.

26 So, even Joppke and Morawska acknowledge that their critique of the 'national model' notion 'is not to deny significant institutional variations of integrating immigrants across states, which reflect historically particular state-and-nation-building experiences'. Christian Joppke and Ewa Morawska, note 20, p. 30.

27 In this section, the categorization laid down in Stephen Castles and Mark Miller, note 10, is followed. See also Stephen Castles, 'How nation-states respond to immigration and ethnic diversity' (1995) 21(3) *Journal of Ethnic and Migration Studies* 293; Piaras MacEinrí, 'Integration Models and Choices', note 22.

multicultural and assimilationist models, the UK and France, respectively, have been taken to be national examples of these models and the integration framework of each of these jurisdictions is outlined. Added to the description of these models is a consideration of the emerging concept of interculturalism and an exploration of the argument that there is a convergence among European countries towards an assimilationist-style model of 'civic integration'.

The Exclusionary Model

The exclusionary model does not represent a model for integration as such, and is better described as reflecting an 'anti-integration standpoint'.[28] This model sees immigrants as temporary and merely of economic value. An emphasis on ethnic origin and a homogeneous culture leads to a refusal to accept immigrants and their descendants as participating members of the national polity. In legal terms, this is translated into the incorporation of immigrants in certain sectors of society (principally, the labour market) and the denial of access to other sectors (welfare systems, citizenship and political participation). The exclusionary model is typically associated with countries which in the past recruited 'guestworkers', such as Germany, Switzerland and Austria, but, as MacEinrí observes, all European states have used variations of this model at different stages for different types of migrants.[29] It is widely accepted that exclusionary policies are 'anachronistic' and 'difficult to reconcile with prevailing market principles, to say nothing of democratic norms'.[30]

The Multicultural Model

Under the multicultural model, 'immigrants are granted equal rights in all spheres of society, without being expected to give up their diversity, although usually with an expectation of conformity to certain key values'.[31] Castles and Miller identify two main variants of multiculturalism: the *laissez-faire* approach typical of the USA, whereby the existence of ethnic communities is accepted, but it is not seen as the role of the state to ensure social justice or to support ethnic cultures; and multiculturalism as official policy, as exemplified by Canada, Australia and Sweden, whereby the state becomes involved in protecting cultural difference and securing equal rights for minorities.[32] In the European context, the UK has been seen as the epitome of the multicultural model.[33] The UK's emphasis on

28 Piaras MacEinrí, note 22, p. 216.

29 Piaras MacEinrí, note 22, p. 218.

30 Stephen Castles and Mark Miller, note 10, p. 280.

31 Ibid., p. 252.

32 Ibid.

33 Although the Netherlands and Sweden have also constituted examples of multiculturalism.

multiculturalism is tied to the classical liberal origins of its legal and political system and its complex relationship with its former colonies. The essence of the British approach to incorporating migrants into the structures of British society was described in 1966 by the then Home Secretary Roy Jenkins as: '(n)ot a flattening process of assimilation, but ... equal opportunity accompanied by cultural diversity in an atmosphere of mutual tolerance'.[34] The emphasis has been on race relations legislation to combat individual and institutional racism, coupled with an acceptance of cultural difference and the formation of ethnic communities. Immigrants have traditionally been placed under little pressure to take on 'mainstream' British values.

The current reality is that multiculturalism is itself a contested concept, in the UK and elsewhere, particularly since the September 11 attacks of 2001 and the London bombings of 2005. As Cesari observes, 'In the United Kingdom, the shock of the 7 July subway attacks by "homegrown bombers" led to increased questioning of the entire possibility of cultural difference'.[35] Multiculturalism has faced attacks from all sides of the political spectrum,[36] with feminists questioning whether multiculturalism is bad for women,[37] liberals arguing that equality and multiculturalism are incompatible,[38] and others arguing that multiculturalism reifies ethnic difference while failing to lead to genuine equality.[39] The trend since the 1990s has been a move away from multiculturalism.[40] In the UK, multiculturalism has come under sustained criticism with concerns over the radicalization of young British Muslims provoking a backlash against the concept.[41] Many commentators

34 Address by Roy Jenkins MP to a meeting of the Voluntary Liaison Committees, 23 May 1966.

35 Jocelyne Cesari, 'The Securitisation of Islam in Europe' (Justice and Home Affairs, Challenge Papers, April 2009). See, for example, on recent debates, Bhikhu Parekh, *Rethinking Multiculturalism: Cultural Diversity and Political Theory* (Harvard University Press, 2002); Amanda Wise and Selvaraj Velayutham, *Everyday Multiculturalism* (Palgrave Macmillan, 2009).

36 Dominic McGoldrick, 'Multiculturalism and its discontents' (2005) 5(1) *HRLR* 27.

37 See, for example, Joshua Cohen, Matthew Howard and Martha Nussbaum (eds), *Is Multiculturalism Bad for Women? Susan Muller Okin with Respondents* (Princeton University Press, 1999).

38 See, for example, Brian Barry, *Culture and Equality: An Egalitarian Critique of Multiculturalism* (Harvard University Press, 2002).

39 See Piaras MacEinrí, 'Integration Models and Choices', note 22, p. 224.

40 See generally, for example, Alana Lentin and Gavan Titley, note 15; Will Kymlicka, 'Multculturalism: Success, Failure, and the Future' (Migration Policy Institute, Europe, 2012).

41 See in particular the controversial article by David Goodhart: David Goodhart, 'Too Diverse?' (2004) *Prospect* (February 2004, http://www.prospectmagazine.co.uk/2004/02/toodiverse/), widely re-published under the title 'The Discomfort of Strangers'. On these debates in the Netherlands, see Mieke Maliepaard, Marcel Lubbers and Mérove Gijsberts, 'Generational differences in ethnic and religious attachment and their interrelation. A study among Muslim minorities in the Netherlands' (2010) 33(3) *Ethnic and Racial Studies* 451.

have called for a move beyond multiculturalism towards a more comprehensive framework to deal with the systemic discrimination and structural inequality faced by first and second generation immigrant communities.[42]

Development of a Policy Framework for Integration in the UK: Part of the Shift Away from Multiculturalism?

There has been a marked retreat from the strong form of multiculturalism traditionally practiced in the UK in recent years. By way of example, as will be further discussed in Chapter 7, individuals are now required to pass a 'Life in the UK' test, evincing a certain level of knowledge of British society, before they will be granted indefinite leave to remain or citizenship. In 2011, Conservative Prime Minster David Cameron expressed the view that multiculturalism has fostered extremist ideology, directly contributing to home-grown Islamic terrorism. Mr Cameron said that Britain must move away from 'passive tolerance' to adopt a policy of 'muscular liberalism' to enforce the values of equality, law and freedom of speech across all parts of society.[43] This reflects the culmination of the gradual erosion of the multicultural model through an emphasis in the New Labour years in government on 'community cohesion'.[44] The views expressed by Mr Cameron also reflect a European-wide retreat from the idea of multiculturalism, and echoed the comments of the German Chancellor Angela Merkel in October 2010, to the effect that multicultural policies in Germany had been a 'failure'.[45]

Despite the UK's long engagement with race relations, discrimination and community cohesion, 'integration' has not been viewed as a distinct public policy area in need of development. The only official specific integration policy which existed prior to 2012 was that relating to refugees.[46] In this context, the elaboration

42 See, for example, Gerard Delanty, 'The Limits of Diversity: Community beyond Unity and Difference', in Flemming Christiansen and Ulf Hedetoft (eds), *Multiple Belongings in Europe and Asia* (Ashgate, 2004), p. 45. In a similar vein, see Yasmin-Alibhai-Brown, *True Colours: Public Attitudes to Multiculturalism and the Role of Government* (Institute for Public Policy Research, 1999). See also Robert Miles, *Racism After Race Relations* (Routledge, 1993), who argued in 1993 that the idea of race relations reified the concept of 'race' and orders social relations in a racialized form (p. 6).

43 'Cameron: My War on Multiculturalism', *The Independent*, 5 February 2011.

44 See, for example, 'Community Cohesion: A Report of the Independent Review Team (chaired by Ted Cantle)' (Home Office, 2002); and 'Our Shared Future: Report from the Commission on Integration and Cohesion' (Commission on Integration and Cohesion, June 2007). Also see generally, on community cohesion, Ted Cantle, *Community Cohesion: A New Framework for Race and Identity* (Palgrave Macmillan, 2008).

45 'Germany wakes up to failed ideal of multiculturalism', *Irish Times*, 18 October 2010.

46 See, for example, Sarah Spencer (ed.), 'Refugees and Other New Migrants: a review of the evidence on successful approaches to integration' (Centre on Migration Policy and Society ('COMPAS'), Oxford, 2006).

of a specific integration strategy can in itself be seen as part of the shift away from a *laissez faire* model which promotes diversity, towards a greater emphasis on common values. Eric Pickles, Minister for Communities and Local Government, launched the new strategy for integration, 'Creating the Conditions for Integration', in February 2012.[47] The short policy paper contains little detail on a programme of action, but presents the five elements of the Government's approach to integration. It emphasizes the subsidiary role of central government in integration and states that 'government will only act exceptionally'[48] – for example, in providing kick-start funding to integration projects and in promoting liberal British values.[49] Along with the emphasis on localism, a mainstreaming approach is mandated, whereby all government departments would take integration into account in the course of their work.[50]

Aside from stating, rather vaguely, that 'integration is achieved when neighbourhoods, families and individuals come together on issues which matter to them',[51] the strategy does not set out a clear vision of exactly what integration means or what exactly is required of individuals living in an 'integrated society'. Rather than setting out a rigid model or definition of integration, it sets out five 'key factors' which are presented as contributing to integration. These are 'Common Ground', 'Responsibility', 'Social Mobility', 'Participation' and 'Tackling Extremism and Intolerance'. These domains reflect the multi-dimensional nature of integration. The strategy is not, as a whole, overly focused on the idea of cultural integration whereby migrants are expected to 'fit in' to a rigid British identity. This fits with the traditional approach taken in practice to integration questions in British policy. In addition, the acknowledgement of the socio-economic dimensions of integration under the 'Social Mobility' heading is progressive and reflects an aspect of integration, often downplayed by states, in which the state plays a key role including through the education system. As a whole, the paper has been commended for its 'generally sensible, evidence-based' content.[52]

That said, there are a number of references in the strategy which, particularly when seen in the context of wider immigration and counter-terrorism policy and discourse, contradict and undermine this generally sensible approach and introduce elements of coercive integration, which has been described as 'liberal coercion'.[53]

47 'Creating the Conditions for Integration' (Department of Communities and Local Government, 2012) (hereinafter, 'Creating the Conditions').

48 Creating the Conditions, p. 9.

49 Creating the Conditions, p. 9.

50 Creating the Conditions, p. 9.

51 Creating the Conditions, p. 2.

52 Ben Gidley, 'Creating the Conditions for Integration', COMPAS Oxford blog, 28 February 2012, available at http://compasoxfordblog.co.uk/2012/02/creating-the-conditions-for-integration/.

53 Shamit Saggar and Will Sommerille, 'Building a British Model of Integration in an Era of Immigration: Policy Lessons for Government' (Migration Policy Institute, 2012), p. 11.

The most striking of these is in the 'Common Ground' section. Alongside the ideas of supporting a community 'Big Lunch' and a community music day as examples given of how government will act to develop a 'clear sense of shared aspirations and values', we find reference to recent reforms in the immigration system related to strengthened mandatory language and integration requirements for those seeking to enter the UK and to settle in the UK.[54] The paper also confirms that other ideas which are being considered in terms of increasing 'common ground' include looking at how the settlement and citizenship process and Life in the UK Test can better promote an understanding not just of the English language, but also of British life and of the values and principles which underlie British society.[55] The implications of mandatory language and integration testing will be considered in detail throughout the rest of this book; for now, it suffices to highlight the vast ideological gap between proposing community events and interactions to promote common ground and mandatory legal tests imposed on migrants, linked to immigration status and rights. The appearance of integration testing in the integration strategy needs to be seen in the broader context of the invocation of 'integration' as a justification for making it more difficult for migrants to enter the UK and to settle in the UK.

Unlike the French policy framework, which will be discussed below, the paper is quite vague about what British values and principles encompass, aside from generic references to 'democracy, rule of law, equality of opportunity and treatment, freedom of speech and the rights of all men and women to live free from persecution of any kind'.[56] The only specific example given in the 'common ground' section is a recognition of the importance of Christianity, and faith generally, in the 'heritage and culture' of the UK, which has resulted in the Government taking action to protect the freedom to pray at council meetings and other public occasions.[57] The annex to the document refers to British values as including treating everyone fairly and a sense of belonging to Britain, leading one to question whether the reason for the absence of specific reference to values in the main body of the text is that these values in fact conflict with the whole enterprise of developing a rigid, planned integration policy.

Another problematic aspect of the strategy, the section on 'Extremism and Intolerance', focuses on religious extremism and intolerance. While governmental support for greater action against religious hate crime is clearly to be welcomed, the narrow focus of the section (on religious extremism and intolerance) fuels the idea of a 'clash of civilizations' which has hastened the retreat from multiculturalism worldwide. In contrast, nowhere in the document are the pernicious effects for integration of more generalized racism and discrimination highlighted. The leanings of this section should also be seen in the broader context of the Government's

54 Creating the Conditions for Integration, pp. 10–11.

55 Creating the Conditions for Integration, p. 11.

56 Creating the Conditions, p. 16.

57 Creating the Conditions, p. 16.

counter-terrorism strategy, which Gearty has criticized as ultimately targeted at mainly fighting Muslim-inspired extremist speech, and seizing upon a version of British values which is 'narrow, complacent and wholly unquestioning'.[58]

Overall then, despite the relatively holistic, community-centred nature of the integration strategy as a whole, two of its central features are the acceptance in principle of mandatory forms of integration imposed by government on individual migrants and its further erosion of the central importance of the 'passive tolerance' (to use David Cameron's words) encapsulated in the multicultural model of integration. While the integration policy framework is not nakedly assimilationist, and retains elements of traditional multicultural values, it constitutes a further shift towards the type of 'flattening process' decried by Roy Jenkins in 1966. This is particularly evident when integration policy is viewed in the context of wider governmental discourse on issues of belonging and multiculturalism.

The Assimilationist Model

Pursuant to the assimilationist model, migrants are expected to actively take on the culture and language of the majority population and renounce their own ethnic or cultural identity. Assimilation effectively requires a 'one-sided process of adaptation'.[59] Modern concepts of assimilation, while more subtle than older formulations, follow this basic definition, with Alba and Nee, for example, defining assimilation as the 'decline of an ethnic distinction and its corollary cultural and social differences'.[60] While forms of assimilation have been used in most immigration countries, today France is most closely associated with the assimilation model. The assimilationist thrust of the French state's attitude to its immigrant communities is based on France's commitment to a republican conception of citizenship and resulting strict policy of secularism.[61]

The French model of republican citizenship is based on a strict conception of equality between citizens.[62] The notion of equality has been interpreted in a

58 Conor Gearty, 'Is attacking multiculturalism a way of tackling racism – or feeding it? Reflections on the Government's Prevent Strategy' (2012) 2 *EHRLR* 121.

59 Stephen Castles and Mark Miller, note 10, p. 250.

60 See Richard Alba and Victor Nee, *Remaking the American Mainstream: Assimilation and the New Immigration* (Harvard University Press, 2003). See also Richard Alba, 'Bright and Blurred Boundaries: Second-Generation Assimilation and Exclusion in France, Germany and the United States' (2005) 28(1) *Ethnic and Racial Studies* 20.

61 On French secularism, see, for example, Jacques Robert, 'Religious Liberty and French Secularism' (2003) 2 *Brigham Young University Law Review* 637; Jean Baubérot, *La Laïcité: Entre Passion et Raison* (Seuil, 2004); Eoin Daly 'The ambiguous reach of constitutional secularism in republican France: Revisiting the idea of laïcité and political liberalism as alternatives' (2012) 32(3) *Oxford Journal of Legal Studies* 583.

62 For a summary analysis of the historical construction of the concept of republican citizenship, see Elizabeth Beller, 'The Headscarf Affair: The Conseil D'Etat on the Role of Religion and Culture in French Society' (2003–2004) 39 *Texas International Law Journal*

formalistic and individualistic manner such that differences between citizens are not recognized: racial, religious and cultural differences are subordinate to the individual's status as a 'citizen' within the French 'nation'.[63] One major consequence of this vision of equality is that French political and legal doctrine does not recognize the existence of minorities, and the principles of equality and indivisibility contained in Article 1 of the 1958 Constitution have the direct result that French law prohibits the collection of data relating to ethnic or racial origin. Immigrants are not seen as members of a linguistic or cultural community, but as (potential) members of the French political community. This in turn leads to an assimilationist model for integration.

In its first annual report, the French integration agency, the *Haut Conseil à l'Intégration* explained that 'The French conception of integration must obey a logic of equality and not a logic of minorities'.[64] The Republican model as applied in France rejects the recognition of difference and the idea of *communautarisme* whereby society is divided along ethnic and/or religious lines. In essence, the acceptance of, and participation in, French culture and political society is the main criterion for access to citizenship and participation in the French state. In recent years, the Republican model of citizenship has been used to promote a strong form of state secularism (*laïcité*) and as the basis for a vision of 'social cohesion' and integration, structured around national identity, which requires new migrants, in particular, to prove their acceptance of Republican values.

Criticisms of the French model focus on the discrepancy between the strictly egalitarian legal treatment of all French citizens and the reality of the pervasive ethnic discrimination and social exclusion which exists in French society.[65] Despite the rhetoric of equality attached to the idea of Republican citizenship, large numbers of first and second-generation immigrants have become ghettoized in areas of social deprivation where there is a high immigrant population, high unemployment and a culture of gangs and criminality.[66] The extent of the discrimination experienced by first, second and third-generation migrants has

---

581. See also John Bowen, 'Why did the French Rally to a Law Against Scarves in Schools?' (2008) 68 *Droit et Société* 35, and on the French relationship with multiculturalism, see Cécile Laborde, 'The Culture(s) of the Republic: Nationalism and Multiculturalism in French Republican Thought' (2001) 29(5) *Political Theory* 716.

63 See Mathias Möschel, 'Race judicata: The Ban on the Use of Ethnic and Racial Statistics in France' (2009) 5(2) *European Constitutional Law Review* 197; see also, generally, Olivia Bui Xuan, *Droit Public Francais Entre Universalisme Et Differencialisme* (Economica, 2004).

64 First report of the *Haut Conseil à l'Intégration* (Paris, 1991).

65 Patrick Haenni, '*La France face à ses musulmans: émeutes, jihadisme et dépolitisation*' (2006) 10 *Esprit* 112, p. 112.

66 See, for example, Kriegner-Krynici, 'The Second Generation: The Children of Muslim Immigrants in France', in Tomas Gerholm and Yngve Lithman (eds), *The New Islamic Presence in Europe* (Mansell, 1988), p. 123.

been criticized by various UN treaty monitoring bodies.[67] The precarious nature of social cohesion in ghettoized areas was highlighted by rioting in cities across France in 2005 and 2010,[68] which has been analysed as exposing a French tradition of social ghettoization that contradicts the dominant discourse of strict equality.[69] Recent critiques of assimilation in France have focussed on the debate over the interpretation of the value of *laïcité* (secularism) and the wearing of various forms of religious dress,[70] most significantly the Muslim veil or *hijab*, which will be discussed in greater detail in Chapter 8.

Integration Policy and Assimilation in France

The background to and ideology surrounding the integration landscape in France is completely different to that in the UK, with the concept of 'integration' forming an express and integral part of French political discourse and public policy for more than twenty years.[71] A fierce resistance to normative multiculturalism, constructing a nexus between integration and national identity and the linking of integration with immigration control have been central features of this policy.

In 2011, the *Haut Conseil à l'Integration* conducted a review of French integration policy over the previous two decades which, in the main, reiterated and reinforced these features.[72] It noted that integration is a contested concept, and one which is frequently misunderstood; it is something more than the simple insertion of individual migrants in the receiving society, and something less than assimilation as commonly understood to be the abandonment of the majority of specific cultural characteristics linked to the country of origin.[73] It is presented as 'a process which requires effort from both the host society and the migrant, an open-ness to diversity, which is enriching, but also a support for and the will

67 See, for example, Concluding observations of the Committee for the Elimination of All Forms of Racial Discrimination, UN Doc CERD/C/FRA/CO/16 (18 April 2005), para. 12; Concluding observations of the Human Rights Committee, UN Doc CCPR/C/FRA/CO/4 (31 July 2008) at para. 25.

68 See, for example, BBC News, 'France vows to restore order after rioting in Grenoble', 17 July 2010.

69 Patrick Haenni, note 65.

70 See, for example, Patrick Weil's discussion of *laïcité* and the decision of the Stasi Commission to recommend a law banning the headscarf in schools in '*Lever le voile*' (2005) 45(1) *Esprit* 54.

71 See generally, Patrick Simon, 'French National Identity and National Identity: Who Belongs to the National Community?' (Migration Policy Institute, 2012).

72 *Haut Conseil à l'Intégration*, '*La France sait-elle encore intégrer les immigrés?*' (HCI, *Rapport au Premier Ministre*, 2011) (hereinafter, '*La France sait-elle encore intégrer les immigrés?*').

73 '*La France sait-elle encore intégrer les immigrés?*', p. 14.

to guarantee and create a common democratic culture'.[74] As will be seen below, this definition is quite similar to that in use in the EU's Common Basic Principles on Integration, however, the emphasis in French policy has traditionally been on the 'common culture' element rather than cultivating diversity.[75] This remains the case, in spite of recent efforts to recognize the importance of reconciling the idea of a society open to diverse cultures with the 'indivisible' Republic.[76] The links to national identity are clear: 'integration has as its object the valuing of what unites French people and what has the potential to do so'.[77] Integration is seen to come under threat from contestations of the fundamental principles of the Republic, in particular equality between men and women and *laïcité*. In this regard, the HCI specifically mentions the question of the wearing of the Muslim veil in schools and the more recent ban on wearing a *burqa* in public places.[78]

The report notes that the two most important planks of integration policy since 2003 have been the development of the 'welcome and integration contract' for newcomers and the fight against discrimination.[79] Perhaps most revealing, however, are the 'challenges' to integration policy identified by the HCI. These include continued large-scale immigration, including irregular migration; the concentration of migrants in certain areas which may be severely disadvantaged; and 'difficulties of a cultural nature which threaten French society'.[80] The recognition of the links between housing and education policy, social disadvantage and integration is crucial, however the proportion of the report taken up with the discussion of these points is much less than the overall discussion of the 'problems' of immigration and perceived counter-cultural practices (primarily, those viewed as fundamentalist Muslim practices).

Overall, while this review of integration policy recognizes the importance of the socio-economic and anti-discrimination dimensions of integration, as well as the problem of 'ghettoization' faced in France, ultimately, the way forward for integration is seen as a shoring up of Republican values and adherence to a common culture. The nexus between these objectives and social cohesion is insisted upon. The HCI concludes that while French people are open to controlled

74 '*La France sait-elle encore intégrer les immigrés?*', p. 13, referring to Haut Conseil à l'Intégration, *Le bilan de la politique d'intégration 2002–2005* (HCI, *Rapport au Premier Ministre*, 2006), p. 22.

75 Benoît Normand (Secretary General of the HCI), '*L'intégration menacée? Quelle efficacité pour les politiques d'intégration? Cinquante ans de politiques publiques d'intégration*', *La France Plurielle, Cahiers Francais* No. 352, available at http://www.hci.gouv.fr/IMG/pdf/Cahiers_Francais_integration-2.pdf.

76 See the two volumes of the *Rapport au Premier Ministre 2011–2012* (HCI, October 2012).

77 '*La France sait-elle encore intégrer les immigrés?*', p. 14.

78 '*La France sait-elle encore intégrer les immigrés?*', p. 14.

79 Ibid.

80 '*La France sait-elle encore intégrer les immigrés?*', Chapter 2: 'The Obstacles to the Integration Process'.

migration, as well as diversity, they require that immigrants and their children adapt and take on French values and morals. To this end, a 'deepening' of integration is called for, which would, among other things, impart the 'taste of France' to migrants, including its countryside, culture, history, and employment and social codes.[81] Thus, as Carrera observes, integration 'functions as the norm in the hands of the State to oblige the non-national to lose all his/her identities in favour of the one perceived as "mainstream" in the French nation'.[82] This strong, centralized (and, it must be said, assimilationist) vision of integration, with its unapologetic requirement for migrants to demonstrate adherence to specific, identified national values is in stark contrast to the approach taken in the evolving British official integration policy which has concentrated, in the main, on a collaborative, local approach to building integrated communities.

Immigration and integration debates in France are highly politicized, and there are some indications that integration policy could be restructured and reformed under the current Socialist President and government. The Minister of the Interior, Manual Valls, has spoken of his desire to relax the requirements of the 'welcome and integration contract' and its links to the renewal of residence permits.[83] In 2013, Councillor of State Thierry Tuot provided a report to the Prime Minister on the overhaul of integration policy in France.[84] The report was scathing in its criticism of integration policy in France, suggesting a complete failure of policy in this field and that the term 'integration' should be abandoned altogether. In particular, Mr Tuot criticized the constant reference to the symbols, 'supreme values' and 'big concepts' of the 'Republic' and an old-fashioned nationalism as the basis of integration policy.[85] He argued that policy needs to be completely re-oriented in order to pursue the broader objective of an 'inclusive society', based on principles of non-discrimination, detached from immigration policy and conceived as social policy and, above all, avoiding stigmatizing of migrants.[86]

Mr Tuot also made a number of concrete suggestions for reforms which he believes would illustrate a radical change of climate, including, for example, the publication of annual immigration statistics; according citizenship by way of simple declaration to non-citizens who have completed all their schooling in France as well as to those with French children who have been in France for twenty years or more; and a form of earned regularization programme for undocumented migrants who show an effort to integrate.[87] This report is being considered by

81 '*La France sait-elle encore intégrer les immigrés?*', p. 15.

82 Sergio Carrera, *In Search of the Perfect Citizen? The Intersection between Integration, Immigration and Nationality in the EU* (Martinus Nijhoff, 2009), p. 347.

83 '*Valls veut une 'réforme d'ampleur' du contrat d'intégration*', *Le Parisien* (25 April 2013).

84 Thierry Tuot, *Rapport au premier minister sur la refondation des politiques d'intégration: La Grande Nation: Pour une Société Exclusive* (February 2013).

85 Ibid., p.10.

86 Ibid., pp. 14–15 and 21–27 in particular.

87 Ibid., pp. 27–41.

government, however, it is difficult to assess whether the report will have any real impact on integration policy or whether any of the more controversial legal reforms suggested will be taken on board. For the moment, the legal, policy and institutional framework surrounding integration in France remains relatively untouched.

Civic Integration in Europe: The Convergence of Traditional Models

A number of contemporary commentators argue that the integration models of Western liberal democracies are converging around an assimilatory model of 'civic integration', based around mandatory integration requirements.[88] Civic integration policies proceed on the basis that successful incorporation into a host society rests not only on economic integration through employment and political engagement through civic engagement, but also on 'individual commitments to characteristics typifying national citizenship, specifically country knowledge, language proficiency and liberal and social values'.[89] This modern form of assimilation, seen as a rejection of pluralism and diversity, is often presented as the emerging model in many European states.[90] The legal trend throughout Europe towards the use of integration tests as a prerequisite to access to the territory and to residency and social rights as well as imposing language and integration requirements for citizenship reinforces this conclusion.[91] This conceptualization of integration requires immigrants to re-mould themselves in the model of an idealized national citizen, in keeping with the assimilation model. This phenomenon is discussed in detail in the next chapter. It has been argued that this increasing policy convergence may be a by-product of increased cooperation in the field of integration at EU level.[92]

As will be seen in the coming chapters, European states are, in a general way, moving away from a multicultural model and towards integration politics based

88 See, among others, Dora Kostakopoulou, 'The Anatomy of Civic Integration', note 12.

89 Sara Goodman Wallace, 'Integration Requirements for Integration's Sake? Identifying, Categorising and Comparing Civic Integration Policies' (2010) 36(5) *Journal of Ethnic and Migration Studies* 753, 754.

90 Rogers Brubaker, 'The return of assimilation? Changing perspectives on immigration and its sequels in France, Germany, and the United States' (2001) 24(4) *Ethnic and Racial Studies* 531; Christian Joppke and Ewa Morawska, note 20; Christian Joppke, 'Transformation of Immigrant Integration: Civic Integration and Antidiscrimination in the Netherlands, France, and Germany' (2007) 59(2) *World Politics* 243; Dora Kostakopoulou, ibid.

91 Liav Orgad, "Cultural Defence' of Nations: Cultural Citizenship in France, Germany and the Netherlands' (2009) 15(6) *ELJ* 719.

92 Sergio Carrera and Anja Wiesbrock, 'Civic Integration of Third Country Nationals: Nationalism versus Europeanisation in the Common EU Immigration Policy' (CEPS, October 2009).

on a neo-nationalist narrative of the nation state, linked to immigration control. However, over-emphasizing the existence of this new emerging assimilation-like model may fail to recognize the reality of integration as a patchwork of multidimensional frameworks, with integration frameworks comprising a mixed bag rather than representing a specific model.[93] Legal and policy convergence in countries such as France, the UK and Germany, which are traditionally seen as representing different approaches to integration, undoubtedly adds weight to the argument that the traditional models retain little of their analytical or conceptual value. However, while they may not fall neatly into the traditional categorization of integration models, national integration policies and strategies still display significant differences in terms of the objectives and means of integration and the type of language used, often with multiculturalist or assimilationist leanings (as seen in relation to the UK and France above).[94] In addition, there are EU Member States which remain, for the moment, largely untouched by the discourse of 'civic integration'. Ireland is one such country, and the Irish approach to integration is explored further below.

The Emergence of 'Interculturalism'?

As discussed above, integration models based on exclusion, assimilation and multiculturalism have been criticized for a variety of reasons. Recent attempts to develop a new framework for managing cultural diversity have turned to the idea of interculturalism.[95] In the Irish context, for example, the concept of interculturalism has informed policy development in a number of areas. As will be described below, policy guidelines on intercultural education have been published as well as an intercultural strategy for healthcare, and the National Action Plan Against Racism provided an intercultural framework for dealing with racism.[96] Policy documentation from the Department of Education describes the difference between interculturalism and multiculturalism thus:

> While the term "multiculturalism" is sometimes used to describe a society in which different cultures live side by side without much interaction, the term "interculturalism" expresses a belief that we all become personally enriched

93 Herman Kurthen and Barbara Schmitter Heisler, 'Immigrant Integration: Comparative Evidence from The United States and Germany' (2009) 32(1) *Ethnic and Racial Studies* 139.

94 Anja Wiesbrock, *Legal Migration to the European Union* (Martinus Nijhoff Publishers, 2010), at para. 2.6.

95 In the academic sphere, see Thomas Faist, 'Diversity: A New Mode of Incorporation?' (2009) 32(1) *Ethnic and Racial Studies* 171, and Gilles Verbunt, *La Société Interculturelle* (Seuil, 2001).

96 See Department of Education and Skills and Office of the Minister for Integration, *Intercultural Education Strategy 2010–2015*, note 155; Office of the Minister for Children, 'Diversity and Equality Guidelines for Childcare Providers', note 150; and FAS, note 155.

> by coming in contact with and experiencing other cultures, and that people of different cultures can and should be able to engage with each other and learn from each other.[97]

Interculturalism can therefore be seen as multiculturalism with a greater emphasis on 'interaction, understanding, respect and integration between cultures'.[98]

The concept of interculturalism is also receiving attention on a European and an international level. Promotion of intercultural dialogue and management of diversity is one of the main priorities of the Organisation for Security and Co-operation in Europe, the United Nations, the Council of Europe and several other organizations.[99] The Council of Europe has produced a White Paper on Intercultural Dialogue which emphasizes the potential for intercultural dialogue to unify the diverse elements of European societies.[100] Intercultural dialogue is seen as 'a powerful instrument of mediation and reconciliation: through critical and constructive engagement across cultural fault-lines, it addresses real concerns about social fragmentation and insecurity while fostering integration and social cohesion'.[101] It remains to be seen whether the intercultural model can achieve such a lofty ambition, or whether it will ultimately become to be seen as flawed, in a manner similar to the other models discussed. In particular, interculturalism can be criticized as vague and apolitical. As will be seen below, however, it seems destined to become the preferred putative underlying philosophy for integration policy in Ireland, for the near future at least.

Defining Integration: The Council of Europe, UNHCR and European Union Approaches

As already mentioned, integration is an elusive concept. A cursory review of literature discussing integration reveals the complexity and uncertainty surrounding the meaning and use of the term. Overall, there is a 'lack of a clear and generally agreed conceptual framework for integration research'.[102] The following are some of issues which become problematic when assessing the meaning of integration.

---

97 Department of Education and Skills and Office of the Minister for Integration, *Intercultural Education Strategy 2010–2015*, note 155, p. 3.

98 This is the National Consultative Committee on Racism and Interculturalism's definition of interculturalism. See NCCRI, *Spectrum*, January 2008, p. 1.

99 'Annual High-level Tripartite meeting between the Council of Europe, the Organization for Security and Co-operation in Europe, the United Nations and partner organizations Joint Communiqué' (7 July 2008). See www.osce.org/item/32097.html.

100 Council of Europe, *White Paper on Intercultural Dialogue: Living Together as Equals in Dignity* (Strasbourg, 7 May 2008).

101 Ibid., p. 9.

102 See Stephen Castles, Maja Korac, Ellie Vasta, Steven Vertovec, *Indicators of Integration: Mapping the Field* (Report of a Project carried out by the University of Oxford

Is integration a condition or a process? If it is a process, is it a one-way process whereby immigrants are expected to adapt to fit in with a dominant culture and way of life, or a two-way process of adaptation, involving change in values, norms and behaviour for both newcomers and members of the existing society? What are the defining criteria for integration, and how do we know if it has been successfully achieved? The multi-dimensional nature of the integration process makes it difficult to define in any precise way. Integration is related to a wide range of policy areas (for example, education, housing and health) and involves a wide variety of social actors: political decision-makers, public officials, employers, trade unions, co-workers, neighbours and so on. The process is shaped by many factors, including the characteristics of the migrants (for example their skills, language abilities, education and religion) and the characteristics – economic, social, cultural and political – of the milieu which they are attempting to enter.[103]

Approaches to the definition of integration can revolve around identifying the underlying issues and fundamental theoretical questions raised by the concept,[104] or take a more functional approach by identifying expected outcomes.[105] An 'inclusive' approach can be taken, whereby integration is simply seen as the inclusion of new populations into the structures of the host country.[106] On balance, it is possible to conclude that '(T)here is no single, generally accepted definition, theory or model of immigrant and refugee integration. The concept continues to be controversial and hotly debated'.[107] This section considers the definitions of integration put forward by the Council of Europe, UNHCR, the EU and Ireland (providing examples of the way in which regional, international and domestic actors have defined the term) in order to develop a synthesized working definition for the purposes of the rest of the book. Ireland has been chosen as the main national example due to the recent nature of its engagement with the concept of integration and the specific attempts made in recent years to develop an integration framework.

Centre for Migration and Policy Research and Refugee Studies Centre contracted by the Home Office Immigration Research and Statistics Service, December 2002), p. 139.

103 See International Organization for Migration and the National Economic and Social Council, *Managing Migration in Ireland: A Social and Economic Analysis* (IOM, September 2006).

104 See Adrian Favell, *Philosophies of Integration: Immigration and the Idea of Citizenship in France and Britain* (2nd edn, Palgrave, 2001), p. 3.

105 See, for example, Home Office, *Indicators of Integration: Final Report* (Home Office Practice and Development Report, 2004).

106 See, for example, Friedrich Heckmann and Dominique Schnapper (eds), *The Integration of Immigrants in European Societies – National Differences and Trends of Convergence* (Lucius and Lucius, 2003), p. 14; International Organisation for Migration, *Managing Migration in Ireland A Social and Economic Analysis*, note 103, p. 151; and Anja Wiesbrock, *Legal Migration to the European Union*, note 94, p. 16.

107 Stephen Castles, Maja Korac, Ellie Vasta, Steven Vertovec, note 102, p. 114.

Early Definitions of Integration: The Council of Europe Approach

The Council of Europe was one of the first organizations that included integration on its agenda[108] and the European Committee on Migration has produced a significant body of work on immigration and integration, particularly throughout the 1990s.[109] The committee has noted that there is no uniform concept of migrant integration in the receiving European societies. Concepts of integration may differ greatly with regard to their position on the inclusion-exclusion continuum of legal-political rights (for example, possibilities of naturalization, active and passive voting rights), and in offering access to differing degrees to language training, housing, education, the labour market and the social security system.[110] The Council of Europe advocates a broad understanding of the concept of integration. Integration is understood as 'a two-sided process and as the capacity of people to live together with full respect for the dignity of each individual, the common good, pluralism and diversity, non-violence and solidarity, as well as their ability to participate in social, cultural, economic and political life'.[111] According to the Council of Europe's approach, the rationale for integration policies is to allow immigrants to participate fully in the life of the host society, and strategies for integration must include social, political and cultural aspects. While states should respect immigrants' dignity and distinct identity, immigrants also have a responsibility to abide by the laws and respect the basic values of European societies and their cultural heritage. In this way, integration is perceived as a process of mutual responsibility on the part of both the receiving state and the immigrant.

On a practical level, integration and the creation of an environment conducive to integration are viewed by the Council of Europe as key elements in a successful migration management strategy.[112] The most important practical elements of integration policies are identified as being secure residence and related rights, promotion of equal socio-economic and civil and political rights, easy and fair naturalization and the adoption of legal and other measures to combat racial and

---

108 See Rinus Penninx, Dimitrina Spencer and Nicholas Van Hear, *Migration and Integration in Europe: The State of Research* (ESRC Centre on Migration, Policy and Society [COMPAS], University of Oxford, 2008), available at http://www.norface.org/files/migration-COMPAS-report.pdf, p. 7; Kerstin Rosenow, 'The Europeanisation of Integration Policies' (2009) 47(1) *International Migration* 133, p. 139.

109 See, for example, Rainier Baubock, *The Integration of Immigrants* (Council of Europe Consultation); Christoph Hofinger, *Measurements and Indicators of Integration* (Council of Europe, 1998); Council of Europe, *Religion and the integration of immigrants* (Community Relations, 1999); Jan Niessen, *Diversity and cohesion: new challenges for the integration of immigrants and minorities* (Council of Europe, 2000). See also Council of Europe, *Framework for Integration* (2000).

110 Christoph Hofinger, ibid., p. 32.

111 See Council of Europe, *White Paper on Intercultural Dialogue: Living Together as Equals in Dignity* (Strasbourg, 7 May 2008).

112 See Council of Europe, *Towards a Migration Management Strategy* (July 2003).

ethnic discrimination.[113] In addition, recent policy developed by the Council of Europe has emphasized the critical importance, from a human-rights perspective, of its work on integration,[114] as well as the value of 'positive interactions' in giving migrants a voice, empowering them and building their sense of belonging.[115]

UNHCR's Definition of Integration

UNHCR uses a similar formulation in the context of refugee integration, which is defined as a 'dynamic and multifaceted two-way process which requires efforts by all parties concerned, including a preparedness on the part of refugees to adapt to the host society without having to forego their own cultural identity, and a corresponding readiness on the part of host communities and public institutions to welcome refugees and meet the needs of a diverse population'.[116]

UNHCR emphasizes the complex and multi-dimensional nature of the integration process, noting that 'the process of integration is complex and gradual, comprising distinct but interrelated legal, economic, social and cultural dimensions, all of which are important for refugees' ability to integrate successfully as fully-included members of society'.[117] Integration is divided into a three-pronged process of legal, economic and social and cultural integration.[118] Specific rights relating to integration are seen as encompassing: legal residency status; employment; housing rights; education; public relief and health care; social security and labour legislation; family unity; right of access to courts; property rights; freedom of residence and movement and naturalization.[119] UNHCR has also emphasized the importance of the means chosen to promote integration: these can be, on the one hand, targeted support for those who are expected to integrate

113 Ibid. See also *Council of Europe, Framework for Council of Europe Work on Migration Issues 2011–2013* (Proposed by the Secretary General and supported by the Committee of Ministers of the Council of Europe on 15 June 2011) (hereinafter 'Council of Europe Framework'), p. 11 and 13.

114 Council of Europe Framework, p. 6.

115 Recommendation by the Committee of Ministers on interaction between migrants and receiving societies (CM/Rec(2011)1); Andrew Orton, 'Building Migrants' Belonging Through Positive Interaction' (Council of Europe, November 2012).

116 UNHCR Executive Committee, *Conclusion on Local Integration* 7 October 2005, No. 104 (LVI) – 2005, preamble and (k). See also UNHCR, *Note on the Integration of Refugees in the European Union* (May 2007); see also UNHCR's promotional brochure on local integration, 'The Benefits of Belonging: Local Integration Options and Opportunities for Host Countries, Communities and Refugees' (2011).

117 UNHCR, *Note on the Integration of Refugees in the European Union*, ibid., p. 2.

118 See Alexandra Fielden, 'New Issues in Refugee Research: Local integration: an under-reported solution to protracted refugee situations' Research Paper No. 158 (UNHCR, June 2008).

119 Rosa da Costa, 'Rights of Refugees in the Context of Integration: Legal Standards and Recommendations' UNHCR Legal and Protection Policy Research Series (UNHCR, June 2006).

along with clearly identified obligations or expectations and, on the other hand, ensuring integration through mainstream services from the beginning with little or no initial direct support to integrate.[120] UNHCR's concept of integration will be examined in detail in Chapter 4.

The Definition of Integration in the European Union Framework on Integration

The European Commission has noted that, in the context of the EU, 'No Member State has a uniform definition of integration, however they do to a certain extent agree that integration is composed of different elements and that it must be a two-way process involving both immigrants and their local community'.[121] The Commission has summarized the common elements of Member States' integration policies as including respect for fundamental values in a democratic society; the right of the individual to maintain his or her own cultural identity; rights comparable to those of EU citizens and corresponding obligations, and active participation in all aspects of life on an equal footing.[122]

The EU Framework for the Integration of Third Country Nationals in the EU (EU 'Framework on Integration') envisages integration as 'a process of mutual accommodation by both the host societies and immigrants and an essential factor in realizing the full benefits of migration'.[123] The approach taken in the EU Framework on Integration has been to identify 'Common Basic Principles for Immigrant Integration Policy in the EU' (CBPs),[124] which are primarily to assist Member States in formulating integration policies by offering a non-binding guide of basic principles against which they can judge and assess their own efforts and to serve as a basis for Member States to explore how EU, national, regional, and local authorities can interact in the development and implementation of integration policies. Integration is defined in the CBPs thus: 'Integration is a dynamic, two-way process of mutual accommodation by all immigrants and residents of

120 UNHCR, *Mapping Integration: UNHCR's Age, Gender and Diversity Mainstreaming Project on Refugee Integration in Ireland – 2008/2009* (April 2009), p. 9.

121 Communication from the Commission to the Council, the European Parliament, the European Economic and Social Committee and the Committee of the Regions, *Immigration, Integration and Employment* (COM(2003) 336 final), Annex 1, p. 44.

122 Ibid.

123 Communication from the Commission to the Council, the European Parliament, the European Economic and Social Committee and the Committee of the Regions, *Third Annual Report on Migration and Integration* (COM(2007) 512 final), p. 3.

124 Justice and Home Affairs Council Conclusions, *Common Basic Principles on Immigrant Integration*, Council Document 14615/04, Brussels, 19 November 2004. In 2009, the European Parliament reminded Member States, local authorities and immigrants that all points of the CBPs must be applied equally (European Parliament resolution of 2 April 2009 on problems and prospects concerning European citizenship (2010/C 137 E/03), at para. 20.

Member States'.[125] The CBPs are wide-ranging and emphasize the importance of employment,[126] education,[127] access to institutions of the host society on a basis equal to that of EU citizens,[128] participation in the democratic process,[129] and free practice of religion and culture.[130] Reflecting the two-way approach taken in the definition of integration, both the migrants' and the host society's responsibilities in the integration process are acknowledged: for example, CBP 4 states that 'basic knowledge of the host society's language, history, and institutions is indispensable to integration; enabling immigrants to acquire this basic knowledge is essential to successful integration'. Similarly, CBP 2 provides that '(I)ntegration implies respect for the basic values of the European Union'. Frequent interaction between immigrants and Member States' citizens is stated to be a 'fundamental mechanism for integration'.[131]

The CBPs have been further developed in subsequent policy documents, including in the Commission's 2005 and 2011 Agendas for Integration,[132] which make proposals for concrete measures to put the CBPs into practice. The Common Agendas for Integration provide suggestions for action both at EU and national level. They encourage Member States to strengthen their efforts in developing comprehensive national integration strategies and emphasize the role of the EU in contributing to steering and guiding Member States' efforts via different instruments. The CBPs are also elaborated upon in the Handbooks on Integration, which consider in detail various practical issues linked to different CBPs.[133] While the importance of the CBPs as the basis for EU integration policy has been consistently emphasized[134] and the CBPs contain the official EU definition of integration, they constitute only one small part of the multi-faceted EU Framework on Integration. The EU approach to integration will be further discussed in Chapter 6.

---

125 CBP 1.

126 CBP 3.

127 CBP 5.

128 CBP 6.

129 CBP 8.

130 CBP 9.

131 CBP 7.

132 Communication from the Commission to the Council, the European Parliament, the European Economic and Social Committee and the Committee of the Regions of 1 September 2005 – A Common Agenda for Integration – Framework for the Integration of Third-Country Nationals in the European Union (COM(2005) 389 final – Not published in the Official Journal); Communication from the Commission to the European Parliament, the Council, the European Economic and Social Committee and the Committee of the Regions of 20 July 2011 – European Agenda for the Integration of Third Country Nationals (Brussels, 20.7.2011 COM(2011) 455 final).

133 The most recent (and third) edition of the handbook is European Commission, *Handbook on Integration for policymakers and practitioners* (Brussels, 3rd edn, April 2010).

134 See, for example, Council of the EU, *Strengthening of Integration Policies in the EU*, Council Document 10267/07 Luxembourg, 12–13 June 2007, at para. 6.

Defining Integration in the Irish Context: The Conceptual Basis for Irish Integration Policy

The concept of integration is relatively new to Irish policymakers and consequently has not yet generated a significant body of specific policy documentation. In addition, formal integration programmes in the form of language courses, civic orientation courses, integration contracts or tests do not as yet form part of the Irish integration landscape (other than the basic civic orientation course provided for resettled refugees).[135] To date, official discourse appears to embrace the two-way approach discussed above in the context of the Council of Europe, UNHCR and EU definitions. One of the first policy documents in the area of integration (dating from 2000) adopted a wide-ranging and inclusive working definition of the concept of (refugee) integration, stating that: 'Integration means the ability to participate in Irish society to the extent that a person needs and wishes in all of the major components of society, without having to relinquish his or her own cultural identity'.[136] It was also acknowledged that integration is not a static concept but a process which undergoes constant change as society evolves, and that integration is a two-way process that places an obligation on both refugees and on society.[137] As regards specific integration issues, the report identified the following key practical issues: language skills, employment, training, recognition of skills and qualifications, education, accessing mainstream health services, health issues, accommodation, naturalization and citizenship and family reunification.[138] Integration policy, insofar as it existed at all, was based on this report for eight years.

The rapid rise in immigration in the years following the publication of this policy document resulted in an increased focus on integration. In 2007, the Houses of the Oireachtas (Parliament) Joint Committee on European Affairs produced a 'Report on Migration and Integration Policy in Ireland', which considered the integration practices of other European countries. The fairly sparse conclusions of the committee related primarily to the importance of language teaching and the necessity for a single government department with responsibility for integration.[139] This recommendation was acted upon in 2007 with the creation of a new position of Minister of State with special responsibility for Integration (referred to generally as the 'Minister for Integration'). Upon his appointment as Ireland's first Minister

135 This contrasts with practice in most EU Member States, which usually combine a number of mandatory and/or voluntary integration measures of this type. See Anja Wiesbrock, *Legal Migration to the European Union*, note 94, pp. 606–700.

136 *Integration: A Two-Way Process*, Report to the Minister for Justice, Equality and Law Reform by the Interdepartmental Working Group on the Integration of Refugees in Ireland (Department of Justice Equality and Law Reform, 2000).

137 Ibid.

138 Ibid.

139 Houses of the Oireachtas Joint Committee on European Affairs, *Report on Migration and Integration Policy in Ireland* (March 2007).

for Integration in 2007, Conor Lenihan described his task as twofold: 'making sure that there are no barriers to migrants succeeding in Irish society; and bringing the Irish population to the point of maturity and understanding what the issues are'.[140] This two-way approach reflects Ireland's acceptance of the EU common framework for the integration of third-country nationals. The EU Common Basic Principles are used as a benchmark for Irish integration policy,[141] as part of a general trend whereby '(p)olicy to combat racism and foster a more inclusive and intercultural society in Ireland are increasingly influenced by policy at EU level, including policy relating to integration'.[142]

This trend is continued in the Statement on Integration Strategy and Diversity Management ('Migration Nation') published by the Office of the Minister for Integration ('OMI') in 2008.[143] This key document, which reiterates the major influence which the EU Common Basic Principles have had and continue to have on Irish integration developments, outlines the principles intended to underpin Irish integration policy. The statement sets out these principles as follows:

- A partnership approach between the Government and non-governmental organizations, as well as civil society bodies, to deepen and enhance the opportunities for integration;
- A strong link between integration policy and wider state social inclusion measures, strategies and initiatives;
- A clear public policy focus that avoids the creation of parallel societies, communities and urban ghettoes, i.e. a mainstream approach to service delivery to migrants; and
- A commitment to effective local delivery mechanisms that align services to migrants with those for indigenous communities.[144]

The central features of the policy statement are its mainstreaming approach to the provision of services for new communities;[145] its situation of integration policy in the context of the general social inclusion and equality framework;[146] and its insistence on a two-way model of integration.[147] Other notable features include the emphasis placed on respect for cultural differences and the lack of emphasis on identity or 'values' issues. The practical areas of language education, interpretation

140 'Vigorous economy key to integration of migrants, says Minister', *Irish Times*, 4 January 2008.

141 Houses of the Oireachtas Joint Committee on European Affairs, note 139, p. 11.

142 Editorial, National Consultative Committee on Racism and Interculturalism Journal: *Spectrum*, Issue 15, September 2007.

143 Office of the Minister for Integration, *Migration Nation: Statement on Integration Strategy and Diversity Management* (May 2008).

144 Ibid., pp. 9 and 10.

145 Ibid., p. 16.

146 Ibid.

147 Ibid., p. 18.

and translation, information provision, and funding arrangements information, are identified as the key areas crucial to integration success, rather than areas relating to culture or values.[148] The statement has been characterized as enshrining an intercultural approach for this reason.[149] Migration Nation constitutes a skeletal conceptual framework for the development of integration policy in Ireland.

The Fragmented Nature of Integration Policy in Ireland

In addition to the body of policy documentation specifically based on integration, integration-related concerns have emerged in other major policy areas. The National Action Plan Against Racism 2005–2008 (NPAR) and the National Action Plan for Social Inclusion 2007–2016 (NPSI) lay down integration policies and goals. NPSI provides that one of the high level goals to be achieved in the context of social inclusion is the integration of migrants and specifically the development of a 'strategy aimed at achieving the integration of newcomers in our society'.[150] NPAR is the bedrock of Irish integration policy and provided the guiding principles for Migration Nation,[151] and has importance as 'a blueprint for an overall integration agenda'[152] even though the life span of the plan is now officially over (and no anti-racism strategy has been put in place to replace it).[153] In parts, it reads more like an integration plan than an anti-racism plan, providing an 'intercultural framework' with the objectives of protection, inclusion, provision, recognition and participation.[154] In the sphere of education, Guidelines for Intercultural Education in Primary Schools and an Intercultural Education Strategy 2010–2015 have been published[155] and in health, an Intercultural Strategy for Healthcare has been

148 Ibid., pp. 34 and 35. Although it also states that 'serious social upheaval can be anticipated' as a result of immigration (at 35) and that 'we cannot focus on "rights" to the exclusion of "responsibilities" [of migrants]' (p. 36).

149 For example, in An Garda Síochána, *Diversity Strategy and Implementation Plan 2009–2012: Beyond Legal Compliance* (May 2009), at i.

150 See *National Action Plan for Social Inclusion 2007–2016* (February 2007), p. 15, Goal 12. See also International Organisation for Migration and the National Economic and Social Council, note 102, Chapter 8: 'Implications for Social Policy: Health, Social Welfare and Migrants'.

151 See *The National Action Plan Against Racism 2005–2008: Not an End, Just a Beginning* (2009), p. 7.

152 Ibid.

153 The final report in relation to NPAR is contained in *The National Action Plan Against Racism 2005–2008: Not an End, Just a Beginning* (2009).

154 See *Planning For Diversity: The National Action Plan Against Racism 2005–2008*, p. 27.

155 Department of Education and Skills and Office of the Minister for Integration, *Intercultural Education Strategy 2010–2015* (2010). Also in the field of child care and education, see Office of the Minister for Children, 'Diversity and Equality Guidelines for Childcare Providers' (Office of the Minister for Children, December 2006) and FAS, 'Guidelines for Interculturalism' (FAS, January 2009). These publications are not

devised.[156] In a similar vein, An Garda Síochána, the national police force, has published a Diversity Strategy which draws on the NPAR and Migration Nation to promote an intercultural approach to diversity management.[157]

There is an acknowledged need to go beyond these piecemeal policy documents towards a more comprehensive integration framework.[158] The International Organization for Migration observed in 2006 that integration policy would need to be built on a widely shared vision of how integration might contribute to a dynamic, secure and socially cohesive Irish future.[159] While it has been seen that broadly speaking a mainstreaming, intercultural approach drawing on EU integration policy is endorsed in the policy documentation, a more developed, specific vision of integration still seems to be lacking. Aside from Migration Nation, the only integration-specific document to emanate from the former Office of the Minister for Integration related to the specific group of resettled refugees.[160] These refugees are a highly selected group of migrants and it is difficult to extrapolate general principles from the policy approach to the integration of this group. Since its establishment, the OMI appeared to perceive its role as facilitating integration at grassroots level through the funding of sporting groups, NGOs and faith-based community groups, rather than developing an overarching integration framework which could be used to inform the action of other state bodies.[161]

---

immigration-specific. See also Oireachtas Library and Research Service, 'Understanding the Challenges of Immigration for Education Provision' (Spotlight No. 1, 2008).

156 Launched by the HSE on 21 February 2008. Furthermore, in 2010, the Arts Council, the Irish Government Agency for developing the arts, launched a cultural diversity strategy: The Arts Council, 'Cultural Diversity and the Arts: Policy and Strategy' (The Arts Council, 2010).

157 An Garda Síochána, note 149, p. i.

158 See speech of An Tánaiste Michael McDowell, where he expressed the view that 'The challenge now, of course, is to extend our horizons; to go beyond anti-racism measures as we begin to understand the totality of initiatives needed to work towards societal cohesion'. See also Dublin City Council, *Towards Integration: A City Framework* (Dublin City Council, 2008).

159 See International Organization for Migration and the National Economic and Social Council, note 102. See also National Economic and Social Council, *Migration Policy*, NESC Report No. 115 (2006). This was reiterated in OECD, *Economic Survey of Ireland* (April 2008).

160 Louise Kinlen, 'The Reception, Orientation and Integration of Resettled Refugees in the Irish Context' (Office of Minister for Integration, February 2008).

161 This view is reinforced by the following statement of the Office in the *United Nations International Convention on the Elimination of All Forms of Racial Discrimination Combined Third and Fourth Reports by Ireland as Required under article 9 of the Convention on the legislative judicial, administrative or other measures adopted to give effect to the provisions of the Convention* (Office of the Minister for Integration, 21 December 2009), p. 12. Also see the contribution of the Minister for Integration, Mary White, at the EU Ministerial Conference on Integration, where she emphasized the role of sport in integration ('Minister White T.D., attends the European Ministerial Conference on

The decentralized approach taken thus far to integration is also reflected in the focus on the development of integration strategies by local authorities rather than by the OMI.[162] This trend would suggest that the current fragmented approach to integration will probably continue into the future. This emphasis on localism is quite similar to that recently put forward in the UK, as discussed above, and contrasts with the highly centralized nature of French integration policy as based around a Republican conception of citizenship and society. This is a somewhat narrow approach to integration which suggests a reluctance to tackle the deeper issues attaching to integration. However, as has been seen in both the UK and French contexts, the elaboration of centralized strategies and 'principles' for integration seems to somehow inevitably lead to a discourse of cultural integration and coerced integration and away from integration as a social process. Viewed in this way, perhaps the fragmented, localized approach to integration illustrated by the Irish example is as close to an inclusive, participatory approach to integration as could be hoped for.

The Impact of the Financial Crisis on Integration Strategy in Ireland

One of the major reasons for the lack of progress in the field of integration since the establishment of the OMI has been the impact of the financial difficulties which Ireland has been experiencing since late 2007. The financial crisis and dramatic rise in unemployment resulted, in April 2009, in a return to net emigration for the first time since 1995.[163] These developments have meant that integration is no longer as immediate an issue as it was between 2000 and 2007 and it has slipped down the political agenda. The harsh budgetary measures necessitated by the financial crisis have impacted on the equality and integration infrastructure through, for example, the closing of the National Consultative Committee on Racism and Interculturalism and the cuts in funding for the Human Rights Commission and Equality Authority.[164] The plans set out in Migration Nation to establish new

Integration in Zaragoza, Spain', *Press Release of the Office of the Minister of Integration* (19 April 2010)).

162 See, for example, Dublin City Council, 'Towards Integration: A City Framework' (2009); Cork City Council, 'Integration Strategy – Connecting Communities' (2008); Limerick City and County Councils, 'Integrating Limerick – Integration Plan 2010 – 2012' (2010).

163 Central Statistics Office, *Population and Migration Estimates, April 2009* (CSO, September 2009). The statistics showed that immigration from all non-Irish groups showed a decline, with those from the EU 12 countries showing the greatest fall. See the analysis contained in Central Statistics Office, *Population and Migration Estimates April 2010* (CSO, 21 September 2010).

164 See 'Budget cuts will severely limit effectiveness of State watchdogs', *Irish Times*, 11 November 2009. Prior to the 2009 budget, the CEO of the Equality Authority resigned in protest when its budget was halved. His account of this is contained in Niall Crowley, *Empty Promises: Bringing the Equality Authority to Heel* (Farmar, 2010).

integration structures, including a standing Commission on Integration and a Task Force to establish future policy needs, have been shelved (although a Ministerial Council on Integration was established in 2010).[165] The NPAR has not been replaced by a new strategy and so the state currently has no formal anti-racism strategy in place. This state of affairs resulted in 2011 in the following findings of the Migration Integration Policy Index:

> The boom transformed Ireland into a country of immigration but, with the crisis, net emigration has returned for the moment. Government is restricting family access to work, increasing fees and cutting funds, including for the Equality Authority, which may undermine its anti-discrimination work. These exacerbate the effect of the crisis on immigrants, who are already more likely to lose jobs. ... These and other restrictions mean that ... Ireland's policies are still not halfway favourable for integration, below Canada, the UK, and the US and new labour migration countries (Spain and Portugal).[166]

The most significant of the integration 'casualties' of the economic recession and the consequent reorientation of government policy was the decision made by the newly elected Fine Gael-Labour coalition government in March 2011 to abolish the position of the Minister for Integration. While this clearly indicates that integration (along with immigration matters generally) has slipped down the policy agenda, the full implications of this move for the development of integration policy is still uncertain. The OMI has become the 'Office for the Promotion of Migrant Integration', a small unit within the Department of Justice and Equality. In these circumstances, the further development of integration policy in Ireland seems unlikely, even though research conducted by the Economic and Social Research Institute shows that Irish attitudes towards immigrants are becoming ever more negative.[167]

Conflicting Messages Contained in Irish Integration Discourse

It was noted above that Migration Nation does not enter the controversial terrain of cultural integration in any detail. Moreover, Irish state institutions and politicians generally employ a rhetoric of inclusion and interculturalism when talking about

---

165 See announcement on the website of the Office for the Minister for Integration: http://www.integration.ie/website/omi/omiwebv6.nsf/page/aboutus-structures-overview-en (27 May 2010). The Ministerial Council was launched in September 2010 ('Minister White announces details of the newly established Ministerial Council on Integration', *Press Release of the Office of the Minister of Integration* (22 September 2010)).

166 British Council and Migration Policy Group, Migration Integration Policy Index III (2011), available at www.integrationindex.eu.

167 ESRI, *Annual Monitoring Report on Integration* (2012).

integration issues.[168] However, at times conflicting discourses emerge.[169] Irish politicians frequently conflate the ideas of integration and assimilation. For example, in July 2007, when commenting on the decision of An Garda Síochána to ban turbans from its official uniform, then Minister for Foreign Affairs Dermot Ahern spoke of the need for newcomers to 'assimilate' into Irish society, arguing that it was important that people who 'come to our country have to assimilate into our own culture and our own norms in society'.[170] The Minister for Integration, Conor Lenihan, said:

> If we are to take integration seriously, people who come here must understand our way of doing things. When the President and Ministers travel to the Middle East, they accept cultural requirements of the country and the culture they are operating in. It is a vice versa situation with regard to Ireland.[171]

The ban on the wearing of the Sikh turban by on-duty members of the Garda Síochána has been strongly criticized as failing to reflect government's stated commitment to integration, as well as sending out contradictory messages as to the meaning of integration.[172]

---

168 See, for example, An Garda Síochána, note 149; Conor Lenihan, *An important year for integration* (Metro Eireann, 17 January 2008); 'Lenihan stresses positive contribution of migrants', *Irish Times*, 21 January 2008.

169 On the importance of public discourse on integration processes, see European Commission, 'Handbook on Integration for policymakers and practitioners' (Brussels, 3rd edn, April 2010), p. 55.

170 'Gardaí deny turban ban is based on race or religion', *Irish Times*, 24 August 2007. In a case taken by a Sikh member of the Garda Reserve under the Employment Equality Act 1998 (as amended), the High Court ultimately found that membership of the Garda Reserve is not within the scope of the Employment Equality Act and is not employment within the meaning of that legislation, nor was training to be a member of that Reserve training or experience for or in relation to employment or a course of vocational training within the meaning of the Employment Equality Act. The Equality Officer did not, therefore, have jurisdiction to consider the complainant's claim that he had been treated less favourably in accessing employment, in his conditions of employment and in relation to training for employment and/or in relation to vocational training due to his religion and his ethnicity in that he was prohibited from wearing his turban and so was unable to complete his training and become a member of the Garda Reserve. *Commissioner of An Garda Síochána v Oberoi* [2013] IEHC 267.

171 'Granting Special Status Doesn't Help Integration', *Sunday Independent*, 19 August 2007.

172 See Steven Loyal writing in the *Irish Times*, 'Getting our heads around reality of multiculturalism', *Irish Times*, 22 August 2007. See also, for example, 'Gardaí deny turban ban is based on race or religion', *Irish Times,* 24 August 2007. See generally, Siobhán Mullally and Darren Donovan, 'Religion in Ireland's 'public squares': education, the family and expanding equality claims' (2011) *Public Law* 284.

Another example of this underlying discourse was the comments of the then Fine Gael spokesman on immigration and integration, Brian Hayes (now Minister of State for Public Service Reform and the Office of Public Works), who expressed the view that children attending schools without a satisfactory grasp of English should be 'segregated' from their classmates.[173] Similarly, when Ruairi Quinn, then Labour Party spokesman on education and science (now Minister for Education and Skills), was asked for his opinion on the wearing of Muslim headscarves in schools, his response could not be said to endorse an intercultural approach: 'Nobody is formally asking them to come here. In the interests of integration and assimilation, they should embrace our culture'.[174] These incidents illustrate not only the lack of awareness of Irish politicians of the nuances of the meaning of integration and the terminology involved but also perhaps an underlying tendency towards a philosophy of cultural assimilation among Irish politicians.[175]

Common Threads in Defining Integration

While the detail of the Council of Europe, UNHCR, EU and Irish approaches to defining integration differ somewhat, each of the approaches discussed follows a basic pattern: each begins by identifying a basic definition of the concept of integration and then goes on to identify a range of integration issues. This reflects the multidimensional nature and complexity of the concept. There is some convergence among the definitions on the meaning of the concept of integration: it is seen as a two-way process composed of different elements. The emphasis on a bi-directional approach indicates a subtle, inclusive understanding of integration. A two-way approach implies that integration is not about all members of a society, new and existing, becoming the same, but about an arrangement of unity despite the existence of difference:[176] unity is achieved through mutual acceptance and accommodation. However, as Carrera observes in the context of the EU, '(t)he paradigm of a positive, two-way process does not appear to be one that is easily implemented in practice'.[177] State measures taken in the field of integration often place a greater emphasis on migrants', rather than existing members',

173 Brian Hayes subsequently said that he regretted his use of terminology: 'Hayes regrets 'segregation' remark', *Irish Times*, 21 August 2008.

174 'Muslim Anger at Opposition Calls for School Ban on Hijab', *Irish Independent*, 2 June 2008.

175 See Niall Crowley and Migrant Rights Centre of Ireland, *Hidden Messages, Overt Agendas: A Migrant Rights Centre of Ireland Pamphlet* (9 March 2010). In response to this pamphlet, see *Minister Curran Responds to Pamphlet Entitled 'Hidden Messages/ Overt Agendas* (Office of the Minister for Integration, 9 March 2010), available at http://www.integration.ie/website/omi/omiwebv6.nsf/page/CDKR-83DPR21831599-en.

176 See Ulrike Davy, 'Integration of Immigrants in Germany: A Slowly Evolving Concept' (2005) 7 *EJML* 123.

177 See Sergio Carrera, 'Towards an EU Framework on the Integration of Immigrants',

responsibilities throughout the integration process. This has been the case in relation to the integration and immigration policies of a number of European countries, in which the trend is towards conceiving integration as an obligation on the immigrant which must be fulfilled in order to gain access to the territory of the state for example, or to obtain citizenship.

The definitions studied above attempt to divide the conceptual analysis of integration into manageable parts by looking at its various dimensions, for example by viewing the concept in terms of legal, economic and social integration, or breaking the concept down to a multi-faceted framework. While the categorization varies, the common thread underlying the definitions is that integration is relevant to and should underpin more general policies in state and society. A developed conception of integration should reflect this broad base. For the purposes of the present research, perhaps the most useful conclusion to draw from the overview in this chapter of the concept of integration is that integration should be recognized as an umbrella term suggesting a set of possible and overlapping processes and spheres.[178] This is discussed further below in developing a working definition of integration for the purposes of this book.

Wider Perspectives on Integration

Placing integration within the context of the broader themes and clashes of interests which it involves reveals its complexity and significance and illustrates the wide jurisprudential, political and cultural debates into which integration fits. With this is mind, this section seeks to identify connections between integration and broader themes and frame the debate on the meaning of integration in its broad interdisciplinary context. The connections identified will be used to inform the analysis in subsequent sections and throughout the book.

Links between Integration and National Identity

Integration policy is inextricably linked to national identity and a society's conception of itself.[179] Sackmann sums up this issue well: '(t)he self-conception of the respective country of immigration provides a framework for the perception of its migrants'.[180] This can also be expressed as the somewhat simplistic question:

---

in Sergio Carrera (ed.), *The Nexus Between Immigration, Integration and Citizenship in the EU* (Challenge Collective Conference Volume, April 2006), p. 5.

178 Stephen Castles, Maja Korac, Ellie Vasta, Steven Vertovec, note 102, p. 126.

179 In an explicit example of this, the former French President and French Prime Minister directed that national identity underpin French integration policy. *Lettre de mission du Président de la République et du Premier ministre au ministre de l'immigration, de l'intégration, de l'identité nationale et du développement solidaire* (31 March 2009).

180 See Rosemarie Sackmann, Bernhard Peters, Thomas Faist (eds), note 6, p. 2.

what are the defining characteristics of the society into which migrants are expected to integrate?[181] How do we reconcile the desire to continue a common national life with the fact of increasing fragmentation along ethnic and other lines?[182] Favell observes that struggles between majority populations and immigrants or minority groups over political rights or social and welfare entitlements reveal the complexities of belonging.[183] Examples of these struggles are specific political conflicts about access to housing, to welfare benefits or education; the question of voting rights for non-nationals; or the creation of special cultural rights for ethnic minorities.

The perspective of the nation state remains essential to understanding immigration and integration issues. Ward affirms that: '(T)he situation of the "other" cannot readily be distinguished from that of the European polity of nation states which accompanied the ideology of the Enlightenment'.[184] The jurisprudential construction of refugees and migrants as 'others' is a direct consequence of the philosophy and politics of identity which form the basis of the nation state.[185] The legitimacy of 'national identity' can be questioned, with the nation state dependant on a mythical commonalty that must seek to identify and distinguish 'others'. National identity can thus be seen as a flawed ideological construct which perpetuates racism, xenophobia and exclusion. However, this reaction simplifies the relevant issues to a great degree and also fails to take seriously the fact that political communities do build boundaries, some of which might be argued as a necessity in building some sort of social cohesion, solidarity and community.[186] More fundamental, from an integration perspective, is the extent to which national identity in states which have experienced extensive migration for a long time encompasses the migrant experience and embraces this diversity, or whether it seeks to push back against this to cling to the pre-existing mythical commonalty.[187] Open forms of citizenship constructed around universal values of human and democratic rights that all communities share could constitute a core set of values for society to unite around.[188] Xanthaki has argued that if a multiplicity of cultures

181 See Piaras MacEinrí, 'Integration into What? From de Facto Assimilationism to Ghettoisation: Challenges for the State and Civil Society', Presentation at Trinity Immigration Initiative Migration Research Fair, 27 September 2007.

182 Attracta Ingram, 'Citizenship and Diversity' in *Mosaic or Melting Pot? Living with Diversity: Proceedings of a Conference on Cultural Diversity* (Royal Irish Academy, 2003).

183 Adrian Favell, 'To belong or not to belong: the postnational question', note 8, p. 211.

184 Ian Ward, 'Identifying the European Other' (2002) 14(23) *IJRL* 219, p. 219.

185 Ibid. See also Patricia Tuitt, *False Images : Law's Construction of the Refugee* (Pluto Press, 1996).

186 Adrian Favell, 'To belong or not to belong: the postnational question', note 8, p. 210.

187 Sara Goodman Wallace, note 84.

188 Arun Kundnani, note 13, p. 8.

and minorities are recognized as equal partners in an on-going process of evolution of a national identity, it is possible for society to evolve *with* the participation of minorities.[189] Few modern European states, however, seem willing to make space for this dialogic, multicultural form of belonging whereby minority groups are seen as 'negotiators' rather than 'imitators'. Nonetheless, on a practical level, while the concept of national identity is open to criticism, it remains a significant influencing factor on the development of law and policy, particularly on issues relating to integration.

Management of Difference and Diversity in Democratic Societies

Schnapper argues that '(i)ntegration is first and foremost a value *per se*, insofar as it rests on the fundamentally democratic notion that, in spite of divergences of their beliefs and their experience and their allegiances, people who have respect for what is right and, in particular, for human rights can live in harmony'.[190] This viewpoint reflects the importance of the concept of integration in one of the fundamental issues faced by modern democratic states: maintaining social cohesion in increasingly diverse societies. Identifying the bases of social unity in diverse societies and delineating the parameters of common spaces are recognized as important factors for the smooth functioning and internal stability of states.[191] Integration can be characterized as both a political and a social necessity, essential for avoiding the formulation of urban ghettoes, born of poverty, exclusion and ethnic apprehension, where social and ethnic disadvantage are compounded.[192] The demands of immigrant groups for political inclusion and recognition may lead states to consider whether the recognition of difference leads to a fragmentation of society. In this way, concerns over 'integration' could be seen in another sense as concerns over 'disintegration'. This is one of the most controversial dimensions of integration, leading to scapegoating of racialized minorities as threats to social order,[193] and, in Kundnani's view, exposing a fear and anxiety of behalf of Western states in relation to those who are defined as 'aliens', whether migrants, asylum seekers or 'Muslim extremists'.[194]

On a practical level, an important task for states is deciding on appropriate responses to the sometimes conflicting claims of minority communities of immigrant origin and of members of the majority population. State responses to

189 Alexandra Xanthaki, 'Multiculturalism and International Law: Discussing Universal Standards' (2010) 32(1) *Hum Rts Q* 21.

190 Dominque Schnapper in Bernard Lewis and Dominique Schnapper (eds), *Muslims in Europe* (Pinter Publications, 1994), p. 159.

191 See Will Kymlicka, *Multicultural Citizenship* (1995), p. 9; Ulrike Davy, note 171, p. 123.

192 Bernard Lewis and Dominique Schnapper (eds), note 190, p. 159.

193 Alana Lentin and Gavan Titley, note 15, p. 194.

194 Arun Kundnani, note 13, p. 1.

the diversity created by immigration cover a wide spectrum, broadly reflecting the theoretical models discussed above, from exclusion to interculturalism. Immigrants arrive in the receiving society with cultural and religious practices and beliefs which may differ from or even clash with those of the majority population. Female genital mutilation, arranged marriages and multiple marriages are some of the issues which may arise. Rightly or wrongly, some beliefs and practices may be met with discomfort or hostility by members of the majority population. Religious dress has been a particular focal point for such problems in European states. Overall, '(t)he issue is starkly posed whether the immigrants or new citizens should be allowed to continue their practices, or whether they should be required to follow laws and practices ... that effectively require their abolition'.[195] The correct balance to be drawn on this issue constitutes one of integration's most problematic and intractable aspects, especially as the problem of integration is increasingly presented as one of compatibility with western societies and democracy.[196] The challenge consists in considering and analysing the real issues experienced in diverse communities without problematizing immigration or constructing the newcomers as social enemies.[197] The question does arise as to why 'difference' needs to be managed at all: this may just be an extension of the neo-assimilationist agenda brought about by the resurgence of exclusionary forms of national identity, as discussed above.

Connecting Integration, Social Inclusion and Equality

Questions of integration are intricately linked with questions of social policy, social inclusion and equality. Viewed in a broad sense as 'the inability to participate effectively in economic, social, political and cultural life, and ... alienation and distance from the mainstream society',[198] social exclusion is the opposite of integration. The overarching aim of integration policy can be seen as to 'avoid the creation of a socially excluded underclass'[199] with all the attendant social problems which this creates. This is essentially a social inclusion goal which involves acknowledging the links between poverty and marginalization and a commitment to addressing these issues. The implication of these connections between integration and social inclusion is that 'cultural' dimensions of integration should not be over-emphasized such that the role of social policy in integration is

195 Henry Steiner, Philip Alston and Ryan Goodman, *International Human Rights in Context* (3rd edn, Oxford University Press, 2007), p. 616.

196 Lentin and Titley, note 15 p. 194.

197 See Anastassia Tsoukala, 'Looking at Migrants as Enemies' in Didier Bigo and Elspeth Guild (eds), *Controlling Frontiers: Free Movement Into and Within Europe* (Ashgate, 2005).

198 Anver Saloojee, 'Social Inclusion, Anti-Racism and Democratic Citizenship' (Laidlaw Foundation, 2003), p. 3.

199 International Organization for Migration and the National Economic and Social Council, note 103, at 150.

neglected. It is arguable that integration discourse should focus on the issues of poverty and the consequent marginalization of immigrants, rather than on cultural differences. This point is made by Fournier and Yurdakul in their critique of the Muslim headscarf debates in France and Germany. [200] In their view, the political and legal debate over religious symbolism and the perceived failure of cultural integration has removed questions of socio-economic inequality from the political arena in France and Germany. They argue that the ghettoization and exclusion of immigrant communities through structural inequalities and lack of social mobility leading to poverty are the real issues. The unequal distribution of resources and structural inequalities faced by immigrants are masked by the segregation by states of immigrant groups into certain sectors and under certain themes, such as religious rights and equality before the law. On this analysis, the real challenge for states is a social policy one: to ensure the true and effective integration of immigrants at a socioeconomic level.[201]

Saloojee makes a similar connection between racial discrimination, disadvantage and exclusion, observing that 'those who are disadvantaged, marginalized and "othered" in society do not have access to valued goods and services and are consequently excluded'.[202] She argues that, viewed in a broad sense as encompassing an anti-racism discourse, social inclusion presents a radical alternative to the dominant discourses on how to ensure the social cohesion of communities containing immigrant groups. Social inclusion as a concept is 'fully capable of both recognizing the politics of difference and transcending its narrow confines precisely because it embraces an inclusive vision, which suggests that a common purpose and shared community can be achieved through inter-group solidarity'.[203] Seen in this light, social inclusion provides an escape route from the restrictive conceptual framework of integration 'models' in the form of multiculturalism or assimilation and places integration in its broader societal context.

The links between integration and social inclusion are explicitly recognized in each of the policy frameworks in Ireland, the UK and France. One of the high-level goals laid down by the Irish National Action Plan for Social Inclusion is the development of a strategy aimed at achieving the integration of newcomers in Irish society.[204] This objective is placed in the context of the crucial importance of building and supporting sustainable communities, particularly those that are subject

200 Pascale Fournier and Gökçe Yurdakul, 'Unveiling Distribution: Muslim Women with Headscarves in France and Germany', in Michal Bodemann and Gökçe Yurdakul (eds), *Migration, Citizenship and Ethnos* (Palgrave, 2006), pp. 167–185.

201 Ibid., p. 185.

202 Anver Saloojee, note 195, p. 9.

203 Ibid., p. 18.

204 See *National Action Plan for Social Inclusion 2007–2016* (February 2007), Goal 12, p. 15.

to disadvantage.[205] This inclusion of integration in the NPSI is a manifestation of the trend, as observed by Fanning, that the Irish debate on integration has been to date 'principally shaped by social policy norms rather than debates about multiculturalism'.[206] Fanning identifies a family resemblance between social inclusion goals and prevalent definitions of integration within Irish social policy debates which has been informed by similar sociological understandings of the inequalities that cause poverty and those resulting from racism.[207] These connections are made explicit in Migration Nation, which emphasizes a 'clear commitment to including integration in the overall social inclusion framework of planning and resource provision'.[208] In addition, the 'core integration services' of housing, employment, health, education, social supports, community development and training[209] identified in Migration Nation reflect the social inclusion goals contained in NPSI, which relate to education, employment and participation, income support and housing and health. The connections are also explicit in the British document, *Creating the Conditions for Integration*, which was praised above for specifically recognizing the socio-economic dimension of integration in its 'Social Mobility' section. While, as mentioned above, French policy is often criticized as neglecting the connections between the perceived 'failure' of integration among some groups and social exclusion and marginalization, recent governmental reviews of integration policy have included an acknowledgment that one of the principal difficulties faced by integration policy is the concentration of immigration in very specific disadvantaged areas.[210] This discussion demonstrates the way in which 'integration' issues are not only confined to immigrants but raise questions relevant to existing structures, inequalities and exclusion in the host society.

Developing a Working Definition of Integration

The difficulties inherent in defining the concept of integration are apparent from the above discussion, with the indeterminate nature of the concept meaning that any definition of integration inevitably has quite a strong normative dimension. Nevertheless, it is useful to identify relevant policy areas and desired outcomes of the integration process, using these as a starting point for discussion, without diving

205 Ibid., p. 15.

206 Bryan Fanning, 'Integration and Social Policy' in Bryan Fanning, *Immigration and Social Change in the Republic of Ireland* (Manchester University Press, 2007) 237, p. 237.

207 Bryan Fanning, 'Integration and Social Policy', ibid., p. 239.

208 Office of the Minister for Integration, *Migration Nation: Statement on Integration Strategy and Diversity Management*, note 143, p. 15.

209 Ibid., p. 26.

210 '*La France sait-elle encore intégrer les immigrés?*', p. 34, for example.

too deeply into the conceptual difficulties surrounding the term 'integration'. The 'EU Handbook on Integration for practitioners and policy-makers', for example, employs a pragmatic approach, observing that policy-makers in the field prefer to concentrate on practical outcomes such as social and economic mobility, education, health, housing, social services, and societal participation, rather than enter into familiar debates about multiculturalism or assimilation.[211] The 2007 Handbook identifies two processes as critical to improving immigrants' outcomes: the elimination of inequalities, and the acquisition of competences.[212] Similarly, the Migrant Integration Policy Index, which measures integration policies in 27 EU Member States and four non-EU states,[213] does not attempt to define the concept of integration but simply identifies seven key policy areas: labour market access, family reunion, long-term residence, political participation, access to nationality, anti-discrimination and education, and uses 'policy indicators' in each area to create a picture of migrants' opportunities for participating in European societies.[214] In a similar vein, in the UK the initial objective in establishing a framework for a common understanding of refugee integration was not to *define* integration as such but rather to identify the key factors that appear to contribute to the process of integration for refugees in the UK along with indicators of integration to assist in policy development.[215] This approach has been replicated there in respect of more general integration policy.

These pragmatic approaches are based on a broad-based working definition of integration as a social phenomenon cutting across intersecting policy fields. The advantages of this approach from the point of view of states are clear: adopting a working definition of integration allows all actors in host countries to have a common reference point and goal.[216] Da Costa observes, in the context of refugee integration, that '(W)hile such a definition will be a living text ... it encourages States to formulate and work towards a national vision ... and develop a common strategy for accommodating and managing a diverse population'.[217] In addition, from the perspective of this book, there are cogent reasons in favour of outlining a working definition of integration at the outset. First, the most relevant policy areas must be identified in order to provide a frame of analysis for the relevant legal instruments at the national, regional and international level. Second, a working definition may partially neutralize the negative connotations which could be attached to the concept of integration. Overall, a clear definition

211 European Commission: Directorate General for Justice and Home Affairs, *Handbook on Integration for Policy-makers and Practitioners* (2nd edn, May 2007), p. 10.

212 Ibid., p. 10.

213 Canada, the United States, Norway and Switzerland.

214 See British Council and Migration Policy Group, Migration Integration Policy Index III (2011), available at www.integrationindex.eu.

215 Home Office, *Indicators of Integration: Final Report* (Home Office Practice and Development Report, 2004).

216 Rosa da Costa, note 119, p. 30.

217 Ibid.

of the assumptions on which it will proceed is necessary to provide a conceptual framework for this book.

Having ascertained the need to develop a working definition of integration, how is such a definition to be shaped? As Mathew Gibney argues in exploring ways to look at the ethics and politics of asylum, a conceptual framework for thinking about integration issues should be both practically relevant and theoretically sound.[218] A broad-based understanding of the concept of integration, combined with an awareness of the relevant policy areas and intended outcomes of the integration process, provides such a framework. In addition, the working definition should be structured in a way that reflects the legal nature of the analysis. It needs to fit in with the core concern of the book, which is to explore the relationship between integration and law.

The term 'integration' will generally be used in this book in the sense of an on-going two-way process involving a series of interlinked spheres. On top of this foundational meaning, taking into account the exploration of the meaning of integration undertaken in this chapter, it is suggested that an analysis of integration and law can be broken into 'functional' and 'wider' perspectives. The way in which black-letter legal rules determine access to fundamental rights and key entitlements related to integration such as a secure legal status, housing, education, healthcare, access to social benefits and family reunification, is termed the 'functional' perspective. The 'wider' perspective is the way in which law intervenes in the broader societal themes identified in the previous section as including national identity, responses to diversity in society, social policy and equality.

The working definition of integration upon which this book will proceed is therefore as follows:

> Integration is an on-going, multidimensional, two-way process between, on the one hand, migrants and, on the other hand, existing members of the receiving society along with the receiving state itself. This process involves a series of interlinked spheres, which, for the purposes of this book, will be characterized as forming part of "functional" or "wider" perspectives on integration. "Functional" aspects of integration include first of all protecting fundamental rights and secondly providing a legal status which acts as a gateway to the core policy areas of housing, health, education, social welfare and family reunification. "Wider" aspects of integration connect to these functional themes but place integration in its broader thematic context. These are aspects of integration with wider connections to the broader themes of national identity, responses to diversity in society, social policy and equality – most importantly, approaches to citizenship and the place of culture and religion in public space.

218 Matthew J. Gibney, *The Ethics and Politics of Asylum: Liberal Democracy and the Response to Refugees* (Cambridge University Press, 2004).

The next chapter will discuss the nature of the interaction between law and integration in greater depth.

Conclusion

This chapter has explored the various ways in which integration is framed in official and academic literature and commentary. It has shown that integration can be understood in terms of models, definitions and broad social themes. It was found that most conceptualizations of integration provide a basic definition of the term and then proceed to identify various categories of issues with implications for integration (such as education, housing and citizenship). The connections between integration and wider social themes were then highlighted. Drawing on these findings, a working definition of integration appropriate to an analysis of the concept in a legal context was proposed. This was necessary in order to define the scope of the book. However, the indeterminacy of the concept of integration means that it can be given a spectrum of meanings depending on the purpose and context in which it is being defined. Thus it will be seen in the next chapter that the traditional narratives of integration explored in this chapter – within which, despite differences, integration is broadly conceived as a process of social inclusion and cohesion – have been sidelined by governments seeking to use integration as a legal means of immigration and social control.

Chapter 3
Exploring the Relationship between Integration and Law

Introduction

The conceptual foundations of integration were explored in the previous chapter. This chapter builds on that analysis to explore the relationship between integration and law in greater detail. It does this first by looking at the nature of the interaction between integration and law. A variety of ways in which law interacts with integration are considered. Both functional and wider elements of the relationship are identified in an expansion of the working definition of integration suggested in the previous chapter. Family reunification is used as an illustration of the broad nature of the nexus between integration and law, encompassing functional and wider perspectives. This general discussion then moves to the more specific way in which immigration law and integration have been linked in many European states, in the form of integration requirements for entry, residence and family reunification.

Having identified a number of dimensions to the relationship between integration and law, the chapter asks what factors influence the legal approach to integration. The role of national 'public philosophies' in shaping the approach to integration (and more broadly in addressing issues related to the governance of a diverse society) is examined. Finally, the chapter introduces one of the central ideas of the book, that 'external influences' on integration – through the normative development of the concept in the EU and in international law settings – are central to a comprehensive understanding of integration and law.

The Complexity of the Interaction between Integration and Law

The idea was put forward in the previous chapter that the relationship between integration and law can be characterized in terms of functional and wider perspectives. From the 'functional' viewpoint, law defines the framework within which integration does or does not happen by regulating the legal and social conditions of migrants' everyday lives: it 'sets the legal and political framework within which other aspects of integration occur'.[1] The rights of non-citizen groups are increasingly defined in terms of their membership of legal and administrative

1 See British Council and Migration Policy Group, Migration Integration Policy Index III (2011), available at www.integrationindex.eu.

categories, and law thus defines migrants' rights and obligations and grants or restricts access to essential elements of the integration process. Black-letter legal rules may constitute instruments of or barriers to integration, even where that may not be their primary object. Legal status is one of the key determinants of integration for a number of reasons. Legal status creates a variety of restrictions on decision-making, self-sufficiency, and the capacity of migrants to benefit from basic economic, political, social, and cultural opportunities and services.[2] Moreover, as Hofinger has observed, the 'prolongation of legal differences between citizens of a state and migrants reinforces social discrimination against the latter', thus forming part of the root causes of the racism, stereotyping and marginalization which are anathema to integration.[3] Policies on citizenship, family reunification and the determination of legal status linked to rights of access to services are all dimensions of the integration process.

Legal mechanisms for controlling access to social rights via the labour market or welfare need not be aimed at integration or designed with integration in mind to have a powerful impact on immigration and integration, creating 'outsiders' and 'insiders' in the process. The effects of these legal mechanisms constitute a defining feature of integration policy as well as perceptions of identity and who 'belongs' in a state. Also in the realm of concrete legal rules, the trend in European legal systems towards the use of integration as a norm in both immigration law and citizenship law are the subject of a burgeoning body of literature.[4] The normative use of integration in these countries, as discussed further below in this chapter, reveals the propensity of governments to manipulate the indeterminate concept of integration for use as a mechanism of immigration control and as a means to promote discourses on national identity. The notion of integration as a gradual process of inclusion contained in national integration policies is turned on its head, and conceptualized in legal terms as a mandatory condition of access to the territory and to a secure immigration status in the territory.

Integration also interacts with law in a wider sense. The first way in which integration interacts with law in this broad sense is in its guise as a policy issue. Integration issues are often intensely politicized, and the legislature and executive

2 Immigrant Council of Ireland, 'Getting On: From Immigration to Integration' (ICI, May 2008), p. 6.

3 Christoph Hofinger, *Measurements and Indicators of Integration* (Council of Europe, 1998), p. 29.

4 See, for example, Sergio Carrera, *In Search of the Perfect Citizen? The Intersection between Integration, Immigration and Nationality in the EU* (Martinus Nijhoff, 2009), p. 441; Elspeth Guild, Sergio Carrera and Kees Groenendijk (eds), *Illiberal Liberal States: Immigration, Citizenship and Integration in the EU* (Ashgate, 2009); Saskia Bonjour, 'Between Integration Provision and Selection Mechanism. Party Politics, Judicial Constraints, and the Making of French and Dutch Policies of Civic Integration Abroad' (2010) 12(3) *EJML* 299; Ricky Van Oers, Eva Ersboll and Dora Kostakopoulou (eds), *A Re-Definition of Belonging? Language and Integration Tests in Europe* (Martinus Nijhoff Publishers, 2010).

enjoy a substantial measure of latitude in determining policy relating to integration. These policy choices must, however, be made within the normative constraints imposed by international and EU law as well as domestic constitutional provisions and any discussion of integration is therefore posited in an environment of multiple legal mechanisms which constrain governmental action.

Secondly, integration is fundamentally a social phenomenon and depends on numerous factors outside the control of law and policy such as (*inter alia*) ethnic, linguistic and cultural affinities within the population, the wealth of the state and the 'integration history' of the state.[5] The discussion as to the relationship between integration and law can thus be seen as a microcosm of the larger issue of the paradoxical relationship between law and society. Law is itself a social phenomenon, and is as such restrained and influenced by society while at the same time exerting authority over society; it is simultaneously an independent social formation and also interdependent with other social formations.[6] In this way, there is a two-way process of influence between law and the public to which it addresses its rules, such that '(L)aw is causally determined by the societal structure but can also be viewed as a more active instrument for shaping future behaviour and social forms'.[7] In the context of integration, a similarly complex relationship exists: the legal approach to integration issues is conditioned by conceptions of national identity and the organizational principles of the society in question; however the legal approach and its success or failure in promoting integration will in turn contribute to shaping these ideas.

The functional and wider elements of the integration/law dynamic frequently overlap. States may respond to the demands of specific ethnic or religious groups by providing for group-differentiated measures, in the form of what Kymlicka refers to as 'polyethnic rights'.[8] This includes what has been described as 'the most controversial demand of ethnic groups'[9]: exemptions from laws and regulations that disadvantage them given their religious or cultural practices. For example, in the UK, Sikh men are exempt from the requirement to wear a safety helmet on a construction site and from the requirement to wear a helmet on a motorcycle,[10] and in Ireland, Jewish shops had an exemption from evening opening hours legislation

5 Matthew J. Gibney, *The Ethics and Politics of Asylum: Liberal Democracy and the Response to Refugees* (Cambridge University Press, 2004). See also Elizabeth Mestheneos and Elizabeth Ioannidi, 'Obstacles to Refugee Integration in the European Union Member States' 15 *JRS* 304.

6 Denis Galligan, *Law in Modern Society* (Oxford University Press, 2007).

7 Vilhelm Aubert (ed.), *Sociology of Law: Selected Readings* (Penguin, 1969), p. 14.

8 Will Kymlicka, *Multicultural Citizenship* (1995), p. 30.

9 Ibid., p. 31.

10 Introduced by the Motor-Cycle Crash Helmets (Religious Exemption) Act 1976, now section 16 of the Road Traffic Act 1988. For a discussion of these issues in the UK context, see Mark Hill, 'Is Nothing Sacred? Clashing Symbols in a Secular World' [2007] *Public Law* 488.

due to the fact that they closed on Saturdays.[11] Kymlicka observes that these rights are usually intended to promote integration into the larger society.[12] Black-letter legal rules thus frame wider debates relating to the place of religion in the public sphere and the co-existence of different ethnic, cultural and religious communities.

Finally, laws delineate the parameters of the common spaces of society and impose limits on freedom of action in the private sphere, providing the starting point for answering the question, 'What are migrants supposed to integrate into?' For example, legal rules and decisions often prohibit multiple marriages and arranged marriages[13] and the law in liberal democracies does not generally provide for punishment for adultery or permit domestic violence. These rules are generally applicable notwithstanding the existence of contradicting religious or cultural beliefs within particular communities.

Integration as a Part of Immigration Law in European Legal Systems

Perhaps the most important integration trend in Europe from a legal perspective concerns the use of integration as a norm in immigration and citizenship law – as a condition of entry to the state or access to social welfare, migration status or citizenship. This trend has often been said to have been encouraged or at least legitimized by EU law and policy.[14] The use of integration as a norm in citizenship law is discussed in Chapter 7. In relation to immigration law, these measures – adopted in France, Germany, the Netherlands and Denmark for example – can be divided into two broad categories: the 'external' and 'internal' dimensions of the use of integration as a mechanism of immigration control.[15] The external dimension of integration as a means of immigration control involves 'integration abroad', whereby integration tests are used as a selection and control measure at a distance for individuals seeking to gain access to the territory of the state.[16]

11 See *Quinn's Supermarket v Attorney General* [1972] IR 330, in which the Supreme Court considered a challenge to the provisions of a Ministerial Order which exempted the proprietors of Kosher shops from a ban on evening opening.

12 Will Kymlicka, note 8, p. 31.

13 See Máire Ní Shúilleabháin, 'Accommodating Cultural Diversity under Irish Family Law' (2002) 9(1) *DULJ* 175, where the writer argues that increased immigration and cultural diversity in Ireland creates a need for the reassessment of legal rules affecting the family.

14 Kees Groenendijk, 'Pre-departure Integration Strategies in the European Union: Integration or Immigration Policy?' 13(2011) *EJML* 1.

15 Sergio Carrera and Anja Wiesbrock, 'Civic Integration of Third Country Nationals: Nationalism versus Europeanisation in the Common EU Immigration Policy' (CEPS, October 2009).

16 Saskia Bonjour, note 4.

These are 'pre-departure' integration strategies.[17] There are significant differences between the types of pre-departure integration strategies followed by different countries, which is shown, for example. by Bonjour's comparison of French and Dutch integration abroad mechanisms.[18] She argues that the Dutch programme is much more stringent than the French, with France requiring only participation in an evaluation and course that are organized and financed by the French state, while the Dutch government has made entry conditional upon passing a test and does not offer paid-for training courses.[19] In contrast to these external strategies, the internal dimension involves the use of integration contracts and tests as a prerequisite to access to social protection and/or security of residence.

Countries which employ integration as a tool of immigration law use variants of the external and internal dimensions of integration as a mandatory legal process. Germany and the UK, for example, do not include a civic integration component in their integration abroad test, for which a language test is the sole pre-entry requirement.[20] At the other end of the spectrum, France has made the grant of a visa for family reunification subject to an examination of the applicant's knowledge of the 'values of the Republic' as well as the French language.[21] In a similar vein to France, the Netherlands requires knowledge of both language and society at both the pre-departure stage and within the Netherlands (the passing of which is necessary for application for a long-term residence permit and naturalization),[22] as does Denmark. In the UK, there are language requirements for some economic migrants and for family migrants,[23] while knowledge of life in the UK, including

17 Kees Groenendijk, 'Pre-departure Integration Strategies in the European Union: Integration or Immigration Policy?', note 14.

18 Saskia Bonjour, note 4. See also, on the Netherlands, Karin de Vries, *Integration at the Border: The Dutch Act on Integration Abroad and International Immigration Law* (Hart, 2013).

19 Ibid. Note that a Dutch District Court found in 2012 that the denial of family reunification for the sole reason that the applicant has failed the integration test abroad, is not in compliance with Article 7(2) of the Directive. Rb Den Haag zp Den Bosch AWB 12/9408 (23 Nov. 2012).

20 Anja Wiesbrock, 'Discrimination Instead of Integration? Integration Requirements for Immigrants in Denmark and Germany', in Elspeth Guild, Sergio Carrera and Kees Groenendijk (eds), *Illiberal Liberal States: Immigration, Citizenship and Integration in the EU* (Ashgate, 2009) 299, p. 305.

21 *Loi relative à la maitrise de l'immigration, à l'intégration et à l'asile* no. 2007–1631 of 20 November 2007. Article 1 inserts a new provision into the French immigration code to the effect that every non-EU national over 16 and under 65 years old will be evaluated in their country of residence on their degree of knowledge of the French language and the values of the Republic.

22 In relation to family migrants, see Betty de Hart, Tineke Strik & Henrike Pankratz, Netherlands Summary Report, *Family Reunification: A barrier or facilitator of integration?* (January 2013), pp. 6–9.

23 In relation to family migrants, see Statement of Changes in Immigration Rules Cm 7794 (October 2010, came into force 29 November 2010), and Part 8 of the Immigration

history and the functioning of institutions, is required for access to indefinite leave to remain in the UK (long-term residence).[24] The type of required knowledge of the society also varies, with the Dutch test focussing on practical issues such as knowledge of the geography of the Netherlands and the health-care system while the French test can encompass more explicitly 'national identity' centred questions such as questions related to secularism and the exercise of citizenship.[25]

With regard to the internal dimension, France and Denmark have followed a contractual approach whereby migrants are required to enter into an integration contract in order to gain access to security of residence. In Denmark, while the signing of a contract is not strictly mandatory, failure to sign will result in the delay of the acquisition of a permanent residence permit.[26] In France, the objective of assimilating migrants into French Republican identity is not disguised, with the degree of integration being evaluated by reference to the requirements outlined in the contract and the commitment of the individual to respect the principles and values governing the French Republic. Carrera argues that these legal developments in France have strengthened the juridical nexus between integration and immigration, and have led to the emergence of a neo-Republican integrationist doctrine.[27]

The personal scope of these integration measures, in particular those relating to 'integration abroad', illustrates both the objectives of the measures and the concepts of identity and 'otherness' which they enshrine. EU migrants are exempt from such requirements and any attempt to impose integration requirements on EU citizens would be contrary to EU law. In the case of the Netherlands and Germany, migrants entering the Netherlands from 'developed' countries – for example, Switzerland, the US, Canada, Japan, South Korea, Australia and New Zealand – are largely exempt from integration requirements (although in the

---

Rules, for example, paragraphs 281(i)(a)(ii); 290(vii)(a) and 295A (i)(a)(ii). In relation to the complex system of language requirements for economic migrants within the points-based system, see generally Appendix B to the Immigration Rules ('English language') and for commentary, see Bernard Ryan, 'The Integration Agenda in British Migration Law', in Elspeth Guild, Sergio Carrera and Kees Groenendijk (eds), *Illiberal Liberal States: Immigration, Citizenship and Integration in the EU* (Ashgate, 2009), 277.

24 See Chapter 7. For commentary, see Bernard Ryan, 'The Integration Agenda in British Migration Law', ibid., p. 285; Bernard Ryan 'Integration Requirements: A New Model in Migration Law' (2008) 22(4) *Journal of Immigration Asylum and Nationality Law*.

25 Sergio Carrera and Anja Wiesbrock, 'Civic Integration of Third Country Nationals: Nationalism versus Europeanisation in the Common EU Immigration Policy', note 15, pp. 12–16.

26 Ibid., pp. 21–23.

27 Sergio Carrera, 'Nationality, Immigration and 'the Republican Integration' in France', in Elspeth Guild, Kees Groenendijk and Sergio Carrera, 'Understanding the Contest of Community: Illiberal Practices in the EU?', in Elspeth Guild, Sergio Carrera and Kees Groenendijk (eds), *Illiberal Liberal States: Immigration, Citizenship and Integration in the EU* (Ashgate, 2009) 315, p. 333.

case of Germany the requirement is simply a language test).[28] This confirms that the requirements are culturally based, suggesting not only that certain types of migrants (i.e. those from rich, developed countries) are considered more desirable than others, but also that it is presumed that migrants from developed countries can fit more easily into the social fabric of the receiving state.[29]

In addition to the direct form of differential treatment, certain ethnic groups are disproportionately affected by the measures. In relation to the Netherlands for example, the Turkish and Moroccan communities have been the most affected by the high costs involved and the literacy levels required to undergo the tests.[30] Human Rights Watch has criticized the 'integration abroad' measures contained in the Integration Abroad Act adopted by the Netherlands as discriminatory and in violation of the principle of non-discrimination contained in the European Convention on Human Rights (ECHR) and the International Convention on the Elimination of All Forms of Racial Discrimination (ICERD), arguing that the intended effect of the measures is the reduction of immigration of family migrants of these groups.[31] In its 2010 concluding observations on the state report submitted by the Netherlands, the CERD Committee echoed Human Rights Watch's concerns.[32] In addition, the way in which these integration abroad measures are, in the main, targeted at family migrants is of note, as this results in a 'double hit' for integration: integration becomes a mandatory process for family migrants and also makes family reunification more difficult, potentially hindering the integration of the family member already in the receiving country.

28 In the case of the Netherlands, see Leonard F.M. Besselink, 'Integration and Immigration: The Vicissitudes of Dutch 'Inburgering', in Elspeth Guild, Sergio Carrera and Kees Groenendijk (eds), *Illiberal Liberal States: Immigration, Citizenship and Integration in the EU* (Ashgate, 2009) 241, p. 250. In relation to Germany, see Anja Wiesbrock, 'Discrimination Instead of Integration? Integration Requirements for Immigrants in Denmark and Germany', in Elspeth Guild, Sergio Carrera and Kees Groenendijk (eds), *Illiberal Liberal States: Immigration, Citizenship and Integration in the EU* (Ashgate, 2009), p. 305.

29 Although see Besselink's argument, ibid.

30 Human Rights Watch, 'The Netherlands: Discrimination in the Name of Integration: Migrants Rights Under the Integration Abroad Act' (May 2008). See generally, Karin de Vries, note 18, Chapter 8, 'The Right to Equal Treatment: Direct Differential Treatment on Grounds of Nationality and Residence Purpose'.

31 Ibid.

32 The Netherlands, UN Doc CERD/C/NLD/CO/17–18 (25 March 2010), para. 5.

Replication of the Civic Integration Model: Integration as a Feature of Irish Immigration Law?

As already seen in the previous chapter in the context of policy, Ireland is 'beyond the dominant European narrative' when it comes to integration.[33] Irish legislation contains no express reference to integration, and there are no language or 'knowledge of society' tests attached to the application process for family reunification, long-term residence or citizenship. The Immigration, Residence and Protection Bill 2010 proposed the introduction of the concept of 'integration' into Irish legislation. Section 141 of the 2010 Bill gave the Minister the power to make regulations relating to immigration matters, and such regulations could provide for:

> (a) the classes of foreign nationals to whom entry permissions, residence permissions, enhanced residence permissions or long-term residence permissions (referred to as "permissions") of particular categories may be granted; and
>
> (b) such conditions attaching to the different categories of such permissions as the Minister considers appropriate.

A class of foreign nationals to whom a particular category of permission applied was to be specified by reference to 'such matters as the Minister considers appropriate'. In specifying categories of permission or conditions of permission, the Minister was to have regard to whether the entry into or presence in the state of a foreign national or a class of foreign nationals to whom a permission of a category specified in those regulations may be granted would contribute to (*inter alia*) 'the promotion of successful social integration of foreign nationals into the State'.[34] Interestingly, the same section provided that the Minister must have regard to 'the enrichment and strengthening of the cultural and social fabric of the State',[35] which seemed to acknowledge the benefits and enrichment brought by immigration. These legislative references to integration, and their recognition of the impact of immigration rules on integration, would have constituted a new departure in Irish law.

Even more significant than this general recognition of integration as an important policy consideration in the development of immigration law, however, was the provision in section 46 of the 2010 Bill, on long-term residency, which provided that the Minister would grant long-term resident status to individuals satisfying the requirements set out therein. These requirements included that the person concerned had satisfied the Minister that he or she has made reasonable

33 Alana Lentin and Gavan Titley, *The Crises of Multiculturalism* (Zed Books, 2011), p. 206.

34 Section 141(4)(e) of the Immigration, Residence and Protection Bill 2010.

35 Section 141(4)(d) of the Immigration, Residence and Protection Bill 2010.

efforts, while resident in the state, to 'socially integrate'.[36] This term was not defined in the Bill and this vague condition was effectively a tool to allow the Minister to retain a high level of discretion over the granting of long-term residency. These provisions of the 2010 Bill reflect the practice, discussed (and criticized) in this section, by European states of using integration as a condition to access legal status and entitlements, and illustrate the replication of the civic integration model in different states around Europe. This Bill failed to pass through Parliament before the dissolution of the 30th Dáil on 2 February 2011 and thus lapsed before it could be adopted. It remains to be seen whether these elements of the legislation pertaining to integration will be retained in future proposals. In 2012, responding to the European Commission's Green Paper on family reunification, Ireland stated that while it did not operate language or integration testing, it can 'see the rationale for doing so'.[37]

The Effects of Coercive Integration Measures: A Narrowing of the Frame of Analysis and the Need to Move beyond This

As a result of the adoption of these legal measures, the interaction between integration and law is increasingly considered within the 'integration as a condition in immigration law' frame of analysis, with the concept of integration seen as a means used by states as a vehicle for discrimination and assimilation, as well as a means of immigration control.[38] This shift has led to an extensive analysis of this direct link between integration and immigration law. Carrera and Wiesbrock conclude that:

> Integration … is not regarded as a process of social inclusion and equalisation of rights and freedoms, but rather as a state requirement for the TCN to disappear into the homogenous national wholeness and another way for the state to promote national identity and nationalism within and beyond its territorial borders.[39]

Guild, Groenendijk and Carrera echo this, characterizing these integration practices in immigration and citizenship laws as illiberal practices in liberal regimes.[40] This

36 Section 46(3)(d)(iii) of the Immigration, Residence and Protection Bill 2010.

37 European Commission, 'Summary of Stakeholder Responses to the Green Paper on the Right to Family Reunification of Third-Country Nationals' (2012), p. 11.

38 See Ricky Van Oers, Eva Ersboll and Dora Kostakopoulou, 'Mapping the redefinition of belonging in Europe', in Ricky Van Oers, Eva Ersboll and Dora Kostakopoulou (eds), *A Re-Definition of Belonging? Language and Integration Tests in Europe* (Martinus Nijhoff Publishers, 2010) 307, p. 318.

39 Sergio Carrera and Anja Wiesbrock, note 15, p. 4.

40 Elspeth Guild, Kees Groenendijk and Sergio Carrera, 'Understanding the Contest of Community: Illiberal Practices in the EU?', in Elspeth Guild, Sergio Carrera and Kees Groenendijk (eds), *Illiberal Liberal States: Immigration, Citizenship and Integration in the EU* (Ashgate, 2009) 1, p. 3.

transformation of integration into a means of social exclusion and insecurity for non-EU migrants undermines the narratives of integration propounded by – *inter alia* – UNHCR, the Council of Europe and the EU, which emphasize the two-way, holistic and gradual nature of the integration process. Lochak points out the inverted nature of the concepts of integration in use in immigration law, arguing that, in the French case, the stigma attached to integration 'obligations' cannot but have the effect of marginalizing immigrant groups more than ever, ultimately constituting a barrier to real integration.[41] In particular, the notion of 'integration abroad' abandons the idea of integration as a multi-faceted two-way process, by requiring individuals to prove their capacity for integration before even entering the territory of the state.

Ostensibly, 'civic integration' through integration tests and contracts simply requires individuals being admitted to the territory of the state to demonstrate a minimum commitment to adapting to the society which they are entering. However, the way in which the tests are framed and targeted suggests that the real objectives are to control certain types of immigration and compel migrants to accept elements of national identity (more than likely relinquishing their own in the process) without acknowledging the role of members of the receiving society or the receiving state itself in facilitating social and economic integration. Integration thus becomes both a tool of immigration control and a mechanism for controlling identity – sending a message that certain types of migrant, who are presumed to hold values different from those of members of the receiving society, will not be accepted in the receiving state if they do not accept the state's imagined national identity.[42]

The examination of integration as a mandatory norm has become the prism through which the interaction between integration and law is currently predominantly discussed in the academic sphere, and constitutes a valuable source of academic commentary on integration and law. These analyses have focussed on integration as a 'border practice' employed by states:[43] to shore up the state's external borders against migrants, who are characterized as potentially dangerous threats to social cohesion, or internal borders between citizens and non-citizens. It has been shown in this chapter, however, that the interactions between integration and law are more far-reaching than the border practice of express references to integration in immigration and citizenship law. In addition, as discussed briefly above (and as it will be seen in the course of this book), integration has not yet

41 Danièle Lochak, '*L'intégration comme injonction. Enjeux idéologiques et politiques liés à l'immigration*' (2006) 64 *Cultures et Conflits* 131, p. 133.

42 See Liav Orgad, ''Cultural Defence' of Nations: Cultural Citizenship in France, Germany and the Netherlands' (2009) 15(6) *ELJ* 719; Elspeth Guild, Kees Groenendijk and Sergio Carrera, 'Understanding the Contest of Community: Illiberal Practices in the EU?', in Elspeth Guild, Sergio Carrera and Kees Groenendijk (eds), *Illiberal Liberal States: Immigration, Citizenship and Integration in the EU* (Ashgate, 2009), 1, note 40, p. 11.

43 Lentin and Titley, note 33, p. 204.

entered all European legal systems in the form of integration conditions, tests or contracts (Ireland, for example, remains a notable exception). The idea of this book, therefore, is to move beyond this framework for discussing the relationship between integration and law, using the broader frame of analysis outlined in the first two chapters. Rather than ask questions such as: 'Are these requirements in response to concrete problems of immigrant integration?' or 'Do they enable, or actually inhibit, integration?',[44] this book attempts to outline a legal framework for examining integration, with the intention of showing that governments do not have a monopoly over defining what integration actually means.

As an example of the broader approach which this book takes to the study of integration and law, the next section considers the regulation of family reunification in Ireland, the UK and France.

A Broader Look at Integration and Law: Family Reunification

As seen above, the 'normativity' of integration is frequently expressed through black letter rules in the legal systems of European countries.[45] As discussed, in France, the Netherlands and Denmark for example, the satisfaction of integration 'conditions' as a pre-condition to legal migration and to accessing certain legal statuses has become an accepted part of immigration law and policy. Aside from this express linkage of immigration law and integration, however, all European legal systems contains legal rules which have a direct impact on integration, in particular in the key integration domain of family reunification (as taken here to mean the process whereby family members who are separated due to forced or voluntary migration regroup in a country other than the country of origin of one or more of the family members). The connections between legal classification, immigration status and integration in the context of family reunification constitute an example of a 'functional' element of integration as referred to in Chapter 2.

Family reunification is treated by scholars and immigrant advocates as a key element of the integration process and as essential for the wellbeing of migrants.[46]

44 Sara Goodman Wallace, 'Integration Requirements for Integration's Sake? Identifying, Categorising and Comparing Civic Integration Policies' (2010) 36(5) *Journal of Ethnic and Migration Studies* 753.

45 Sergio Carrera, *In Search of the Perfect Citizen? The Intersection between Integration, Immigration and Nationality in the EU* (Martinus Nijhoff, 2009).

46 See Kate Jastram and Kathleen Newland, 'Family Unity and Refugee Protection', in Erika Feller, Voller Turk and Frances Nicholson (eds), *Refugee Protection in International Law* (Cambridge University Press, 2003), p. 555. In the refugee context, see UNHCR Executive Committee, *Conclusion on Local Integration* 7 October 2005, No. 104 (LVI) – 2005, para. 2. In the Irish context, see Immigrant Council of Ireland, 'Getting On: From Immigration to Integration' (ICI, May 2008), p. 148.

The socio-political consequences of the failure to facilitate family reunification have been emphasized by the International Labour Organization in the following terms:

> Prolonged separation and isolation lead to hardships and stress situations affecting both the migrants and the families left behind and prevent them from leading a normal life. The large numbers of migrant workers cut off from social relations and living on the fringe of the receiving community create many well-known social and psychological problems that, in turn, largely determine community attitudes towards migrant workers.[47]

However, official policy relating to integration often ignores this dimension of family reunification, most likely due to the perception that 'more generous family sponsorship provisions tend to raise the overall costs of integration and dilute the economic benefits produced by the original labour entrants'.[48]

Family Reunification in Ireland: Complexity and Differentiation

Irish official discourse on integration has to date avoided reference to family reunification as a potential tool for integration, reflecting policy and practice in many European states.[49] In legal terms, the lack of emphasis on family reunification in Ireland is highlighted by the fact that outside the field of refugee law, there is no legislative provision for family reunification. The legal position relating to family reunification in Irish law depends on the legal classification of the person concerned.[50] Different rules apply to Irish citizens, nationals of EU Member States, refugees and other categories of non-EU migrants who want their family members to join them in Ireland.[51]

47 International Labour Conference, 59th session, 1974, Report VII (I), *Migrant Workers*, 1973, 27.

48 International Organization for Migration and the National Economic and Social Council, *Managing Migration in Ireland: A Social and Economic Analysis* (IOM, September 2006), p. 158.

49 UNHCR noted in a recent report on integration that none of the European countries researched for the report emphasized facilitation of family reunification as part of their integration efforts. UNHCR, 'Mapping Integration: UNHCR's Age, Gender and Diversity Mainstreaming Project on Refugee Integration in Ireland – 2008/2009' (UNHCR, 2009), p. 10.

50 On the fragmentation of family reunification rules in the EU generally, see Anne Staver 'Free Movement and the Fragmentation of Family Reunification Rights' (2013) 15(1) *EJML* 69.

51 It should be noted that in the Irish system, nationals of European Economic Area countries are treated the same as EU nationals for the purposes of family reunification.

EU migrants are in the most favourable position in relation to family reunification due to the protection afforded by EU law,[52] followed by refugees whose family reunification regime is grounded in statute.[53] In contrast, the family reunification of Irish citizens and non-EU citizens is based on ministerial discretion and is consequently fraught with uncertainty for applicants (except in a limited range of exceptions determined by EU law, particularly in the wake of the *Zambrano*,[54] *McCarthy*,[55] *Dereci*[56] and other recent rulings of the CJEU).[57] In judicially reviewing decisions by the Minister for Justice on family reunification the Irish courts have been influenced by the difficulty in reconciling the conflicting interests at the centre of family reunification disputes, and the approach, in relation to the family reunification of non-national spouses, has been that 'a state is not bound to respect the choice of residence made by married couples'[58] – even where one of the couple is a citizen of the state. In the words of Fennelly J in the Supreme Court, 'The legitimate interest of the State in the control of immigration frequently conflicts with claims of migrants based on family reunification'.[59]

A cursory look at the rules relating to each of the categories thus reveals an anomaly: EU citizens exercising their right to free movement in Ireland, along with recognized refugees, are better off in family reunification terms than Irish citizens. The lack of legislative provision for family reunification does not seem to be of pressing concern to legislators. The Immigration, Residence and Protection Bill 2010 provided the Minister for Justice with the power to make regulations which could have provided for conditions relating to 'the extent to which foreign nationals may enjoy family reunification in the State', however the Bill did not provide for family reunification in the primary legislation.[60] As mentioned, this Bill lapsed in February 2011 but is likely to be resurrected in the course of the current Parliament.[61]

52 The seminal case being Case 127/08 *Metock* [2008] ECR I-6241.

53 Section 18 of the Refugee Act 1996 (as amended).

54 Case C-34/09 *Zambrano v Office National de l'Emploi (ONEm)* (Judgment of 8 March 2011).

55 Case C-434/09 *McCarthy v Secretary of State for the Home Department* (Judgment of 5 May 2011).

56 Case C-256/11 *Murat Dereci and Others v Bundesministerium für Inneres* (Judgment of 15 November 2011).

57 Other recent decisions include: Case C-40/11 *Iida* (Judgment of 8 November 2012); Cases C-356/11 and C-357/11 *O, S* and *Maahanmuuttovirasto* (Judgment of 6 December 2012); Case C-87/12 *Kreshnik Ymeraga and Others v Ministre du Travail, de l'Emploi et de l'Immigration* (Judgment of 8 May 2013).

58 *TC v Minister for Justice, Equality and Law Reform* [2005] 4 IR 109.

59 *TC v Minister for Justice, Equality and Law Reform* [2005] 4 IR 109, *per* Fennelly J at 111.

60 Section 141(2)(b)(x) of the Immigration, Residence and Protection Bill 2010.

61 In its 2011 concluding observations on Ireland's state report, the CERD Committee regretted the lapse of the Bill as well as the provision in that Bill that family reunification

The differentiated rules applied to different groups of applicants for family reunification in Ireland have a variety of rationales, none of which are directly related to integration. In the case of EU migrants, the rationale for the right to family reunification in EU law relates to the objectives of the single market and the realization of the free movement of persons. In the case of refugees, the entitlement to family reunification is linked to the inability of the refugee to return to their country of origin. Nevertheless, the rules in relation to these two categories are both indirectly related to integration concerns in the sense of constituting an acknowledgement that individuals find it difficult to settle and integrate in a country without their family unit. The position in relation to Irish citizens and non-EU citizens, on the other hand, is bound up with the concerns of immigration control and the desire to maintain a high degree of executive control over the immigration and asylum systems. Overall, despite the importance of family reunification as a functional aspect of integration, the law in this area is fragmented and restrictive, and unconnected to the idea of facilitating family reunification as a means to further integration. The legal regime for family reunification in Ireland remains characterized by a patchwork of differentiated rules and policies – shaped partly by EU law, partly by international refugee law, and mainly by the principle of executive discretion in the field of immigration law.

Family Reunification in the UK: Discouraging or Encouraging Integration?

Similar to Ireland, in the UK, family reunification policy is not presented as complementary to integration. In contrast, in recent years, the drive to reduce net migration has led to further restrictions being placed on family migration, making it more difficult for people to join their relatives in the UK.

For those categories of migrant who are still allowed to bring dependents to the UK to live with them, there is a stated 'clear focus' in the Immigration Rules on family migration on 'whether the relationship is genuine, that the sponsor can properly support their partner and any dependants financially, and that the partner is able to integrate into British society'.[62] Both the increased financial threshold for being allowed to sponsor a dependent (introduced in 2012)[63] and the enhanced language requirement to be satisfied by family members when they are applying for a visa or permission to remain in the UK (introduced in 2010)[64] have thus been justified in terms of 'facilitating' integration. In particular, the financial requirement is justified on the dual grounds that it will ensure that such

could be provided for in a statutory instrument (para. 26). UN Doc CERD/C/IRL/CO/3–4 (10 March 2011), para. 15.

62 Home Office, 'Statement of Intent, Family Migration' (June 2012), p. 6.

63 Ibid., p. 6; Statement of Changes in Immigration Rules HC 194 (June 2012).

64 Statement of Changes in Immigration Rules Cm 7794' (October 2010, came into force 29 November 2010), and Part 8 of the Immigration Rules, for example, paragraphs 281(i)(a)(ii); 290(vii)(a) and 295A (i)(a)(ii).

family members 'do not become a burden on the taxpayer and allows sufficient participation in everyday life to facilitate integration'.[65] In this approach we again see an emphasis on conditions unilaterally imposed on the migrant, justified in the name of integration, to limit the entitlement to a right viewed by human rights and migrant-led organizations as key to successful integration. This stems from the clear manipulation of the idea of integration to fit with the ultimate immigration policy goals of promoting 'skilled' migration and reducing net migration overall. This also reflects other European states' (including France's) approach of linking selective migration to successful integration.[66]

There have been a number of human rights challenges to these amended rules, in which the courts have considered the balance struck between the legitimate aims of the rules (promoting integration, protecting the economic interests of the UK) and the interference with family life. These challenges followed the Supreme Court decision in *Quila v Secretary of State*,[67] in which a paragraph of the Immigration Rules which set the eligible age for spouses to join their partner in the UK at twenty one, with the stated aim of reducing forced marriages, was found to be a disproportionate interference with family rights under Article 8 ECHR when applied to unforced marriages.[68] This aspect of the Rules was subsequently amended to require a minimum age of 18.

In *MM, Javed and Majid v Secretary of State*,[69] decided in July 2013, the High Court found that the stringent financial requirements introduced in 2012 severely restricted the ability of sponsors on low incomes to bring their spouses to the UK to live with them. The minimum income requirement, together with one or more of four other financial requirements of the rules, would amount to a disproportionate interference with family rights, even when considered in light of the legitimate aim of safeguarding the economic welfare of the UK.[70] While Blake J accepted in principle that the families of migrants could and should be encouraged by the terms of admission to integrate, the features of the rules did not represent a fair balance between the competing interests.[71] The Court did not strike down the rules but urged the Secretary of State to adjust them in order to satisfy the requirements of proportionality.

The result in *MM* contrasts with the finding of the Court of Appeal in *R (Bibi and others) v Secretary of State*,[72] which was a challenge to the enhanced language

65 Home Office, 'Statement of Intent, Family Migration', p. 16.

66 See Kees Groenendijk, 'Pre-departure Integration Strategies in the European Union: Integration or Immigration Policy?', note 14, p. 15.

67 [2012] 1 AC 241.

68 For commentary on this decision, see Yvonne Tew, 'And they call it puppy love: young love, forced marriage and immigration rules' (2012) 71(1) *Cambridge Law Journal* 18.

69 [2013] EWHC 1900 Admin.

70 Ibid., paras 126–147.

71 Ibid., para. 142.

72 [2013] EWCA Civ 322.

requirement, applicable to most foreign spouses, which was introduced in 2010. The Court of Appeal allowed for a wide margin of appreciation in this case, revealing a reluctance to interfere with matters of integration, which it considered as a part of social policy to be primarily determined by the government. Maurice Kay LJ was of the view that: '(t)he pre-entry test was conceived as a benign measure of social policy with the purpose of facilitating the integration of non-English-speaking spouses',[73] and did not constitute a 'colossal'[74] interference with family life, as, according to him, '(i)t involves a relatively simple test, satisfaction of which will generally be achievable within a relatively short time'.[75] The Court's interpretation of the language requirement as a relatively minor interference with family life, together with its acceptance of the government's arguments as to the necessity of the test in terms of integration, thus resulted in the rejection of the challenge to the rules. The Court also rejected the idea that exempting individuals from English-speaking countries from the requirement amounted to direct discrimination.

In these decisions, the UK courts have supported the position of the government that integration can be a legitimate aim of mandatory requirements in immigration rules. They have also endorsed the idea that integration policy is a field in which governments should be given a wide margin of appreciation. However, these cases also show that the human rights implications of incorporating integration-related measures into immigration rules must be taken into account if the rules are to be justified and proportionate. This reinforces the arguments for a human-rights based paradigm of integration which are discussed in the next chapter.

Family Reunification as an Illustration of the Nexus between Integration and Law: The View from France

As mentioned above, under French law, family reunification is expressly subject to an evaluation of the applicant's language skills as well as knowledge of the 'values of the Republic' (language being tested through oral and written tests and knowledge of values being tested orally through a ten-minute interview in a language the person understands).[76] These values are defined as 'in particular, equality between men and women, *laïcité*, the rule of law, the fundamental freedoms, the security of persons and property, as well as the exercise of citizenship that is permitted notably through obligatory and free education'.[77] If this evaluation reveals insufficient knowledge, then the applicant is obliged to follow a language course of at least 40 hours or a three-hour course on Republican

73 Ibid., para. 30.

74 Para. 27.

75 Ibid.

76 Article R311-30-2 of the Immigration Code ('*Code de l'entrée et du séjour des* étrangers *et du droit d›asile*'), to be read together with Article L211-2-1.

77 Article R311-30-2 and R311-22 of the Immigration Code.

values (and is then re-tested in the case of language skills).[78] If there are children involved in the family reunification, the parents must, in signing the integration and welcome contract for the family,[79] follow a course (of at least half a day) on the rights and obligations of parents in France.[80]

French law thus explicitly incorporates an integration dimension, which expressly includes both language and values elements. However, as is also clear from the review of Irish and UK law, laws do not need to explicitly acknowledge the connection to have a real impact on integration, once the complexity of integration is recognized. This section started from the assumption that migration status plays a key role in integration. Viewed in this way, in Ireland and the UK (as well as in France), the legal barriers to access to legal status via family reunification contradicts the rhetoric of social inclusion, interculturalism, social mobility and participation contained in official integration policy, with non-EU migrants in a precarious position in this legal domain due to the operation of a largely discretionary family reunification regime (in Ireland) and the imposition of financial and language requirements imposed (in the UK).

An 'Integration and Law' Paradigm?

'Legal integration' is sometimes seen as a discrete aspect of the integration process. UNHCR, for example defines legal integration as the legal process and framework whereby refugees are granted a progressively wider range of rights and entitlements by the host state broadly commensurate with those enjoyed by citizens and '(a)ffirms the particular importance of the legal dimension of integration'.[81] At the other end of the spectrum of the idea of 'legal integration' is the study of the use of integration as a mandatory norm in immigration and citizenship law, discussed in detail above. However, both of these approaches underestimate the pervasive nature of the influence of law on integration, particularly when integration is viewed in its broad context as discussed in Chapter 2. Some examples illustrate this point. National constitutional law provides the legal parameters for integration policy, outlines the fundamental rights of citizens and non-citizens and provides the framework for the mediation of conflicting interests. National constitutions

78 Articles R311-30-4, R311-30-6 and R311-30-9 of the Immigration Code, with *Arrêté du 1er décembre 2008 relatif à l'évaluation dans leur pays de résidence du niveau de connaissance, par les étrangers, de la langue française et des valeurs de la République et aux formations prescrites dans ces domaines conformément aux articles R. 311-30-1 à R. 311–30–11 du code de l'entrée et du séjour des étrangers et du droit d'asile*.

79 As required by Article L311-9-1 of the Immigration Code.

80 Article R311-30-12 of the Immigration Code.

81 UNHCR Executive Committee, *Conclusion on Local Integration* 7 October 2005, No. 104 (LVI) – 2005.

often disclose the values of the society into which immigrants will be integrated,[82] and provide some indication of the extent to which ethnic, cultural and religious diversity is welcomed, tolerated or discouraged from a legal point of view. Immigration law divides migrants into legal categories, giving the individual a legal status which will define the extent of access to the employment market, social welfare benefits, and services such as education and health services. Governments may decide to deal with discrimination based on race or xenophobia by developing anti-discrimination and equality legislation. Laws may define acceptable public behaviour or dress in certain ways. On the basis of legal provisions, governments determine the conditions of access to citizenship including language requirements and knowledge of the host society. Legal provisions can thus constitute both barriers to and instruments of integration and have a direct effect on migrants' outcomes in terms of social mobility, economic stability, societal participation, health and education.

As was seen from the section above on integration as part of immigration law in European legal systems, the literature exploring the interactions between integration and law is expanding. In addition, Chapter 2 showed that the traditional theoretical models are inadequate for coping with the complexity of integration processes. The idea of 'integration and law', if given a broader meaning than that ascribed to it by UNHCR or in the use of integration as a mandatory norm in immigration law, could become a useful analytical tool. A paradigm of integration viewed through the prism of law, or 'integration and law' leads away from circular discussions on the meaning of integration and towards a more meaningful debate on how integration operates in practice. 'Integration and law', as conceived in terms of the interaction of law with the functional and wider perspectives delineated in Chapter 2, forms the basis of this book. A key element of the 'integration and law paradigm' proposed in this book is the use of different legal frameworks to develop an alternative narrative of integration to the neo-nationalist, values-promoting paradigm, in use at the national level in many European countries, whereby migrants are required to pass integration tests and sign integration contracts. The 'external influences' on national integration law and policy, as described briefly below, thus form a central part of the analysis in both parts II and III of the book.

The Role of Public Philosophy in Shaping the Legal Framework for Integration

What are the factors that shape the legal approach to integration at the national level and what are the distinctive legal approaches that arise from these factors? The legal approach to integration on a national level is conditioned by a complex

82 On the constitutional expression of national identity, see, for example, Anthony D. Smith, *National Identity* (Penguin, 1991).

combination of social, historical, political and legal factors.[83] Heckmann and Schnapper maintain that certain consistencies and common characteristics in integration policies are not the result of a conscious strategy but derive from basic socio-structural principles and institutions or the social order of a country.[84] Thus, for example, Permoser and Rosenberger argue that the strong recognition of religious citizenship and the role that this plays in integration in Austria stems from the historical legacy of the multi-ethnic Austro-Hungarian Empire and its tolerant attitudes, as well as the traditions of consociational democracy and corporatism that characterize the political system.[85] The approach to integration issues may also be determined by the sense of nationhood or concept of citizenship. Constitutions can be seen as the legal expression of important elements of political and social philosophy as well as national identity.[86] They frame discussions about a shared conception of the common good and a desired form of life that is put forward as authentic.[87] Jurgen Habermas has observed that constitutional discourse enables the participants to clarify the way in which they want to understand themselves as citizens of a specific republic, as inhabitants of a specific region, as heirs to a specific culture, which traditions they want to perpetuate and which they want to discontinue, how they want to deal with their history, with one another and so on.[88] Thus, for example, Article 1 of the French Constitution of 1958 enshrines the fundamental principles of the French Republic, including *laïcité* and equality before the law, and in the same vein, the Turkish Constitution of 1982 declares the secular nature of the Turkish Republic.[89] The 'multicultural' foundations of Canada

83 Wiesbrock, for example, counts the country's historical, political, legal and cultural framework, and the nature and extent of immigration flows as among the multiple influences that shape national legislation in the area of immigration and integration. Anja Wiesbrock, *Legal Migration to the European Union* (Martinus Nijhoff Publishers, 2010), p. 728.

84 Friedrich Heckmann and Dominique Schnapper (eds), *The Integration of Immigrants in European Societies – National Differences and Trends of Convergence* (Lucius and Lucius, 2003), p. 11.

85 Julia Mourao Permoser and Sieglinde Rosenberger, 'Religious Citizenship as a Substitute for Immigrant Integration? The Governance of Diversity in Austria?', in Elspeth Guild, Sergio Carrera and Kees Groenendijk (eds), *Illiberal Liberal States: Immigration, Citizenship and Integration in the EU* (Ashgate, 2009), 149.

86 See Thomas J. Barron, Owen Dudley Edwards and Patricia J Storey (eds), *Constitutions and National Identity* (Quadriga, 1993), in particular D. W. Harkness, 'The Constitutions of Ireland and the Development of National Identity', p. 304. Cf. Sujit Choudhry, 'Globalization in Search of Justification: Toward a Theory of Comparative Constitutional Interpretation' (1999) 74 *Indiana Law Journal* 819; Bruce Ackerman, 'The Rise of World Constitutionalism' (1997) 83 *Virginia Law Review* 771.

87 Jurgen Habermas, 'The European Nation State: Its Achievements and its Limitations: On the Past and Future of Sovereignty and Citizenship' (1996) 9 *Ratio Juris* 125, p. 125.

88 Ibid., p. 124.

89 Article 2, 'Characteristics of the Republic' of the Constitution of Turkey 1982.

are acknowledged in the Canadian Charter of Rights and Freedoms.[90] Article 1 of the Basic Law of Germany 1949 expressly constitutionalizes the respect for human dignity, reflecting the legacy of the Second World War.[91] Similarly, the legacy of apartheid is clear in Article 1 of the South African Constitution of 1996, which includes the values of 'human dignity, the achievement of equality and the advancement of human rights and freedoms' and 'non-racialism and non-sexism' among the founding values of the state. In this way, as Habermas observes, every constitutional order, legal community and democratic process for actualizing basic rights is permeated by ethics.[92] In the integration context, the permeation of ethics throughout the constitutional order is significant, because 'ethical-political decisions are an unavoidable part of politics, and because their legal regulation expresses the collective identity of a nation of citizens, they can spark cultural battles in which disrespected minorities struggle against an insensitive majority culture'.[93]

In practice, the expression of the legal and political identity of states contained in constitutions has a demonstrable impact on constitutional adjudication. For example, in the Canadian case of *Multani v Commission Scolaire Marguerite-Bourgeoys*,[94] the Canadian Supreme Court struck down an order of a school authority that prohibited a Sikh child from wearing a kirpan to school as a violation of freedom of religion under the Canadian Charter of Rights and Freedoms. A large part of the reasoning of the court revolved around the importance of adhering to Canadian values of multiculturalism and religious tolerance.[95] Similarly, in the South African case of *MEC for Education: Kwazulu Natal v Pillay*,[96] the Supreme Court of South Africa held that a school's refusal to allow an exemption from the school code which prohibited the wearing of any jewellery for a Hindu student who wished to wear a nose stud was discriminatory, even though the wearing of the stud was not a mandatory religious practice but a voluntary cultural practice. In coming to this conclusion, the Court emphasized the centrality to the South African constitutional project of the positive commitment to the accommodation of religious and cultural diversity, 'which not only affirms diversity, but promotes and celebrates it'.[97] These cases demonstrate the importance of constitutional identity in adjudicating issues related to integration.

90 Article 27, Canadian Charter of Rights and Freedoms 1982.

91 Article 1, 'Human dignity', of the Basic Law of Germany 1949.

92 Jurgen Habermas, note 95, p. 125.

93 Jurgen Habermas, note 95, p. 125.

94 [2006] 1 SCR 256, 2006 SCC 6. However, see also *Alberta v Hutterian Brethren of Wilson Colony* [2010] 1 LRC 349, 2009 SCC 37, in which it was found to be permissible to require Hutterites to be photographed to attain driver's licences, against their religious beliefs.

95 Ibid., at para. 79, for example. (Judgment of McLachlin C.J. and Bastarache, Binnie, Fish and Charron J.J. delivered by Charron J.)

96 Case CCT 51/06, [2007] ZACC 21, 7 October 2007.

97 Ibid., at para. 65, *per* Langa CJ.

Finally, integration measures may be influenced by the societal definition of the immigration situation (for example, 'The US is a country of immigration'). These ideologies are transformed into legal and institutional measures affecting the integration of immigrants.[98] It has been shown that integration is composed of different elements covering a wide spectrum of issues ranging from labour market participation and social mobility to cultural and religious issues. The ideological and political foundations of the state in question will determine which aspects of integration are emphasized, and these then enter the legal landscape through legal measures and institutional practice.[99]

Illustrations of the Impact of Public Philosophy in the European Setting

Favell suggests that a state's 'public philosophy' provides the frame for response to ethnic dilemmas in liberal democracies.[100] The notion of a 'public philosophy' is a way of characterizing the widespread political beliefs and ideas that underpin everyday politics in western liberal democratic societies. French public philosophy, for example, is traditionally based on the idea of universalist Republican citizenship, while British public philosophy is conditioned by classic liberalism and the idea of citizenship and incremental social progress through the pragmatism and flexibility of political and legal institutions.[101] The public philosophy of a state will form the background to the consensus for talking about integration issues and will shape the contours of the legal framework for integration. Accordingly, the UK and France have traditionally formed contrasting ideas about the correct framework for policy responses to integration issues due to their contrasting public philosophies. Favell characterizes the UK as promoting the integration of ethnic minorities into a tolerant multi-national state, via the management strategy of race relations and multiculturalism, while France is viewed as envisaging the integration of *immigrés* into a universalist national community, via access to full participatory political *citoyenneté*.[102] The previous chapter explored some of the concrete manifestations of these public philosophies in the integration policies and models followed in each.

Favell goes on to recognize that integration policies in UK and France have important similarities in that the policy framework in both countries relies on a good deal of 'mystificatory discourse'[103] in order to sustain a political consensus

---

98 Ibid.

99 International Organization for Migration and the National Economic and Social Council, *Managing Migration in Ireland: A Social and Economic Analysis* (IOM, September 2006), p. 152.

100 Adrian Favell, *Philosophies of Integration: Immigration and the Idea of Citizenship in France and Britain* (2nd edn, Palgrave, 2001).

101 Friedrich Heckmann and Dominique Schnapper, note 92, p. 12.

102 Adrian Favell, note 108, p. 115.

103 Adrian Favell, note 108, p. 120.

that is unresponsive to the social facts and demands of the situation. He concludes that states promote a centralized ideological consensus around culture and value issues while failing to address the real causes behind failure of integration: poverty and inequality.[104] This can be seen in practice in the renewed emphasis in western liberal democracies on questions of religious and cultural difference, charged by a linking of the ideas of failed integration and Islamic fundamentalism. This change in emphasis has arguably contributed to the revival of the concept of 'assimilation' and a move away from particularistic models of assistance towards greater universalism and a common civic culture.[105] The focus shifts from attempting to ensure equality between immigrants and the host society, to the 'flattening' process whereby the true goal of integration is to make all members of a society the same. From a legal viewpoint, this is translated into measures such as restrictions on religious dress in public places[106] and conditions attached to the acquisition of citizenship.[107]

As mentioned in the previous chapter, the trend towards the use of integration conditions in European states, among other factors, may indicate that differences between states' approaches to integration are diminishing, or perhaps have always been overstated. However, as Wiesbrock emphasizes in her overview of integration measures of the UK, the Netherlands, Denmark, Sweden and Germany, despite the trend towards increasingly restrictive integration measures in European countries, there are still major differences between the countries in terms of their objectives and means used to achieve these objectives.[108] Thus, in Sweden and to a certain extent in the UK, the main objective of integration is to promote the socio-economic inclusion and independence of immigrants within the context of a society based on the principle of diversity. On the other hand, in Denmark, the Netherlands and Germany, the assimilation of immigrants has been officially cited

104 This line of argument is echoed by Pascale Fournier and Gökçe Yurdakul, in 'Unveiling Distribution: Muslim Women with Headscarves in France and Germany', in Michal Bodemann and Gökçe Yurdakul (eds), *Migration, Citizenship and Ethnos* (Palgrave, 2006).

105 See, for example, Rogers Brubaker, 'The return of assimilation? Changing perspectives on immigration and its sequels in France, Germany, and the United States' (2001) 24(4) *Ethnic and Racial Studies* 531; Christian Joppke, 'The retreat from multiculturalism in the liberal state: theory and policy' (2004) 55(2) *British Journal of Sociology* 237. The idea of the failure of multiculturalism is strongly disputed by thinkers such as Will Kymlicka. See Will Kymlicka, 'Immigrants, Multiculturalism and Canadian Citizenship', in Will Kymlicka (ed.), *Finding Our Way: Rethinking Ethnocultural Relations in Canada* (Oxford University Press, 1997); Will Kymlicka, 'Multiculturalism: Success, Failure and the Future' (Migration Policy Institute, 2012).

106 The types of restrictions that are being applied in European states are examined in Chapter 8.

107 See Chapter 7.

108 Anja Wiesbrock, *Legal Migration to the European Union*, note 91, p. 673.

as the aim of integration policies.[109] The underlying public philosophy of states thus retains an important role in determining the shape of integration measures in law and policy.

The Role of External Legal Influences in Shaping the Legal Approach to Integration

While this chapter has focussed on the ways in which the public philosophy of a state influences the contours of integration, paradigms of integration are being developed in different arenas outside the traditional framework of the nation state, in ways which could fundamentally alter national approaches to integration. One of the central arguments put forward by this book is that 'external' legal influences on integration constitute a rich resource for the development of a comprehensive understanding of integration, and much of the rest of this text will be dedicated to examining these influences. Integration has been conceptualized in a legal setting in the context of the European Union, the European Court of Human Rights and UN human rights and refugee law bodies. Chapters 4, 5 and 6 respectively will consider in detail the legal conceptions of integration under construction within the UN setting, under the rubric of the European Convention on Human Rights and at the EU level.

Conclusion

This chapter has highlighted the manner in which the law interacts with integration in a number of different ways and on a number of different levels. It considered a specific aspect of 'integration and law' in the form of the use of integration as a mandatory process and condition in immigration law but argued that this new dynamic in the immigration law of European states should not obscure the complexity of the relationship between integration and law (as illustrated by the example of the impact of law on family reunification). It was suggested that the idea of 'integration and law', based on the working definition set out in Chapter 2, constitutes a useful analytical tool for capturing the complexities of this relationship. Finally, it considered the important influence of national public philosophy on the framing of integration while noting that much of the rest of this book will be dedicated to trying to understand other, external influences on the development of an integration and law paradigm.

109 Ibid., pp. 673–674.

PART II
Legal Foundations of Integration

Chapter 4

The International Legal Framework for Integration: The UN Treaty Regime

Introduction

Inextricably linked to immigration, integration is by nature an issue with international dimensions, especially in the context of an ever-more integrated and globalized world. In the legal domain, migration has had a profound effect on national legal systems, importing international concerns into national legal frameworks.[1] These effects are not limited to the national level and it will be seen in Chapter 6 that international human rights law also exerts a strong influence on EU law through the general principles of EU law, limiting the discretion of states in the manner in which they implement EU immigration law. This chapter shows that international law does not contain specific provisions on the integration of migrants. Nonetheless, state approaches to integration must stay within the boundaries permitted by international refugee and human rights norms. The international legal framework is thus a key element in assessing the domestic and EU integration frameworks and in the development of a comprehensive understanding of integration and law.

This chapter investigates the legal and conceptual framework for integration contained in international refugee and human rights law. First, the primary ways in which the 1951 UN Refugee Convention[2] (together with its 1967 Protocol,[3] the '1951 Refugee Convention') is intertwined with the integration of refugees will be considered in detail. The 1951 Convention provides a comprehensive set of integration-related rights for recognized refugees and is the only international instrument to explicitly address integration as a broad-based objective in itself, as it does in Article 34. In addition, the 1951 Convention establishes an incremental approach to the granting of these rights, linked to the degree of legal integration of the refugee in the State Party. Secondly, the impact on integration of the

1 See Jacqueline Bhabha, 'Rights Spillovers: The Impact of Migration on the Legal System of Western States', in Elspeth Guild and Joanne Van Selm (eds), *International Migration and Security: Opportunities and Challenges* (Routledge, 2005) 28, p. 42.

2 UN General Assembly, *Convention Relating to the Status of Refugees*, 28 July 1951, United Nations, Treaty Series, vol. 189, p. 137

3 UN General Assembly, *Protocol Relating to the Status of Refugees*, 31 January 1967, United Nations, Treaty Series, vol. 606, p. 267.

International Covenant on Civil and Political Rights (ICCPR),[4] the International Covenant on Social, Cultural and Economic Rights (ICESCR)[5] and the International Convention on the Elimination of All Forms of Racial Discrimination (ICERD)[6] will be examined. These instruments constitute the core minimum of human rights entitlements that generally apply to all persons within the territory of State Parties, regardless of legal or migration status. The application of these treaties to integration will be outlined and the development of the concept of integration (if any) by the relevant treaty monitoring bodies will be considered. As Xanthaki has noted in the context of exploring the meaning of 'multiculturalism', the UN bodies have refrained from explaining in precise terms the meaning of the concept of integration, reflecting practice in international law of avoiding sharp and tight definitions that may limit flexibility in the applying instruments to different circumstances.[7] Rather, as is the case with multiculturalism, 'an analysis of the elements of the concept appears more practical and desirable'.[8] Finally, in Europe, migrants benefit from the protection of a powerful regional human rights mechanism in the form of the European Convention on Human Rights (ECHR),[9] and the next chapter will outline the use of the concept of integration as an element in the legal reasoning of the European Court of Human Rights (ECtHR) in its jurisprudence on the scope of a non-citizen's right to family and private life under Article 8 of the ECHR.

It will be seen that, while international law does not provide a comprehensive legal framework for integration, a number of ways in which international law impacts on national integration frameworks can be identified. These are outlined in detail in the conclusion to this chapter. The concepts of integration under construction by the UN treaty bodies are particularly significant as they are developed outside the context of the nation state at a supranational level. They represent a normative development of integration which is independent of any national public philosophy of integration. In addition, these concepts are developed in the context of human rights protection and thus constitute, at their heart, rights-based conceptions of integration. For these reasons, they constitute a valuable resource for the interpretation of integration, removed from the identity and 'values' politics which often hinder national integration policy and practice,

4 UN General Assembly, *International Covenant on Civil and Political Rights*, 16 December 1966, United Nations, Treaty Series, vol. 999, p. 171.

5 UN General Assembly, *International Covenant on Economic, Social and Cultural Rights*, 16 December 1966, United Nations, Treaty Series, vol. 993, p. 3.

6 UN General Assembly, *International Convention on the Elimination of All Forms of Racial Discrimination*, 21 December 1965, United Nations, Treaty Series, vol. 660, p. 195.

7 Alexandra Xanthaki, 'Multiculturalism and International Law: Discussing International Standards' (2010) 32(1) *Hum Rts Q* 21, p. 24, also citing Patrick Thornberry, *Indigenous Peoples and Human Rights* (Manchester University Press, 2002), p. 51.

8 Ibid.

9 Council of Europe, *European Convention for the Protection of Human Rights and Fundamental Freedoms*, 4 November 1950, ETS 5.

and a counterpoint to the trend towards viewing integration and law through the prism of integration as immigration control. In particular, the paradigm of integration as the progressive realization of equal rights as national citizens, which it is argued is emerging from the universal treaty regime, could provide the basis for the development of inclusive and holistic integration policies.

Integration in International Refugee Law

Local integration is commonly referred to as one of the three durable solutions available to refugees, the other two being resettlement and voluntary repatriation. UNHCR notes that this solution is based on the 'assumption that refugees will remain in their country of asylum permanently and find a solution to their plight in that state'.[10] While there is no formal definition of 'local integration', it is generally conceived of as a process with three interrelated dimensions: legal, economic and social.[11] The 1951 Refugee Convention places considerable emphasis on the integration of refugees. It provides for social and economic rights which are expressly designed to assist integration[12] and in Article 34 calls on Contracting States to facilitate the 'assimilation and naturalization' of refugees. Hathaway argues that, in essence, local integration is conceived of by UNHCR as the granting of some form of durable legal status to a refugee that allows him or her to stay in the country of first asylum on an indefinite basis, and to participate fully in the social, economic and cultural life of the host community.[13] He maintains that, so conceived,

> local integration is not really distinguishable from the primary solution envisaged by the Refugee Convention, namely simple respect for refugee rights. That is, the rights which are said to be the hallmarks of the solution of local integration are essentially the same rights which actually accrue by virtue of refugee status

---

10 UNHCR, *Global Consultations on International Protection: Local Integration*, 25 April 2002 EC/GC/02/6.

11 See UNHCR Executive Committee, *Conclusion on Local Integration* 7 October 2005, No. 104 (LVI) – 2005 at (k); Jeff Crisp, 'The local integration and local settlement of refugees: a conceptual and historical analysis', New Issues in Refugee Research – Working Paper No. 12 (UNHCR, April 2004), p. 1; Alexandra Fielden, 'Local integration: an under-reported solution to protracted refugee situations', New Issues in Refugee Research – Working Paper No. 158 (UNHCR, June 2008), p. 1. See the discussion of UNHCR's definition of integration at 2.2.2.

12 See UNHCR Executive Committee, *Conclusion on Local Integration*, note 11, at (k): 'the 1951 Convention and its 1967 Protocol set out rights and minimum standards for the treatment of refugees that are geared towards the process of integration …'.

13 James Hathaway, *The Rights of Refugees Under International Law* (Cambridge University Press, 2005), p. 978.

> itself. Even the economic and social aspects of local integration add little substantive content to the rights already guaranteed by the Convention.[14]

In other words, the 1951 Convention itself contains the principal rights necessary to ensure local integration. This gives concrete expression to the viewpoint, considered in previous chapters, that 'integration' is perhaps nothing more than the full realization of rights.

Nevertheless, it should be noted that, due mainly to the reluctance of Contracting States to take measures that might imply the acceptance of the long-term or permanent residence of refugees,[15] the international community has paid relatively little attention to local integration and has preferred to focus mainly on voluntary repatriation as a solutions strategy.[16] Until the mid 1990s, industrialized states generally acknowledged that those who were granted refugee status would remain on their territory indefinitely and consequently granted refugees a wide range of rights. Since then however, there has been a tendency among European states in particular to grant temporary and limited forms of protection.[17] Despite this retrenchment on the behalf of industrialized states from local integration, UNHCR has reiterated on numerous occasions that integration is the principal durable solution for refugees in the industrialized world.[18] Reflecting the increasingly prevalent idea that the integration of refugees should be promoted, and that refugees have integration needs distinct from those of other categories of migrant, the Migration Policy Group, together with UNHCR, has developed a refugee integration tool (separate from the MIPEX tool discussed in previous chapters) to evaluate refugee integration policies in EU Member States.[19]

---

14 Ibid.

15 See Rosa da Costa, 'Rights of Refugees in the Context of Integration: Legal Standards and Recommendations', UNHCR Legal and Protection Policy Research Series (UNHCR, June 2006), p. 11; also UNHCR, *Global Consultations on International Protection: Local Integration*, note 10, p. 1.

16 UNHCR, *Global Consultations on International Protection: Local Integration*, note 10, p. 1.

17 This was particularly the case regarding refugees fleeing the former Yugoslavia in the 1990s. See Jeff Crisp, note 11. See also, for example, Gregor Noll, *Negotiating Asylum: The EU Acquis, Extraterritorial Protection and the Common Market of Deflection* (Martinus Nijhoff, 2000); and James Hathaway, 'The Emerging Politics of Non-Entrée' (1992) 91 *Refugees* 40.

18 See UNHCR Executive Committee, *Conclusion on Local Integration*, note 10, at preamble and (d) and UNHCR, *Note on the Integration of Refugees in the European Union* (May 2007). See also Sarah Dryden-Peterson and Lucy Hovil, 'Local integration as a durable solution: refugees, host populations and education in Uganda', New Issues in Refugee Research – Working Paper No. 93 (UNHCR, September 2003); Susan Banki, 'Refugee integration in the intermediate term: a study of Nepal, Pakistan, and Kenya', New Issues in Refugee Research – Working Paper No. 108 (UNHCR, October 2004).

19 A User's Guide to the tool has been published, entitled *EU support for integration:*

A special emphasis has been placed by UNHCR on the integration of 'resettled' refugees – refugees who have been selected and transferred from a state in which they have sought protection to a third state which has agreed to admit them (as refugees) with permanent residence status – and resettlement has taken on a renewed importance in the European context with the adoption of the Joint EU Resettlement Programme in 2012.[20] The UNHCR Resettlement Handbook emphasizes the point that opportunities for resettled refugees to become citizens and to enjoy full and equal participation in society represent an overarching commitment by governments to refugee integration.[21] In addition, it highlights that family reunification is crucial to refugee integration and that relatives and ethnic community networks can play key roles in successful refugee integration.[22] UNHCR has sought to draw the attention of states to the specific integration needs of resettled refugees, and to encourage integration programmes that focus on a two-way exchange in order to create welcoming communities and foster positive integration.[23] The human rights dimension of integration is thus recognized as being particularly important in the case of resettled refugees. The emphasis on an inclusive and long-term process of integration for resettled refugees reflects the permanent nature of their settlement, which is legally recognized from the time of their arrival, and also the pragmatic reality that these refugees are specifically selected for resettlement in the receiving state.

In terms of the legal framework, the 1951 Convention provides for integration in three ways: Article 34 requires Contracting States 'as far as possible' to 'facilitate the assimilation and naturalization of refugees' (assimilation in this context being understood as non-coercive integration); the Convention sets out a wide range of substantive entitlements to be accorded to refugees which lay the foundations of refugee integration; and finally, the substantive rights provided for in the Convention are granted incrementally, linked to legal integration within the state. Each of these will be considered below.

What about beneficiaries of international protection? A User's Guide to EU Standards, Funds and Cooperation.

20 UNHCR, *Resettlement Handbook* (2011), p. 3. The Joint EU Resettlement Programme was established by Decision No. 281/2012/EU of the European Parliament and of the Council, amending Decision No. 573/2007/EC establishing the European Refugee Fund for the period 2008 to 2013 as part of the General programme 'Solidarity and Management of Migration Flows (OJ L92, 29 March 2012).

21 Ibid.

22 Ibid.

23 Ibid., p. 70. See also the guidelines and recommendations put forward by UNHCR and other stakeholders: UNHCR, *Refugee Resettlement: An International Handbook to Guide Reception and Integration* (2002); International Organization for Migration, *Resettlement Services Handbook*; ICMC, *Paving the Way: A Handbook on the Reception and Integration of Refugees in Europe*.

The Scope of Beneficiaries of the 1951 Convention

In UNHCR's view, 'the 1951 Convention provisions that are not linked to lawful stay or residence would apply to asylum seekers in so far as they relate to humane treatment and respect for basic rights, including *non refoulement*'.[24] An asylum seeker can possibly avail themselves of the rights contained in articles 3 (non-discrimination), 4 (religion), 5 (rights granted apart from this Convention), 7 (exemption from reciprocity), 8 (exemption from exceptional measures), 12 (personal status), 16 (access to courts), 20 (rationing), 22 (public education), 31 (refugees unlawfully in the country), and 33 (*non-refoulement* principle). Thus asylum seekers benefit from a far narrower range of integration-related entitlements than recognized refugees.

As regards beneficiaries of complementary protection, while UNHCR has consistently advocated for this group to be accorded the same access to integration facilities as Convention refugees,[25] there is no legal obligation on Contracting States in this regard under the 1951 Convention. This also applies more generally to the range of rights to which refugees become progressively entitled in the host state and states have a wide discretion as to which rights are to be afforded to those with complementary protection.

Facilitation of 'Assimilation' and Naturalization under Article 34 of the 1951 Convention

Article 34 of the 1951 Convention provides:

> The Contracting States shall as far as possible facilitate the assimilation and naturalization of refugees. They shall in particular make every effort to expedite naturalization proceedings and to reduce as far as possible the charges and costs of such proceedings.[26]

The extent of Contracting States' obligations under Article 34 and the meaning of 'assimilation' are key issues here. In its first sentence, Article 34 imposes a general duty on Contracting States to, as far as possible, facilitate assimilation

24 UNHCR, *Reception Standards for Asylum Seekers in the European Union* (July 2000), p. 5; UNHCR, *Global Consultations on International Protection/Third Track: Reception of Asylum-Seekers, Including Standards of Treatment, in the Context of Individual Asylum Systems*, 4 September 2001, EC/GC/01/17.

25 See UNHCR, *Note on the Integration of Refugees in the European Union*, note 18, p. 1. The ECRE has made similar recommendations: see ECRE, 'Good Practice Guide on the Integration of Refugees in the European Union' (Recommendation 13).

26 Article 34 is reinforced by the Statute of the UNHCR which 'calls upon Governments to co-operate with the UNHCR in the performance of his functions concerning refugees falling under the competence of his Office', especially by: … 'promoting the assimilation of refugees, especially by facilitating their naturalisation'.

and naturalization. While the word 'shall' indicates that this is a duty, rather than a recommendation, it is explicitly a duty to 'facilitate' rather than an obligation of result, and thus constitutes quite a minimalist legal obligation.[27] This reflects the fact that integration strategy and naturalization – in particular the latter – are generally conceived of as matters within the sovereign discretion of states (despite the evolution of the international law of citizenship, as discussed in Chapter 7). The second sentence of Article 34 provides two examples of potential ways of facilitating naturalization by requiring Contracting States to make every effort to expedite naturalization proceedings and to reduce as far as possible the charges and costs of such proceedings. Despite the rather minimalist nature of the obligations which it imposes, Article 34 represents the only major international treaty provision to specifically impose duties on states regarding integration assistance and naturalization and as such can be accurately described 'a provision without precedent in international law'.[28]

As regards the obligation to facilitate assimilation, the use of the term 'assimilation' is problematic, as this term has come to be understood as suggestive of forced assimilation or coercion. Mirroring current debates as to the meaning of 'integration', at the time of the drafting of the Convention, the *ad hoc* drafting committee considered the meaning of the obligation to facilitate assimilation at some length, with the representative of Israel expressing the view that 'the word "assimilation", well known in sociology, bore a rather unpleasant connotation closely related to the notion of force'.[29] UNHCR's position is that the term is to be understood in the sense of integration into the economic, social and cultural life of the country and not in the sense of forced assimilation; and furthermore, that this was the interpretation intended by the original drafters of the 1951 Convention.[30] This view is supported by Grahl-Madsen's view on the meaning of this part of Article 34:

> What is meant … is in fact the laying of foundations … so that the refugee may familiarize himself with the language, customs and way of life of the nation among whom he lives, so that he – without any feeling of coercion – may be more readily integrated in the economic, social and cultural life of his country of refuge.[31]

---

27 James Hathaway, *The Rights of Refugees Under International Law*, note 13, p. 987.

28 See Atle Grahl-Madsen, 'Commentary on the 1951 Refugee Convention, Articles 2–11 and 13–37' (1963, re-published by the Division of International Protection of the UNHCR, 1997) p. 244 and James Hathaway, ibid., p. 981.

29 UN Doc E/AC.32/SR.39, p. 26. See also Grahl-Madsen, p. 147.

30 See UNHCR, *Global Consultations on International Protection: Local Integration*, note 10, p. 2, footnote 3: '(T)he international community has always rejected the notion that refugees should be expected to abandon their own culture and way of life, so as to become indistinguishable from nationals of the host community'.

31 Atle Grahl-Madsen, note 28, p. 147.

He lists some examples of the means which may be employed for the purpose of facilitating integration, including language courses, vocational adaptation courses, and 'stimulation of social contacts between refugees and the indigenous population'.[32] More recent literature emphasizes the need to adopt a regime of rights which generally accords refugees the same rights as permanent residents or nationals, thus contributing to their self-reliance and cultural integration.[33] Unfortunately, however, the absence of a monitoring body for the 1951 Convention has meant that the concept of assimilation or integration remains normatively undeveloped.

The naturalization aspect of Article 34 is also significant since access to citizenship is an issue traditionally viewed as lying firmly within the discretion of sovereign states. Furthermore, acquisition of citizenship is seen as a key factor in successful integration. The concepts of assimilation and naturalization as contained in Article 34 are inter-related, and to the extent that integration can be viewed as a stage that precedes naturalization, measures to facilitate integration have an important knock-on effect: to facilitate an eventual process of naturalization.[34] The linkage of the two concepts is made explicit in Article 34's housing of both assimilation and naturalization. This linkage of integration and access to citizenship contrasts with the practice of many European states of using integration tests as a prerequisite to naturalization (rather than viewing naturalization as facilitating integration).[35] Naturalization is particularly important in the refugee context as refugees, unlike other most other non-citizens, lack an effective nationality. Nevertheless, Article 34 cannot be said to contain a strong legal obligation as regards naturalization. Article 34 does not give rise to an *entitlement* to naturalization in any circumstances. This is made clear in the negotiations of the original drafters of the Convention, and Grahl-Madsen records that it was stressed in the discussions that naturalization is a matter of such a delicate nature that in every case the final decision must rest with the organs of the state concerned.[36] It was felt that without establishing formal obligations in this respect, it would be acceptable to request states to facilitate to the fullest possible extent the naturalization of refugees. [37] Despite the qualified nature of the Article 34 duty, which would probably not preclude a requirement for refugees to pass integration or language tests to access citizenship (once these tests were not set at such an reasonably high level of difficulty as to effectively deny citizenship), Hathaway has argued that Article 34 is breached where a Contracting State simply does not allow refugees to secure its citizenship, and fails to provide a persuasive

32 Ibid.

33 Rosa da Costa, note 15, p. 29.

34 See Anna Low, 'Local Integration: A Durable Solution for Refugees?' (2006) 25 *Forced Migration Review* 64.

35 See further, Chapter 7.

36 Atle Grahl-Madsen, note 28, p. 145.

37 Ibid.

justification for this exclusion.[38] The duty contained in Article 34 to facilitate the naturalization of refugees should primarily be viewed therefore as a means to *promote* access to citizenship in host countries.

Refugee Rights and Minimum Standards of Treatment: The Foundations of Integration

The UNHCR's Executive Committee's 'Conclusion on Local Integration' notes that the 1951 Convention and its 1967 Protocol set out rights and minimum standards for the treatment of refugees that are geared towards the process of integration.[39] The bulk of the 1951 Convention is dedicated to enumerating the entitlements that flow from refugee status, in spite of which judicial and academic commentary has focussed primarily on the interpretation of the definition of a 'refugee' and the core duty of *non-refoulement*.[40] The rights laid down in the Convention include basic rights such as the right to *non-refoulement*,[41] non-expulsion,[42] and access to the courts.[43] It also protects a number of civil rights such as freedom of association. Of particular importance in the integration context, however, is the range of socio-economic rights guaranteed by the Convention, which contribute to refugees' economic and social integration, and which are rarely specifically accorded to migrants in such explicit terms in international law. The rights to work[44] and to own property[45] are supplemented by the right to the same treatment as nationals as regards public relief and assistance,[46] and in relation to labour legislation and social security.[47] In this way, the 1951 Convention goes some way towards requiring the inclusion of refugees within the economic and social fabric of the host state. Furthermore, the Convention guarantees to refugees the free practice of religion and freedom, including as regards the religious education of their children,[48] reinforcing the position that refugees may not be forcibly assimilated into the culture of the host society.

---

38 James Hathaway, *The Rights of Refugees Under International Law*, note 13, p. 989.

39 UNHCR Executive Committee, *Conclusion on Local Integration*, note 11, at (d).

40 James Hathaway, *The Rights of Refugees Under International Law*, note 13, p. 2.

41 Article 33.

42 Article 32.

43 Article 16.

44 Articles 17 (wage-earning employment), 18 (self-employment) and 19 (liberal professions).

45 Article 13.

46 Article 23.

47 Article 24.

48 Article 4.

Incremental Granting of Rights under the 1951 Convention

The third way in which the 1951 Convention is linked with integration is the way in which rights are attributed under the Convention. Entitlements are granted on an incremental basis, related to the length of the refugee's residence in the state and the strength of the connection between the refugee and the state.[49] The core minimum rights are granted to refugees who are simply 'present' in the territory under a state's jurisdiction, and include the rights to *non-refoulement*, to non-discrimination and of access to the courts.[50] The majority of rights are reserved for those who are 'lawfully present',[51] or who are 'lawfully staying'.[52] Finally, a few rights only accrue when the refugee is habitually resident in the territory of the host state (that is to say, has resided there for an extended period). For example, Article 17(2) provides that restrictive measures imposed on aliens or the employment of aliens for the protection of the national labour market shall not be applied to a refugee who has been resident for three years in the country.[53] Thus, '(A)s the refugee's relationship to the asylum state is solidified over the course of this five-part assimilative path, the Convention requires that a more inclusive range of needs and aspirations be met'.[54]

Rights which enable the economic and social integration of refugees are thus granted as the refugee becomes progressively integrated in legal terms. This reflects the notion of integration as a bi-directional incremental process: as the refugee becomes progressively more embedded in the host society, the host society must make more efforts to accommodate the refugee and ensure that their integration is facilitated. This analysis is supported by that of Anna Low who, on the basis of UNHCR's experience in Mexico, Uganda and Zambia, emphasizes the incremental nature of integration, stating that local integration policies can grant refugees a progressively wider range of rights and entitlements generally

49 This is pointed out in UNHCR, *Reception Standards for Asylum Seekers in the European Union*, p. 5.

50 Article 3 (non-discrimination), Article 4 (religion), Article 16 (access to the courts), Article 22 (public education), Article 27 (identity papers) and Article 33 (prohibition of *refoulement*).

51 Article 18 (self-employment), Article 26 (freedom of movement) and Article 32 (expulsion).

52 See, for example, Article 15 (freedom of association), Article 19 (liberal professions), Article 21 (housing).

53 Article 17(2) also applies to refugees who have a spouse or children possessing the nationality of the country of residence. As regards rights which accrue to habitually resident refugees, Article 7 (2)–(5) provides that the principle of legislative reciprocity laid down in Article 7(1) ceases to apply after three years' residence. See also Article 14 (artistic rights and industrial property); and Article 16(2) ('A refugee shall enjoy in the Contracting State in which he has his habitual residence the same treatment as a national in matters pertaining to access to the Courts, including legal assistance and exemption from *cautio judicatum solvi*').

54 James Hathaway, *The Rights of Refugees Under International Law*, note 13, p. 156.

commensurate with those enjoyed by local citizens.[55] These include freedom of movement, access to education and the labour market, access to public services and assistance, including health facilities, the possibility of acquiring and disposing of property and the capacity to travel with valid documentation and 'over time the process should lead to permanent residence rights and perhaps ultimately the acquisition of citizenship in the country of asylum'.[56] While recognizing that certain fundamental rights are to be afforded to all notwithstanding their legal status or embedded-ness in the state, the incremental granting of rights under the 1951 Convention also encapsulates the idea of integration as the progressive realization of equality. This links in to the development of a similar narrative in general international human rights law, which will be discussed for the remainder of this chapter.

The Role and Value of International Human Rights Law in Addressing Integration Issues

Moving on from international refugee law to international human rights standards, a preliminary issue to be considered is that of the role and value of international human rights law in the context of integration. Is integration an issue within the remit of international human rights law? As noted above, there are no specific provisions in the international human rights treaties on integration. Moreover, while a secure legal status is generally seen as a prerequisite to successful integration, the type of legal residency status to be granted to migrants is not provided for by an unqualified, explicit provision in international law. In addition, as mentioned in Chapter 2, integration is often seen as a matter peculiarly within the discretion of individual states due to its links with national identity and the fundamental organizational principles of particular states. However, international human rights law has a significant role in the context of integration. The formal legal status of a non-citizen may represent a barrier to their integration into the host society. International human rights law, with its core content of rights applicable to all persons regardless of their legal status or any other prerequisite, provides the legal limits and framework within which integration policy must operate.[57]

On a fundamental level, international human rights law involves a reshaping of the relationship between the state and persons within its jurisdiction. By accepting human rights duties which transcend the state, the state loses a degree of control over the treatment of immigrants and non-citizens, such it is no longer permitted to treat immigrants within its jurisdiction in ways which are contrary to its obligations under international human rights law. Through the engagement of supranational

55 Anna Low, note 34, p. 65.

56 Anna Low, note 34, p. 65.

57 See generally, Economic and Social Council, 'The rights of non-citizens: Final report of the Special Rapporteur', UN Doc E/CN.4/Sub.2/2003/23 (May, 2003).

norms, the importance of the distinction between the individual as citizen and as foreigner, which is so central to the notion of state sovereignty as well as to national integration policies, begins to be broken down. As Guild observes:

> The individual as a holder of rights, which transcend the state's power of definition, is central to the concept of international human rights. The individual has rights because he or she exists in the human rights tradition, not because he or she forms part of the group which negotiated the constitutional settlement between the rulers and the ruled.[58]

The existence of international norms therefore provides not only a constraint on the way in which states deal with migrants and integration issues, but a challenge to perception of the relationship between the state and persons within its borders, shifting the focus from a state/citizen nexus of rights and responsibilities to a state/individual nexus. Integration paradigms which are based on narrow conceptions of national identity and a strict dichotomy between the citizen and others are thus put under significant pressure by international human rights norms. In these ways, the supranationalization of core rights of individuals and duties of states has a direct impact on national integration policy.

A further function of international human rights law in the field of integration is to provide a neutral framework for deciding on the correct balance to be struck between the competing interests which emerge in diverse societies. In essence, integration forms part of a broader question – how do people who disagree profoundly over various matters live together? Human rights principles provide a broad framework within which to balance the competing claims of different groups. It is undoubtedly the case that the 'clashes' of culture or tradition which may arise in multicultural societies – for example, debates over wearing religious dress in public spaces – raise serious human rights issues which can be resolved by reference to international norms. International human rights law has the potential to provide differing cultures with a common vocabulary and foundation on which to address these issues. Human rights law can provide a strong platform for shared values in multicultural, diverse societies, providing a guide for governments attempting to construct the parameters of a common societal space.[59]

58 Elspeth Guild, 'Cultural and Social Identity: Immigrants and the Legal Expression of National Identity', in Elspeth Guild and Joanne Van Selm (eds), *International Migration and Security: Opportunities and Challenges* (Routledge, 2005), p. 108.

59 See, for example, Morten Kjaerum, 'Human Rights for Immigrants and Immigrants for Human Rights', in Elspeth Guild and Joanne Van Selm (eds), *International Migration and Security: Opportunities and Challenges* (Routledge, 2005), 51, in particular pp. 61–63.

The Impact of Universal Human Rights Mechanisms: Focus on the ICCPR, ICESCR and ICERD

Universal human rights instruments protect many of the rights which arise in the integration context including, for example, education, housing, freedom of religion and non-discrimination. The universal standards enshrined in the ICCPR and the ICESCR constitute the core rights that should, in principle, be available to all persons regardless of nationality or immigration status (in addition to the protections contained in the Convention Against Torture). In addition, specialized treaty rights under the auspices of ICERD, the Convention on the Elimination of All Forms of Discrimination Against Women (CEDAW),[60] the Convention on the Rights of the Child (CRC)[61] and the Convention on the Protection of All Migrant Workers and Members of Their Families (CMW)[62] form a second level of protection for members of these groups. The in-depth analysis in this chapter is confined to the ICCPR, the ISCER and ICERD. The principal rationale for the selection of these particular instruments is one of universality. As mentioned above, the ICCPR and the ICESCR apply to all persons in State Parties thereto and thus apply to all migrants in those states. In addition, ICERD applies to all victims of racial discrimination, as very widely defined in Article 5 as 'any distinction, exclusion, restriction or preference based on race, colour, descent, or national or ethnic origin', and so applies to all non-citizen migrants.

The CMW will not be considered in detail in this chapter. The CMW is an ambitious document aiming to protect both legally resident and illegally resident migrant workers and represents substantive normative progress in the elaboration of binding guarantees of protection specifically addressed to migrants.[63] Many of its provisions are innovative in nature and are directly relevant to the integration prospects of migrant workers.[64] Article 44, while not providing for a *right* of family reunification for documented migrant workers, encourages State Parties to facilitate family reunification and to protect the unity of the family. Integration

60 UN General Assembly, *Convention on the Elimination of All Forms of Discrimination Against Women*, 18 December 1979, United Nations, Treaty Series, vol. 1249, p. 13.

61 UN General Assembly, *Convention on the Rights of the Child*, 20 November 1989, United Nations, Treaty Series, vol. 1577, p. 3.

62 UN General Assembly, *International Convention on the Protection of the Rights of All Migrant Workers and Members of their Families*, 18 December 1990, A/RES/45/158.

63 See Nafziger and Bartel, 'The Migrant Workers Convention: Its Place in Human Rights Law' (1991) 25(4) *International Migration Review* 771, p. 776.

64 Article 49 provides thus that where separate authorizations to reside and to engage in employment are required by national legislation, the states of employment shall issue to migrant workers authorization of residence for at least the same period of time as their authorization to engage in remunerated activity.

is specifically mentioned in Article 45 which concerns access to education.[65] However, the emergence and normative development of this Convention has been, and continues to be, a very slow process.[66] In addition, the potential influence of the CMW is hampered by the low number of ratifications of the Convention, combined with the complete absence of Western industrialized states from the list of signatories and State Parties.[67] No EU Member State is a party to the CMW. Finally, a cursory examination of the few concluding comments of the Committee on Migrant Workers reveals a limited relevance to integration. The comments do not enter into a detailed consideration of integration, or social and economic rights of migrant workers. The focus of the concluding observations is on the right to effective procedures and developing comprehensive immigration frameworks rather than ensuring the integration of migrant workers.[68] The closest the committee comes to discussing integration as such is in relation to the elimination of discrimination against migrant workers – where the committee has emphasized the need to combat social marginalization and stigmatization of migrant workers.[69] These constraining factors have limited the potential of the CMW as a mechanism with the ability to effect meaningful change in the position of migrant workers and influence the shape of national integration policies and it is for these reasons that the CMW is not examined in the same way as the ICCPR, the ISCER and ICERD in this chapter.

This chapter focuses on the development of the concept of integration by the treaty bodies established under the ICCPR, the ICESCR and ICERD. This will be done primarily through an analysis of their concluding observations on State Reports up to 1 January 2013,[70] although the general comments of the Human Rights Committee (CCPR) and the Committee on Economic, Social and Cultural Rights

---

65 Article 45(2) provides that 'States of employment shall pursue a policy … aimed at facilitating the integration of children of migrant workers in the local school system, particularly in respect of teaching them the local language'.

66 For an analysis of the drafting process by one of the drafters, see Juhnai Lonnroth, 'United Nations International Convention on the Protection of All Migrant Workers and Members of Their Families in the Context of International Migration Policies: An Analysis of Ten Years of Negotiation' (1991) 25(4) *International Migration Review* 710. At the time of writing, the Convention has 35 signatories and 46 parties, most of these being labour-sending rather than receiving states.

67 Patrick Taran, 'Status and Prospects for the UN Convention on Migrants' Rights' (2000) 2 *EJML* 85.

68 See, for example, Mali, UN Doc CMW/C/MLI/CO/1 (31 May 2006), para. 18; Ecuador, UN Doc CMW/C/ECU/CO/2 (15 December 2010), paras 28 and 35; Egypt, CMW/C/EGY/CO/1 (25 May 2007), paras 48 and 49.

69 See, for example, Egypt, para. 21(b); Ecuador, para. 20.

70 The most recent concluding observations on the country reports for every State Party to the ICCPR, the ICESCR and the ICERD at 1 January 2013 have been examined. In the case of those countries for which the most recent concluding observations date from 2010 to 2013, the previous set of concluding observations have also been examined.

(CESCR) and the general recommendations of the Committee on the Elimination of Racial Discrimination (the CERD Committee) will also be referenced. While the CCPR and the CERD Committee have the competence to consider individual complaints, the views of the CCPR have not, to date, specifically referred to the concept of integration and the ICERD individual complaints procedure is rarely used. In contrast, integration-related issues as well as the concept of integration itself are expressly referred to by the committees in their concluding observations and it will be seen that there has been a certain development of the concept of integration in these concluding observations. For these reasons, the article concentrates on the concluding observations of the committees. While it must be acknowledged that concluding observations are generally understood as not having binding effect *per se*, nevertheless, as outputs of a treaty body, they have a 'notable authority, albeit unspecified', in particular where they purport to interpret treaty provisions.[71] For these reasons, this part of the chapter concentrates on the concluding observations of the committees.

It will be seen that, broadly speaking, while the CCPR and the CESCR refer to integration-related matters they rarely do so under the banner of 'integration' and integration in itself is evidently not among the primary concerns of these committees. Despite this, we shall see that the CCPR and the CESCR make many observations which are related (even if for the most part indirectly) to integration. In contrast, the CERD Committee conceives of integration in terms of an objective in itself and a relatively nuanced conception of integration is under construction in its concluding observations.

The International Covenant on Civil and Political Rights

The ICCPR has been described as 'probably the most important human rights treaty in the world',[72] principally owing to its protection of a large number of rights and its universal coverage.[73] Article 2(1) of the ICCPR lays down the general requirement of non-discrimination in respect of the rights laid down in the Covenant, providing that each State Party must ensure the rights in the Covenant

71 See Michael O'Flaherty, 'The Concluding Observations of the United Nations Human Rights Treaty Monitoring Bodies' (2006) 6(1) *HRLR* 27, pp. 32–37. See also Christian Tomuschat, *Human Rights: Between Idealism and Realism* (Oxford University Press, 2003), in particular p. 149.

72 Sarah Joseph, Jenny Schultz and Melissa Castan, *The International Covenant of Civil and Political Rights: Cases, Materials and Commentary* (2nd edn, Oxford University Press, 2004), p. 4.

73 In addition, Article 28 of the ICCPR creates a supervisory body in the form of the Human Rights Committee, which may hear individual complaints under the Optional First Protocol. Thus a form of individual legal remedy is available for persons whose rights under the Covenant are violated, in contrast to the position under many other international human rights instruments.

to 'all individuals within its territory and subject to its jurisdiction'. In its General Comment No. 15 on the position of aliens under the Covenant, the CCPR clarified the precise position relating to non-citizens as follows: 'the general rule is that each one of the rights of the Covenant must be guaranteed without discrimination between citizens and aliens'.[74] General Comment No. 15 outlines in detail the fundamental rights of non-citizens including the rights to life; to liberty and security of the person; to freedom of thought, conscience and religion; and (where they constitute a minority) to enjoy their own culture, to profess and practice their own religion and to use their own language.[75] There are two exceptions to this general principle of non-discrimination: political rights explicitly guaranteed to citizens[76] and freedom of movement.[77]

As Wiesbrock has observed, the principle of non-discrimination is essential to the integration process as it prohibits states from denying migrants access to employment, housing and education which would significantly undermine their integration.[78] Also essential are the freedoms to maintain cultural and religious identity, which allow migrants to preserve their cultural traditions and prohibit forced assimilation.[79] Other protections in this category are fundamental freedoms such as religion, marriage and the protection of private and family life.[80] The freestanding equality guarantee contained in Article 26, the protection of the right of minorities to enjoy their own culture, to practice their religion and to use their own language contained in Article 27, and the protection of private and family life provided for by articles 17 and 23 have particular significance in a discussion of integration and these articles will be briefly examined before turning to the development of the concept of integration by the CCPR in its concluding observations on State Reports. It will be seen that the concept of integration employed by the CCPR in its concluding observations is quite under-developed. Nonetheless, it is argued that the CCPR's approach can be characterized as defining integration in terms of the progressive realization of rights for immigrants and their families. Other features of the CCPR's approach include the subordinate role of Article 27 (in comparison to Article 26) in the normative development of integration, and the contrasting way in which integration is dealt with by the CCPR in relation to wealthy and poorer countries.

74 CCPR General Comment No. 15, 'The position of aliens under the Covenant' (11 April 1986), p. 1.

75 For a full list of the relevant rights, see ibid., p. 2.

76 See Article 25, which provides that every 'citizen' shall have the right to participate in public affairs, to vote and hold office, and to have access to public service.

77 Article 12 (4) states that no one shall be arbitrarily deprived of the right to enter 'his own country'.

78 Anja Wiesbrock, *Legal Migration to the European Union* (Martinus Nijhoff Publishers, 2010), p. 708.

79 Ibid.

80 Ibid.

Article 26: Equality

It has been observed that equality and non-discrimination 'constitute the dominant single theme' of the ICCPR.[81] The equality guarantee contained in Article 26 enshrines these values,[82] providing a three-limbed protection: equality before the law; equal protection of the law; and a prohibition of discrimination on any grounds such as race, colour, sex, language, religion, political or other opinion, national or social origin, property, birth or other status.[83] Article 26 is somewhat unique among non-discrimination guarantees in that it is a free-standing equality norm, meaning that a claim of discrimination contrary to Article 26 need not be linked to another Covenant right. Article 26 governs the allocation of all public goods and thus protects against discrimination in relation to social and economic rights as well as civil and political rights. The application of Article 26 to social and economic as well as civil and political rights was confirmed in the seminal case of *Broeks v The Netherlands*.[84]

Article 26 therefore requires that all public goods be distributed to everyone without distinction. This includes distinction as to nationality[85] or citizenship[86] (once admitted, migrants must be given the same treatment as nationals unless there are reasonable and objective grounds to justify a more restrictive application) and thus has obvious implications for integration. Policies which discriminate against migrants or non-citizens in the field of education or employment, for example, are potentially in breach of Article 26. Moreover, policies and laws which do not discriminate against non-citizens as such, but which may affect non-citizens, may fall foul of Article 26 for other reasons, including on the basis of discrimination on the grounds of religion for example. The wide reach of Article 26 was illustrated

81 Bertie G. Ramcharan, 'Equality and Non-Discrimination', in Louis Henkin (ed.), *The International Bill of Rights: The Covenant on Civil and Political Rights* (Columbia University Press, 1981).

82 'All persons are equal before the law and are entitled without discrimination to the equal protection of the law. In this respect, the law shall prohibit discrimination and guarantee to all persons equal and effective protection against discrimination on any grounds such as race, colour, sex, language, religion, political or other opinion, national or social origin, property, birth or other status'.

83 See Manfred Nowak, *UN Covenant on Civil and Political Rights – CCPR Commentary* (Engel, 1993), p. 463, and CCPR General Comment No. 18, 'Non-Discrimination' (10 November 1989).

84 (172/84) CCPR/C/29/D/172/1984 (1987). The principle that Article 26 can apply in the case of social and economic rights has been affirmed in – *inter alia* – *Johannes Vos v Netherlands* (786/97) CCPR/C/66/D/786/1997 (1999); *Wackenheim v France* (854/99) CCPR/C/75/D/854/1999 (2002) (employment); and *Arieh Hollis Waldman v Canada* (694/1996) CCPR/C/67/D/694/1996 (1999) (education subsidies).

85 See *Gueye v France* (196/1985) CCPR/C/35/D/196/1985 (1989); and *Griffin v Spain* (493/1992) CCPR/C/53/D/493/1992 (1995).

86 See CCPR General Comment No. 15, note 74, para. 2 – as affirmed in *Karakurt v Austria* (965/2000) CCPR/C/74/D/965/2000 (2002).

by the concluding observations of the CCPR for Ireland in 2000, in which the CCPR expressed concern that exemptions under the Employment Equality Act 1998, which allow religious bodies directing hospitals and schools to discriminate in certain circumstances on the ground of religion in employing persons whose functions are not religious, may result in discrimination contrary to Article 26 of the Covenant.[87]

In principle, therefore, Article 26 could constitute a powerful tool for immigrants seeking to establish their entitlement to equal treatment as nationals of the host state. However, the jurisprudence of the CCPR on Article 26 has a number of limitations which weakens it in this regard. First, the committee's approach to the issue of indirect discrimination, which is of particular relevance in the context of subtle discriminatory treatment of first or second-generation immigrants, has been criticized as inadequate.[88] In particular, Hathaway accuses the committee of engaging in superficial analysis in cases involving allegations of discrimination against non-citizens.[89] The second limitation of the views of the CCPR on individual communications is the wide margin of appreciation afforded to states in some situations in determining whether differential treatment constitutes 'discrimination' (which is prohibited) or a reasonable and objective differentiation (which is permitted).[90] For example, in *Singh Bhinder v Canada*,[91] the committee found that while a rule requiring all persons to wear hard hats in certain jobs indirectly discriminated against Sikhs, it accepted, without question or analysis of the subtle issues involved, the state's assessment that the rule was 'reasonable and directed towards objective purposes that are compatible with the Covenant', as it was necessary on the basis of safety.[92]

87 Un Doc A/55/40 (21 July 2000), para. 22.

88 Tufyal Choudury, 'Interpreting the Right to Equality Under Article 26 of the International Covenant on Civil and Political Rights' (2003) 1 *EHRLR* 24, p. 33.

89 James Hathaway, *The Rights of Refugees Under International Law*, note 13, p. 135. See *Oulajin and Kaiss v The Netherlands* (406/1990 and 426/1990), CCPR/C/46/D/406/1990 and 426/1990 (1992), for example.

90 As confirmed in General Comment No. 18, 'not every differentiation of treatment will constitute discrimination, if the criteria for such differentiation are reasonable and objective and if the aim is to achieve a purpose which is legitimate under the Covenant'. CCPR General Comment No. 18, note 83, para. 13.

91 (208/1986) CCPR/C/37/D/208/1986 (1989).

92 Ibid., para. 6.2. The position of the committee on the reasonableness of differentiation on the basis of citizenship is not altogether clear: contrast the results in *Oord v The Netherlands* (658/1995) CCPR/C/60/D/658/1995 (1997) – and *Karakurt v Austria* (965/2000) CCPR/C/74/D/965/2000 (2002).

Article 27: Minority Rights

Article 27 is 'the only expression of the right to an identity in modern human rights conventions intended for universal application',[93] making it an important element of the international legal framework for integration. Article 27 provides:

> In those States in which ethnic, religious or linguistic minorities exist, persons belonging to such minorities shall not be denied the right, in community with the other members of their group, to enjoy their own culture, to profess and practise their own religion, or to use their own language.

Article 27 protects the rights of individuals who are members of a minority which 'exists' in a State Party.[94] The article therefore applies to all individuals who belong to a minority: they need not be citizens or permanent residents, and can be migrant workers or even visitors.[95] Article 27 thus clearly imposes obligations on states in respect of all migrants belonging to an ethnic, linguistic or cultural minority.[96] The exact scope and nature of these obligations is not, however, altogether clear from the Convention itself. Poulter observes that 'Article 27 is ... expressed in such vague and general terms that its precise ambit and content have been the subject of much speculation'.[97] In particular, he notes that the significance of the use of negative language in the formulation of Article 27, in contrast to the positive formulation used in the bulk of the other articles of the Covenant, left the door open for restrictive interpretations of the scope of the article.[98] This problem was remedied to a certain extent by the adoption of the Declaration on the Rights of Persons Belonging to National or Ethnic, Religious

93 Patrick Thornberry, *International Law and the Rights of Minorities* (Oxford University Press, 1991), p. 142.

94 The existence of an ethnic, religious or linguistic minority in a given State Party does not depend on a decision by that State Party, but requires to be established by objective criteria.

95 CCPR General Comment No. 23, 'The rights of minorities (Art. 27)' (8 April 1994), p. 2. See also General Comment No. 15, note 74, at para. 7, which states that 'in those cases where aliens constitute a minority within the meaning of Article 27, they shall not be denied, in community with other members of their group, to enjoy their own culture, to profess and practice their own religion and use their own language'.

96 Prior to the adoption of this General Comment there was a widely-held view that Article 27 implicitly excluded aliens who did not acquire the nationality of the host state from its scope. See Patrick Thornberry, note 93, pp. 171–172.

97 Sebastian Poulter, 'The Rights of Ethnic, Linguistic and Cultural Minorities' (1997) 3 *EHRLR* 254.

98 Ibid.

and Linguistic Minorities in 1992 (the 'Minority Declaration')[99] and the CCPR's General Comment No. 23 in 1994.

The Minority Declaration goes a considerable distance towards clarifying the obligations of State Parties as regards minority rights. For example, it provides that '(P)ersons belonging to minorities have the right to participate effectively in cultural, religious, social, economic and public life',[100] and that '(N)ational policies and programmes shall be planned and implemented with due regard for the legitimate interests of persons belonging to minorities'.[101] Importantly, it clarifies that measures taken by states to ensure the effective enjoyment of the rights contained in the Declaration shall not (*prima facie*) be considered contrary to the principle of equality contained in the Universal Declaration of Human Rights (UDHR).[102] General Comment No. 23 further delineates the precise nature of the obligation contained in Article 27, explaining that it imposes both negative and positive obligations on State Parties, and concerns relations between the State Party and individuals and also between private actors.[103] Importantly, the concept of culture as contained in the Covenant is not a narrow one. Drawing parallels between Article 27 and the references to cultural rights contained in the UDHR[104] and the ICESCR,[105] Thornberry states that 'the right to enjoy culture in Article 27 means all aspects of that culture; what is at stake is the ability of ethnic minorities to preserve their cultural identity and their cultural inheritance, *their own culture*'[106] and the General Comment confirms that 'culture manifests itself in many forms'.[107]

The expansive reach of Article 27 has a number of implications for integration. The first of these is that any integration policy which forced migrants who are members of a minority to forsake their culture, language or religion in favour of that of the host state would violate Article 27. This echoes the views of UNHCR regarding forced assimilation or integration by coercion in the case of refugees. Indeed, as explained in General Comment No. 23, 'positive measures by States may also be necessary to protect the identity of a minority and the rights of its members to enjoy and develop their culture and language and to practise their religion, in community, with other members of the group'.[108] Article 27 would therefore seem to require the same type of two-way definition of integration as that

99 Declaration on the Rights of Persons Belonging to National or Ethnic, Religious and Linguistic Minorities (Adopted by General Assembly resolution 47/135 of 18 December 1992).

100 Minority Declaration, Article 2(2).

101 Minority Declaration, Article 5(1).

102 Minority Declaration, Article 8(3).

103 CCPR General Comment No. 23, note 95, p. 2.

104 Article 27(1) of the UDHR.

105 Articles 13–15 of the ICESCR.

106 Patrick Thornberry, note 93, p. 187.

107 General Comment No. 23, note 95, at para. 7. See generally, Xanthaki, note 7, pp. 24–28.

108 CCPR General Comment No. 23, note 95, para. 6.2.

propounded by the Council of Europe, the European Union and UNHCR. Article 27 does not, however, go so far as to prohibit all measures designed to integrate members of minorities into a host society, so long as such measures respect the individual's right to an identity as a member of a minority. Thornberry suggests that 'Article 27 is ultimately no barrier to assimilation *per se* but only assimilation contrary to the wishes of the members of the minority'.[109] However, Article 27 certainly implies that, in implementing integration programmes, states are under a positive obligation to enable minorities to both participate in the host society and also retain their own distinctive identity. It also, as Xanthaki argues, appears to support a 'multiculturalist' approach to integration.[110]

At the very least, there is considerable doubt as to the legitimacy, under Article 27, of imposing integration 'tests' or 'contracts', which would require the migrant to demonstrate their adherence to the majority culture, language or religion, as a pre-condition to accessing the territory of the State Party or to accessing a secure legal status. In practice, however, integration tests formulated by European states generally focus on knowledge of society, history or democratic values, rather than requiring migrants to commit to cultural integration or to expressly take on the supposed cultural values of existing citizens, and in this sense are probably not 'coercive' enough, or close enough to 'forced assimilation', to engage Article 27. While these tests may not violate the letter of Article 27, they certainly contradict the multicultural ethos underlying the provision.

Articles 17 and 23: The Protection of Private and Family Life

The importance of family reunification in the integration process is well established, and was outlined in detail in the previous chapter. Protection of the family and its members is provided for by articles 17 and 23 of the ICCPR. Article 17 of the ICCPR provides for the right of every person to be protected against arbitrary or unlawful interference with – *inter alia* – his or her privacy, family and home. Article 23(1) provides that the family is 'the natural and fundamental group unit of society and is entitled to protection by the society and the state'.[111] On the basis of these articles, the CCPR has, like the European Court of Human Rights in the context of the ECHR, found in respect of individual communications that the deportation of a non-citizen may constitute a breach of family rights under the ICCPR, depending on the circumstances of the case.[112] Articles 17

109 Patrick Thornberry, note 93, p. 206.

110 Xanthaki, note 7.

111 In particular, Article 24 specifically protects the rights of the child to such measures of protection as are required by his status as a minor, on the part of his family, society and the state.

112 *Madafferi v Australia*, CCPR/C/81/D/1011/2001 (2004); *Winata v Australia*, CCPR/C/72/D/930/2000 (2001); *Dauphin v Canada*. However, in contrast, see *AS v Canada*, CCPR/C/12/D/68/1980 (1981). In the deportation context, see *Stewart v Canada*,

and 23, therefore, set an outer boundary for the immigration decisions of State Parties where family rights are involved. However, unlike the ECtHR (as will be examined in the next chapter), the CCPR has not used integration as an element in its reasoning in its views on individual complaints, and has focussed on family rights. A finding that a deportation breaches the ICCPR on the grounds of the right to family life is rare, and appears to require exceptional circumstances. These exceptional circumstances existed in *Dauphin v Canada*,[113] in which the ICCPR found that the fact that the individual in question had resided in Canada since he was two years old, had close ties to Canada and no family ties to Haiti meant that the drastic effects on the author of the proposed deportation was disproportionate to the legitimate aims pursued by the State Party. Here, the CCPR found that there was a violation of articles 17 and 23(1) of the ICCPR.

The Concept of Integration in the Concluding Observations of the Human Rights Committee: The Progressive Realization of Equal Rights

Express and Indirect References of the CCPR to Integration: Articles 2 and 26

Express references of the CCPR to integration are sparse and arise only in the European context.[114] Express references to integration are linked to the equality guarantee contained in Article 26, and to manifestations of xenophobia and racism. Sweden, for example, is exhorted to improve 'the application of laws punishing racially motivated crimes' and 'the integration into society of members of minority groups' in the context of the CCPR's noting of persistent manifestations of racism and xenophobia.[115] Similarly, while the committee noted the measures taken by Lichtenstein to promote equality and integration of non-citizens, it also expressed its concern over the persistence of xenophobic attitudes towards Muslims and people of Turkish origin in particular which raises issues under articles 2 and 26.[116] This express linkage between integration and Article 26 was taken a step further in relation to Slovakia, when the committee was concerned by the 'slow pace of integration' of those who had been granted asylum and refugee status and recommended that Slovakia should take should take 'concrete measures' to

---

CCPR/C/58/D/538/1993; *Canepa v Canada*, CCPR/C/52/D/558/1998; *Rajan and Rajan v New Zealand*; and *Sahid v New Zealand*, CCPR/C/77/D/893/1999.

113 CCPR/C/96/D/1792/2008 (UNHRC, 2009).

114 Although, note that in the committee's 2011 concluding observations on Ethiopia's state report, it recommended that the State Party should strive to promote the integration of refugees and asylum seekers, including by developing the out-of-camp policy as much as possible. Ethiopia, UN Doc CCPR/C/ETH/CO/1 (19 August 2011), at para. 13. It remains to be seen whether this trend will be further developed in forthcoming concluding observations on other African countries, for example.

115 Sweden, UN Doc CCPR/C/SWE/CO/6 (7 May 2009) at para. 13.

116 Lichtenstein, UN Doc CCPR/CO/81/LIE (12 August 2004) at para. 9.

promote their integration in the State Party, 'to ensure equal access to employment, education, housing and health'.[117] Integration is thus seen as a prerequisite to the full enjoyment of equality.

In addition to its comments and recommendations in respect of migrants, refugees and asylum seekers, the committee has also invoked the concept of integration in the context of Roma and national minorities, insisting on the necessity to integrate members of the Roma community[118] and national minorities in a manner which is respectful of their cultural identity[119] in order to enable such persons to fully enjoy their rights under the Covenant – including through engaging in dialogue with the concerned groups and civil society.[120] The elaboration of integration plans for such groups will not in themselves satisfy the committee in circumstances where there is evidence of widespread discrimination in practice.[121] The committee's concept of integration as a process which respects the individual's right to a cultural identity is reinforced by the fact that integration must be conducted in the context of attempts to raise awareness of discrimination and promote tolerance.[122]

The non-discrimination guarantees contained in articles 2 and 26 have also formed the basis for concerns expressed by the committee regarding the treatment of migrants and migrant workers which do not expressly refer to integration but which nonetheless constitute integration-related issues. The committee has frequently expressed general concerns about hate speech and other manifestations of discrimination, xenophobia and racism directed at immigrant-origin communities.[123] More specifically, the CCPR has expressed concern at the level of discrimination in employment experienced by persons of migrant origin,[124]

117 Slovakia, UN Doc CCPR/C/SVK/CO/3 (20 April 2011), at para. 9. See also, Czech Republic, para. 18.

118 See Finland, UN Doc CCPR/CO/82/FIN (2 December 2004) at para. 15. On the extensive discrimination suffered by the Roma and the way in which this impedes effective access to Covenant rights, see also, for example, the concluding observations on the reports submitted by Moldova, UN Doc CCPR/C/MDA/CO/2 (2009), para. 27, Albania, UN Doc CCPR/CO/82/ALB (2 December 2004) at para. 21; Bulgaria UN Doc CCPR/C/79/Add.24 (3 August 1993) at para. 8; Czech Republic, UN Doc CCPR/CO/72/CZE (27 August 2001) at paras 8–11; Germany, UN Doc CCPR/C/DEU/CO/6 (12 November 2012), at para. 17.

119 Portugal, UN Doc CCPR/CO/78/PRT (2003), para. 20.

120 See, for example, Georgia, UN Doc CCPR/C/GEO/CO/3 (15 November 2007) at para. 17.

121 Bulgaria, para. 7.

122 Bulgaria, para. 7 and Serbia UN Doc CCPR/C/SRB/CO/2 (24 March 2011), at para. 22.

123 Australia, UN Doc CCPR/C/AUS/CO/5 (7 May 2009) at para. 26; Russian Federation, UN Doc CCPR/C/RUS/CO/6 (24 November 2009) at para. 11; Germany, UN Doc CCPR/C/DEU/CO/6 (12 November 2012), at para. 18.

124 France, UN Doc CCPR/C/FRA/CO/4 (31 July 2008) at para. 25; The Netherlands, UN Doc CCPR/CO/72/NET (27 August 2001); Portugal, UN Doc CCPR/C/PRT/CO/4 (23 November 2012), at para. 5.

and the lack of representation of racial and other minorities in public life[125] and in the judiciary.[126] The committee has also recognized that the legal status of migrant workers may raise serious concerns under articles 2 and 26, reflecting the importance of the relationship between integration and law which is the focus of this book. In relation to Thailand, the committee commented on the 'lack of full protection of the rights of registered and unregistered migrant workers in Thailand, particularly with regard to liberty of movement, access to social services and education, and access to personal documents. The deplorable conditions in which migrants are obliged to live and work indicate serious violations of articles 8 and 26 of the Covenant'.[127] In addition, observations made by the CCPR in relation to Roma and national minority issues under the rubric of articles 2 and 26 also have application in the case of immigrant communities, for example, in the case of the issue of the de facto segregation of some Roma children in schools in Europe which has been referred to by the CCPR as raising concerns under articles 26 and 27.[128]

References of the CCPR to Integration-Related Matters Outside the Article 26 Context

Aside from the express and indirect references to integration in the context of non-discrimination and equality under articles 2 and 26, the areas of concern to the CCPR regarding non-citizens and ethnic minorities are wide-ranging but often relate to more basic civil rights than those usually associated with integration. Issues relating to the determination of immigration or asylum status, and the process for dealing with immigration and asylum applications are frequently raised by the CCPR.[129] In Europe, the concerns of the CCPR in this regard include detention for the purposes of asylum and immigration law and the conditions of

125 France, UN Doc CCPR/C/FRA/CO/4 (31 July 2008) at para. 26; Serbia, UN Doc CCPR/C/UNK/CO/1 (14 August 2006) at para. 21; and Croatia, UN Doc CCPR/C/HRV/CO/2 (4 November 2009) at para. 18.

126 United Kingdom of Great Britain and Northern Ireland, UN Doc CCPR/C/GBR/CO/6 (30 July 2008), para. 8.

127 Thailand, UN Doc CCPR/CO/84/THA (8 July 2005), para. 23. See also the concerns of the committee in relation to the treatment of Haitians in the Dominican Republic, involving mass expulsion violating articles 7, 12(4) and 13, the issue of the living and working conditions of Haitian workers and the failure to protect Haitians from serious human rights abuses such as forced labour. Dominican Republic, UN Doc CCPR/CO/71/DOM (26 April 2001), paras 17 and 18 in particular.

128 See, for example, Croatia, UN Doc CCPR/C/HRV/CO/2 (4 November 2009) at para. 19.

129 The extensive comments often made on the application of refugee law are linked to the lack of a monitoring body for the 1951 Refugee Convention.

such detention[130] as well as the conduct of asylum and deportation procedures.[131] Outside Europe and North America, the concerns of the committee relating to immigration and asylum procedures are even more basic. For example, in relation to Mali, the committee has expressed its concern at:

> reports of the hardship suffered by some 6,000 Mauritanian refugees who, for the last 10 years, have been living in the west of the country (Kayes region), are not registered, possess no identity papers and whose right to physical security is not sufficiently protected.[132]

The issue of the ill-treatment of minorities by the police is also a pervasive concern of the CCPR, particularly in the European context. This encompasses includes both the police treatment of immigrant and ethnic groups in a physical sense and the stopping of individuals by the police on a discriminatory basis, and as such may raise issues under articles 2 and 7.[133]

Freedom of religion, as protected by Article 18, is also a right which the committee has examined in connection with migrant and ethnic groups. It will be seen in Chapter 8 that issues of religious freedom have become a significant

---

130 This can raise issues under articles 7, 9, 10 and 13: see, for example, Belgium, CCPR/CO/81/BEL (12 August 2004); Greece, UN Doc CCPR/CO/83/GRC (25 April 2005); Ireland, UN Doc CCPR/C/IRL/CO/3 (30 July 2008); Sweden, UN Doc CCPR/C/SWE/CO/6 (7 May 2009); and Australia, UN Doc CCPR/C/AUS/CO/5 (7 May 2009).

131 Which can raise an issue under articles 6 and 7: see, for example, Belgium, CCPR/CO/81/BEL (12 August 2004), para. 14; Switzerland, UN Doc CCPR/C/CHE/CO/3 (3 November 2009); Russia, UN Doc CCPR/C/RUS/CO/6 (24 November 2009), para. 17 (returning foreign nationals to countries in which torture is allegedly practiced while relying on diplomatic assurances).

132 Mali, UN Doc CCPR/CO/77/MLI (16 April 2003), para. 20. In the Asia-Pacific region, see Democratic Republic of Korea (UN Doc CCPR/CO/72/PRK (27 August 2001), para. 21); Thailand (UN Doc CCPR/CO/84/THA (8 July 2005), para. 17); and Japan (UN Doc CCPR/C/JPN/CO/5 (30 October 2008), para. 25. Again, similar issues arise in the Middle East/North Africa region in relation to Algeria (UN Doc CCPR/C/DZA/CO/3 (12 December 2007), para. 22); Morocco (UN Doc CCPR/CO/82/MAR (1 December 2004), para. 13); and Libya (UN Doc CCPR/C/LBY/CO/4 (15 November 2007), para. 18); and in Latin America and the Caribbean in relation to Barbados (UN Doc CCPR/C/BRB/CO/3 (11 May 2007), para. 10).

133 See, for example, Belgium, UN Doc CCPR/C/BEL/CO/5 (16 November 2010); Czech Republic, UN Doc CCPR/CO/72/CZE (27 August 2001), paras 14 and 15; Greece, UN Doc CCPR/CO/83/GRC (25 April 2005), para. 9; Italy, UN Doc CCPR/C/ITA/CO/5 (24 April 2006), para. 11; Portugal, UN Doc CCPR/CO/78/PRT (5 July 2003), para. 8; Slovakia, UN Doc CCPR/CO/78/SVK (22 August 2003), para. 11; Norway, UN Doc CCPR/C/NOR/CO/5 (25 April 2006), para. 17; Australia, UN Doc CCPR/C/AUS/CO/5 (7 May 2009), para. 1.

integration issue worldwide.[134] In 2010, the committee involved itself in the discourse surrounding controversial political issues in Switzerland, expressing the view that the adoption of a proposed referendum aimed at prohibiting the construction of minarets on mosques would bring the State Party into non-compliance with its obligations under the Covenant.[135] This referendum was passed in 2010. The committee's observations have also covered the lack of official recognition of mosques,[136] discrimination in state subsidies between schools on the basis of religion,[137] the special or established position of a religion in some states,[138] and the existence of a denominational education system.[139]

Finally, the CCPR has frequently commented on family reunification in the context of the privacy and family rights protected by articles 17 and 23 of the ICCPR. The CCPR has criticized the family reunification regimes in a number of European countries. It has suggested (in the case of Belgium) that Article 17 requires that aliens, the majority of whose ties are to the host state, are not to be expelled under any circumstances.[140] This provides added protection against deportation to migrants who are integrated into the host country in which they live, and goes further than the jurisprudence of the ECtHR on Article 8 ECHR's protection of private and family life (which will be discussed in detail in the next chapter).

The fact that integration is not explicitly linked to these rights, while it is linked expressly to equality in a small number of cases, illustrates a concept of integration which is posited in a framework of the progressive realization of rights, with the objective of migrants obtaining equality with members of the majority population. This ties in with UNHCR's conception of integration as the granting of a progressively wider range of rights and entitlements generally commensurate with those of local citizens.

The Subordinate Role of Article 27 ICCPR in the Context of Integration of Migrants

As noted above, the protection of the right of members of minorities to 'enjoy their own culture, to profess and practise their own religion, or to use their own language' contained in Article 27 is an important component of the international legal framework relating to integration. The CCPR is in favour of measures

134 See also, for example, the discussion in Siobhán Mullally, 'Civic Integration, Migrant Women and the Veil: At the Limits of Rights?' (2011) 74(1) *Modern Law Review* 27.

135 Switzerland, UN Doc CCPR/C/CHE/CO/3 (3 November 2009), para. 8.

136 Belgium, CCPR/CO/81/BEL (12 August 2004), para. 26.

137 Canada, UN Doc CCPR/C/CAN/CO/5 (20 April 2006), para. 21 (discusses Canada's failure to respond to the views of the CCPR in *Waldman v Canada*).

138 Denmark, UN Doc CCPR/C/DNK/CO/5 (29 October 2008), para. 5; Georgia, UN Doc CCPR/C/GEO/CO/3 (15 November 2007), para. 15.

139 Ireland, UN Doc CCPR/C/IRL/CO/3 (30 July 2008), para. 22.

140 UN Doc CCPR/CO/81/BEL (12 August 2004), para. 25.

'envisaged or taken to promote the integration of minorities and the protection of their rights and to guarantee respect for their cultures and dignity'.[141] Issues relating to the preservation of the culture and language of national minorities are frequently considered within the framework of Article 27 and this may provide important guidance in the context of immigrant-origin minorities. The committee has emphasized, for example, the point that all religious and ethnic minorities (whether or not they are officially recognized as national minorities) should be able in practice to enjoy their own culture and to use their own language,[142] although these comments are generally made in the context of countries with significant national minority groups such as Albania, Thailand and Turkey. Articles 26 and 27 are often linked in the committee's consideration of discrimination against national minorities. In relation to Moldova for example, the committee argued that:

> The State party should increase its efforts to translate its international commitments under articles 26 and 27 of the Covenant into practical achievements for its minorities, including the Gagauz and the Roma in rural communities.[143]

The committee also provides an insight into the correct interpretation of 'integration' in noting, in the context of observations made under Article 27 along with Article 26, the need to integrate the Roma in a manner respectful of their cultural identity.[144] Latvia, which has a large Russian minority without Latvian citizenship, is urged to facilitate the integration process by enabling non-citizens who are long-term residents of Latvia to participate in local elections and to limit the number of restrictions on non-citizens in order to facilitate participation in public life.[145]

Nevertheless, in general, the committee does not refer to Article 27 as a benchmark in matters relevant to the integration of migrants or second and subsequent generation migrant communities.[146] The committee does not place

---

141 Democratic Republic of the Congo, UN Doc CCPR/C/COD/CO/3 (26 April 2006), para. 26 (in the context of the marginalization, discrimination and even persecution of pygmies in DRC).

142 Albania, UN Doc CCPR/CO/82/ALB (2 December 2004), para. 21 (all members of ethnic and linguistic minorities, whether or not they are recognized as national minorities), Croatia, CCPR/CO/71/HRV, 30 April 2001, para. 22, Estonia CCPR/CO/77/EST (15 April 2003), para. 16 (primarily in relation to the Russian-speaking minority).

143 Moldova, UN Doc CCPR/CO/75/MDA (26 July 2002), para. 19. See also Ireland, UN Doc CCPR/C/IRL/CO/3 (30 July 2008), para. 23.

144 Germany, UN Doc CCPR/CO/80/DEU (4 May 2004), para. 21(a). See also Greece, UN Doc CCPR/CO/83/GRC (25 April 2005), para. 18(a).

145 Latvia, UN Doc CCPR/CO/79/LVA (2003), para. 18. See also Estonia, UN Doc CCPR/C/EST/CO/3 (4 August 2010).

146 For a fuller discussion of whether 'new minorities', including refugees and asylum seekers, are entitled to minority rights, see Stephanie E Berry, 'Integrating Refugees: The

the same emphasis on the preservation of the culture and language of minorities resulting from recent immigration as it does in respect of national minorities, and does not refer for example to an obligation to provide an opportunity for migrant children to receive instruction in and of their languages, which it does in the case of national minorities.[147] The CCPR appears to conceive of integration issues as primarily related to equality rather than to minority and cultural rights when it comes to immigrant-origin, rather than national, minorities. An examination of the concluding observations relating to the country reports of the United Kingdom and the United States of America (both countries with significant immigrant-origin ethnic groups) illustrates this point. Racial minorities' issues are generally discussed in terms of Article 26 rather than Article 27. In the case of the UK, issues relating to negative public attitudes towards Muslims, the low degree of ethnic minority representation in the judiciary and racial profiling by the police are all considered in the context of Article 26 rather than Article 27.[148] In relation to the United States, racial segregation in schools and racial discrimination were dealt with under Article 26 while aboriginal peoples' rights' issues, including issues relating to culture, are dealt with under Article 27.[149] The upshot of this is that while Article 27 and the cultural rights of minorities protected thereunder provide a basic framework which integration policies must respect, Article 27 does not constitute the full picture from an integration perspective. As shown in Chapters 2 and 3, integration stretches beyond the Article 27 concerns of minority language, culture and religion (the primary concerns of Article 27) to all-encompassing social issues. The treatment of the concept of integration by the CCPR in its concluding observations suggests that the essence of integration lies in immigrants and their descendants progressively achieving equal treatment and outcomes as existing members of society, rather than centring round a narrow culture-based core. National integration policies which centre on testing cultural integration on a superficial level without connecting integration to state responsibilities in respect of equality of inclusion are diametrically opposed to this approach.

The CCPR's Approach to Integration Linked to the Wealth of the State Party

The contrasting way in which the ideas discussed in this section are developed in the European/North American/Australian contexts and elsewhere is striking. As noted above, the concept of integration is not expressly mentioned in the

---

Case for a Minority Rights Based Approach' (2012) 24(1) IJRL 1 pp. 22–24.

147 See, for example, Macedonia, UN Doc CCPR/C/MKD/CO/2 (3 April 2008) para. 19; Serbia, UN Doc CCPR/C/UNK/CO/1 (14 August 2006), para. 22; Austria, UN Doc CCPR/C/AUT/CO/4 (30 October 2007), para. 21.

148 United Kingdom of Great Britain and Northern Ireland, UN Doc CCPR/C/GBR/CO/6 (30 July 2008), paras 16, 8 and 29 respectively.

149 United States of America, UN Doc CCPR/C/USA/CO/3 (15 September 2006), paras 22, 23, 24 and 27 respectively.

observations of the CCPR relating to the African, Asian, Latin American or Middle-Eastern/North-African regions.[150] In the context of most European countries, basic procedural safeguards and rights are, generally speaking, assured (or at least theoretically provided for) for refugees, immigrants and non-citizens, meaning that the committee moves on to the next stage in the progressive realization of equal rights as the host population, which is their integration into the host state. Integration is simply not on the agenda in the same way in most African, Asian, Middle Eastern and Latin American countries, reflecting the links between integration and state expenditure, and also the fact that these State Parties are in the main more significant migrant-sending rather than migrant-receiving countries. In its concluding observations on Africa in particular, the CCPR seems reluctant to get involved in these matters because of the enormous financial burden faced in recent years by some African countries, such as Tanzania, in accommodating large numbers of refugees.[151] In addition, in the case of African, Asian and Latin American states, the committee is in general more preoccupied with the treatment of indigenous minorities than minorities of recent immigrant origin.

The International Covenant on Economic, Social and Cultural Rights

In terms of its content, the ICESCR is a crucial international legal source of integration-related rights. It contains some of the most significant and wide-ranging international legal provisions establishing economic, social and cultural rights, including rights relating to work in just and favourable conditions, to social protection, to an adequate standard of living, to the highest attainable standards of physical and mental health, to education and to enjoyment of the benefits of cultural freedom and scientific progress. In addition, Article 2(2) imposes an obligation of non-discrimination as to the rights set down in the ICESCR: the Covenant rights apply to everyone, including non-nationals, regardless of legal status and documentation.[152] Thus, in principle, the ICESCR provides migrants with the tools necessary to maintain self-reliance and an acceptable standard of life in order that they can contribute actively to the life of the country and the community and live amongst the host population without discrimination.[153] Consequently, the

150 With the exception of the Democratic Republic of Congo, which was recommended to provide detailed information in its next report on measures envisaged or taken to promote the integration of minorities. UN Doc CCPR/C/COD/CO/3 (2006), para. 26.

151 See, for example, Tanzania, UN Doc CCPR/C/79/Add.97 (18 August 1998), at para. 3.

152 CESCR General Comment No. 20, 'Non-discrimination in Economic, Social and Cultural Rights (art. 2, para. 2)' (UN Doc E/C.12/GC/20, 10 June 2009), para. 30 on 'nationality'.

153 Rosa da Costa, note 15, p. 31. According to Wiesbrock, the acquisition of social, economic and cultural rights are essential to the integration process as they ensure that migrants become part of the host society (Anja Wiesbrock, note 78, p. 708).

risk of becoming economically and socially marginalized should be reduced and integration should be facilitated.

A number of articles which protect integration-related rights will be discussed below. The development of the concept of integration by the CESCR in its concluding observations on State Reports will then be assessed. The analysis of the concluding observations reveals that integration as a standalone concept is even less developed in the context of the ICESCR than in the case of the ICCPR. Nonetheless, the CESCR has recognized the impact of national legal and administrative rules on the integration of migrants. Furthermore, the CCPR's approach of conceiving integration in terms of the progressive realization of rights for immigrants and their families is mirrored in the observations of the CESCR. Finally, the CESCR appears to endorse a multicultural approach to integration.

The Right to Work: Articles 6, 7 and 8

The right to work is contained in articles 6, 7 and 8, which are inter-related.[154] Access to the labour market is a key integration issue as it provides both a means for financial stability and a way of improving language skills and establishing contacts with the local community. Article 6 provides for the basic right of everyone to gain his living by work which he freely accepts or chooses, although it clearly does not constitute an absolute and unconditional right to obtain employment.[155] Article 7 then goes on to elaborate a more extensive right of everyone to enjoy just and favourable conditions of work and a decent living for themselves and their families, including 'Equal opportunity for everyone to be promoted in his employment to an appropriate higher level',[156] and 'rest, leisure and reasonable limitation of working hours and periodic holidays with pay'.[157] This is a far-reaching provision with the potential to extend into relationships between private individuals,[158] although the committee has not elaborated on the meaning of the article by way of General Comment. Article 8 addresses the right of all persons to join trade unions (of their choice).

States Parties are under an obligation to respect the right to work by refraining from denying or limiting equal access to decent work for all persons (including

154 CESCR General Comment No. 18, 'The Right to Work (art. 6)' (UN Doc E/C.12/GC/18, 6 February 2006), para. 1. On the right to work, see generally, Haina Lu 'The personal application of the right to work in the age of migration' (2008) 26(1) *Netherlands Quarterly of Human Rights* 43–77.

155 CESCR General Comment No. 18, ibid., para. 6.

156 Article 7(c).

157 Article 7(d).

158 Indeed, Craven notes that this provision has been the subject of some controversy as it is debatable whether 'rest and leisure' are sufficiently fundamental to be established as human rights. Matthew Craven, *The International Covenant on Economic, Social and Cultural Rights: A Perspective on its Development* (Oxford University Press, 1995), p. 226.

members of minorities and migrant workers).[159] In its General Comment on the right to work contained in Article 6, the CESCR emphasizes the importance of the *accessibility* of the labour market. The committee refers to Article 2 of International Labour Organization Convention No. 111, to the effect that State Parties should 'declare and pursue a national policy designed to promote, by methods appropriate to national conditions and practice, equality of opportunity and treatment in respect of employment and occupation, with a view to eliminating any discrimination in respect thereof', and the committee concludes that 'even in times of severe resource constraints, disadvantaged and marginalized individuals and groups must be protected by the adoption of relatively lowcost targeted programmes'.[160] These provisions can thus be seen as an important legal instrument for successful integration, particularly as national constitutions rarely contain such detailed provisions on socio-economic rights such as the right to work.

Other Integration-Related Rights Protected by the ICESCR

Article 11 incorporates a wide range of concerns relating to the lives of all residents of States Parties; in particular food, clothing and housing.[161] The CESCR has devoted particularly extensive attention to the right to adequate housing, which is 'of central importance for the enjoyment of all economic, social and cultural rights'.[162] As explained by the committee, the right to adequate housing goes beyond a basic right to shelter:

> the right to housing, should not be interpreted in a narrower restrictive sense which equates it with, for example, the shelter provided by merely having a roof over one's head ... Rather it should be seen as the right to live somewhere in security, peace and dignity ...[163]

Finally, Article 15 provides (*inter alia*) for the right of everyone to take part in cultural life. This confers a right on every person to participate in the cultural life of the society of the State Party. In relation to migrants, the CESCR's view is that State Parties should pay particular attention to the protection of the cultural identities of migrants as well as their language, religion and folklore, and of their right to hold cultural, artistic and intercultural events. State Parties should not prevent migrants

---

159 CESCR General Comment No. 18, note 154, para. 23.

160 Ibid., para. 12(b)(i).

161 Craven notes that Article 11 can be seen as the epitome of economic, social and cultural rights and is clearly dependent for realization on the economic resources of the state concerned. Matthew Craven, note 158, p. 350.

162 CESCR General Comment No. 4, 'The Right to Adequate Housing' (13 December 1991), para. 1.

163 CESCR General Comment No. 4, ibid., para. 7. The 'adequacy' of housing must be assessed by reference to security of tenure, availability of services, affordability, habitability, accessibility, location and cultural adequacy.

from maintaining cultural links with their countries of origin.[164] Together with Article 27, Article 15 provides a minimum standard with which integration policies must conform in order to remain in compliance with international law. Article 15 should also be read in conjunction with the aims of education as expressed in Article 13 to 'enable all persons to participate effectively in a free society, promote understanding, tolerance and friendship among all nations and all racial, ethnic or religious groups'. This vision reflects the general emphasis in international law of interaction between groups living within the same state and the preference for a multicultural model of societal relations.[165]

Limitations on the Transformative Potential of the ICESCR in the Integration Context

Despite its clear applicability to the integration needs of immigrants and refugees, the ICESCR suffers from some limitations which have enabled State Parties to justify evading the full extent of their obligations and which limit its ability to have a real impact on the integration prospects of individuals. The ICESCR is normatively underdeveloped in comparison to the ICCPR, primarily due to the fact that there has, until now, been no individual complaints procedure in place in relation to the ICESCR.[166] Secondly, the justiciability and extent of the enforceability of socio-economic rights is still matter of debate and controversy in many of the State Parties to the ICESCR.[167] Finally, while it would not apply to European states, Article 2(3) permits developing countries to determine the extent to which they would guarantee the economic rights recognized in the Covenant to non-nationals.

164 CESCR General Comment No. 21, 'The Right of Everyone to Take Part in Cultural Life' (UN Doc E/C.12/GC/21, 21 December 2009), para. 34. See Roger O'Keeffe, 'The Right to Take Part in Cultural Life under Article 15 of the ICESCR' (1998) 47(4) *ICLQ* 904.

165 See Xanthaki, note 7, p. 35.

166 The Optional Protocol to the ICESCR, adopted on 10 December 2008 and opened for signature on 24 September 2009, provides for an individual complaints procedure. The Optional Protocol is not yet in force as it has not yet had the requisite number of ratifications or accessions. For an overview of the committee's background, mandate and workings, see Philip Alston, 'The Committee on Economic, Social and Cultural Rights', in Philip Alston (ed.), *The United Nations and Human Rights: A Critical Appraisal* (Oxford University Press, 1992).

167 See generally, Conor Gearty and Virginia Mantouvalou, *Debating Social Rights* (Hart Publishing, 2010). See also, in the Irish context (against the enforcement of socio-economic rights through the courts) Adrian Hardiman, 'The Role of the Supreme Court in our Democracy', in Joe Mulholland (ed.), *Political Choice and Democratic Freedom in Ireland* (2004); and for the opposing view, see Gerry Whyte, 'The Role of the Supreme Court in Our Democracy: A Response to Mr Justice Hardiman' (2008) 28 *DULJ* 1.

Integration in the Concluding Observations of the Committee on Economic, Social and Cultural Rights: An Underdeveloped Concept

The importance of the acquisition of social, economic and cultural rights in terms of the integration process was highlighted above. However, despite the fact that the CESCR regularly comments in its concluding observations on the social, cultural and economic rights of migrants and asylum seekers, there has been even less development of the concept of integration by the CESCR than the CCPR.

Non-Discrimination and the Impact of Legal and Administrative Rules

In its concluding observations, the CESCR consistently refers to discrimination suffered by immigrants and members of ethnic minorities in the fields of housing,[168] employment,[169] health care[170] and education.[171] Discrimination against migrants in the area of access to and conditions of employment in particular, appears as a key concern of the committee across its concluding observations.[172] Access of migrant children to education of all levels is also a pervasive theme of the concluding observations,[173] with issues including segregated schooling and the provision of intensive language training for migrant children.[174] These are spheres which were identified as key functional aspects of integration in Chapter 2.[175]

The impact of legal and administrative rules on migrants' enjoyment of social and economic rights has also been expressly recognized by the committee.

168 See, for example, Cyprus, UN Doc E/C.12/CYP/CO/5 (12 June 2009), para. 21.

169 See note 172 below.

170 See, for example, the United Kingdom UN Doc E/C.12/GBR/CO/5 (12 June 2009), para. 27 (access to health care for asylum seekers).

171 See note 173 below.

172 Thus, for example, Cyprus is urged to 'ensure strict control over the terms of employment and working conditions of migrant workers by strengthening financial and human resources of the labour inspectorate' (UN Doc E/C.12/CYP/CO/5 (12 June 2009), para. 14), while in relation to the Republic of Korea, the committee expresses its concern that migrant workers are subject to exploitation, discrimination and unpaid wages (UN Doc E/C.12/KOR/CO/3 (17 December 2009), para. 21). See also the concluding observations in relation to Nigeria, which discusses the expulsion of up to half a million Chadian workers 'in inhuman and undignified circumstances' (UN Doc E/C.12/1/Add.23 (13 May 1998), para. 11).

173 See, for example, Tanzania, UN Doc E/C.12/TZA/CO/1–3 (13 December 2012), at para. 28, where the committee reminds Tanzania that refugee children should have access to primary education.

174 On segregated schooling, see United Kingdom of Great Britain and Northern Ireland, UN Doc E/C.12/1/Add.79 (5 June 2002), para. 42 (segregation along religious lines); and Bosnia, UN Doc E/C.12/BIH/CO/1 (24 January 2006), para. 50 (segregation along ethnic lines). On the provision of intensive language training, see Lichtenstein, UN Doc E/C.12/LIE/CO/1 (9 June 2006), para. 36.

175 See the working definition set out in Chapter 2.

Overlapping with the work of the CCPR, the CESCR has emphasized the manner in which immigration measures relating to family reunification may interfere with the right to enjoy family life.[176] The potentially discriminatory impact of restrictions on family reunification was noted in relation to the UK for example, the committee observing (in the context of changes to the Immigration Rules that were subsequently repealed):[177]

> the increase of age from 18 to 21 for foreign partners to join their British partners has a discriminatory effect on some groups, in particular ethnic minorities and women. (arts 10 and 2)[178]

The committee has also commented that administrative obstacles to the enjoyment of the social and economic rights of immigrants and asylum seekers should be removed.[179] In the case of social assistance, the committee advocates universal coverage of the social security system so as to include asylum seekers and newly-arrived immigrants.[180] The committee expressed concern in the case of Austria that social assistance benefits provided to asylum seekers are often considerably lower than those received by citizens of the State Party – an observation which is applicable across Europe.[181] As noted above, the committee has observed that the legal status of certain groups (especially asylum seekers and undocumented workers but also migrant workers and non-citizens more generally), can constitute a barrier to their enjoyment of the rights enshrined in the Covenant. This link between immigration processes and the enjoyment of ICESCR rights was made explicit in the committee's concluding observations on Italy's state report, in which the committee drew attention to the fact that it was concerned about:

> the excessive time taken by the authorities to renew residence permits in the State Party, which may restrict, inter alia, freedom of movement and access to social services by migrant workers and their families.[182]

Notwithstanding the applicability of these observations to integration-related issues, the observations and recommendations illustrate that the primary focus of the committee is to ensure that the rights provided therein are secured on

176 Denmark, UN Doc E/C.12/1/Add.102 (14 December 2004), paras 16 and 29; Cyprus, UN Doc E/C.12/CYP/CO/5 (12 June 2009), para. 18.

177 In light of the UK Supreme Court decision in *Quila v Secretary of State* [2012] 1 AC 241, as discussed in Chapter 3.

178 The United Kingdom, UN Doc E/C.12/GBR/CO/5 (12 June 2009), para. 26.

179 Cyprus, note 172. See also, Republic of Korea, UN Doc E/C.12/KOR/CO/3 (17 December 2009), para. 10.

180 Australia, UN Doc E/C.12/AUS/CO/4 (12 June 2009), para. 20.

181 Austria, UN Doc E/C.12/AUT/CO/3 (25 January 2006), para. 15.

182 Italy, UN Doc E/C.12/1/Add.103 (14 December 2004), para. 17. See also, Monaco, UN Doc E/C.12/MCO/CO/1 (13 June 2006), para. 18.

the territory of the State Party without discrimination rather than focussing on integration *per se*. Thus, as in the case of the CCPR (and even more so than in the case of the CCPR), the concept of integration only therefore enters the work of the CESCR in a subsidiary role. Moreover, only in few instances are the observations of the committee explicitly linked to the concept of integration and, reflecting the pattern in the concluding observations of the CCPR, explicit references to integration only appear in observations relating to European country reports.

The Beginnings of an Integration Paradigm in the Work of the CESCR

Despite the limited nature of its interpretation of the concept of integration, the Committee for Economic, Social and Cultural Rights has made some strong statements on the desirability of integration and has developed the beginnings of a concept of integration. Thus, in connection with Cyprus, the committee observed:

> The Committee is [further] concerned that while third country migrants represent a large percentage of the island's population and legally live in the country, the State Party has not yet adopted an effective policy for their integration. (arts 6 and 7)[183]

Accordingly, the committee encouraged Cyprus to 'adopt and implement an effective integration policy for lawful immigrants', although it failed to outline what such an integration policy would entail.[184] In its concluding observations on Lichtenstein, the committee called on the State Party to:

> continue and intensify its efforts to promote ethnic and religious tolerance, e.g. by including this subject in school curricula and through training of teachers and public awareness campaigns, and to adopt a comprehensive strategy for the integration of persons of a different ethnic origin or religion.

In a similar vein, the committee noted the efforts made by the government of Switzerland to integrate foreign workers and their families',[185] and recommended that 'the State Party take concrete measures to address the unemployment situation of vulnerable groups among the population, to promote their integration into the labour market'.[186] This concept of integration seems to operate on the assumption that integration is a process of social inclusion, including inclusion in the labour market. Slightly more indirectly from the perspective of integration, Portugal is urged to 'intensify its efforts to create a culture of tolerance and to eliminate all forms of discrimination, in so far as they affect women, Roma, asylum seekers and

183 Cyprus, UN Doc E/C.12/CYP/CO/5 (12 June 2009), para. 14.
184 Ibid.
185 Switzerland, UN Doc E/C.12/1998/SR.39 (26 November 1998), para. 7.
186 Switzerland, UN Doc E/C.12/CHE/CO/2 (26 November 2010), para. 9.

immigrants'.[187] This approach seems to stem from the perception that it is difficult for immigrant or minority groups to enjoy their Covenant rights if no effort is made to integrate such persons into the host society. Thus integration functions as a prerequisite to, as well as the result of, the enjoyment of ICESCR rights. This reflects the approach of the CCPR that effective attempts to 'integrate' migrants are necessary in order to ensure that their human rights are protected. This is also reflected in the comments of the committee relating to the manner in which legal status, or lack of such legal status, may affect the ability of migrant workers or non-citizens to enjoy economic, social and cultural rights. The committee has frequently expressed concern that non-citizens[188] or categories of non-citizens such as migrant workers[189] or refugees[190] are denied the full protection of the ICESCR.

A Multicultural Approach

Another dimension of the committee's approach to integration is its preference for a multicultural approach. By way of example, the CESCR is 'encouraged by the development of programmes to promote multiculturalism and the recognition being placed on the racial and cultural differences' in Australia.[191] It consistently advocates State Parties to intensify their efforts to create a culture of tolerance and respect for cultural diversity and to eliminate all forms of discrimination, including in so far as they affect asylum seekers and immigrants.[192] This reflects the CESCR's view that 'the protection of cultural diversity is an ethical imperative, inseparable from human dignity',[193] especially given that:

> Culture has no fixed borders. The phenomena of migration, integration, assimilation and globalisation have brought cultures, groups and individuals

187 Portugal, UN Doc E/C.12/1/Add.53 (1 December 2000), para. 18.

188 Latvia, UN Doc E/C.12/LVA/CO/1 (7 January 2008), para. 37; and Lichtenstein, UN Doc E/C.12/LIE/CO/1 (9 June 2006), paras 11 and 25.

189 Poland, UN Doc E/C.12/1/Add.82 (19 December 2002), para. 15. In the Asian context, the situation of migrant workers, refugees and North Koreans in China is criticized (UN Doc E/C.12/1/Add.107 (13 May 2005), paras 14 and 15.

190 In the African concluding observations, there are references to the situation of refugees in camps who are denied access to basic economic and social rights (Kenya, UN Doc E/C.12/KEN/CO/1 (19 November 2008), para. 13; and Senegal, UN Doc E/C.12/1/Add.62 (24 September 2001), para. 33 for example).

191 Australia, UN Doc E/C.12/1993/9 (3 June 1993), para. 5.

192 Portugal, UN Doc E/C.12/1/Add.53 (1 December 2000) para. 18; Spain, UN Doc E/C.12/1/Add.99 (7 June 2004) para. 25; Sweden, UN Doc E/C.12/SWE/CO/5 (18 November 2008), para. 16; Macedonia UN Doc E/C.12/MKD/CO/1 (24 November 2006), para. 48.

193 CESCR General Comment No. 21, note 164, para. 40.

> into closer contact than ever before, at a time when each of them is striving to keep their own identity.[194]

As noted in the context of Article 27 of the CCPR, integration tests which require migrants to demonstrate cultural assimilation do not fit with this paradigm. Linked to this, and in common with the CCPR, the CESCR has expressed concern over the existence of racist and xenophobic attitudes across Europe in particular; however, it has not expressly linked these comments to the concept of integration.[195]

The International Convention on the Elimination of all Forms of Racial Discrimination

ICERD defines racial discrimination in Article 1, paragraph 1, as:

> any distinction, exclusion, restriction or preference based on race, colour, descent, or national or ethnic origin which has the purpose or effect of nullifying or impairing the recognition, enjoyment or exercise, on an equal footing, of human rights and fundamental freedoms in the political, economic, social, cultural or any other field of public life.

Article 5 sets out a non-exhaustive list of human rights to which the broad non-discrimination principle applies, which includes economic, social and cultural as well as civil and political rights. Of particular relevance to the integration process in this list are the right to nationality (Article 5(d)(iii)), the right to education and training (Article 5(e)(v)) and the right to equal participation in cultural activities (Article 5(e)(vi)). ICERD is therefore a treaty with considerable potential to protect migrants against the multiple forms of discrimination which they often face and provide the foundation for a human rights-based approach to integration. However, the application of the non-discrimination guarantee to non-citizens has been problematic as, in Article 1(2), ICERD indicates that states may make distinctions between non-citizens and citizens as long as they treat all non-citizens similarly, providing: 'this Convention shall not apply to distinctions, exclusions, restrictions or preferences made by a State Party to this Convention between citizens and non-citizens'.[196] Article 1(2) is further defined in Article 1(3), which states that:

194 CESCR General Comment No. 21, note 164, para. 41.

195 Austria, UN Doc E/C.12/AUT/CO/3 (25 January 2006), paras 9 and 21; Denmark, UN Doc E/C.12/1/Add.102 (14 December 2004), para. 13; Poland, UN Doc E/C.12/1/Add.82 (19 December 2002), para. 13; Spain, UN Doc E/C.12/1/Add.99 (7 June 2004) paras 8 and 25.

196 Thus, '[t]he text is ambiguous about whether non-citizens are included within the scope of the Convention and the extent to which non-citizens are protected under the

> Nothing in this Convention may be interpreted as affecting in any way the legal provisions of States Parties concerning nationality, citizenship or naturalization, provided that such provisions do not discriminate against any particular nationality.

The CERD Committee clarified the correct implication of these provisions and the position of non-citizens under ICERD in 2004 in its General Recommendation No. 30. It states that Article 1(2) 'must be construed so as to avoid undermining the basic prohibition of discrimination'.[197] It goes on to explain that as regards the rights referred to in Article 5, they are, in principle (subject to some minor exceptions in the case of political rights), to be enjoyed by all persons, whether citizens or not.[198] Under ICERD, differential treatment based on citizenship or immigration status constitutes discrimination if such differential treatment is not based on objective criteria, justified by reference to a legitimate aim and proportionate to the aim pursued.[199] Significantly, the CERD Committee in General Recommendation No. 30 does not confine itself to these general statements but goes on to make specific recommendations in a wide range of areas, including protection against hate speech and racial violence, access to citizenship and the protection of economic, social and cultural rights. These include recommendations that states pay greater pay greater attention to the issue of multiple discrimination faced by non-citizens,[200] that they ensure that immigration policies do not have the effect of discriminating against persons on the basis of race, colour, descent or national or ethnic origin,[201] and to remove obstacles that prevent the enjoyment of economic, social and cultural rights by non-citizens, notably in the areas of education, housing, employment and health.[202] The Convention, as interpreted by the committee, therefore affects both the functional and wider dimensions of integration as set out in Chapter 2.

While ICERD provides for both an inter-state complaints procedure (Article 11) and an individual complaints procedure (Article 14), the CERD Committee

---

Convention'. Drew Mahalic and Joan Gambee Mahalic, 'The Limitation Provisions of the International Convention on the Elimination of All Forms of Racial Discrimination' (1987) 9 *Hum Rts Q* 74.

197 CERD Committee General Recommendation No. 30, 'Discrimination Against Non Citizens' (1 October 2004), para. 2.

198 Ibid., at para. 3.

199 Ibid., at para. 4.

200 Ibid., at para. 8.

201 Ibid., at para. 5.

202 Ibid., at para. 29. States are also recommended to avoid segregated schooling and different standards of treatment being applied to non-citizens on grounds of race, colour, descent, and ethnic or national origin in elementary and secondary school and with respect to higher education (para. 31).

works principally by analysing and commenting on reports by states.[203] It takes a broad approach to its mandate and '(i)t will consider an issue if it can find even a minimal racial element'.[204] The next section considers the development of the concept of integration by the CERD Committee through its concluding observations. It will be seen that the CERD Committee places a considerable emphasis on the importance of an appropriately constructed integration policy. The CERD Committee has emphasized the point that, fundamentally, integration policies should not discourage members of minority groups from maintaining their cultural identity. A number of key aspects of promoting integration have also been identified by the committee, including access to nationality, political participation and protection of social and economic rights.

The Extensive Development of the Concept of Integration in the Concluding Observations of the Committee on the Elimination of Racial Discrimination

The approach of the CERD Committee to the concept of integration is markedly different to that of the committees examined above. 'Integration' is frequently expressly referred to throughout the concluding observations of the committee. It is seen by the committee as a goal in its own right, an objective to be fulfilled in order to comply fully with the terms of ICERD. This fits with the objectives of the Convention to promote racial equality and push states to construct inclusive and politically inclusive societies: ICERD requires an integrationist multicultural drive on the behalf of State Parties.[205] This has led to a more significant development of the standalone concept of integration in itself by the CERD Committee than in the case of the other committees examined above.

Integration as an Objective of ICERD

In a number of its concluding observations, the CERD Committee requests that states do more to facilitate the integration of immigrant and minority groups, with varying degrees of concern. For example, concern is expressed at acts of violence and expressions of racial hatred in Bulgaria which are seen as linked to the insufficiency of measures taken to guarantee the integration of Bulgarian

---

203 Article 14 of the Convention sets out a procedure for dealing with communications 'from individuals or groups of individuals … claiming to be victims of a violation' by a State Party of rights under the Convention. Acceptance of this procedure is optional and many states have not opted to be party to this provision. Consequently, the individual petition procedure has not generated a significant body of case law.

204 Dominic McGoldrick, *Human Rights and Religion: The Islamic Headscarf Debate in Europe* (Hart Publishing, 2006), p. 259.

205 Article 2(e) specifically provides that 'Each State Party undertakes to encourage, where appropriate, integrationist multiracial organizations and movements and other means of eliminating barriers between races, and to discourage anything which tends to strengthen racial division'.

citizens regardless of their race, nationality or ethnic origin;[206] while France is called on to strengthen its policy for the integration of immigrants and population groups of immigrant origin especially in the field of housing.[207] In other instances, the committee commends states for their commitment to integration[208] and for increasing their integration efforts.[209] The mere existence of integration policy in a state is not, however, sufficient to satisfy the demands of ICERD. States are required to move beyond paying lip-service to the idea of integration towards ensuring that effective measures to facilitate the integration of minority groups are put into place.[210] This is illustrated by the remarks of the committee in respect of Finland:

> The Committee notes the State Party's continued commitment to the integration of persons of foreign origin. Nevertheless, it remains concerned that despite such efforts, de facto discrimination against persons of foreign origin, including Somalis, persists in a number of areas. It is particularly concerned about the lower employment rate among persons of immigrant origin, especially women, and the difficulties that persons with an immigrant background and aliens continue to face when trying to access service places, such as bars and restaurants.[211]

The CERD Committee's concluding observations also shed some light on what the concept of integration entails within the remit of the Convention. The committee is

---

206 Bulgaria, UN Doc CERD/C/304/Add.29 (23 April 1997), para. 9.

207 France, UN Doc CERD/C/FRA/CO/16 (18 April 2005), para. 12. See also for example the Netherlands, which is requested to pursue the effective implementation of measures to facilitate the integration of minority groups in Dutch schools (UN Doc CERD/C/64/CO/7 (10 May 2004) para. 10); and Zambia, in relation to which the committee is concerned that the local integration of Angolan refugees is not encouraged by the relevant refugee legislation (UN Doc CERD/C/ZMB/CO/16 (27 March 2007), para. 14).

208 Sweden, UN Doc CERD/C/SWE/CO/18 (21 August 2008), para. 17.

209 See Ukraine, UN Doc CERD/C/UKR/CO/18 (19 October 2006), para. 3; Estonia, UN Doc CERD/C/EST/CO/7 (19 October 2006), para. 4. Argentina is recommended to 'continue its efforts to acknowledge and integrate the persons of African descent in the State Party, along with migrants of African descent, and to achieve the full development and enjoyment of their human rights'. Argentina, CERD/C/ARG/CO/19–20 (29 March 2010), para. 24.

210 See Spain, UN Doc CERD/C/64/CO/6 (28 April 2004), para. 10; France as discussed above; Sweden, as discussed above where the state's commitment to integration is noted but the State Party is recommended to intensify its efforts to combat discrimination against persons of foreign origin (para. 17).

211 Finland, UN Doc CERD/C/FIN/CO/19 (13 March 2009), para. 19. See also similar comments in the concluding observations on Finland's State Report in 2012, in which the committee states that Finland should take 'concrete measures' to implement its integration legislation and policies 'in order to foster the integration of immigrants with regard to employment, housing, education and social and healthcare services'. Finland, UN Doc CERD/C/FIN/CO/20–22 (31 August 2012), at para. 16.

at pains to emphasize the point that integration does not imply or allow for forced assimilation.[212] Furthermore, integration policies should not discourage members of minority groups (whether national minority or immigrant groups) from expressing their culture, using their mother tongue or preserving and developing their identity.[213] In the case of Denmark, for example, the committee made it clear that even national measures intended to prevent marginalization and ghettoization should not have as a side-effect an 'assimilationist effect that leads to the loss of cultural identities by those affected'.[214] Overall, the CERD Committee favours a multicultural approach to dealing with diversity.[215] In its concluding observations on Namibia's report, the committee is quite clear in what this means for State Parties from an integration perspective:

> Recalling that the principle of non-discrimination requires that the cultural characteristics of all ethnic groups be taken into consideration, the Committee urges the State Party to ensure that its integration policies and programmes respect and protect the cultural identities of persons belonging to national or ethnic minorities within its territory.[216]

The complexity of integrating the immigrant population is also recognized by the committee, without implying more leeway for states in respect of their integration obligations.[217] In relation to Portugal, the committee expressed its distaste for the phenomenon of 'two-speed integration' whereby European immigrants are apparently more easily integrated than those from Africa, for example.[218] Discrimination is considered by the committee to be inimical to integration.[219]

---

212 See, for example, the observations of the committee in relation to Turkmenistan, UN Doc CERD/C/TKM/CO/5 (27 March 2007), para. 12; Germany, UN Doc CERD/C/DEU/CO/18 (21 August 2008), para. 20; and Japan, UN Doc CERD/C/304/Add.114 (27 April 2001), para. 15.

213 Denmark, UN Doc CERD/C/DEN/CO/17, 19 October 2006, para. 22.

214 Denmark, UN Doc CERD/C/DNK/CO/18–19 (20 September 2010).

215 In relation to Australia, for example, the committee 'encourages the State party to develop and implement an updated comprehensive multicultural policy that reflects its increasingly ethnically and culturally diverse society'. Australia, UN Doc CERD/C/AUS/CO/15–17 (13 September 2010).

216 Namibia, UN Doc CERD/C/NAM/CO/12 (19 August 2008), para. 24. Similarly, in relation to the Amazigh people of Tunisia, see Tunisia, UN Doc CERD/C/TUN/CO/19 (23 March 2009), para. 11.

217 Norway, UN Doc CERD/C/NOR/CO/18 (19 October 2006), para. 20.

218 Portugal, UN Doc CERD/C/65/CO/6 (10 December 2004), para. 11.

219 In relation to France, the committee states: 'The Committee notes with regret that, notwithstanding recent policies to combat racial discrimination in housing and employment, persons of immigrant origin or from ethnic groups, within the meaning of the Convention, continue to be the target of stereotyping and discrimination of all kinds, which impede their integration and advancement at all levels of French society'. France, UN Doc CERD/C/FRA/CO/17–19 (23 September 2010), para. 13.

Finally, the committee has emphasized the two-way nature of the integration process, and the importance of maintaining an 'appropriate balance between the responsibilities of the State under the Convention and the responsibilities of immigrant communities'.[220] The committee stated quite clearly in respect of the Netherlands that it was concerned that 'the current policy on integration has effectively shifted the primary responsibility for integration from the State to immigrant communities'.[221] Thus, national integration measures, such as integration tests enshrined in legislation, which place the onus of integration on the immigrant, are not consistent with the approach to integration endorsed by the CERD Committee. In particular, the committee has criticized the civic integration tests which apply to family reunification in the Netherlands on the basis that the test is only required for individuals seeking to enter the Netherlands from certain 'non-Western' countries:

> The Committee notes that, under the Civic Integration (Preparation Abroad) Act, migrants from certain countries requiring a temporary residence permit to enter the Netherlands for family formation or unification must pass the civic integration examination before entering the country. As this requirement applies only to migrants from certain countries, the Committee is concerned that the application of the Act results in discrimination on the basis of nationality, particularly between so-called "Western" and "non-Western" state nationals.[222]

The committee expressed a similar unease in relation to the potential impact of integration contracts which non-EU citizens are required to sign in Lichtenstein, which defines the specific goals of their integration. The committee recommended that the individuals in question should be protected against racial discrimination during the fulfilment of the terms of the contract, 'especially regarding their residency status and freedom of movement and in the areas of employment, education, health care and housing'.[223]

Elements of Effective Integration

In addition to outlining these basic contours of the concept of integration, the committee has identified some key elements of effective integration. Integration programmes, including language courses, appear to be endorsed by the CERD Committee as a means to facilitate integration.[224] Naturalization is also seen as

---

220 The Netherlands, UN Doc CERD/C/NLD/CO/17–18 (25 March 2010), para. 4.

221 Ibid.

222 The Netherlands, UN Doc CERD/C/NLD/CO/17–18 (25 March 2010), para. 5.

223 Lichtenstein, UN Doc CERD/C/LIE/CO/4–6 (23 October 2012), para. 12.

224 In its concluding observations on the Republic of Korea's state report, CERD recommended the provision of adequate information on the country and its traditions and the organization of language courses in order to facilitate the integration of foreign-born

facilitating integration, in contrast to national policies, which often construct naturalization as a reward for completed integration. The importance of naturalization is explicitly recognized in relation to the considerable number of long-term residents in Germany who are eligible for but who have not obtained citizenship. The committee recommends that Germany:

> facilitate acquisition of German citizenship by long-term residents and persons born in Germany in order to promote the integration of such residents as may wish to acquire German citizenship without relinquishing their own.[225]

This illustrates a nuanced approach to the interaction of integration and citizenship which requires that immigrants be allowed to retain their original citizenship without this casting doubt on their commitment to integrating into the host country. In addition, while the acquisition of language is also seen as an important aspect of integration, the committee does not approve of the lack of proficiency in the state language being used as a barrier to naturalization.[226] This indicates that the committee will not allow individual aspects of integration to be interpreted in a way which undermines the overall inclusionary aims of integration. This is also clear in the committee's concerns (in the context of Switzerland) that the lack of definition of integration criteria in the naturalization process could lead municipal assemblies to adopt inconsistent standards and decisions, and effectively use integration as a way to make access to citizenship more limited.[227]

Political and civic integration has also featured as a concern of the committee. In its concluding observations on Latvia, for example, the committee stated that, while recognizing that political rights may be limited to citizens:

> most non-citizens have been residing in Latvia for many years, if not for their whole lives, the Committee strongly recommends that the State Party consider facilitating the integration process by making it possible for all non-citizens who are long-time permanent residents to participate in local elections.[228]

This represents a holistic view of the concept of integration, with the committee reaching outside the confines of international law to recommend voting rights for non-citizens as part of the integration process.[229] Finally, the committee has also

---

female spouses in Korean society. Republic of Korea, UN Doc CERD/C/KOR/CO/14 (17 August 2009), para. 17.

225 Germany, UN Doc CERD/C/DEU/CO/18 (21 August 2008), para. 20. Also on citizenship, see the Concluding Observations relating to Tanzania: Tanzania, UN Doc CERD/C/TZA/CO/16 (27 March 2007), para. 15.

226 See Norway, UN Doc CERD/C/NOR/CO/18 (19 October 2006), para. 19.

227 Switzerland, UN Doc CERD/C/CHE/CO/6 (21 August 2008), para. 18.

228 Latvia, UN Doc CERD/C/63/CO/7 (10 December 2003), para. 12.

229 However, Latvia should perhaps be considered a somewhat atypical case in that, in common with Lithuania, Estonia and other former USSR states, it hosts a significant

expressly linked the protection of social and economic rights with integration. Poland, for example, is exhorted to:

> enhance its efforts towards the full integration of the Roma into Polish society and combat discrimination against the Roma by improving the enjoyment of economic, social and cultural rights, particularly in education, employment and housing.[230]

This approach accords with that of the CCPR and the CESCR in placing the emphasis on the creation of equal opportunities and equal outcomes for migrants as a prerequisite to fully realizing their rights under international human rights law.

Integration as a Global Issue

It should also be noted that, in contrast to the position under the ICCPR and the ICESCR, the concept of integration is referred to by the CERD Committee across the continents and is not seen as solely applicable in the European/North American/ Australian context, albeit that references to integration are more extensive and more common in that context. Integration is perceived by the CERD Committee as a global issue, and one which is particularly important in the refugee context. Thus, Congo, Chad and Ecuador are exhorted to pursue the steps necessary to ensure the integration of refugees in their territory.[231] Senegal is encouraged to facilitate the integration of all refugees living in Senegal and issue them with identity papers as soon as possible.[232] Similarly, concern is expressed that Argentina had not provided information on the existence of policies and programmes to facilitate the socio-economic integration of refugees and asylum seekers.[233] This is evidence of a more wide-reaching and proactive approach to the requirements of integration by the CERD Committee than by the other committees examined. It would also suggest that countries may not use financial circumstances to avoid the issue of integrating refugees and immigrants in the context of their obligations under ICERD.

A Nascent Integration Paradigm in the Work of the UN Committees?

The UN Committees have to date addressed the issue of integration in a haphazard and piecemeal fashion. In the context of the ICCPR and the ICESCR it cannot

minority of Russian citizens who have spent all or nearly all of their lives in Latvia.

230 Poland, UN Doc CERD/C/POL/CO/19 (14 September 2009), para. 4.

231 Congo, UN Doc CERD/C/COG/CO/9 (23 March 2009), para. 18(d); Chad, UN Doc CERD/C/TCD/CO/15 (21 September 2009), para. 18(c); Ecuador, UN Doc CERD/C/ECU/CO/20–22 (24 Oct 2012), at para. 14.

232 Senegal, UN Doc CERD/CSEN/CO/16–18 (24 Oct 2012), at para. 16.

233 Argentina, UN Doc CERD/C/65/CO/1 (2004), para. 13(n).

be said that there has been a comprehensive normative development of the concept of integration by the monitoring committees and express references to integration are quite rare. This is particularly true in the case of the CESCR. However, as illustrated above, the concluding observations of the committees are nonetheless informative from the point of view of integration. The above analysis has attempted to highlight the most pertinent aspects of the work of both the CCPR and the CESCR from an integration perspective. The CCPR in particular frequently comments on integration-related issues, even if it does not always expressly refer to integration. These include family reunification, freedom of religion and from discrimination, xenophobia and racism. It has been argued that the framing of integration by the CCPR mainly in terms of equality under Article 26 rather than in terms of the minority protection provided in Article 27 signals a broad-based conception of integration as the progressive realization of equality between existing and immigrant populations rather than a narrow culture-based conception of integration. Overall, the committees construct integration as a long-term and multi-faceted process of social inclusion, rather than a process of cultural assimilation to be undergone by newcomers.

In contrast to the CCPR and the CESCR, the observations of the CERD Committee reveal a relatively well-defined concept of integration. The basic approach of the CERD Committee is that states are required to ensure that effective measures to facilitate the integration of minority groups (including immigrants) are put into place. These measures may not constitute forced assimilation and must respect the cultural identity of migrants. A two-way conception of integration is favoured whereby a balance is maintained, between the responsibilities of the receiving state and its existing communities on the one hand, and those of the migrant in the integration process on the other. The CERD Committee has also made more specific recommendations in relation to the role of political participation, access to nationality status and the protection of social and economic rights in the integration process. Finally, the concept of integration is developed across the concluding observations of the CERD Committee, including those on the State Reports of less wealthy states.

The common thread in the work of the three bodies discussed in this section is the emphasis on the protection of the human rights of migrants and the creation of equal opportunities through rights protection. The goal of achieving full legal, civil and socio-economic equality is evident in, for example, the concerns of the CCPR in relation to the expulsion of settled migrants, the CESCR in terms of access to employment and the CERD Committee in the sphere of access to citizenship and political participation. This progressive realization of equality is seen as both a prerequisite to and an objective of integration.[234] The dominant

234 This view is echoed by Anuscheh Farahat, who argues that the principle of 'progressive inclusion' is grounded in international human rights law. Anuscheh Farahat, '"We want you! But …" Recruiting Migrants and Encouraging Transnational Migration Through Progressive Inclusion' (2009) *ELJ* 700.

theme of the observations of the three bodies regarding integration and integration-related issues is the desire to eradicate discrimination against migrants in order that they can enjoy the full protection of the rights guarantees in the treaties. The responsibility of the state in providing the legal conditions for this process of equalization to occur is insisted upon by all of the treaty monitoring bodies. The connection between integration and legally-enforceable rights is underlined in the work of the committees, in stark contrast to the tendency of European governments to characterize integration as related to migration law or as solely raising issues of social policy. The overarching paradigm is thus a rights-based approach to integration, founded on the principles of equality and non-discrimination.

In addition to the equality dimensions of this emerging integration paradigm, a key feature of each of the committees' approaches is that integration policies must be developed against a background of tolerance, diversity and respect for migrants' culture: integration as the adoption of the presumed identity and values of the existing population in the host state has no place in the work of the UN Committees. This overarching paradigm and its function in countering restrictive national discourses on integration was made explicit by the first Special Rapporteur for the human rights of migrants who advocated:

> the development of multicultural patterns of social integration for immigrant minorities, patterns that mitigate exclusion and can stand as alternatives to those forms of integration that attempt to impose certain behavioural norms and promote an increasingly dubious social homogeneity.[235]

Overall, then the approaches of the UN human rights treaty bodies to both the meaning and consequences of integration provide a starting-point for a two-way, human-rights based, notion of integration.[236]

Conclusion

The protection of the fundamental rights of migrants can be seen as a prerequisite to integration as it places them on an equal footing with nationals of the host state at a basic level. In this sense, the human rights treaties discussed above are the

235 Report of the Special Rapporteur, Ms. Gabriela Rodríguez Pizarro, submitted pursuant to Commission on Human Rights resolution 2004/53, E/CN.4/2005/85, 27 December 2004.

236 See, for example, Ricky Van Oers, Eva Ersboll and Dora Kostakopoulou, 'Mapping the redefinition of belonging in Europe', in Ricky Van Oers, Eva Ersboll and Dora Kostakopoulou (eds), *A Re-Definition of Belonging? Language and Integration Tests in Europe* (Martinus Nijhoff Publishers, 2010), p. 326; Sergio Carrera, *In Search of the Perfect Citizen? The Intersection between Integration, Immigration and Nationality in the EU* (Martinus Nijhoff, 2009); Anja Wiesbrock, note 78, p. 734.

cornerstones of a rights-based conception of integration and the starting point for the development of an inclusive integration strategy. More generally, the principles of non-discrimination and equality, which form the dominant philosophical thread running through the treaties, constitute the foundation of a human-rights based integration paradigm.[237] The inherent dignity and 'the equal and inalienable rights of all members of the human family' were recognized in the Universal Declaration of Human Rights as the 'foundation of freedom, justice and peace in the world',[238] and this underlying commitment to equality is reflected in each of the universal human rights instruments discussed above. This provides a framework of equality within which the discussion of integration at the national level must be posited. This is reflected in the development of a nascent integration paradigm in the work of the CCPR, the CESCR and the CERD Committee which is based on non-discrimination and the progressive realization of equality for migrants. It is also reflected in the incremental granting of rights under the 1951 Refugee Convention.

Despite this crucial contribution of international law, international refugee and human rights instruments do not, individually or collectively, provide a comprehensive framework for the development of national integration policies. International law does not contain anything resembling a general 'right' to integration or an obligation on states to facilitate integration, aside from the limited obligation imposed by Article 34 of the 1951 Refugee Convention. Migrants' integration-related rights under international law are fragmented, with migrants having variable rights depending on their status as refugees, migrant workers or family members of these groups, or as members of the sub-categories of women, children or members of a racial minority. In particular, in comparison to other migrants, refugees benefit from a wide range of integration-related rights, tailored to their particular situation, as a matter of settled international law. One consequence of this for national integration law and policy is that national frameworks may have to provide for differentiated forms of integration which take into account specific international obligations to refugees. This fragmentation is reflected in the normative development of integration in international law. It was seen above that in the case of the UN human rights treaty monitoring bodies, the limited development of a conception of integration is in the early stages and is fragmented between the different bodies, with each of the committees examined having a slightly different focus in relation to integration. Finally, in the case of international refugee law, the absence of a monitoring body in the case of the 1951 Convention has meant that the only specific provision relating to integration in international law – Article 34 of the 1951 Convention – is normatively undeveloped.

Despite these critical limitations, it has been shown that international norms potentially have an impact on national integration measures in a number of specific ways, as follows:

237 See, for example, Andrew McColgan, 'Principles of Equality and Protection from Discrimination in International Human Rights Law' (2003) 2 *EHRLR* 157.

238 UDHR, preamble, para. 1.

- International refugee law requires a wide range of integration-related rights to be guaranteed to refugees.
- Article 27 ICCPR, together with Article 15 ICESCR and Article 5(a) ICERD, prohibit forced assimilation. National integration policies may not therefore force members of a minority to forsake their culture, language or religion in favour of that of the host state without violating these provisions. This sets a minimum standard for integration policies.
- The ICCPR, the ICESCR and ICERD provide the basis for an equality-based paradigm of integration, by generally requiring states to provide the rights enshrined therein to all persons in their territory without discrimination on the basis of nationality, race religion or immigration status. An equality-based paradigm of integration is apparent in the concluding observations of the CCPR, the CESCR and the CERD Committee. In addition, all the instruments of international law considered in this chapter support the theory that the more integrated the individual migrant becomes, the wider and stronger his or her rights within the State Party become.
- Given the relatively detailed development of the concept in the concluding observations of the CERD Committee, these concluding observations could be used as a benchmark for integration policy at the national level in order to ensure conformity with best practice in international human rights law.

The evolving integration paradigm in the work of the UN Committees, centred on individual equality, normative multiculturalism and state responsibility for social inclusion, helps to broaden our understanding of the nexus between integration and law. It constitutes an important alternative normative model of integration to the increasing trend among states of using the concept of integration as a 'border practice', as a condition of citizenship and a barrier to the entry of migrants and their families.

Chapter 5
Regional Frameworks for Integration: The Jurisprudence of the European Court of Human Rights

Introduction

All EU Member States are parties to the ECHR and, like the treaties discussed in the previous chapters, the ECHR also forms part of EU law, through the general principles of EU law.[1] Article 6(2) of the Treaty on European Union (TEU) provides both a legal basis and an obligation for the EU to accede to the ECHR, stating that: 'The Union shall accede to the European Convention for the Protection of Human Rights and Fundamental Freedoms'.[2] The ECHR expressly applies to all persons on the territory of State Parties and the rights contained therein therefore extend to immigrants.[3] Articles 3 (freedom from torture and inhuman or degrading treatment or punishment) and 8 (right to family and private life) have had most impact in the field of immigration. The freedom of religion guarantee contained in Article 9 and its interaction with integration will be explored in detail in Chapter 8.

This chapter will focus on the concept of integration under construction by the European Court of Human Rights in the context of its case law interpreting Article 8. The European Court of Human Rights has been grappling with integration issues in a different context to that of national and European policy-makers and legislators: that of the negative obligation of states under Article 8 not to expel long-term residents in certain circumstances; and the positive obligation of states – again under Article 8 – to authorize family reunification in certain circumstances. Academic attention has been focussed to date on the inconsistencies and deficiencies of this jurisprudence from the perspective of immigration law generally.[4] The aim of this chapter, in contrast, is to illustrate the importance of this well-known body

1 See generally, Nuala Mole 'The complex and evolving relationship between the European Union and the European Convention on Human Rights' (2012) 4 *EHRLR* 363.

2 See also the 14th Protocol to the ECHR. See generally, Adam Weiss, 'EU accession to the European Convention on Human process: the state of play and the added value for victims of human rights violations in Europe' (2012) 4 *EHRLR* 391.

3 Article 1 states that 'The High Contracting Parties shall secure to everyone within their jurisdiction the rights and freedoms defined in Section I of this Convention'.

4 See, for example, Nicola Rogers, 'Immigration and the European Convention on Human Rights: Are New Principles Emerging?' (2003) *EHRLR* 53; Charlotte Steinorth, '*Üner v The Netherlands*: Explusion of Long-Term Immigrants and the Right to Respect

of judgments in order to gain an insight into the elusive concept of integration. Together with the previous chapter in relation to the UN treaty bodies, the chapter demonstrates that the concept of integration is being normatively developed in numerous arenas external to the nation state and away from national discourses tied to identity and values. It assesses the concept of integration employed by the European Court of Human Rights, analysing the jurisprudence in terms of two core issues: first, the conception of integration employed in the jurisprudence; and second, the implications of the development of the concept in terms of impacting on the right to remain in a State Party and family reunification.

Taking into Account Integration

The jurisprudence of the Strasbourg Court has established that integration does not give rise to a discrete legal category: immigrants who have spent most or all of their lives in a country remain in the same broad legal category as all immigrants. Nevertheless, the Court now explicitly takes into account the fact of integration in determining whether an expulsion decision violates Article 8 and in this sense integration leads to an increased level of protection from expulsion. Having established these starting points, the chapter goes on to outline the contours of the Court's conception of integration, which emerge quite clearly from the case law. It is argued that, in contrast to the approach of the UN Committees, the Court's integration paradigm appears to place the onus of integration on the migrant rather than focussing on states' responsibilities to ensuring the integration of immigrant communities. However, the aspects of integration which are emphasized, and to some extent the form of the concept itself, depend on the facts of the individual case. In addition, and even more importantly, the weight given to integration considerations in the balancing exercise undergone by the Court in each case is variable. This is because integration in itself is not the primary focus of the Court's reasoning. The implications of the Court's reasoning from the perspective of integration remain for the moment incidental to the broader issues in these cases. This means that the impact of the Court's development of the concept of integration on the key practical issues of the right to remain in a State Party and family unity remains limited.

Finally, it is argued – by reference to the family reunification cases in particular – that these cases are underscored by the wide margin of appreciation afforded to states. In the context of the admissions category, it is suggested that the difficulties of the Court in delineating the extent of the positive obligations of states under Article 8 is illustrative of the fundamental difficulties attached to using international law in the integration sphere. It thus remains questionable whether

---

for Private and Family Life' (2008) 8(1) *HRL Rev* 185; and Thomas Spijkerboer, 'Structural Instability: Strasbourg Case Law on Children's Family Reunion' (2009) 11(3) *EJML* 271.

the ECHR, as interpreted by the European Court of Human Rights (ECtHR), will have a meaningful impact on the integration policies of European states.

Interactions between Article 8 ECHR and Integration

While migrants' human rights are protected by various articles of the ECHR, with the Convention applying to all persons within the jurisdiction of a State Party,[5] the Article 8 expulsion and admission cases involve a direct clash of migrants' desire to reside in a State Party and State Parties' right to control immigration and residence. These two interlinked strands of case law are directly linked to integration in different ways. The expulsion cases have largely concerned 'integrated aliens'[6] and/or second-generation immigrants: migrants who have lived for a long period of time in the host country (in some cases their whole lives), whom the state is seeking to expel from its territory on public order grounds following a criminal conviction. The second category of cases relates to the *positive* obligations inherent in Article 8 and concerns the situation where an applicant in a Contracting State maintains that the refusal of that state to allow the entry of a member of his family fails to respect his family life. While integration is not expressly discussed in these cases in the same fashion, family reunification is a central integration theme and these cases are thus crucial in examining integration more broadly.

The Article 8 ECHR Expulsion Cases: Developing the Concept of Integration

It is well established that a decision to expel a non-national from a Contracting State may raise an issue under Article 8 if it would disrupt family or private life in that state. As noted above, many of these cases which have come before the Court have concerned 'integrated' or second-generation immigrants who have lived for long periods of time in the host state. Integration has thus featured as an important part of the reasoning of the Court in the Article 8 expulsion cases. The Strasbourg Court has placed a strong emphasis on integration, in particular the social aspects of integration, in deciding whether the expulsion fails to respect the individual's private and family life. It will be shown that the Court's jurisprudence has gradually evolved to the point of assessing complex questions of the applicant's social and cultural ties and economic links to the Contracting State, in addition to the more straightforward issue of family ties.

---

5 Article 1 provides that 'The High Contracting Parties shall secure to everyone within their jurisdiction the rights and freedoms defined in Section 1 of this Convention', thus making no general distinction between citizens and non-citizens.

6 A phrase used by Judge Morenilla in his partial dissent to *Nasri v France* (1996) EHRR 458 (para. 4); see also dissenting opinion of Judge Martens in *Boughanemi v France* (1996) 22 EHRR 228 (para. 1).

The Court assesses these applications on a case-by-case basis rather than treating long-term immigrants as a special category whose expulsion would require exceptional circumstances.[7] This case-by-case approach led to particularly haphazard results in the early cases, which were described as 'a source of embarrassment for the Court' and a 'lottery'.[8] No clear thread of logic underlining the importance either the seriousness of the offence or the applicant's degree of integration or the looseness of the family ties is apparent in these cases, with the Court emphasizing different factors in each case.[9] Since the 2001 judgment in *Boultif v Switzerland*[10] however, the Court has followed a more structured approach, applying a defined set of criteria to each case.[11] At least three of these criteria are indirectly linked to the degree of integration of the individual in the host state: the duration of the individual's stay, his or her family situation and difficulties that would be faced by the spouse in the country of origin. This last criterion incidentally introduces a further integration dimension into the discussion (along with that of the degree of integration of the person whom it is proposed to expel) as it essentially seeks to ascertain how difficult it would be for the spouse to integrate into the country of origin. Regarding the duration of stay criterion, the Grand Chamber in *Üner v The Netherlands*[12] explained its rationale as the assumption that the longer the individual stays, the closer the ties between the individual and the host state must be.[13] In addition, the Grand Chamber in *Üner* added two further criteria to the list of matters to be considered in these cases:

- The best interests and well-being of the children, in particular the seriousness of the difficulties which any children of the applicant are likely to encounter in the country to which the applicant is likely to be expelled; and

7 On this point, see the judgments of Judge Martens and Judge Morenilla in *Nasri*. It was definitively confirmed that the Court would not follow this approach in *Üner v The Netherlands* (2007) 45 EHRR 14.

8 Comments of Judge Martens in *Boughanemi v France* (1996) 22 EHRR 228 (para. 4).

9 Charlotte Steinorth, '*Üner v The Netherlands*: Explusion of Long-Term Immigrants and the Right to Respect for Private and Family Life' (2008) 8(1) *HRL Rev* 185, p. 186.

10 *Boultif v Switzerland* (2001) 33 EHRR 50.

11 These criteria include: the nature and seriousness of the offence committed; the duration of the individual's stay in the country from which he will be expelled; the time elapsed since the committing of the offence and the applicant's conduct during that period; the nationalities of the various persons concerned; the applicant's family situation; and the seriousness of the difficulties the spouse would be likely to encounter in the country of origin.

12 (2007) 45 EHRR 14.

13 Ibid., at para. 58.

- The solidity of social, cultural and family ties with the host country and the country of destination.[14]

In light of the above, the Court accepted as 'self-evident' that special regard should be had to the position of immigrants who had spent all or most of their life in the host country, had been brought up there and received their education there.[15] The question is therefore how this 'special regard' is to be exercised, and to what extent it will impact on the outcome of cases. The principles laid down in *Üner* were applied by the Grand Chamber in *Maslov v Austria*,[16] which concerned an exclusion order based on offences committed by the applicant (a 20-year-old man who had lived in Austria since the age of six) while he was a juvenile. The Court stated:

> In short, the Court considers that for a settled migrant who has lawfully spent all or the major part of his childhood and youth in the host country very serious reasons are required to justify expulsion. This is all the more so where the person committed the offences underlying the expulsion measure as a juvenile.[17]

In *Üner* then, the ECtHR placed increased emphasis on the fact of integration by including it as one of the express criteria to be applied by the courts.[18] This was of course really nothing new as integration had implicitly been considered since the early cases – which looked at the links of the immigrant and their families to the host country including – *inter alia* – whether they were educated in the country, and the links to the country of origin including knowledge of the language and the presence of family in that country. Since *Boultif*, in particular, the Court had looked at the social ties which the person had established in the host country.[19] However, the express recognition in *Üner* of a requirement to consider a person's social and cultural ties opens the door to a balancing exercise of a complexity which had not existed before this. The significance of this development is two-fold: it constitutes an acknowledgement that courts can become involved in assessing integration issues and the extent of a person's integration; and also indicates the basic implications of integration in terms of the ECHR – integration has the potential to impact on the legal security of the residence of certain immigrants in certain circumstances. Thym expresses this point well:

14 Ibid.

15 Ibid.

16 Application No. 1638/03, Judgment of the Grand Chamber of 23 June 2008.

17 Ibid., at para.75. For a commentary, see ECHR case comment (2008) 6 EHRLR 781.

18 This built in particular on the Court's judgment in *Benhebba v France* (Application No. 53441/99) Judgment of 10 July 2003.

19 See *Benhebba v France*; *Radovanovic v Austria* (2005) 41 EHRR 6; *Keles v Germany* (2007) 44 EHRR 12.

> The resulting proportionality test will be much more complex than in cases concerning the "simple" protection of family life and cover criteria whose interaction is not always straightforward in a plurilateral balancing exercise. Decisive factors will include the integration into the labour market, dependence on social assistance, language skills as an indicator of social integration, criminal behaviour, and links with the country of origin or their absence and the duration of the stay in the host country. Here, the eight Boultif criteria may only be a starting point for a complex jurisprudence which the Court has only started to develop.[20]

How integration is conceived by the Court and how the integrated status of some immigrants has affected the Court's analysis of their case in practice will now be considered.

The Scope and Content of the Integration Criterion

It is clear that integration is one of the criteria to be considered by the Court, but the question of the scope and content of the conception of integration remains. Indications as to the content of the Court's conception of integration are provided throughout the jurisprudence. *Slivenko v Latvia*[21] – a case involving considerations different from those of the others under discussion here as none of the applicants had been convicted of any criminal offence – contains an interesting discussion of the applicant's integration in Latvia.[22] The applicants were a family who had resided in Latvia almost all their lives but had become stateless when Latvia regained its independence in 1991, and were required to leave the country under a deportation order issued in respect of them as members of the family of a retired Russian military officer. The Court rejected the claim of the Latvian Government that the applicants had not been sufficiently integrated into Latvian society.[23] The Court first observed that the applicants had spent virtually all their lives in Latvia. It accepted that the applicants were not of Latvian origin, and that they arrived and lived in Latvia – then part of the USSR – in connection with the service of members of their family in the Soviet armed forces, however, these factors

---

20 Daniel Thym, 'Respect for Private and Family Life under Article 8 ECHR in Immigration Cases: A Human Right to Regularize Illegal Stay?' (2008) 57 *ICLQ* 87, p. 92.

21 *Slivenko v Latvia* (2004) 39 EHRR 24.

22 Daniel Thym presents an interesting analysis of *Slivenko v Latvia*, arguing that the Court re-conceptualizes family and private life; 'the Court restricts its formerly wide understanding with a new focus on the "nuclear family" of spouses and minor children, while at the same time broadening the protective reach of Article 8 ECHR to the network of personal, social and economic relations that make up the private life of every human being'. Daniel Thym, note 20, p. 88.

23 *Slivenko v Latvia*, para. 88.

were outweighed by the genuine and strong personal, social and economic links in Latvia.[24]

In conclusion, the Court found that 'at all times they were sufficiently integrated into Latvian society',[25] and that, in the circumstances, Article 8 was breached. This view of integration suggests that integration has occurred where the immigrant or settler forges personal, social and economic ties with the host society by living among the community, being educated and working in this community. In other words, simply being in the country on a long-term basis and living and working among its citizens was seen as the main indicator of integration. The Court did not require the applicants to reject or renounce their country or language of origin in order to evidence their integration.

This approach has not been echoed in the cases involving convicted criminal offenders, as will be seen below. *AH Khan v UK*[26] provides a striking example of the contrasting approach of the Court in these cases. Here, it was decided that despite living in the UK from 1978 to 2010, the applicant had not achieved 'a significant level of integration into British society',[27] due to his limited family life with his six children, further impeded by the time he had spent in prison, his lack of a lengthy or consistent employment history, and his marriage in and travel to Pakistan on one other occasion. This 2011 decision forms part of a recent trend towards a 'toughening' of the stance of the Court in respect of settled migrant criminal offenders.[28] It should also be noted that *Slivenko* was also somewhat unusual in that the Court has rarely discussed 'integration' as such, but has used the vocabulary of 'ties to the host country' and 'ties to the country of origin'. Overall, the Court has viewed a number of key factors as relevant in their consideration of integration. These are: the acquisition of nationality, links to the country of nationality, language, and labour market integration.

Attempts to Acquire Nationality

One of the questions which the Court asks is as to the reasons why the individual did not have nationality of the host country – most importantly, the issue of whether they were entitled to nationality of the host country and if so, whether they made efforts to obtain such nationality. In *Boughanemi v France*,[29] Court stated that the applicant 'kept his Tunisian nationality and, so it would seem, never manifested a wish to become French. It is probable, as the Government pointed out, that

24 *Slivenko v Latvia*, para. 123.

25 *Slivenko v Latvia*, para. 123.

26 *AH Khan v UK* (Application No. 6222/10) Judgment of 20 December 2011.

27 *AH Khan v UK* (Application No. 6222/10) Judgment of 20 December 2011, para. 41.

28 See UK Human Rights Blog, 'Man can be deported despite living in UK since age of three', 15 April 2012, commenting on *Balogun v UK* (discussed below).

29 (1996) 22 EHRR 228.

he retained links with Tunisia that went beyond the mere fact of his nationality. Before the Commission he did not claim that he could not speak Arabic, or that he had cut all his ties with his country of birth, or that he had not returned there after his deportation."[30] In *Kaya*, the Court did not accept the applicant's claim that even had he applied for German nationality, he would have been unsuccessful.[31]

This approach places great symbolic importance on the acquisition of nationality as an indicator of integration. However, it can effectively result in the penalization of those who do not choose to become naturalized citizens for whatever reason, and it fails to recognize the reality (admittedly changing but which still persists) of migrants in countries such as France and Germany maintaining their original nationality even through to the second generation of migrants, a tradition stemming from the initial belief that such workers were temporary 'guestworkers'.[32]

Links to the Country of Nationality

The Court assesses the strength of the applicant's links to the country of nationality asking questions such as: have they got family in the country of origin? Did they often return there, or holiday there? The rationale for this is that the interference with private and family life is not so drastic where the person has real links with the country of origin.[33] This ties in with the consideration of the duration of the individual's stay in the host country, however – as can be seen from the cases – the fact that the applicant has lived virtually all his or her life in the host state does not always mean that the links to the country of origin have been severed in the view of the Court. The jurisprudence shows that relatively tenuous links have been seen to establish significant ties to the country of origin.

If one takes *Baghli v France* by way of example, this becomes clear. The applicant entered France in 1967 at the age of two and, with the exception of the period he spent doing his military service in Algeria, lived there until he was excluded in 1994. He had received all his schooling there and worked there for several years. Nevertheless, the fact that he had done military service in Algeria, had been on holidays there and had 'never suggested that he cannot speak Arabic', coupled with his lack of desire to become French, led the Court to the conclusion that the applicant had preserved ties with his native country.[34] Similarly, in *Üner v The Netherlands*, the Grand Chamber opined that:

---

30 See also *C v Belgium* (Application No. 21794/93) Judgment of 7 August 1996, and *Baghli v France* (2001) 33 EHRR 32.

31 *Kaya v Germany* (1998) 28 EHRR 1, para. 64.

32 For a discussion of the long-term effects of the early policies in France and Germany, see Pascale Fournier and Gökçe Yurdakul, 'Unveiling Distribution: Muslim Women with Headscarves in France and Germany', in Michal Bodemann and Gökçe Yurdakul (eds), *Migration, Citizenship and Ethnos* (Palgrave, 2006).

33 See *C v Belgium* (Application No. 21794/93) Judgment of 7 August 1996; *Dalia v France* (2001) 33 EHRR 26.

34 *Baghli v France* (2001) 33 EHRR 32, para. 48.

> while it is true that the applicant came to the Netherlands at a relatively young age, the Court is not prepared to accept that he had spent so little time in Turkey that, at the time he was returned to that country, he no longer had any social or cultural (including linguistic) ties with Turkish society.[35]

In short, the Court attempts to determine whether the nationality of that country is merely a legal fact or if it reflects certain emotional and social links,[36] in order to ascertain whether the person has become so 'estranged' from the country that they would not be able to settle there if deported there.[37] On the basis of the above cases, it seems that the Court will readily imply these emotional and social links and will rarely conclude that the estrangement is so complete as to render settling in the country of nationality impossible.[38]

The importance of the assessment of the links to the country of nationality is clearly illustrated in two separate judgments involving two brothers whom the UK was seeking to deport.[39] Both men had British children, were unmarried in the UK, and lived in the family home with their mother and brothers – who were all naturalized British citizens. Both had committed serious offences: the older brother had been convicted of robbery and the younger brother of the importation of a large quantity of heroin (both had significant criminal records). Both had lived in the UK since 1978 and both cases were assessed solely on the basis of 'private' rather than 'family' life. Despite the similarity of the circumstances of the two cases, the Court found that the deportation of the younger brother was disproportionate to the aim pursued and constituted a violation of Article 8, while that of the older brother was permissible. The principal difference between the two cases was that while the younger brother had never returned to Pakistan after leaving in 1978, the older brother had returned twice, once to enter into an arranged marriage (although he claimed to have lost all contact with his wife and was not aware of her whereabouts) and once more on a visit. The Court concluded that the older brother had 'therefore maintained some level of connection to his country of origin and was not deported as a stranger to the country'.[40] The Court found that the deportation was allowable, even though it had not concluded that the

---

35 *Üner v. Netherlands* (2007) 45 EHRR 14, para. 63. See also *C v Belgium* (Application No. 21794/93) Judgment of 7 August 1996.

36 *Dalia v France* (2001) 33 EHRR 26, para. 53. See also *Baghli v France* (2001) 33 EHRR 32, para. 48; *Boulchekia v France* (1998) 25 EHRR 686, paras 46 and 50.

37 *Keles v Germany* (2007) 44 EHRR 12, para. 62.

38 For the same situation with regard to nationality and links to the country of origin, see also *Beldjoudi v France* (1992) 14 EHRR 801, in which the Court also accepted that the applicant had no links to Algeria apart from that of nationality. See also *AA v the UK* (Application No. 8000/08) Judgment of 20 September 2011.

39 *AW Khan v UK (*Application No. 47486/06) Judgment of 12 January 2010; *AH Khan v UK* (Application No. 6222/10) Judgment of 20 December 2011.

40 *AH Khan v UK* (Application No. 6222/10) Judgment of 20 December 2011, at para. 41.

older brother applicant had maintained or developed any meaningful connection to Pakistan.

For the sake of completeness, it is necessary to refer to *Mehemi v France*[41] – one of the few cases in which the Court accepted that the applicant had no links with the country of origin other than nationality. This was a somewhat exceptional situation in that the applicant had been born in France and had had French nationality until he was a year old, losing it only because his father failed to complete the correct formalities. He was also married to a French national and had three children, minors, of French nationality. In the circumstances, the Court was compelled to accept that he had no links with Algeria beyond nationality.[42]

Language

A further subsidiary question which is linked to the consideration of the extent of the individual's ties to the host country is the extent of the individual and the affected family members' linguistic ties to the country of nationality. In many cases the Court has employed the applicant's knowledge of the language of their country of nationality as a relevant factor in the balancing process, with linguistic ties featuring in the Court's reasoning to varying effect.[43] In *Kaya v Germany*, the applicant went to great lengths to protest that he knew no Turkish; however the Court placed importance on the fact that he had written letters to his mother from prison in Turkish, even though he insisted that he had dictated them to a cell-mate. In *Beldjoudi*, emphasis was placed on the fact that the applicant appeared not to know Arabic (he had been born and educated in France) in concluding that he had no links with Algeria apart from that of nationality.[44] In addition, his wife could not be expected to follow her husband to Algeria, 'a State whose language she probably does not know'.[45] In the same vein, in *Keles v Germany*, while the Court presumed that the applicant was familiar with the Turkish language, the applicant's children could not be expected to follow him to Turkey,[46] even though they were Turkish nationals and probably spoke some Turkish, as:

41 *Mehemi v France* (1997) EHRR 6.

42 A similar approach was taken in *Maslov*, in which the Grand Chamber noted that the applicant did not speak Bulgarian and could not read or write the Cyrillic alphabet and further, 'It has not been shown, nor even alleged, that he had any other close ties with his country of origin' (para. 97).

43 See, for example, *Baghli v France*; *Dalia v France*.

44 Para. 77.

45 *Beldjoudi v France* (1992) 14 EHRR 801, at para. 78.

46 The applicant's spouse, however, was Turkish and having arrived in Germany at the age of ten, it was 'assumed that she has sufficient links which would allow her to re-integrate into Turkish society' (para. 63).

> Even if the children should have knowledge of the Turkish language, they would necessarily have to face major difficulties with regard to the different language of instruction and the different curriculum in Turkish schools.[47]

In these circumstances, Article 8 was violated by the applicant's expulsion.[48]

Labour Market Integration

In a number of cases the Court has looked at the extent of the applicant's integration into the labour market of the host country, thus bringing economic links into the equation. The Court often takes into account whether a person had worked in the host country as part of the analysis of their ties to the host country.[49] In *Üner*, the Grand Chamber considered whether the applicant who had lived in Germany since age twelve had integrated into the labour market.[50] In *Kaya v Germany*, the Court considered that even though the applicant had been born and spent all his life in Germany, it could not overlook the fact that he was not integrated into the labour market as had never worked, but lived off money extorted from his former partner.[51] Finally, as pointed out above, the fact that the husband/father has been working in Latvian companies post-independence was also considered to be an indicator of integration in *Slivenko v Latvia*.[52] On one level, this is an interesting endorsement of inclusion in the labour market as an important instrument of integration and recognizes, to an extent, that occupational or economic ties form a part of integration. However, it seems unfair to consider this in the abstract without looking at the background causes of unemployment and marginalization. In addition, it seems that this consideration carries more weight in its negative sense as further illustration of the lack of contribution on the part of the applicant to the host society: there are few examples of where positive engagement in the labour market was seen as a significant factor which rendered the individual more integrated and thus more difficult to remove from the host country.[53]

---

47 *Keles v Germany* (2007) 44 EHRR 12, para. 66.

48 For similar reasoning, see *Amrollahi v Denmark* (Application No. 56811/00) Judgment of 11 July 2002, in which it was accepted that the applicant's mother tongue was Farsi however the Court concluded that in spite of this the applicant could not be considered to have maintained strong ties to Iran. In addition, and most significantly, the wife spoke none of the language. See also *Maslov*, where it was accepted that the applicant did not speak Bulgarian as he was a member of the Turkish minority in Belgium.

49 See, for example, *C v Belgium* (Application No. 21794/93) Judgment of 7 August 1996; *Baghli v France* (2001) 33 EHRR 32. However, it was not a significant factor in either of these cases and no violation of Article 8 was found in either case.

50 *Üner v Netherlands* (2007) 45 EHRR 14, para. 65.

51 Ibid.

52 *Slivenko v Latvia* (2004) 39 EHRR 24.

53 In *C v Belgium* (Application No. 21794/93) Judgment of 7 August 1996 the Court acknowledged that the applicant had established social ties in Belgium, amongst other

An Emerging Integration Paradigm in the Article 8 ECHR Expulsion Cases

The above analysis reveals a specific conception of integration which appears to be a composite of strong links to the host country and an absence of strong links to country of origin. The Court is involved in a double-sided inquiry looking at two fundamental questions:

1. how integrated is the applicant and his family in the host country and to what extent does the expulsion consequently interfere with private and family life in that country; and
2. how difficult would it be for the applicant and his family to re-integrate into the country of nationality?

This approach would seem to require migrants to relinquish the identity of their country of origin in order to secure their place in the host society. This is problematic from a number of perspectives. First, it runs contrary to modern conceptions of integration which stress that immigrants are entitled to maintain their cultural and linguistic identity.[54] In terms of international human rights law, this view of integration would appear incompatible with – *inter alia* – the rights of minorities as guaranteed by Article 27 of the International Covenant on Civil and Political Rights and the interpretation of the concept of integration in the concluding observations of the CERD Committee.[55] The CERD Committee, in particular, is at pains to emphasize that integration does not imply or allow for forced assimilation and that members of minority groups should not be discouraged from expressing

---

things by working there for a number of years (para. 32). However, this was outweighed by the seriousness of the offences in question and his persisting links to Morocco (paras 34 and 35). However, see *Boultif v Switzerland* (2001) 33 EHRR 50, where the applicant had worked as a painter and at various other jobs and had the possibility of further employment. This, along with his exemplary conduct in prison, mitigated fears that he constituted a danger to public order and security for the future (para. 51). Similarly, in *Keles v Germany* (2007) 44 EHRR 12 a violation of Article 8 was found, and the fact that he had been employed for a certain period of time in Germany was referred to, although this was not considered by the Court as one of the particular factors which leaned in favour of the applicant. See also *AA v the UK* (Application No. 8000/08) Judgment of 20 September 2011.

54 See Council of Europe, *White Paper on Intercultural Dialogue: Living Together as Equals in Dignity* (Strasbourg, 7 May 2008), p. 6; UNHCR's definition of integration as set out in UNHCR Executive Committee, *Conclusion on Local Integration*, note 11, at preamble and (k); and in the EU sphere, Justice and Home Affairs Council Conclusions, *Common Basic Principles on Immigrant Integration*, Council Document 14615/04, Brussels, 19 November 2004.

55 In relation to Article 27 of the ICCPR and integration, see the concluding observations of the Human Rights Committee in relation to Albania (UN Doc CCPR/CO/82/ALB (2 December 2004), at para. 21); Germany (UN Doc CCPR/CO/80/DEU (4 May 2004), at para. 21); and Greece (UN Doc CCPR/CO/83/GRC (25 April 2005), at para. 18).

their cultural identity.[56] On a practical level, the ECtHR's approach also fails to recognize the increasing reality of dual nationalities and transnational belonging and identities.[57]

Another conclusion which follows on from this is that the ECtHR places the onus of integration squarely on the migrant. The migrant is seen as the sole agent of integration with responsibility for establishing links with the host country. This is clear particularly in relation to the Court's consideration of an individual's integration into the labour market. The state is not seen as having any responsibility for undertaking to integrate the person into the fabric of the host society. This is partly explicable by the fact that the Court focuses on social and personal integration. However, for a different slant on this question, see the comments of Judge Morenilla in his partial dissent in *Nasri v France*:

> A State which, for reasons of convenience, accepts immigrant workers and authorises their residence becomes responsible for the education and social integration of the children of such immigrants as it is of the children of its "citizens". Where such social integration fails, and the result is antisocial or criminal behaviour, the State is also under a duty to make provision for their social rehabilitation instead of sending them back to their country of origin, which has no responsibility for the behaviour in question and where the possibilities of rehabilitation in a foreign social environment are virtually non-existent.[58]

In this view, the Court, through these judgments, allows governments to abdicate their responsibility for education and social integration to a state in which the person concerned has, in most cases, never lived or lived for a very short period of time. However, to follow Judge Morenilla's reasoning would involve the Court in complex issues of social and economic rights, and social exclusion, a course which it would be unlikely to favour. In this way, the cases under discussion highlight the limitations of reliance on civil and political rights to deal with what at root may be social and economic problems.[59] The rather one-sided conception of integration being developed by the Court also constitutes a point of divergence from most definitions of integration, which emphasize the 'two-way' nature of

---

56 See the concluding observations of the CERD Committee in relation to Turkmenistan (UN Doc CERD/C/TKM/CO/5 (27 March 2007)), Germany (UN Doc CERD/C/DEU/CO/18 (21 August 2008)), Japan (UN Doc CERD/C/304/Add.114 (27 April 2001)) and Denmark (UN Doc CERD/C/DEN/CO/17 (19 October 2006)).

57 On transnationalism and dual citizenship, see, for example, Nancy Poner, 'Engagement Across National Borders: Then and Now' (2006–2007) 75 *Fordham Law Review* 248; and Linda Bosniak, 'Multiple Citizenship and the Postnational Transformation of Citizenship' (2001–2002) 42 *Virginia Journal of International Law* 979, p. 981.

58 1996) EHRR 458, para. 3 of partly dissenting opinion of Judge Morenilla.

59 See Ann Sherlock, 'Deportation of Aliens and Article 8 ECHR' (1998) *ELR* 23, p. 29.

the integration process. It was seen above that the conceptions of integration contained in the concluding observations of the CCPR, the CESCR and the CERD Committee emphasize the responsibilities of the host state to ensure access to education, citizenship and the institutions of the host society, as opposed to solely focussing on the individual migrants' responsibility in the integration process. This divergence in approach stems partly from the different context in which the Court is considering the concept of integration: that of the proposed deportation of individuals rather than the examination of state law and policy undertaken in the concluding observations of the UN treaty monitoring bodies. This narrow frame of analysis makes it very difficult for the ECtHR to develop a holistic concept of integration.

The Prominence of the Dissenting Judgments in the Article 8 Expulsion Cases

The comments of Judge Morenilla quoted above form part of the strong line of dissents which have characterized the Article 8 immigration case law since its inception. One of the distinctive features of this jurisprudence is the high degree of disagreement between the judges of the Strasbourg Court on fundamental aspects of the legal reasoning to be employed in determining these cases. In the early cases, the divisions centred round two fundamental points. The first of these was the uncertainty caused by adopting a case-by-case approach and the unpredictability this was causing. This has been remedied to a certain degree by the development of the *Boultif* criteria as discussed above. The second, more fundamental, area of disagreement concerned the correct approach to the legal status of long-term immigrants in these circumstances, with a number of judges passionately arguing that such individuals should be protected against deportation save in the most extreme circumstances. Over ten years since the first wave of cases, it now appears to be settled that this will *not* be the approach taken by the Court, with the Court's reasoning proceeding on the assumption that long-term immigrants do not form a discrete legal category.[60]

More recently, the case law remains characterized by deep disagreement. In the Grand Chamber's judgment in *Üner*, the three dissenting judges (Judges Costa, Zupancic and Turmen) found, in contrast to the majority, that an assessment of the criteria pointed to a violation of Article 8. This is illustrative of the new difficulties posed by the development of a set of criteria without a clear indication of the relative weight of these criteria: a key issue which is discussed further in the next section. More fundamentally, the minority opinion referred back to the old question of the status of long-term residents, arguing that 'foreign nationals – in any case those who, like Mr Üner, have been residing legally in a country – should

---

60 This being said, the Court sees 'little room for justifying an expulsion of a settled migrant on account of mostly non-violent offences committed when a minor' (*Maslov v Austria*, Application No. 1638/03, Judgment of the Grand Chamber of 23 June 2008, para. 81).

be granted the same fair treatment and a legal status as close as possible to that accorded to nationals'.[61] The minority further argues that the majority judgment fails to construe Article 8 in the light of other international texts dealing with the rights of long-term immigrants.[62] This continuing debate over such a foundational issue reflects the indeterminacy of international law relating to the legal status and rights of non-citizens.

The Relative Weight of Integration in the Balancing Exercise

Leaving aside for a moment the precise scope and meaning of the integration criterion, it is unclear how much weight it will actually be given in the balancing exercise undertaken by the Court in each case. The failure to address this lacuna has been seen as one of the major failings of the *Üner* judgment.[63] One of the key factors which may tip the balance in favour of the state is the severity of the offence in question. In *Boulchekia v France*,[64] the fact that the applicant had been living in France since the age of two, and had received all his education in France was outweighed by the severity of the crime of aggravated rape which he had committed as a minor.[65] The Court has viewed drugs offences as particularly serious, affording governments a considerable margin of discretion in dealing with drug offenders by deportation.[66] In his concurring opinion in *Balogun v UK*, in which the Court decided that the applicant (a repeat serious drug offender) could be deported to Nigeria despite having lived in the UK since the age of three, Judge de Gaetano stated:

61 *Üner v Netherlands* (2007) 45 EHRR 14, minority opinion, para. 5.

62 According to the minority judges, these texts included the Conclusions of the Presidency of the Tampere European Council on 15 and 16 October 1999; The Council of Europe Committee of Ministers Recommendation Rec (2000)15, Parliamentary Assembly Recommendation 1504 (2001) and Committee of Ministers Recommendation Rec (2002); and the 1989 United Nations Convention on the Rights of the Child. See also *Maslov v Austria* (Application No. 1638/03) Judgment of the Grand Chamber of 23 June 2008, in which the Grand Chamber found that there had been a violation of Article 8. Judge Steiner dissented from the majority's assessment of the proportionality of the measure on the basis that the possibility would be open to the applicant after a period of time to request that the authorities reverse their decision.

63 See Charlotte Steinorth, note 9.

64 *Boulchekia v France* (1998) 25 EHRR 686.

65 See also *Boughanemi v France* (1996) 22 EHRR 228. Conversely, in *Moustaquim v Belgium* (Application No. 12313/86) Judgment of 18 February 1991 the Court emphasized the minor nature of the offences in question in deciding that the expulsion would breach Article 8 (para. 44). In *Ezzhoudi v France*, the offences were similarly minor, and this played a large part in the reasoning of the Court.

66 *Amrollahi v Denmark* (Application No. 56811/00) Judgment of 11 July 2002, para. 37; see also for example *Dalia v France* [2001] 33 EHRR 26, para. 92.

> the decisive factor … is the seriousness of the offences committed after the applicant had become an adult. The applicant knew perfectly well that, although he could be considered as a settled migrant, as an alien he had no "absolute right" to stay in the United Kingdom, and he must have known that in the event of serious brushes with the law, he risked being expelled.[67]

However, the severity of the offence has not consistently trumped the other considerations. If we compare a number of judgments this becomes apparent. In *Mehemi v France*, the applicant received a permanent exclusion order after being convicted of cannabis dealing – a serious crime in the view of the Court. However, he had been born in France and had two French children and an Italian wife. It was found that, despite the severity of the offence, his family life would be disproportionately interfered with by the expulsion. In contrast, in *Baghli v France* the severity of the offence (the 'severity' of which was questionable: the applicant had been sentenced to three years imprisonment, two of which were suspended, for dealing in a small quantity of heroin) was not similarly outweighed by the other circumstances of the case, even though, as in *Mehemi*, the applicant had entered France aged two, and 'his main family and social ties are in France'.[68] The Court laid emphasis on the fact that in this case the exclusion was for the determinate period of ten years, and thus would constitute less of an interference with the applicant's rights.[69] The real difference between these two cases appears to be the family status of the applicant: the applicant in *Baghli* was unmarried and had no children. Nevertheless, the family status of the applicant will not always be determinative either. For example, in *Üner* the applicant had a Dutch partner and two sons in the Netherlands, with Dutch nationality. However, the Court did not accord as much weight to this as it had in previous cases, adopting a rather dismissive approach to the issue of the proposed splitting up of the applicant's family.[70]

One of the outstanding issues in relation to this case law is thus the relative weight of the various factors. While integration is an important factor, it has been seen that it is often outweighed by the seriousness of the crime or the situation of the other members of the family. Many of the inconsistencies in the case law arise from the *ad hoc* approach to the balancing exercise undertaken in each case, to the extent that:

> The present approach of the ECtHR, … leaves both prospective applicants and national authorities with little guidance as to whether an expulsion of a long-term immigrant will be deemed a proportionate measure. It would thus be

67 *Balogun v UK* (Application No. 602386/99) Judgment of 10 April 2012.

68 *Mehemi v France* (1997) EHRR 6, at para. 48.

69 Judges Costa and Tulkens issued strong dissents on this point, noting that ten years is long enough for a person's family and social life in the host country to be obliterated.

70 Para. 64.

> preferable for the ECtHR to take a clear stance as to whether it gives primary significance to the legitimate interests of States in securing public order or to the right of long-term immigrants to remain in their host country.[71]

If the Court were to assign greater weight to the criterion of 'the solidity of social, cultural and family ties with the host country and the country of destination', long-term immigrants would almost certainly enjoy greater security of residence in the host country.

The Article 8 ECHR Admission Cases: Limited Consideration of Integration in the Context of Family Reunification

The typical admission case has concerned the situation where an applicant in a Contracting State maintains that the refusal of that state to allow the entry of a member of his family (most often a child) fails to respect his right to family life. In conceptual terms, the distinguishing feature of these cases is therefore that they concern a positive obligation on the part of the state rather than the negative obligation at play in the expulsion cases. As the Court has reiterated:

> the essential object of Article 8 is to protect the individual against arbitrary action by the public authorities. There may in addition be positive obligations inherent in effective "respect" for family life. However, the boundaries between the State's positive and negative obligations under this provision (art. 8) do not lend themselves to precise definition. The applicable principles are, nonetheless, similar. In both contexts regard must be had to the fair balance that has to be struck between the competing interests of the individual and of the community as a whole; and in both contexts the State enjoys a certain margin of appreciation.[72]

This passage suggests that the principles to be applied in relation to the negative and positive obligations contained in Article 8 are broadly similar. In the early admission cases in particular, however, the Court took a very restrictive approach towards applicants making this type of claim, affording states a wide margin of appreciation in determining whether a positive obligation existed at all. The Court stated in *Abdulaziz, Cabales and Balkandali*, the first of these cases, that:

> as far as positive obligations are concerned, the notion of "respect" is not clear-cut: having regard to the diversity of the practice followed and the situations

71 Charlotte Steinorth, note 9, p. 196.

72 *Abdulaziz, Cabales and Balkandali v United Kingdom* (1985) EHRR 471, para. 67.

> obtaining in the Contracting States, the notion's requirements will vary considerably from case to case.[73]

The jurisprudence of the Court shows that the state's right to control the entry of non-nationals into its territory will rarely be outweighed by the circumstances of the individual applicants. First, the Court has been clear in its position that Article 8 does not impose on a state 'a general obligation to respect the choice by married couples of the country of their matrimonial residence and to authorize family reunion in its territory'.[74] In assessing the circumstances of the applicants, the Court will consider whether admission is the only way to develop true family life: are there are insurmountable obstacles to setting up family life in the country of origin? This is a high hurdle for applicants to overcome, as illustrated by *Gul v Switzerland*[75] and the subsequent case of *Ahmut v The Netherlands*.[76] In its harsh decision in *Gul*, the Court found that while the circumstances of the family in question were compelling and 'very difficult from the human point of view',[77] there was no such obligation in this case as there were 'strictly speaking, no obstacles preventing them from developing family life in Turkey'.[78] A similar approach was taken in *Ahmut v The Netherlands*,[79] in which the father had actually obtained Dutch nationality.[80]

It seems that one circumstance in which the Court will find that insurmountable obstacles to settling in the country of origin exist is where the applicant(s) have started a family in the host country and other children have been born or substantially brought up in that country. Here the Court acknowledges that the state's decision effectively requires the applicants to choose between their children in the host country and those in the country of origin, compelling an impossible

73 *Abdulaziz, Cabales and Balkandali v United Kingdom* (1985) EHRR 471, at para. 67.

74 *Abdulaziz, Cabales and Balkandali v United Kingdom* (1985) EHRR 471; *Gul v The Netherlands* (1996) 22 EHRR 93; *Ahmut v The Netherlands* (1996) 24 EHRR 62; *Sen v The Netherlands* (Application No. 31465/96) Judgment of 21 December 2001.

75 (1996) 22 EHRR 93. It is particularly difficult for applicants to succeed where the separation was caused by a deliberate and voluntary decision on the behalf of the parent or parents, as was the case in *Ahmut*.

76 (1996) 24 EHRR 62.

77 Para. 42.

78 Para. 42. In a strong dissenting opinion, Judge Martens criticized what he viewed as the artificial distinction drawn by the majority between positive and negative obligations, and stated that there had to be a limit to the Court's deference to domestic immigration law and policy (para. 9).

79 (1996) 24 EHRR 62.

80 There were four dissenting judges in this case, including Judge Valticos who stopped just short of accusing the Dutch government of racism, given that the father in this case was a Dutch national.

choice which does not respect the applicants' right to family life.[81] This formed the basis of the reasoning of the Court in *Sen v The Netherlands*[82] and *Tuquabo-Tekle v The Netherlands*,[83] which seemed to signal a shift towards a less restrictive attitude of the Court towards these cases.[84] However, the limited number of cases which make it past the admissibility stage illustrates how difficult it remains to succeed in these cases.[85] Even where cases, such as *Darren Omoregie v Norway*,[86] proceed to judgment on the merits of the individual case, it is still very unlikely that the Court will hold in favour of the applicant.

Integration is not as significant an issue in the admission cases as in the expulsion cases considered above. This is understandable, as the child has not, for the most part, entered the receiving country yet and so no question of his or her integration could arise. The Court considers the extent of the child's 'cultural and linguistic links' to the country of *origin* in determining the viability of developing family life in that country.[87] It also considers the child's degree of dependence on the parents,[88] and in this context, the age of the children may be an important factor.[89] Interestingly however (and as touched upon in the previous paragraph), in cases of split families where there are children who have been brought up in the host country, the Court may also consider their degree of integration in the host country in order to ascertain the impact on them of moving to the country of origin to join the other members of the family. In *Sen v the Netherlands*, the Court considered that the two children who had been born and had grown up in the Netherlands and were receiving their schooling there had few or no links to the country of origin aside from the legal fact of nationality, and in these circumstances the most appropriate way to develop true family life was to allow the entry of the son who was in Turkey.[90] In this limited sense, there is a certain degree of overlap here with the expulsion cases considered above.

It seems that it is only in a very narrow set of circumstances that the Court will compel a state to authorize family reunification on the basis of Article 8.

81 *Sen v The Netherlands*, para. 41.

82 Application No. 31465/96, Judgment of 21 December 2001.

83 Application No. 60665/00, Judgment of 1 December 2005.

84 See Nicola Rogers, note 4, p. 64. See also *Rodriguez da Silva and Hoogkamer v the Netherlands* (Application No. 50435/99) Judgment of 31 January 2006.

85 See, for example, *Benamar v. the Netherlands* (dec.), Application No. 43786/04, 5 April 2005; *I.M. v. the Netherlands* (dec.), Application No. 41266/98, 25 March 2003; and *Chandra and Others v. the Netherlands* (dec.), Application No. 53102/99, 13 May 2003.

86 *Darren Omoregie v Norway* (Application No. 265/07) Judgment of 31 July 2008.

87 *Gul v The Netherlands* (1996) 22 EHRR 93, para. 42; *Ahmut v The Netherlands* (1996) 24 EHRR 62, para. 69; *Sen v The Netherlands*, para. 37.

88 See, for example, *Sen v The Netherlands*, para. 37.

89 See *Tuquabo-Tekle v The Netherlands* (Application No. 60665/00) Judgment of 1 December 2005, para. 49; and *Benamar v. the Netherlands, I.M. v. the Netherlands* and *Chandra and Others v. the Netherlands* discussed above.

90 Para. 40.

Furthermore, even though the Court has insisted that the same principles are applicable in the case of the negative and positive obligations under Article 8, it is clear that the Court is reluctant to first of all find that a positive obligation exists at all and secondly that the positive obligation is breached. This is consistent with the general observations made above in relation to the difficulties inherent in identifying and enforcing positive obligations in international law. Overall, the analysis of the family reunification judgments of the ECtHR in this section confirms that in the specific field of family reunification, states are relatively unconstrained by the ECHR in their formulation of law and policy, and – more generally – that states have a wide margin of appreciation in matters relating to the entry and residence of non-nationals.

As noted above, the Article 8 case law has been criticized both from within the Court itself and by academic commentators for its incoherence and instability.[91] These difficulties have stemmed from the high degree of deference shown to domestic immigration policy in the judgments of the Court, which has led to conceptual confusion to the point where 'it is difficult to extrapolate clear principles identifying the application of Article 8'.[92] States are thus free to decide on the most appropriate way to deal with the key integration issue of family reunification, providing they stay within the generous margin of appreciation delineated by the Court in *Sen* and *Tuquabo-Tekle*. This is perhaps indicative of the broader difficulties faced when applying international law in the integration context. Integration is by its nature an area involving the progressive realization of rights, of positive rights involving complex and delicate issues of social policy closely related to issues of national identity and sovereignty. The focus of international law on negative obligations of states and on leaving states with a wide margin of appreciation thus may limit the applicability of international human rights law in the integration context.

The Influence of the Normative Development of Integration by the European Court of Human Rights

The readiness of the Court in recent cases to explicitly protect long-term residents under the heading of private life involves it in a complex and nuanced balancing exercise which includes integration as one of the express criteria to be considered by the Court. This makes explicit the integration analysis in which the Court had been implicitly engaging since the early cases. While the jurisprudence relating to what actually constitutes 'integration' is very much in its infancy, the implications of this move extends beyond the circumstances of the applicants in these cases and

91 In addition to the comments of the dissenting judges referred to above, see Catherine Dembour, 'Human Rights Law and National Sovereignty in Collusion: The Plight of Quasi-nationals at Strasbourg' (2003) 21 *Netherlands Quarterly of Human Rights* 63.

92 Nicola Rogers, note 4, at 53.

signifies the start of a normative development of the concept of integration by the European Court of Human Rights.

Nevertheless, the impact of the developing concept of integration on the outcome of the expulsion cases is variable and in some cases unclear, as the integration criterion is only one element of a complex balancing exercise undertaken by the Court. In addition, it has been seen that the specific context in which the Court considers integration has led to some differences in the emerging integration paradigm employed by the Court and those put forward by the UN CCPR, CESCR and CERD Committees, for example. The one-sided approach of the Court to the notion of 'integration', placing the onus of integration principally on the individual concerned, has been criticized here. This integration paradigm conflicts with those being developed by the UN treaty monitoring bodies, which it was shown above have focussed on a holistic, rights-based and equality-based vision of integration involving obligations on the part of the state as well as of the migrant.

It also remains to be seen whether the increased emphasis of the Court on the integration criterion in the expulsion cases influences the Court's approach to key integration issues such as family reunification and in turn whether this filters down to legislators and policymakers at the national level. As the admissions cases clearly demonstrate, the Court continues to operate within the constraints of Article 8 and in the awkward space between international obligations and states' margin of appreciation in immigration matters, which raises the question of how far the ECtHR can hope to influence state practice in this sphere, particularly where the circumstances relate to the positive obligations of states. Taking Ireland and the UK as examples, the influence of the Article 8 case law on judicial decision-making in the sphere of expulsions and family reunification has been very significant in Ireland,[93] and has led to the amendment of the Immigration Rules in the UK to codify the factors relevant in Article 8 'balancing' exercises, for example.[94] As well as taking into account the ways in which Article 8 can be raised in asylum applications and standalone applications for leave to remain, the

93 *Oguekwe v Minister for Justice, Equality and Law Reform* [2008] 3 IR 795; *N v Minister for Justice, Equality and Law Reform* [2008] IEHC 8; *A v Minister for Justice, Equality and Law Reform* [2009] IEHC 245; *I(S) v Refugee Appeals Tribunal* [2009] IEHC 8. See generally, Siobhán Mullally and Liam Thornton, 'The Rights of the Child, Immigration and Article 8 in the Irish Courts', in Ursula Kilkelly (ed.), *The ECHR and Irish Law* (2nd edn, Jordans, 2009), p. 146.

94 See paragraph 395C of previous versions of the Immigration Rules; Home Office, *Statement of Intent: Family Migration*, June 2012 (hereinafter, 'Statement of Intent'); Statement of Changes to the Immigration Rules HC 194. See House of Commons Library research briefing: Melanie Gower, *Article 8 of the ECHR and Immigration Cases* (15 June 2012). For commentary, see UK Human Rights Blog, 'Article 8 and a half – wider than thought, but will it work?', 13 June 2012; and ILPA, *UKBA consultation on Family Migration: a consultation, response from Immigration Law Practitioner's Association (ILPA)* (October 2011).

amended rules deal with the application of Article 8 in the context of deportation following criminal conviction. The way that the balancing test has been interpreted in the new rules in the UK means that in circumstances where a foreign national criminal has received a custodial sentence of less than four years, deportation will not be proportionate if 'they have been continuously resident in the UK for at least the last 20 years (excluding any period of imprisonment) and they have no social, cultural or family ties with their country of origin, **or** they are aged under 25 years and have spent at least half of their life residing continuously in the UK (excluding any period of imprisonment) and they have no social, cultural or family ties with their country of origin'.[95] Where the sentence is longer than four years, on the other hand, deportation will very rarely be disproportionate.[96] The Immigration Rules thus take advantage of the lack of clarity in the Court's decisions on the relative weight of the seriousness of the offence and other factors including integration.

However, outside these direct effects of the Court's jurisprudence, the human rights-based approach underpinning its decisions does not appear to have influenced the developing national integration policies discussed in Chapter 2. These policies do not conceive of nationality, for example, as a tool for integration, and they do not mention family reunification. Similarly (on the bright side) integration policy in the UK and Ireland does not require migrants to relinquish all connection to their country of nationality, which is one of the key elements of the Court's analysis of integration.

Conclusion

The interpretation of integration by the ECtHR is limited in the sense that it is rooted in the narrow field of application of Article 8 ECHR on the right to family and private life. In addition, the Court does not often explicitly look at 'integration' in such terms but usually refers to the 'social ties' or 'links' of the applicant. The one-sided nature of the analysis of integration by the ECtHR, whereby the onus of integration appears to rest on the migrant, has also been identified as problematic. The jurisprudence of the ECtHR thus pursues a somewhat different vision of integration to that employed by the UN treaty monitoring bodies. Nonetheless, it is clear that the ECHR requires State Parties to consider the degree of integration of non-citizens whom they are seeking to expel from their territory prior to their expulsion, as part of a matrix of factors to be considered pursuant to Article 8's protection of private and family life. This contrasts with the use of integration as a legal barrier to immigration in the law of certain countries and as endorsed in some

95 Statement of Intent, para. 68; paragraphs 396, 397, 398, 399 and 399A of the Immigration Rules.

96 Statement of Intent, para. 68; paragraphs 396, 397, 398, 399 and 399A of the Immigration Rules.

aspects of EU law. In addition, the ECHR places some limits on state discretion in the sphere of family reunification.

The last two chapters have shown that the interpretation of the concept of integration by the UN treaty bodies and by the European Court of Human Rights constitutes a valuable, legal, contribution to the emerging discourse on the nature, scope and implications of integration. The approaches of these international law bodies to both the meaning and consequences of integration provide a starting-point for the positive, human-rights based, notion of integration advocated by academic commentators.[97]

97 See, for example, Ricky Van Oers, Eva Ersboll and Dora Kostakopoulou, 'Mapping the redefinition of belonging in Europe' in Ricky Van Oers, Eva Ersboll and Dora Kostakopoulou (eds), *A Re-Definition of Belonging? Language and Integration Tests in Europe* (Martinus Nijhoff Publishers, 2010, p. 326; Sergio Carrera, *In Search of the Perfect Citizen? The Intersection between Integration, Immigration and Nationality in the EU* (Martinus Nijhoff, 2009); Anja Wiesbrock, *Legal Migration to the European Union* (Martinus Nijhoff Publishers, 2010), p. 734.

Chapter 6
Regional Frameworks for Integration: Concepts of Integration in EU Law and Policy

Introduction

Understanding the legal framework for integration constituted by EU law is central to understanding integration in EU Member States. In strictly legal terms, EU law constitutes a significant body of norms affecting integration in all Member States. On a more abstract level, the EU provides a supranational dimension to citizenship and belonging, potentially leading to a cosmopolitan openness towards the 'other' at the national level.[1] The transformative potential of EU law in the field of migration and integration has been witnessed in the case of EU citizens. EU law relating to the free movement of workers has altered the status of EU migrant workers and their families in a legal sense with a consequent change in the way in which such migrants are perceived. Nationals of EU Member States living and working in other Member States have been gradually transformed from 'immigrants' subject to the conditions of entry and residence imposed by the state, to EU citizens, entitled to equal treatment and the same respect as the host population.[2] It has thus been seen that EU law can in itself constitute an instrument of integration.

This chapter examines the conceptual and legal framework formed by EU law and policy in respect of the integration of both non-EU national migrants (referred to in this chapter as 'third-country nationals' or 'TCN's)[3] and EU citizen migrants exercising their right to free movement within the EU (referred to in this chapter as 'EU citizen migrants' or 'EU migrants'), with the primary aim of determining whether EU law and policy contains a coherent paradigm of integration. EU

1 Dora Kostokopoulou, 'European Union Citizenship: Writing the Future' (2007) 13(5) *ELJ* 623, pp. 628–629.

2 See Dora Kostakopoulou, 'European Citizenship and Immigration after Amsterdam: Silences, Openings and Paradoxes' (1998) 24(4) *Journal of Ethnic and Migration Studies* 639; Elspeth Guild, 'Cultural and Social Identity: Immigrants and the Legal Expression of National Identity', in Elspeth Guild and Joanne Van Selm (eds), *International Migration and Security: Opportunities and Challenges* (Routledge, 2005) 101, p. 107.

3 For a detailed examination of 'The Community Acquis on Legal Migration', see generally, Anja Wiesbrock, *Legal Migration to the European Union* (Martinus Nijhoff, 2010), chapter 2.

integration law and policy in respect of TCNs can be split into three separate but interlinked spheres: (i) specific integration policy; (ii) concepts of integration contained in general immigration law; and (iii) concepts of integration in asylum law. Each of these spheres will be examined in the part of the chapter dealing with TCNs. In contrast, in the case of EU citizen migrants, there is no specific integration policy, and the analysis is confined to the framework for integration formed by the law relating to free movement, equal treatment and EU citizenship. The bulk of the chapter is devoted to the approach to the integration of TCNs enshrined in EU law and policy.

It will be argued that EU law and policy encompasses a number of conceptions of integration (largely dependent on the legal classification of the individual concerned), such that no coherent paradigm of integration can be identified in the EU framework. This is an idea echoed by Kostakopoulou, Carrera and Jesse, who identify the 'competing frames' of the conception consistently applied to nationals of Member States, based on equal rights, agency and participation in political communities, juxtaposed against what they describe as the new conception of integration applicable to third-country nationals which centres on migration control and the preservation of the alleged homogeneity of national bodies.[4] It is argued in this chapter that the concepts of integration in EU law and policy are still more complex and numerous than these frames of reference. This lack of coherence is due in part to the preoccupation of Member States with maintaining tight control over the area of migration and citizenship and the treatment of TCNs in particular. This control has been eroded in certain limited cases due to the demands of international law (refugees) and economic self-interest (students, researchers and highly skilled workers).[5] The analysis contained in this chapter points to the conclusion that the lack of a coherent integration paradigm in EU law and policy undermines its potential to provide an alternative approach to integration to that based on national public philosophies of integration. The scope for EU law and policy to influence the scope and content of integration at the national level is therefore quite constrained. This ultimately weakens the transformative potential of EU law in the field of integration.

Integration Policy for TCNs: The EU Framework on Integration

Prior to the adoption of the Lisbon Treaty, there was no explicit legal basis for the development of EU co-operation in the field of integration. As will be discussed further below, the harmonization of the laws and regulations of

4 Ibid., p. 168.

5 Kostakopoulou, Carrera and Jesse, 'Doing and Deserving: Competing Frames of Integration in the EU', in Elspeth Guild, Sergio Carrera and Kees Groenendijk (eds), *Illiberal Liberal States: Immigration, Citizenship and Integration in the EU* (Ashgate, 2009) 167, p. 168.

Member States relating to integration remains excluded under the amended Treaty on the Functioning of the European Union (TFEU).[6] It is arguable that even if such competence existed, harmonization in the field of integration would be undesirable due to the cultural and legal differences between the Member States and their various groups of immigrants.[7] Furthermore, Member States use widely differing definitions and notions of key concepts, including the concept of 'integration' itself, which would render agreement on binding policy very difficult to achieve. It has been argued that the vocabulary of integration is 'inappropriate to a polity in which there is: (i) a plurality of cultures and sub-cultures; (ii) no shared definition of a 'common life'; and (iii) multiple definitions of communal 'homes' formed at national, subnational and supranational levels of governance'.[8] In short, the question of what migrants are expected to integrate into is particularly indeterminate on the level of the EU.

Nevertheless, a significant body of soft law (policy) has emerged on the specific theme of integration of TCNs, and a common policy framework has been developed which is intended to serve as a guide for national policies. This specific integration policy framework applies to TCNs only. The so-called 'Framework for the Integration of Third-Country Nationals in the EU' (EU Framework on Integration) comprises several substantive and institutional mechanisms: the Common Basic Principles on integration (CBP's), three Handbooks on Integration for Policy Makers and Practitioners, three Annual Reports on Migration and Integration, the National Contact Points on Integration (NCPIs) and the European Fund for the Integration of Third Country Nationals (EIF). Political debate on integration takes place at Ministerial Conferences on Integration.[9] In addition, in 2009, two instruments of exchange and information were introduced to support the framework: the European Website on Integration and the European Integration Forum. The EU Framework on Integration is thus evolving in different institutional settings and through various means.

The Origins of EU Integration Policy

The impetus for the development of a specific EU integration policy for TCNs started with the entry into force of the Treaty of Maastricht, which provided for

6 Article 79.4 TFEU provides: 'The European Parliament and the Council, acting in accordance with the ordinary legislative procedure, may establish measures to provide incentives and support for the action of Member States with a view to promoting the integration of third-country nationals residing legally in their territories, excluding any harmonization of the laws and regulations of the Member States'.

7 See Katja Ziegler, 'Editorial: Integrating Integration' (2005) 7 *EJML* 119.

8 Dora Kostakopoulou, 'Integrating Non-EU Migrants in the European Union: Ambivalent Legacies and Mutating Paradigms' (2002) 8 *Columbia Journal of European Law* 181, p. 188.

9 These have taken place in 2004 (Groningen), 2007 (Potsdam), 2008 (Vichy) and 2010 (Zarazoga).

the possibility of co-ordination in immigration and asylum matters by identifying areas of common interest. The Treaty of Amsterdam conferred full competence on the Union to develop policies in the field of freedom, security and justice, and one of the tasks of the newly created Directorate General for Justice and Home Affairs was to examine options for developing policies on the integration of migrants and refugees.[10] The basis for policy development in the sphere of integration was set out by the 1999 Tampere European Council. The conclusions of the Tampere Council – in the context of setting out the political guidelines for the EU immigration framework – favoured an inclusive integration policy based on equal treatment and a secure legal status, particularly in the case of long-term residents. The Council requested the creation of a uniform set of rules through which 'fair treatment' of all TCNs residing legally in the EU Member States should be ensured.[11] This fair and equal treatment paradigm of integration[12] envisaged that a 'vigorous integration policy' should aim at granting legally resident TCNs rights and obligations comparable to those of EU citizens[13] and granting long-term resident TCNs 'a set of uniform rights which are as near as possible to those enjoyed by EU citizens'.[14] However, despite this broad mandate, aside from the creation of National Contact Points on Integration in 2002,[15] 'the integration aspects of the Tampere conclusions did not advance very fast and … integration had never been fully developed by the Commission'.[16]

The development of an EU integration policy was revived in 2003 by the Commission's Communication on Immigration, Integration and Employment, which presents a broad-based, inclusive conception of integration, emphasizing its economic and human rights dimensions. The importance of immigration in the context of the demographic change (ageing and decline) of European populations is emphasized, and the Communication points out that '(T)he successful integration of immigrants is both a matter of social cohesion and a pre-requisite

10 For a comprehensive overview of the political and legal evolution of EU integration policy, see Helene Urth, 'Building a Momentum for the Integration of Third-Country Nationals in the European Union' (2005) 7 *EJML* 163, p. 164.

11 Tampere European Council 15 and 16 October 1999: Presidency Conclusions, para. 18.

12 This phrase is coined by Sergio Carrera, in *Benchmarking Integration in the EU: Analyzing the Debate and Moving it Forward* (Bertelsmann Foundation, 2008), p. 8. See also Sergio Carrera, *In Search of the Perfect Citizen? The Intersection between Integration, Immigration and Nationality in the EU* (Martinus Nijhoff, 2009), p. 49.

13 Ibid.

14 Tampere European Council 15 and 16 October 1999: Presidency Conclusions, para. 21.

15 The National Contact Points were endorsed by the Thessaloniki European Council. See Thessaloniki European Council 19 and 20 June 2003: Presidency Conclusions, p. 10.

16 Helene Urth, note 10, p. 167.

for economic efficiency'.[17] The Communication stresses the need for a two-way, holistic approach to integration, which is based on mutual rights and obligations of the immigrant and the host society and takes into account not only the economic and social aspects of integration but also issues relating to cultural and religious diversity, citizenship, participation and political rights. Key elements in holistic integration policies are also identified, including integration into the labour market,[18] education and language skills[19] and housing and urban issues.[20] Some of the observations made in the Communication are quite far-reaching, and touch on sensitive national sovereignty issues such as access to citizenship. For example, it is stated that 'It is widely recognized that acquiring nationality is a means of facilitating integration, although it need not be the ultimate aim of the integration process'.[21]

Development of the Framework on Integration

Integration received renewed attention in the Hague Programme[22] which, significantly, identified integration as a separate policy area to that of 'migration management' and a high-priority area for attention by the EU.[23] More generally, the Hague Programme emphasized the human rights dimension of migration while at the same time restating the major concerns of security and fighting terrorism.[24] This focus was somewhat inevitable given the shift which had taken place since the terrorist attacks of September 11, 2001 and other events such as the Madrid bombings of 2004, which had led to the emergence and development of anti-immigrant and anti-Muslim discourses at the national level.[25] The Hague Programme takes a step back from the Tampere paradigm and does not reiterate

---

17 Communication from the Commission to the Council, the European Parliament, the European Economic and Social Committee and the Committee of the Regions, *Immigration, Integration and Employment* (COM(2003) 336 final), p. 17.

18 Ibid., at para. 3.3.1.

19 Ibid., at para. 3.3.2.

20 Ibid., at para. 3.3.3.

21 Ibid., p. 22.

22 Brussels European Council 4 and 5 November 2004: Presidency Conclusions, Annex 1 – 'The Hague Programme: Strengthening Freedom, Security and Justice in the European Union' (hereinafter, the 'Hague Programme').

23 Communication from the Commission to the Council and the European Parliament, *The Hague Programme: Ten priorities for the next five years* (COM(2005) 184 final).

24 See, for example, Thierry Balzacq and Sergio Carrera, 'The Hague Programme: The Long Road to Freedom, Security and Justice', in Thierry Balzacq and Sergio Carrera (eds), *Security Versus Freedom: A Challenge for Europe's Future* (Ashgate, 2006), p. 1.

25 The importance of the security discourse in the Hague Programme is explicit: 'The security of the European Union and its Member States has acquired a new urgency, especially in the light of the terrorist attacks in the United States on 11 September 2001 and in Madrid on 11 March 2004' (The Hague Programme, p. 3).

the aims of the Tampere Programme in relation to a more vigorous integration policy and the near-equal treatment of TCNs; the furthest it goes in this respect is to state that:

> While recognising the progress that has already been made in respect of the fair treatment of legally resident third-country nationals in the EU, the European Council calls for the creation of equal opportunities to participate fully in society.[26]

The Programme stated that greater co-ordination of national integration policies and EU initiatives were needed and that a framework based on common basic principles should form the foundation for future initiatives in the EU. This framework is intended to assist the EU in helping Member States to better their integration policies, with the express aim of creating equal opportunities to participate fully in society and removing barriers to integration.[27]

The Common Basic Principles, adopted soon after the Hague Programme in 2004, are expressly not intended to form the basis for a binding EU policy on integration. They are principally intended to 'assist Member States in formulating integration policies by offering them a simple non-binding but thoughtful guide of basic principles against which they can judge and assess their own efforts'.[28] While the effectiveness of the CBPs is limited by their non-binding nature, the principles are centrally important as they delineate the contours of the EU approach to integration. As Pratt observes, these principles 'provide a first definition of what we mean by integration in the EU'.[29] Integration is defined as a 'dynamic, two-way process of mutual accommodation by all immigrants and residents of Member States';[30] and the basic requirements of integration laid down: respect for the basic values of the European Union,[31] including the diversity of cultures and religions;[32] and a basic knowledge of the host society's language, history and institutions.[33] The introduction of these requirements, contained in CBPs 2 and 4.2, have been interpreted as representing a new departure in EU integration

26 The Hague Programme, p. 10.

27 See The Hague Programme, at para. 1.5, Communication from the Commission to the Council and the European Parliament, *The Hague Programme: Ten priorities for the next five years* (COM(2005) 184 final).

28 Justice and Home Affairs Council Conclusions, *Common Basic Principles on Immigrant Integration*, Council Document 14615/04, Brussels, 19 November 2004 (hereinafter, the 'Common Basic Principles' or the 'CBPs'), Common Basic Principle 8.

29 Sandra Pratt, 'Immigration, Integration and Citizenship: Latest Developments and the EU's Role', in Sergio Carrera (ed.), *The Nexus Between Immigration, Integration and Citizenship in the EU* (CEPS, 2006) 10, p. 10.

30 Common Basic Principle 1.

31 CBP 2.

32 CBP 8.

33 CBP 4.

policy by introducing a nexus between integration and the adoption of 'values' which was absent from previous integration discourse in the EU context and from the fair and equal treatment paradigm contained in the Tampere Programme.[34] For some commentators, this represented the start of the transmission of national discourses and categories of integration to the EU level.[35] However, the 'culture and values' principles constitute just one dimension of the CBPs. A number of key integration issues which emphasize the state's role in the integration process are also identified, including access to employment,[36] education[37] and access to institutions on an equal basis to national citizens.[38] Finally, a number of ways to enable integration are outlined, including frequent interaction between immigrants and Member State citizens;[39] mainstreaming integration policies and measures;[40] and developing clear policy goals, indicators and evaluation mechanisms.[41]

Aside from the argument that the CBPs represented a paradigm shift in EU integration policy towards a more culture and values-centred concept of integration, they can be criticized as being vague and depoliticized,[42] a criticism which could apply to EU integration policy generally. CBP 2, for example, which refers to respect for the 'basic values' of the EU, does not specify what these values are.[43] Indeed, it is arguable that the inherent vagueness of any policy guidelines aimed at all Member States, with their diverse migration experiences and immigration, citizenship and integration practices, makes it almost impossible for such guidelines to espouse a clear vision of what integration actually encompasses. This effectively leaves Member States free to fill in the gaps with their own national conception of integration, detracting from the added value of the elaboration of EU guidelines.

The CBPS are fleshed out and built upon by the Commission's 2005 Communication on the Framework for the Integration of Third Country Nationals in the European Union, which contains proposals for concrete measures to put the

34 Sergio Carrera and Anja Wiesbrock, 'Civic Integration of Third Country Nationals: Nationalism versus Europeanisation in the Common EU Immigration Policy' (CEPS, October 2009), pp. 8 and 9; Dora Kostakopoulou, Sergio Carrera and Moritz Jesse, 'Doing and Deserving: Competing Frames of Integration in the EU', in Elspeth Guild, Kees Groenendijk and Sergio Carrera, *Illiberal Liberal States: Immigration, Citizenship and Integration in the EU* (Ashgate, 2009), 167, p. 183.

35 Kostakopoulou, Carrera and Jesse, ibid., p. 180.

36 CBP 3.

37 CBP 5.

38 CBP 6.

39 CBP 7.

40 CBP 10.

41 CBP 11.

42 Piaras Mac Einrí, 'Integration Models and Choices', in Bryan Fanning (ed.), *Immigration and Social Change in the Republic of Ireland* (Manchester University Press, 2007), p. 231.

43 Although these are elaborated upon in later documents, as will be discussed below.

CBPs into practice, both at national and at EU level. It stresses the links between the legal framework constituted by the legislative instruments on the conditions of admission and stay of TCNs and integration policy, and the supportive role of the anti-discrimination legislation in the context of integration. In relation to the 'new', values-centred, aspect of EU integration discourse contained in CBPs 2 and 4.2, the Commission's recommendations in relation to the national level include 'strengthening the integration component of admission procedures'[44] and 'assuring that all residents, including immigrants, understand, respect and benefit from common European and national values'.[45] However, the Communication also emphasizes other wider and more inclusive dimensions of integration, stating that '(t)he promotion of fundamental rights, non-discrimination and equal opportunities for all are key integration issues' and stressing the need to eliminate structural barriers to integration.[46]

A number of EU mechanisms which support the integration framework are also referred to in the Commission's Communication. These include the NCPI and Annual Reports,[47] as referred to above, as well as the Handbook for Integration, which contains examples of good practice and lessons learned by policy-makers across the Member States.[48] Another supporting mechanism is the European Fund for the Integration of Third Country Nationals, which aims to support national efforts in enabling TCNs to fulfil conditions of residence and to facilitate their integration, through *inter alia* the development of transnational co-operation

44 Communication from the Commission to the Council, the European Parliament, the European Economic and Social Committee and the Committee of the Regions of 1 September 2005 – A Common Agenda for Integration – Framework for the Integration of Third-Country Nationals in the European Union (COM(2005) 389 final – Not published in the Official Journal), p. 7.

45 Ibid., p. 16.

46 Ibid., pp. 3 and 4.

47 There have been three Annual Reports on Migration and Integration: Communication from the Commission to the Council, the European Parliament, the European Economic and Social Committee and the Committee of the Regions of 16 July 2004, *First Annual Report on Migration and Integration* (COM(2004) 508 final – Not published in the Official Journal); European Commission Staff Working Document of 30 June 2006 – *Second Annual Report on Migration and Integration* (SEC(2006) 892 – Not published in the Official Journal); and Communication from the Commission to the Council, the European Parliament, the European Economic and Social Committee and the Committee of the Regions of 11 September 2007, *Third Annual Report on Migration and Integration* (COM(2007) 512 final – Not published in the Official Journal).

48 There have been three editions of the Handbook on Integration: European Commission, *Handbook on Integration for Policy-makers and Practitioners* (Brussels, November 2004), European Commission, *Handbook on Integration for Policy-makers and Practitioners* (Brussels, 2nd edn, May 2007), European Commission, *Handbook on Integration for Policy-makers and Practitioners* (Brussels, 3rd edn, April 2010).

networks and benchmarking techniques.[49] These mechanisms represent a move to a 'more structured approach to exchange of information, best practices and monitoring of Member States policy development'.[50]

The move towards a more structured approach to the sharing of 'best practices' is reflected in the production of three editions of the Handbook on Integration, the product of technical seminars held by national ministries involved in integration. These Handbooks avoid theoretical questions relating to integration and focus on approaches to the improvement of practical 'outcomes' of immigrants, based on the idea that:

> Integration policies aim to bring about, over time, a convergence of societal outcomes for all. This requires the active involvement of all citizens and residents; those with and without an immigrant background. They can contribute to the social, economic, cultural and civic life of society by using their skills and competencies.[51]

However, the commentary in the Handbook's third edition on 'the naturalization process' demonstrates the way in which this method of co-operation can lead to the sharing and replication of integration strategies which conflict with the fundamental EU definition of integration as a two-way process of mutual accommodation by immigrants and the host community. The section on integration and language tests for access to citizenship outlines the different approaches taken by Member States, thereby implicitly endorsing the use of such tests as an acceptable means of pursuing the aims of integration, and also implying that citizenship represents a reward for integration rather than a tool in the integration process.[52] This represents the transfer of national discourses on integration to the EU level and effectively legitimizes a one-sided conception of integration which places the onus of integration on the migrant. It provides a good illustration of the way in which the sharing of 'best practice' in the sphere of integration brings the risk that the reorientation of integration as a tool for immigration control and a barrier to accessing citizenship, as practiced in some Member States, will be perpetuated in other Member States as 'best practice'.[53]

In parallel to the holding of technical seminars and Ministerial Conferences on integration, the Council and Commission have continued to produce soft law on integration. In 2007, the Council adopted a further set of conclusions on

---

49 Council Decision 2007/435/EC of 25 June 2007 establishing the European Fund for the Integration of third-country nationals for the period 2007 to 2013 as part of the General Programme 'Solidarity and Management of Migration Flows', OJ L 168/18.

50 Helene Urth, note 10, p. 174.

51 European Commission, *Handbook on Integration for Policymakers and Practitioners* (Brussels, 3rd edn, April 2010), p. 8.

52 See, for example, ibid., p. 113.

53 Sergio Carrera, *Benchmarking Integration*, note 12, p. 62.

strengthening integration policies in the EU.[54] The Conclusions recognize the social inclusion aspect of integration policy and invite the NCPI to consider approaches to integration that involve society as a whole: including exploring how integration programmes and policies can contribute to the prevention of social alienation and radicalization.[55] The 2008 Communication on a Common Immigration Policy in Europe: Principles, Tools and Actions[56] contains the Commission's 'blueprint' for developing a common EU immigration policy. Ten principles are identified which provide the foundation on which the immigration policy should be based. These relate to three main areas: 'prosperity', 'security' and solidarity', with integration described as 'the key to successful immigration', and interestingly being placed under the heading of 'prosperity'. The Communication confirms the trend of co-operation in the field of integration being based on Member States' exchange of 'best practice' and the development of benchmarking 'indicators' rather than the elaboration of standards or a common shared approach to integration.

A New Legal and Policy Context for Integration?

The adoption of the Lisbon Treaty in 2009, as well as the adoption of the Stockholm Programme, which outlines a roadmap for the EU's work in the area of freedom, security and justice for the period 2010–2014, provided a new legal and policy context for the development of integration policies by the EU.

The Lisbon Treaty: Putting Integration on a Treaty Footing

The Lisbon Treaty inserted Article 79.4 into the TFEU, as follows:

> The European Parliament and the Council, acting in accordance with the ordinary legislative procedure, may establish measures to provide incentives and support for the action of Member States with a view to promoting the integration of third-country nationals residing legally in their territories, excluding any harmonisation of the laws and regulations of the Member States.

54 Council of the EU, *Strengthening of Integration Policies in the EU*, Council Document 10267/07 Luxembourg, 12–13 June 2007 (principle 9).

55 Council of the EU, ibid., at Principle 9.

56 Communication from the Commission to the European Parliament, the Council, the European Economic and Social Committee and the Committee of the Regions, *A Common Immigration Policy in Europe: Principles, Tools and Actions* (COM(2008) 359 final). See also Communication from the Commission to the European Parliament, the Council, the European Economic and Social Committee and the Committee of the Regions, *Strengthening the Global Approach to Migration: Increasing Coordination, Coherence and Synergies* (COM(2008) 611 final).

In addition to the symbolic significance involved in the political act of inserting integration into the TFEU, this provides a clear legal basis for the co-ordination of integration policy at EU level and clarifies that integration will continue to be dealt with by way of policy co-ordination and not by way of legal harmonization.[57] Finally, the strengthened role of the European Parliament helps address democratic deficit concerns in relation to the soft-law mechanisms comprising the Framework on Integration.[58]

The Lisbon Treaty also made the EU Charter of Fundamental Rights binding on Member States,[59] with implications for TCNs and for integration both in terms of the express rights contained therein and the scope of the protection of the Charter. Article 22 of the Charter expressly requires the Union to 'respect cultural, religious and linguistic diversity', reflecting the commitment in Article 2 TEU to the values of pluralism, non-discrimination and tolerance. Article 18 expressly protects the right to asylum, which is not explicit in the constitutions of most Member States. Chapter III of the Charter is devoted to 'Equality', with a prohibition on discrimination on 'any ground such as sex, race, colour, ethnic or social origin, genetic features, language, religion or belief, political or any other opinion, membership of a national minority, property, birth, disability, age or sexual orientation' contained in Article 21. These provisions provide the normative context for the elaboration of integration policy at European level in a similar way to the expression of the 'public philosophy' of nation states in national constitutions. In addition, the majority of the rights set out in the Charter (including those described above) are not limited to EU citizens, bringing TCNs expressly within the scope of its protection in respect of most of the rights contained therein. EU action in the sphere of integration must comply with the rights enshrined in the Charter. This lends further weight to the arguments in favour of an equality-based, rights-based conception of integration at EU level along the lines of that enshrined in the Tampere Programme, however it remains to be seen whether the Charter impacts on the evolution of integration policy in this way in practice, with such an impact (if it happens) likely to be over a long period of time. As Guild points out, the Charter is unique in that it constitutes a bill of rights which is not enshrined in a national constitution or an international human rights treaty. It is a creature of EU law and cannot be modified by any one Member State's authorities, directly constraining Member State action in the sphere of implementation of EU law relating to integration and backed up by the enforcement mechanisms of EU law. This represents another limitation – along with the limitations imposed by

57 See Council of the EU, *The Stockholm Programme – An open and secure Europe serving and protecting the citizens*, Council Document 17024/09, Brussels, 2 December 2009, p. 64, para. 6.1.5.

58 See Sergio Carrera, *In Search of the Perfect Citizen*, note 12, p. 108.

59 Article 6 TEU gives the Charter the same legal value as the Treaties.

international law – on the discretion of Member States in respect of the treatment of TCNs within their territory.[60]

A Mixed Paradigm of Integration in the Stockholm Programme

The European Pact on Immigration and Asylum,[61] which was devised by the French government and adopted by the European Council in 2008, provided a basis for the Stockholm Programme.[62] While the Pact is a political, non-binding document, it is endorsed in the Stockholm Programme and will therefore have a substantial influence on the future direction of immigration and integration policy.[63] Regarding family reunification, the Pact expresses the view that in order to manage family migration 'more effectively', each Member State could take into account in national legislation its own 'reception capacities' and 'families' capacity to integrate', which could be evaluated by, for example, assessing their knowledge of the language.[64] In addition, the original Proposed Pact would have introduced the idea of 'integration contracts' similar to those in use in France and the Netherlands. These proved too controversial and the idea was abandoned, however the rationale behind integration contracts (i.e. exclusion and/or assimilation) persists in the statements relating to integration contained in the Pact. Overall, it has been observed that:

> the Pact … heralds a more conservative approach to immigration, in line with changing public and political attitudes. It looks at immigration policies through the prism of "control first", making this more explicit that in the "past".[65] The pervasive driving forces of the Pact – nationalism and intergovernmentalism – will almost inevitably lead to an emphasis on Member States' self-interest in

60 Elspeth Guild, 'The European Union after the Treaty of Lisbon: Fundamental Rights and EU Citizenship', Global Jean Monnet/European Community Studies Association World Conference, 25–26 May 2010.

61 Council of the EU, *European Pact on Immigration and Asylum*, Council Document 13440/08, Brussels, 24 September 2008.

62 Council of the EU, *The Stockholm Programme – An open and secure Europe serving and protecting the citizens*, Council Document 17024/09, Brussels, 2 December 2009.

63 The Stockholm Programme states that the Pact provides 'a clear basis for further development' in the field of migration. Council of the EU, *The Stockholm Programme – An open and secure Europe serving and protecting the citizens*, Council Document 17024/09, Brussels, 2 December 2009.

64 See Elspeth Guild and Sergio Carrera, 'The French Presidency's European Pact on Immigration and Asylum: Intergovernmentalism vs Europeanisation? Security vs Rights?' (CEPS Policy Brief, September 2008).

65 Elizabeth Collett, 'The EU Immigration Pact – from Hague to Stockholm, via Paris' (European Policy Centre, October 2008).

> controlling immigration to the detriment of an integration paradigm which seeks to respect the interests of TCNs and their families.[66]

The 2008 Council conclusions are similar in tone to the Pact, reiterating the idea that Member States should 'stress respect for the identities of the Member States and the European Union and for their fundamental values, such as human rights, freedom of opinion, democracy, tolerance, equality between men and women, and the compulsory schooling of children', and includes 'the promotion of the fundamental values of the European Union' as one of the principal themes to be explored under the CBPs.[67]

The Stockholm Programme does not specifically invoke the identities of Member States in the same way as the Pact and the 2008 Council Conclusions. However, the theme of the Programme is 'serving and protecting the citizens', raising the questions, first, who is considered to be a citizen and second, what are the implications of falling outside this category? It is clear from the Programme and surrounding documentation that 'citizens' in this context is intended to encompass EU citizens in the legal sense of those holding the nationality of a Member State – excluding TCNs.[68] From an integration perspective, this maintains and widens the gap between EU citizens and TCNs and legitimates legal and policy distinctions based on these categories. The full implications of the focus on the EU citizen in terms of the evolution of actions taken pursuant to the Stockholm Programme remain to be seen.

In addition, while the Stockholm Programme is more subtle, when it comes to promoting nationalism, than the Pact or the subsequent 2008 Council Conclusions, it confirms the integration/values nexus, stating that 'the interconnection between migration and integration remains crucial, inter alia with regard to the fundamental values of the Union'.[69] It provides some guidance as to what the 'values' of the EU are, including respect for the human person and human dignity and for the other rights set out in the Charter of Fundamental Rights and the European Convention on Human Rights;[70] values which are incompatible with crimes against humanity,

---

66 On the nationalist and intergovernmentalist leanings of the Pact, see Elspeth Guild and Sergio Carrera, 'The French Presidency's European Pact on Immigration and Asylum: Intergovernmentalism vs Europeanisation? Security vs Rights?' (CEPS Policy Brief, September 2008).

67 Council of the EU, *Conclusions of the Council and the Representatives of the Governments of the Member States on integration policies in the European Union*, Council Document 15251/08, Brussels, 6 November 2008, p. 4.

68 This is in spite of Carrera and Wiesbrock's convincing arguments in favour of a wider conception of EU citizenship which takes into account the increasingly citizenship-like elements of the status of TCNs in the EU, Sergio Carrera and Anja Wiesbrock, 'Whose European Citizenship in the Stockholm Programme? The Enactment of Citizenship by Third Country Nationals in the EU' (2010) 12(3) *EJML* 337.

69 Stockholm Programme, p. 59.

70 Stockholm Programme, p. 4.

genocide and war crimes;[71] democracy, human rights and the rule of law.[72] While the integration/values nexus contained in the EU approach to TCNs is often criticized, it must be acknowledged that these are quite basic values which would not seem to require cultural assimilation but rather a basic acceptance of universal human rights principles. In addition, the Programme specifically refers back to the fair and equal treatment objectives of the Tampere Programme in its consideration of the position of TCNs and the development of a more vigorous integration policy.[73]

The Stockholm Programme thus seems to blend the Tampere fair and equal treatment paradigm with the newer emphasis on the duty of migrants to adopt the values of the EU, as developed during the course of the Hague Programme. The Action Plan Implementing the Stockholm Programme gives further expression to this mixed paradigm, stating:

> The EU must strive for a uniform level of rights and obligations for legal immigrants comparable with that of European citizens. ... The integration of migrants will be further pursued, safeguarding their rights whilst also underlining their own responsibilities to integrate into the societies in which they live.[74]

In light of this mixed paradigm, the contention that the Tampere Programme is a 'forgotten vision', replaced by a neo-national conception of integration based on conditioned membership is over-stating the problem.[75] Rather, it seems that the newer idea of requiring immigrants to accept a minimum set of common values, which emanates from national integration discourses, has been grafted on to the fair and equal treatment paradigm. The endorsement of the values dimension of integration at EU level could be seen as legitimating Member States' national policies and practices of using integration as a mandatory process and as a tool of immigration law. However, there is as yet no evidence of a strong paradigm of integration as conditioned membership in EU policy itself.[76] The EU Framework on Integration enshrines a holistic approach to integration encompassing social, economic and political, as well as the cultural (or 'values') dimensions of

71 Ibid., p. 12.

72 Ibid., p. 82.

73 Ibid., p. 64.

74 Communication from the Commission to the European Parliament, the Council, the European Economic and Social Committee and the Committee of the Regions, *Delivering an area of freedom, security and justice for Europe's citizens: Action Plan Implementing the Stockholm Programme* (COM(2010) 171 final), p. 7.

75 Dora Kostakopoulou, Sergio Carrera and Moritz Jesse, note 34, p. 184.

76 For the argument that there has been a shift from equal treatment to conditioned membership at the European level, see Dora Kostakopoulou, Sergio Carrera and Moritz Jesse, note 34, p. 168.

integration. Member States may however choose to emphasize some of these dimensions over others.[77]

The mixed paradigm identified above is also reflected in the Commission's Report to the 2010 Ministerial Conference on Integration.[78] The key 'priorities' addressed in the Report include the promotion of common EU values and the development of European modules on integration. The three themes involved in the promotion of European values are fundamental rights, intercultural dialogue and active citizenship, with the aims of providing equal rights and equal opportunities for TCNs along with the participation of immigrants in formulating integration policy and in community and democratic life forming a common thread between the themes.[79] The promotion of 'values' –associated with the new negative framing of integration at national level as transposed to the European stage through the mechanisms of intergovernmental co-operation – is therefore married with the fair and equal treatment model enshrined in the early policy documentation.

The Renewed Common Agenda for Integration: Economic Participation and the Introduction of the Idea of a 'Three Way Process'

Following on from the Stockholm Programme, the Council's Conclusions of 2010 on 'Integration as a Driver for Development and Social Cohesion'[80] took another step back from the values paradigm expressed in the Pact on Immigration and the 2008 Conclusions, instead placing a greater emphasis on the importance of harnessing the potential of migration for building a competitive and sustainable economy. It specifically takes into account 'the economic and financial crisis, the subsequent recovery process', as well as 'EU 2020' with the aim of making sustainable growth possible by 'empowering people in inclusive societies'.[81] In addition to the well-worn concerns of trying to ensure diverse participation in the development of integration strategies and considering tools for the evaluation of integration policies and the development of indicators of integration, the Conclusions underline the importance of issues arising in the context of CBP 3 relating to employment and CBP 5 relating to education, and the 'management of diversity' in both employment and education, with a view to the 'appropriate

77 This is reinforced by the European Parliament's view, which has been to call for the Member States to implement the CBPs, without emphasizing some over others. European Parliament resolution of 2 April 2009 on problems and prospects concerning European Citizenship OJ C 137E/10, at para. 20.

78 European Commission (staff working document), 'The Consolidation of the EU Framework on integration – Report to the 2010 Ministerial Conference on Integration' (SEC(2010) 357 final).

79 Ibid., p. 4, 5 and 6 for example.

80 Conclusions of the Council and the Representatives of the Governments of the Member States on Integration as a Driver for Development and Social Cohesion, Council Document 9248/10 (Brussels, 4 May 2010).

81 Ibid., p. 3.

management of economic immigration' which is 'essential to increasing the EU's competitiveness'.[82]

The 2010 Council Conclusions called on the Commission to develop a new European agenda on integration and, in 2011, an opportunity to evaluate the policy actions undertaken within the framework on integration arose with the presentation of this new common agenda. The new agenda is framed not just by the Stockholm Programme and the Lisbon Treaty but also by the Europe 2020 strategy, which 'highlights the need to design a new agenda for migrant's integration to enable them to take full advantage of their potential' and the contribution of migration to the vitality and competitiveness of the EU,[83] and the renewed Global Approach to Migration and Mobility, which sets out the policy framework for the EU's relations with all non-EU countries.[84] According to the Commission, all actions presented in the 2005 Common Agenda for Integration have been completed, leaving it free to identify new approaches and areas of action.[85] While acknowledging that despite the completion of the previous agenda, the social, economic and political context has changed and not all integration measures have been successful in meeting their objectives, the Commission takes a side swipe at migrants in noting that 'Integration policies also require the will and commitment of migrants to be part of the society that receives them'.[86] However, the 'pressing challenges' identified comprise a socially conscious list and include low employment levels; rising unemployment and 'overqualification'; increasing risks of social exclusion; gaps in educational achievement; and public concerns with the lack of integration of migrants.[87]

The document takes a holistic approach to the question of integration, conceiving it in terms of the creation of favourable conditions for migrants' economic, social, cultural and political participation, 'to realize the potential of migration'.[88] The participative focus of the agenda is clear in the selection of the key areas of focus for the agenda, which include 'Integration through participation' and 'More action at local level'. Reference to values is largely avoided in the agenda, which hones in on enhancing the socio-economic contribution of migrants through acquiring

82 Ibid., p. 5.

83 For detailed information on the Europe 20/20 strategy, see http://ec.europa.eu/europe2020/index_en.htm.

84 Communication from the Commission to the European Parliament, the Council, the European Economic and Social Committee and the Committee of the Regions, *The Global Approach to Migration and Mobility* (COM(2011) 743 final) ('Global Approach to Migration').

85 Communication from the Commission to the European Parliament, the Council, the European Economic and Social Committee and the Committee of the Regions, *European Agenda for the Integration of Third-Country Nationals* (COM(2011) 455 final) ('2011 Integration Agenda').

86 2011 Integration Agenda, p. 2.

87 2011 Integration Agenda, p. 3.

88 Ibid.

language knowledge and participation in the labour market, as well as 'rights and obligations: ensuring equal treatment and a sense of belonging'.[89]

Despite these positive aspects of the renewed agenda for integration, the move away from a 'values' paradigm of integration and the spectre of integration as conditioned membership is accompanied by new, potentially negative developments. A central new plank of the renewed agenda is the idea of the shift from a 'two-way process' of integration to a 'three-way process', involving the migrant's country of origin.[90] The Commission envisages a three-pronged role for the country of origin, comprising pre-departure measures in support of integration; supporting the migrant while in the EU; and to prepare the migrant's temporary or definitive return with acquired experience and knowledge.[91] The Commission's recommendation in this regard is that Member States and countries of origin should ensure 'pre-departure support to migrants in order to facilitate integration to be part of the dialogue and co-operation frameworks between the EU and partner countries. A key element in this regard is to improve methods for recognition of the migrant's qualifications and skills'.[92] While this proposed co-operation fits with the EU's aim to prioritize dialogue and co-operation with partner countries in the EU neighbourhood and farther afield,[93] this could signify the further dilution of individual Member State's responsibilities in terms of integration. While the period 2005–2010 saw a shift towards putting the responsibility for integration onto the migrant, this may now extend to the country of origin. In particular, the reference to pre-departure measures echoes the design of the civic integration models, with their focus on 'Integration Abroad', which have been subject to extensive criticism (as outlined in chapters 2 and 3). Although the agenda suggests that the pre-departure measures are intended to encompass elements such as language tuition and vocational training, as well as pre-departure information, this element of the agenda could result in the EU validation and legitimation of restrictive national practices relating to pre-departure integration. In addition, it is difficult to see how the idea of pre-departure integration and a 'three-way process' fits with the Common Basic Principles for Integration.

The other main way in which the agenda falls short is in respect of its proposed actions for 'The Way Forward', which do not connect back to the broad inclusive statements and actions proposed in the rest of the document. Reflecting the limited nature of the remit of the EU in co-ordinating integration matters, it does not propose any measures for the EU to take in respect of the identified key areas of action. Instead, it confirms that the trend of co-operation through exchange of practices and the development benchmarking and indicators will be continued and further developed, *inter alia*, through the further use and co-ordination of existing

89 2011 Integration Agenda, p. 7.

90 2011 Integration Agenda, p. 11.

91 2011 Integration Agenda, p. 10.

92 2011 Integration Agenda, p. 11.

93 Global Approach to Migration, p. 21.

European platforms such as the National Contact Points, the European Website on Integration and the European Integration Forum.[94]

The further development of joint practices and developing a 'flexible European toolbox', including European modules on integration, raises important issues relating to the scope and nature of such practices and modules. The Commission's Report to the 2010 Ministerial Conference confirmed that the technical seminars which produced the Handbooks will form the basis for this new instrument of co-operation. It was argued above that the Handbooks represent the sharing of information by national policymakers in a rather uncritical manner. The Commission has also selected certain projects focussing on various aspects of integration, which include research on 'integration and naturalization tests'. There would seem to be a real risk therefore that these modules would contain elements which would support national restrictive and coercive conceptions of integration, which contradict the EU's own basic principle of a two-way definition of integration.

The three draft European modules on migrant integration, published by the Commission in 2011, focus on introductory and language courses; 'strong commitment by the receiving society'; and active civil and political participation of immigrants, respectively.[95] The proposed modules deal mainly with practical issues such as the provision of language courses and ways to enhance political participation, rather than on culture and values. Although the draft modules do not expressly embrace the idea of using the modules in a mandatory fashion, the 'incentives structures' component of the 'introductory and language courses' module does not rule out the possibility of introducing fines and sanctions as 'incentives' for completing such courses, as already employed in certain Member States.[96] More generally, the focus on such 'modules' provides support for a conception of integration as achieved through a finite programme, course or module, undertaken by the immigrant. This further erodes long-term, social inclusion visions of integration that involve both the immigrant and the host society.

Finally, the Common Agenda emphasizes the importance of the common European 'indicators' which have been identified in the areas of employment, education, social inclusion and active citizenship.[97] However, the method by which such indicators are identified and the value of developing 'indicators' of integration remain contested issues.[98] Overall, the significant conceptual difficulties and

94 Stockholm Programme, p. 65.

95 European Commission, 'European Draft Modules on Migrant Integration' (9 July 2011).

96 Ibid., pp. 20–21.

97 See Eurostat, 'Indicators of Immigrant Integration, A Pilot Study' (*Methodologies and Working Papers*, 2011).

98 See, for example, Anja Wiesbrock, 'The Integration of Immigrants in Sweden: A Model for the European Union?' (2011) 49(4) *International Migration* 48; Sergio Carrera,

definitional issues involved in such benchmarking have not been addressed by the Commission, which did not take the opportunity provided by the elaboration of the renewed agenda to critically reflect on the use of indicators and benchmarking in the context of integration. In addition, the difficulty mentioned in the previous paragraph in relation to the spread of national, restrictive integration discourses through such forms of co-operation remains wholly unaddressed.

The EU Framework on Integration: A Largely Inclusive, Two-Way Integration Paradigm

The soft law instruments discussed above represent an evolving EU policy on integration. As regards the conceptual foundations of this integration policy, despite criticism of the CBPs dealing with migrants' responsibilities in the integration process,[99] on the whole the relevant instruments propose an inclusive and participatory form of integration centred on the idea of a positive two-way process involving input from both immigrants and members of the host society. It is certainly arguable that the policy documentation is becoming more restrictive. Increasingly prevalent references to the duties of the migrant in the integration process and the onus on the migrant to adopt the 'fundamental values' of the EU as well as those of the Member States can be seen as representing a shift away from the Tampere paradigm of integration as fair and equal treatment towards a model which requires the individual migrant to remake him or herself to resemble an idealized version of existing members of the imagined political community. This is particularly the case in the policy documents emanating from the Council and the Ministerial Conferences, and in the European Pact on Asylum and Immigration, examined above. While the most recent policy documents seem to have retreated from this 'values' paradigm, the idea of a 'three-way process' of integration could be seen as another means by which states can seek to avoid their duties in the integration process, shifting the focus to a third country as well as on to individual migrants. This contrasts with the emphasis of the UN human rights treaty monitoring bodies on state responsibility for ensuring that the conditions for integration are established.

Despite these developments, overall it must be conceded that the Framework on Integration, by and large, represents an attempt to aid policymakers in the construction of two-way, holistic integration policies. The policy documentation

---

Benchmarking Integration in the EU: Analyzing the Debate and Moving it Forward, note 12; Han Entzinger and Renske Biezeveld, *Benchmarking in immigrant integration* (Rotterdam: European Research Centre on Migration and Ethnic Relations, 2003) (for the European Commission); Kingsbury, Davis, Fisher, and Merry (eds), *Governance by Indicators: Global Power through Classification and Rankings* (Oxford University Press, 2012).

99 Sergio Carrera, *Benchmarking Integration*, note 12, p. 15.

does not in itself conceive of integration as a mandatory tool of immigration law or advocate the use of integration 'measures' or 'conditions' (although it does seem to accept the legitimacy of these measures and conditions in some parts). The ultimate aims of integration as the achievement of equal opportunities and participation are consistently emphasized. There has also been a move towards trying to include civil society and other representative voices in the co-ordination of integration policy.[100] Thus, while elements of different paradigms co-exist within the policy framework, overall a broad-based and inclusive paradigm predominates, which resembles in many respects the working definition of integration set out in the second chapter of this book.

In the final analysis, whether or not the policy instruments examined above help to promote an inclusive and human rights-based concept of integration within the EU, the real test for the EU Framework on Integration is whether it can be said to inform the content of binding legislative measures in the field of immigration law, which probably 'have more influence on the actual integration on the societies of member states than the handbooks, lists of good practices, integration websites or National Contact Points figuring in the most recent EU documents on integration policy'.[101] Is the broadly positive, two-way approach to integration envisaged in the Framework translated into binding legal measures? In particular, are the aspirations contained in the Common Basic Principles translated into real measures to promote integration or are they mainly symbolic? The next section will examine the assertion that:

> The Common Basic Principles are complementary to and in full synergy with the Community legislative instruments on the admission and stay of legally residing third-country nationals concerning family reunion and long term residents ...[102]

Integration of TCNs in EU Immigration and Asylum Law

The links between immigration law and integration policy have been consistently emphasized by the Commission and the Council. The Third Report on Migration, for example, notes that the link between legal migration policies and integration strategies needs to be reinforced, and that consolidating the legal framework for the conditions of entry and stay of TCNs is essential to the development of a

---

100 Stockholm Programme, p. 65.

101 Kees Groenendijk, 'Integration Policy and Community Law', in Sergio Carrera (ed.), *The Nexus Between Immigration, Integration and Citizenship in the EU* (CEPS, 2006), 7, p. 8.

102 Council Decision 2007/435/EC of 25 June 2007 establishing the European Fund for the Integration of third-country nationals for the period 2007 to 2013 as part of the General Programme 'Solidarity and Management of Migration Flows', OJ L 168/18.

coherent EU approach to integration.[103] While immigration law measures are not necessarily drafted with the specific intention of addressing integration or creating an immigrant 'other', that is often their effect. EU immigration law measures reveal much about the position of TCNs in the EU legal order and have a powerful impact on the process of integration. Six main Directives have been adopted to date in the field of immigration to the EU: Directive 2003/86/EC on the right to family reunification;[104] Directive 2003/109/EC on a long-term resident status for third-country nationals who have legally resided for five years in the territory of a Member State;[105] Directive 2004/114 on the conditions of admission of third-country nationals for the purposes of study, pupil exchange, unremunerated training or voluntary service;[106] Directive 2005/71 for the facilitation of the admission of researchers into the EU;[107] Directive 2009/50/EC on the conditions of entry and residence of third-country nationals for the purposes of highly qualified employment;[108] and Directive 2011/98/EU on a single application procedure for a single permit for third-country nationals to reside and work in the territory of a Member State and on a common set of rights for third-country workers legally residing in a Member State.[109] In terms of asylum law, the centrepiece of the Common European Asylum System is Directive 2004/83/EC of 29 April 2004 on minimum standards for the qualification and status of third-country nationals or stateless persons as refugees or as persons who otherwise need international protection and the content of the protection granted.[110]

This part of the chapter will begin by assessing two of these measures with close links to integration: the Family Reunification Directive (FRD) and the Long-Term Residents Directive (LTRD). It should be noted that Ireland and the UK opted out of both these Directives and are not therefore bound by their terms.[111] Nevertheless, an examination of these Directives is central to understanding the approach to integration at the EU level. It will be argued that while the FRD and LTRD formed part of the Tampere Programme's drive towards approximating the statuses of EU citizens and TCNs, the content of the Directives and the concept of integration contained within them mutated significantly during the course of Council negotiations, with the end result that the meaning and function of the

103 *Third Annual Report*, note 47.

104 'The Family Reunification Directive', or 'FRD'.

105 'The Long-Term Residents Directive', or 'LTRD'.

106 'The Students Directive'.

107 'The Researchers Directive'.

108 'The Blue Card Directive'.

109 'The Single Permit Directive'.

110 'The Qualification Directive'.

111 The UK and Ireland secured an opt-out from the entire Title IV EC with the 'Protocol on the position of the United Kingdom and Ireland' annexed to the Treaty of Amsterdam (Protocol 4 annexed to the Treaty of Amsterdam). Both have the possibility to opt in to the adoption of any measure adopted under Title IV within three months of a new proposal (Article 3 of the Protocol).

concept of integration contained in these directives diverges from the way it is conceived in the Tampere Programme.[112] The brief examination of these two Directives reveals a gap between the holistic vision of integration contained in the Common Basic Principles and Framework on Integration, on the one hand, and the actual legally binding acts being produced by the EU institutions, on the other. The Students, Researchers and Blue Card Directives (of which Ireland opted in to the Researchers Directive and the UK did not opt in to any) will then be briefly touched on to illustrate that, in contrast to the position under the FRD and LTRD, the fair and equal treatment paradigm of integration has been employed in practice in relation to these special categories of TCN. Finally, the legal concept of integration in the context of refugees and beneficiaries of subsidiary protection will be addressed, by looking first at the relevant provisions of the Qualification Directive and then the position of refugees and beneficiaries of subsidiary protection under the general immigration law measures.

It will be seen that, in terms of integration, the broad legal category of TCNs is split in a dichotomy between beneficiaries of international protection and economic migrants. Refugees occupy a privileged position in relation to access to integration-related rights, as they do in international law and also in most domestic legal systems. Beneficiaries of subsidiary protection similarly enjoy privileged treatment in comparison to other TCNs. Within the category of economic migrants, certain sub-categories benefit from legal rules at EU level which grant them near-equality with nationals of Member States in certain areas. Overall, it will be shown that the legally binding measures relating to integration contain elements of different paradigms. However, the dominant vision of integration contained in the immigration law framework contrasts with that contained in the policy instruments as set out above. The EU legitimates and reinforces discriminatory practices of Member States by utilizing the concepts of integration 'conditions' and 'measures' in its legislation, and EU law's differentiation between different categories of TCNs weakens the position of TCNs as a group. Overall, the transformative potential of EU law in the integration sphere is not realized in the case of TCN migrants.

Notwithstanding these serious deficiencies, recent case law of the Court of Justice of the European Union shows that the Court considers the primary objective of the LTRD, in particular, to be 'the integration of third-country nationals who are settled on a long-term basis in the Member States';[113] and furthermore that the directive 'seeks, by granting the status of long-term resident to such third-country nationals, to approximate the legal status of third-country nationals to that of Member States' nationals'.[114] The CJEU is 'pushing back' against attempts by states to limit the impact of the FRD and LTRD, and is using an inclusive, 'fair and

112 See Sergio Carrera, *Benchmarking Integration*, note 12, p. 9.

113 Case 502/10 *State Secretary Van Justitie v Singh* (Judgment of the CJEU of 18 October 2012), para. 45.

114 Ibid.

equal treatment' concept of integration to do so. National visions of integration, it seems, will not be permitted to usurp the primary integrative function of these directives. While, on this basis, this jurisprudence is welcome, it introduces a further contradiction in the concepts of integration at work within the EU law framework.

Integration as a Mandatory Process in the Family Reunification and Long-Term Residents Directives[115]

The Family Reunification Directive

Family reunification is a key dimension of integration, as pointed out in Chapter 3.[116] As the FRD itself states: 'Family reunification is a necessary way of making family life possible. It helps to create sociocultural stability facilitating the integration of third-country nationals in the Member State, which also serves to promote economic and social cohesion'.[117] It is also a human rights issue, as is clear from the analysis of the international legal framework for integration contained in the previous chapters.[118] However, as mentioned in Chapter 3, for states, a tension arises between the human rights dimension of family reunification and its significance as an immigration issue. This tension underlies the FRD and gives rise to the contradictory approaches contained within the Directive which will be identified below.

The Amsterdam Treaty provided in Articles 63(3) and (4) for the power to adopt measures in respect of TCNs including family reunification. The Directive represents an attempt to realize the fair and near-equal treatment goals set by the Tampere Council.[119] The initial proposal for the Directive was made by the Commission in 1999,[120] and, after two revised proposals were presented,[121] the Directive was finally adopted in 2003. It codifies the right to family reunion, defines who can apply for family reunification, sets out the conditions for admission, gives a certain level of protection against expulsion and provides family members with certain rights of access to the labour market, education and equal treatment. The

115 See generally, the detailed analysis contained in Sergio Carrera, *In Search of the Perfect Citizen*, note 12, p. 102.

116 On the interaction of family reunification and integration, see 9.1.

117 Family Reunification Directive, at Recital 4.

118 In addition to the discussions in the previous chapter, see Ryszard Cholewinski, 'Family Reunification and Conditions Placed on Family Members: Dismantling a Fundamental Human Right' (2002) *EJML* 271.

119 See the Family Reunification Directive, at Recital 3.

120 Proposal for a Council Directive on the right to family reunification OJ C 116 E/66.

121 Revised proposals for a Council Directive on the right to family reunification, OJ C 62 E/99 and OJ C 203 E/136.

provisions of the Directive have been analysed in detail elsewhere[122] and will not be re-examined here. It is sufficient for present purposes simply to observe that the scope and the substance of the Directive were watered down in the course of the legislative process and the conditions for admission expanded, such that the final Directive 'places many objects of a variety of different types in the place of (third-country nationals') family reunification',[123] and 'primarily serves as a means to preserve Member States' interest'.[124] The analysis here will be limited to the approach (or indeed, approaches) to integration embodied in the Directive.

As a measure in itself, the Directive is a positive step for integration, providing TCN immigrants with an EU law basis for the enjoyment of family life within the EU, thus bringing their status closer to that of EU citizens; and a legal status for their family members encompassing a level of access to the institutions of the host society including the labour market and the education system. A positive, participatory concept of integration, reflecting that contained in the policy framework for integration, is contained in the numerous references to integration in the preamble recitals. Recital 3 refers to the Tampere objective of an integration policy linked to rights comparable to those of EU citizens; Recital 4 recognizes that family reunification facilitates integration by providing socio-cultural stability and Recital 15 underlines that the integration of family members must be promoted by granting them a status independent of that of the sponsor, and access to education, employment and vocational training.

However, other references to integration inserted by the Member States during the course of the legislative process espouse a contradictory vision of the concept of integration, its meaning and function. The last subparagraph of Article 4(1) allows Member States the possibility of derogating from the general obligation to authorize the entry and residence of minor children, providing that Member States may verify that children over the age of 12 travelling independently meet a condition for integration laid down in national legislation. This provision was inserted at the insistence of Austria, Germany and the Netherlands in the late stages of the negotiating process.[125] Recital 12 provides the 'justification' for this provision, stating that it is 'intended to reflect the children's capacity for integration at early ages and shall ensure that they acquire the necessary education and language skills in school'. The notion of integration is therefore turned on its head and used not as a means of inclusion, but as a potential barrier to family

122 See, for example, Helen Oosterom-Staples, 'The Family Reunification Directive: A Tool Preserving Member State Interest or Conducive to Family Unity', in Anneliese Baldaccini, Elspeth Guild and Helen Toner (eds), *Whose Freedom, Security and Justice? EU Immigration and Asylum Law and Policy* (Hart Publishing, 2007), p. 234. See also Elspeth Guild, *The Legal Elements of European Identity: EU Citizenship and Migration Law* (Kluwer Law International, 2004), p. 119.

123 Elspeth Guild, *The Legal Elements of European Identity*, ibid., p. 123.

124 Helen Oosterom-Staples, note 122, p. 487.

125 See Kees Groenendijk, 'Legal Concepts of Integration in EU Migration Law' (2004) 6 *EJML* 111.

reunification. In addition, the rationale for the provision seems to be assimilationist in nature: the younger a person is, the easier it will be to make them 'the same' as members of the host society.

This subparagraph of Article 4(1) formed one of the bases for the annulment procedure initiated against the Council by the European Parliament.[126] In its decision upholding the validity of the Directive, the Court of Justice (CJEU) rejected the Parliament's arguments that the provision violated international law, particularly the ECHR and the UN Convention on the Rights of the Child (CRC). It found that the relevant international instruments, while stressing the importance of the best interests of the child, did not create an individual right for family members to enter the territory of a State. Furthermore, the Court emphasized that these international instruments leave a margin of appreciation to states when assessing an application for family reunification. The Court seemed to approach the issue from the viewpoint that the FRD, overall, constitutes a specific restriction of this margin of appreciation of Member States, and that the final subparagraph of Article 4(1) represents one area in which the Member States' margin of appreciation in respect of family reunification under international law remains untouched.[127] The Court also considered whether the integration condition and age limitation violated the right to respect for family life contained in Article 8 ECHR, and concluded that it did not, finding that integration can in itself constitute a 'legitimate aim' for a restriction of right to family life under Article 8(2) ECHR, and accepting the Council's logic that the provision is intended 'to reflect the children's capacity for integration at early ages and is to ensure that they acquire the necessary education and language skills in school'.[128] Importantly, the Court found that integration conditions do not violate the ECHR or the CRC *per se*. Furthermore, it held that integration could be a valid rationale for the imposition by a Member State of a residence condition and/or a waiting period prior to family reunification, as is permitted under Article 8 of the FRD.[129]

126 Case C-540/03 *European Parliament v Council* [2006] ECR I-5769. Also challenged were Article 4(6) which permits Member States to refuse reunification to children over the age of fifteen in certain circumstances, and Article 8, which allows a waiting period of two or three years for family reunification, depending on the circumstances. For commentary on this decision, see Eleanor Drywood, 'Giving with One Hand, Taking with the Other: Fundamental Rights, Children and the Family Reunification Decision' (2007) 32(3) *ELRev* 396; Martin, 'Comments on *European Council v Parliament* (2007) 9(1) *EJML* 148; and Rick Lawson 'Family Reunification and the Union's Charter of Fundamental Rights, Judgment of 27 June 2006, Case 540/03' (2007) 3 *European Constitutional Law Review* 324.

127 Case C-540/03 *European Parliament v Council* [2006] ECR I-5769, at para. 60.

128 Case C-540/03 *European Parliament v Council* [2006] ECR I-5769, at para. 67.

129 The Court found that the provision 'does not have the effect of precluding family reunification, but preserves a limited margin of appreciation for Member States by permitting them to make sure that family reunification will take place in favourable conditions, after the sponsor has been residing in the host State for a period sufficiently long

Nonetheless, this seminal judgment recognized the binding effect of the ECHR, the CRC (for the first time) and other international human rights norms in EU law through the general principles of EU law and underlines the limits that this places on Member States' discretion in using derogations contained in EU immigration law. On this basis, the Court laid down a minimum standard in respect of the concept of integration which may be employed by Member States in determining the nature of integration conditions, holding that:

> The fact that the concept of integration is not defined cannot be interpreted as authorising the Member States to employ that concept in a manner contrary to general principles of Community law, in particular to fundamental rights. The Member States which wish to make use of the derogation cannot employ an unspecified concept of integration, but must apply the condition for integration provided for by their legislation existing on the date of implementation of the Directive ...[130]

The Court also ruled that any integration condition should have, in light of recital 12 of the FRD, the general objective of facilitating integration by making family life possible through reunification. The Court thus laid down a minimum standard for integration conditions used by Member States in implementing the FRD. The Court's concept of integration in this context was rooted in the two-way inclusive conception expressed in the preamble of the FRD rather than in a vision of integration as a tool of immigration control. This vision is also evident in the subsequent judgments of the CJEU in *Chakroun*[131] and *O, S and Maahanmuuttovirasto*,[132] which confirmed that authorization of family reunification is the rule under the Directive and that derogations contained therein must be interpreted strictly, avoiding any undermining of the objective and effectiveness of that Directive.

Despite these positive aspects, the judgment of the Court in *Parliament v Council* also highlights the gap between the aspirational concept of integration presented within the Framework on Integration and the actual legal constraints on Member States' adoption of binding measures connected with integration. In the view of the CJEU, legally binding integration measures are ultimately constrained only by a minimalist obligation to respect fundamental rights and international law as filtered into the EU legal order through the general principles of European law, in addition to the obligation not to deprive the Directive of its *effet utile* (as highlighted in *Chakroun* and *O, S and Maahanmuuttovirasto*). In addition, while the CJEU's conclusion that integration conditions do not of themselves necessarily

---

for it to be assumed that the family members will settle down well and display a certain level of integration' (para. 98).

130 Case C-540/03 *European Parliament v Council* [2006] ECR I-5769, para. 70.

131 Case C-578/08 *Chakroun* [2010] ECR I-0000.

132 Cases C-356/11 and C-357/11 *O, S and Maahanmuuttovirasto* (Judgment of 6 December 2012).

constitute an infringement of the right to family and private life contained in Article 8 ECHR is probably correct, in light of the wide margin of appreciation afforded to states in respect of immigration control, the endorsement of the use of integration conditions and measures does not sit well with the European Court of Human Rights' normative development of integration in the sense of a barrier to deportation, as traced in the previous chapter. The CJEU's analysis of Article 4(1) certainly does not constitute a radical approach to integration or to the legal boundaries of Member State approaches to integration.

In addition to Article 4(1), a second express reference to integration in the body of the FRD is contained in Article 4(5). Article 4(5) relates to restrictions which Member States may place on the admission of spouses. It states:

> In order to ensure better integration and to prevent forced marriages Member States may require the sponsor and his/her spouse to be of a minimum age, and at maximum 21 years, before the spouse is able to join him/her.

It is difficult to see the logic behind this provision. First, ensuring integration and preventing forced marriages are surely separate issues and it is not clear why they are put together in this way to justify age restrictions for the admission and residence of spouses. It is also difficult to see how the age of the spouse could impact on their ability to integrate. As Groenendijk observes, the reasoning here appears to be diametrically opposed to that underlying Article 4(1).[133] While children are expected to integrate better when they are younger, spouses are expected to integrate better when they are older. This internal inconsistency adds to the incoherency of the approach to integration contained in the Directive.

Finally, Article 7(2) allows Member States to require TCNs to comply with integration measures, without indicating the types of measures with which compliance might be required. The distinction between integration 'conditions' and integration 'measures' is not altogether clear from the text, although it seems that integration 'measures' are probably imposed when family reunification has already been granted rather than as a condition of family reunification imposed prior to the admission of the family migrant(s). The provision is silent on the nature of the sanctions which could be imposed for failure to comply with integration measures. Although not as draconian as the integration 'conditions' allowed by Article 4(1), this provision eschews the central idea put forward in the soft law instruments discussed above of a holistic approach to integration based on participation and co-operation, in favour of a conception of integration as a condition which may be imposed by Member States. This places the onus of integration solely on the migrant, in contrast to the soft law instruments.

---

133 Kees Groenendijk, 'Legal Concepts of Integration in EU Migration Law', note 125, p. 119. This contradiction is also criticized by Dora Kostakopoulou, Sergio Carrera and Moritz Jesse, note 34, p. 180.

The concept of integration is used as an instrument of exclusion in the FRD, contrary to the dominant vision of integration as set out in the soft policy mechanisms as discussed above. This leads to the incongruous situation whereby a legal instrument which is intended, among other things, to facilitate the integration of TCNs also allows for the use of the concept of integration as a barrier to their families' access to the EU. The appearance of these conflicting ideas of integration renders the underlying approach to integration incoherent and unsatisfactory. Guild goes further than this, suggesting that:

> Identity politics based on integration are used to justify punish third country nationals for having foreign family members. Implicit is the argument that they should abandon their foreign identities (and families) and start again.[134]

While this statement may seem extreme, it must be acknowledged that the substantive provisions on integration in the FRD come close to presenting at best an assimilationist model whereby diversity is rejected and TCNs must 'fit in'(in a way which the Member State is free to define) or stay out, and at worst is an exclusionary model. Under the FRD, integration becomes a mechanism by which Member States can retain a degree of control over immigration conditions.[135] It is certainly fair to say that Member States' interests in maintaining control of immigration, and the restrictive attitude of some states to the concept of integration, prevailed over the holistic vision of integration contained in the Framework on Integration.

Numerous problems with the application of the Directive, illustrating Member States' diverse approaches to family reunification and their reluctance to concede discretion in this sphere, are set out in the Commission's Report on its implementation, which states that 'the harmonisation of national legislation on family reunification remains rather limited', and that 'in certain cases, the transposition or the application of the directive has been incorrect'.[136] While the Report finds that in practice only a few Member States have introduced integration conditions,[137] this does not detract from the significance of the relevant provisions in terms of their introduction of the concept of integration as a mandatory process of immigration law into EU law. In its Green Paper of 2011, the Commission reminded Member States that in implementing the FRD, its objective to determine the conditions for the exercise of the right to family reunification and to facilitate the

---

134 See Elspeth Guild, *The Legal Elements of European Identity*, note 122, p. 123.

135 Report from the Commission to the European Parliament and the Council on the application of Directive 2003/86/EC on the Right to Family Reunification, 9 October 2008, COM (2008) 610 final (hereinafter, 'FRD Report'). On the implementation of the FRD in Sweden, Germany, Denmark and the Netherlands, see Anja Wiesbrock, *Legal Migration to the European Union*, note 4, p. 363.

136 FRD Report, p. 15.

137 FRD Report, p. 7.

integration of TCNs meeting the conditions should be kept in mind.[138] Integration is thus clearly conceived of by the Commission in terms of the fair and equal treatment paradigm, encompassing the facilitation of family reunification. While the Green Paper recognizes that, in its present form, the FRD itself does not give any precise indication what 'integration measures' should entail and how should they be applied, it reiterates that the admissibility of such measures depends on whether they serve the purpose of facilitating integration and whether they respect the principles of proportionality and of subsidiarity.[139] This reaffirms the view that Member States may not simply impose national approaches of integration which are at variance with the independent conception of integration at work in the Directive as a whole.

The Green Paper asked Member States to give their views on whether integration measures used by them efficiently serve the purpose of integration and whether they would consider it useful to further define these measures at EU level. In addition, it asked whether Member States would recommend pre-entry measures and, if so, how safeguards could be introduced in order to ensure that they do not *de facto* lead to undue barriers to family reunification (such as disproportionate fees or requirements) and take into account individual circumstances such as age, illiteracy, disability, educational level. This fits with the approach of the CJEU that pre-entry measures and integration conditions are not illegal and discriminatory *per se* but that they must not result in disproportionate difficulties in accessing the rights contained in the FRD. In responding to the Green Paper, Member States presented a wide variety of views on integration measures.[140] Tellingly, however, most Member States who answered opposed any definition of integration measures, and any limits placed on countries' ability to introduce such measures.[141]

The Long-Term Residents Directive

The acquisition of a secure legal status and equality of treatment are often characterized as two of the prerequisites for successful integration,[142] as acknowledged in the Tampere Programme. The LTRD is an effort to fulfil this

138 Green Paper on the right to family reunification of third-country nationals living in the European Union (Directive 2003/86/EC) Brussels, 15.11.2011 COM(2011) 735 final.

139 The Green Paper states (p. 4) that 'Decisions on the application for family reunification in relation to passing tests should take into account whether there are available facilities (translated materials, courses) to prepare for them and whether they are accessible (location, fees). Specific individual circumstances (such as proven illiteracy, medical conditions) should also be taken into account'.

140 European Commission, Summary of Stakeholder Responses to the green Paper on the Right to Family Reunification of Third-Country Nationals (May 2012), p. 11.

141 Ibid.

142 See, for example, Jan Niessen, 'Integration, Citizenship and the Benchmarking of Integration in the EU', in Sergio Carrerra (ed.), *The Nexus between Immigration, Integration and Citizenship in the EU* (CEPS, 2006); Kees Groenendijk, 'Legal Concepts of Integration

mandate and the rationale for the Directive is therefore closely linked to integration. As the preamble indicates:

> In order to constitute a genuine instrument for the integration of long-term residents into the society in which they live, long-term residents should enjoy equality of treatment with citizens of the Member State in a wide range of economic and social matters, under the relevant conditions defined by this Directive.[143]

The Directive, the background and provisions of which have been discussed in detail elsewhere,[144] has three key dimensions. First, TCNs who have legally resided in a Member State for five years are entitled to a special secure residence status, which can only be withdrawn on certain limited grounds.[145] Secondly, persons with this status are entitled to equal treatment as nationals in a range of areas such as employment, education, social security, tax advantages and freedom of association (this principle of equal treatment is subject however to the possibility of significant derogations in a number of areas).[146] Finally, TCNs are granted a conditional right to free movement within the EU.[147] As with the FRD, the adoption of the LTRD in itself represents an improvement on the legal position of TCNs residing in the EU. The Directive strengthens the position of TCNs in EU law and from an integration perspective, the creation of a secure status which brings TCNs closer to the privileged status enjoyed by citizens of Member States (particularly as regards the right to free movement) reflects a positive concept of integration involving a process of the legal and social inclusion of immigrants in the structures of the host society.

However, as with the FRD, the inclusive concept of integration underlying the LTRD was manipulated in the course of the negotiating process by Member

---

in EU Migration Law', note 125; and Thomas Gross, 'Integration of Immigrants: The Perspective of European Community Law' (2005) 7 *EJML* 145.

143 Recital 12. Recital 4 also points out that '(t)he integration of third-country nationals who are long-term residents in the Member States is a key element in promoting economic and social cohesion, a fundamental objective of the Community stated in the Treaty'.

144 See, for example, Kees Groenendijk, 'The Long-Term Residents Directive', in Anneliese Baldaccini, Elspeth Guild and Helen Toner, *Whose Freedom, Security and Justice? EU Immigration and Asylum Law and Policy* (Hart Publishing, 2007), p. 429; Sonja Boelaert-Suominen, 'Non-EU Nationals and Council Directive 2003/109/EC on the Status of Third-Country Nationals who are Long-Term Residents: Five Paces Forward and Possibly Three Paces Back' (2005) *CMLR* 42; Louise Halleskov, 'The Long-Term Residents Directive: A Fulfilment of the Tampere Objective of Near-Equality?' (2005) 7(2) *EJML* 181.

145 See Long-Term Residents Directive, Articles 4–10.

146 Long-Term Residents Directive, Article 11.

147 Long-Term Residents Directive, Chapter III: Residence in other Member States.

States attempting to maintain a degree of control over the treatment of TCNs. The clause on integration laid down in Article 5(2), which was inserted primarily as a result of strong advocacy on the part of Germany, Austria and Holland,[148] provides a good example of this.[149] Article 5(2) provides that as one of the conditions for acquiring long-term resident status, 'Member States may require TCNs to comply with integration conditions, in accordance with national law'. No definition of an 'integration condition' is provided and no limitations are set on the extent or nature of the conditions which Member States may set.[150] Thus, in a similar manner to Article 4(1) of the FRD, integration is inverted and used as an instrument of exclusion and assimilation. The assimilatory aim of such integration conditions is even clearer here than in the case of Article 4(1), as in the case of the LTRD, the TCN has already legally resided in the Member States for five years, and therefore must have attained a certain level of integration in the host society already. Integration is not to be measured simply through residence and participation in the host society for a period of time, implying that cultural integration is also required.

Integration 'measures' also feature in the LTRD as a condition that may be placed on long-term resident TCNs' right to free movement within the EU once long-term resident status has been obtained. Article 15(3) provides that 'Member States may require third-country nationals to comply with integration measures, in accordance with national law'. Such integration 'measures' cannot, however, be applied where the TCN concerned has already been required to comply with integration conditions in order to be granted long-term resident status, in accordance with the provisions of Article 5(2).[151] This at least removes the risk of TCNs being required to undergo multiple integration tests and measures. Finally, even if the person has passed integration conditions in the first Member State (in which they obtained long-term resident status), they may still be required to attend language courses in the second Member State. Overall, Article 15(3) could constitute a significant obstacle to the free movement of long-term residents and it stands in stark contrast to the rights of free movement afforded to EU nationals. This undermines the objective of the Directive as a whole to ensure that long-term residents enjoy rights which are 'as near as possible' to those of EU citizens.

In summary, the above analysis reveals a tension between the overall aims of the Directive and the limitations contained in its specific provisions. In this Directive, as well as in the FRD, an undefined concept of integration is inserted by

---

148 Kees Groenendijk, 'Legal Concepts of Integration in EU Migration Law', note 125, p. 120.

149 The provision has been described as the 'Achilles heel' of the Directive. Sonja Boelaert-Suominen, note 138, p. 1023 and Kees Groenendijk, 'The Long-Term Residents Directive', note 144, p. 442.

150 For an analysis of the way in which this has been implemented in Germany, the Netherlands, Sweden and Denmark, see Anja Wiesbrock, *Legal Migration to the European Union*, note 4, p. 343.

151 Article 15(3), second subparagraph.

Member States as a tool to retain a measure of national control over the status of long-term resident TCNs. At a more fundamental level, the LTRD in fact confirms and perpetuates the differential treatment of TCNs in the EU legal framework which is inimical to integration. The provisions on equal treatment laid down in Article 11 have been criticized as embodying a low minimum standard and falling far short of the Tampere commitment to 'near-equality', primarily due to the limitations placed on the right of access to employment and the right to social benefits.[152] The Directive as a whole, perhaps unsurprisingly, does not represent a move away from the assumption that there is a fundamental inequality between TCNs and EU nationals, particularly as regards the right to free movement. Such a move would have been easiest to achieve in this relatively well-accepted category of long-term resident TCNs. In this sense, Halleskov's assertion that '(b)y failing to grant Long Term Residents the foundation necessary for their full integration into the Community – i.e. the right to equal treatment with nationals – the Council signals that the Member States still consider TCNs, even after they have resided and worked legally in a Member State for more than five years and fulfilled the numerous conditions laid down in the Directive, to be second class citizens'[153] is justified.[154] As will be shown in the next section, these problems have been compounded by the reluctance of Member States to transpose the LTRD in a meaningful way, leading to very low numbers of individuals who have managed to take advantage of LTR status – six years after the transposition deadline has passed.[155]

'Push Back' from the Commission and the Court of Justice of the EU on Integration in the LTRD

As mentioned above, the provisions of the LTRD have come under serious criticism, particularly Article 5(2), which raised the possibility of the paradoxical situation arising whereby 'an integration requirement may turn out to be the main obstacle to the full effectiveness of a Directive aiming at the integration of long-term immigrants'.[156] The Commission and the CJEU have been 'pushing back' against this possibility in their monitoring of the transposition of the Directive. In its evaluation report on the LTRD, published in 2011, the Commission 'deplored'

152 For a detailed analysis of the equal treatment provisions, see Louise Halleskov, note 144.

153 Louise Halleskov, note 144, p. 201.

154 Although, see Anja Wiesbrock, 'Granting Citizenship-related Rights to Third-Country Nationals: An Alternative to the Full Extension of European Union Citizenship?' (2012) 14(1) *EJML* 63.

155 For example, the Commission's application report noted in 2011 that only 2000 third-country residents had acquired the LTR permit in France and Germany. In 2009, around four fifths of those third-country nationals having LTR status were living in four Member States: Estonia, Austria, Czech Republic and Italy.

156 Kees Groenendijk, 'The Long Term Residents Directive', note 144, p. 442.

the weak impact which the Directive has had across the Member States, specifically referring back to the primary rationale for the Directive of promoting the integration and non-discrimination of third-country nationals, and particularly of LTRs.[157] In relation to the permissible integration conditions contained in Article 5(2), the Commission reminded states that transposition of this provision must respect the principles of EU law including preserving the *effet utile* of the Directive and proportionality. To this end, 'the nature and level of the knowledge expected from the applicant, ... the cost of the exam, the accessibility of the integration training and tests, the comparison between the integration requirements imposed on a prospective LTR and those applied to prospective citizens (which are expected to be higher)' were all pointed to as indicators in carrying out an assessment of compatibility with EU law.[158] In respect of the integration 'measures' which may be imposed under Article 15(3) in respect of LTRs exercising their intra-EU mobility rights, the Commission is even more forthright in its analysis, stating that national legislation providing that LTR status-holders from another Member State must comply with integration measures 'entailing more than the mere attendance of a language course' (despite the application of an integration condition in the first Member State) is in breach of the Directive.[159]

The Commission concludes its evaluation report with an assurance that it will make full use of its powers under the Treaty and continue to launch infringement proceedings when necessary. The case law of the CJEU to date has supported the views of the Commission. Most importantly from an integration perspective, the Court has confirmed that the concept of integration employed by Member States in implementing the LTRD must respect the boundaries set by the CJEU in *European Parliament v Council*.[160] The approach of the Court in this and the *Chakroun*[161] case has been built on in a number of recent decisions of the Court in which it has used, among other things, the recitals of the LTRD to identify its objectives and inform the interpretation of its substantive provisions and their implementation by Member States.

In *Kamberaj*,[162] the CJEU determined that housing benefit must be interpreted as a 'core benefit' under the LTRD, meaning that the derogation provided for in Article 11(4) thereof, which permits the Member State to limit the social assistance and social benefit made available to long-term resident third-country nationals to 'core benefits', did not apply. The Court arrived at this interpretation of the

---

157 LTRD Application Report, Conclusions.

158 LTRD Application Report, at para. 3.2.

159 Ibid., at para. 3.7. The Commission notes that this is the case in Austria, Estonia, France, Germany and Latvia.

160 [2006] ECR I-5769.

161 Case C-578/08 *Rhimou Chakroun v Minister van Buitenlandse Zaken* [2010] ECR I-01839.

162 Case C-571/10 *Servet Kamberaj v Istituto per l'Edilizia sociale della Provincia autonoma di Bolzano (IPES) and Others*, Judgment of the Court of 24 April 2012.

meaning and scope of concept of 'core benefits' by taking into account the context of Article 11, most importantly, the objective pursued by the LTRD, which was identified as 'the integration of TCNs who have resided legally and continuously in the Member States and equal treatment of such persons'.[163] The Court also stated that the refusal to provide Mr Kamberaj with housing benefit must be interpreted in light of Article 34 of the EU Charter, which recognizes and respects the right to social housing and assistance so as to ensure a decent existence for all those who lack sufficient resources.[164] The Court thus used the provisions relating to access to social assistance under the EU Charter, alongside the overriding objective of integration enshrined in the LTRD, to limit the ability of Member States to deny access for long-term residents to certain rights enjoyed by EU citizens. In doing so, the Court pursues a human rights-based approach as well as reasserting the equal treatment paradigm of integration underlying the Directive as a whole.

The Court took a similar approach in *Commission v Netherlands*,[165] in which it held that the Dutch fees for the issue of a long-term residence permit were disproportionately high, exceeded the measure of discretion allowed to Member States in fixing such charges and ultimately jeopardized the achievement of the objectives of the LTRD. Again, the Court based its reasoning on integration, finding that the principal purpose of the Directive is the integration of TCNs who are settled on a long-term basis in a Member State, as well as the free movement of persons within an internal market area.[166] On this basis, the Court found that the level of the charges imposed had the effect of creating an obstacle to obtaining long-term resident status, undermining the objective and spirit of the Directive.

A third case, *Singh*,[167] concerned one of the key issues raised by the Commission in its application report: the restriction of the personal scope of the LTRD in some Member States caused by their broad reading of the exclusion provided for in Article 3(2)(e) for TCNs who have been admitted solely on temporary grounds.[168] The Commission had noted that some Member States apply a very broad reading of the exception contained in the provision and define the status of certain categories of third-country nationals as temporary, even though their residence permit may be renewed for a potentially indefinite period, without any definite time limit and regardless of the total duration of residence in the Member State. This means that artists, athletes, ministers of religion, social workers, researchers, family members of permanent third-country nationals, low skilled migrant workers or other TCNs

163 *Kamberaj*, at para. 9.

164 *Kamberaj*, at paras 80 and 81.

165 Case C-508/10 *Commission v Netherlands*, Judgment of the Court of 26 April 2012.

166 *Commission v Netherlands*, at para. 66.

167 Case C-502/10 *Staatssecretaris van Justitie v Mangat Singh*, Judgment of the Court of 18 October 2012.

168 Report from the Commission to the European Parliament and the Council on the application of Directive 2003/109/EC concerning the status of third-country nationals who are long-term residents, Brussels, 28.9.2011 COM(2011) 585 final, para. 3.1.

whose stay is unduly labelled 'temporary' may thereby be excluded from EU long-term residence status in some states.[169] In *Singh*, in which the CJEU considered this issue as referred from a Dutch court, the residence permit in question was a fixed period residence permit, the validity of which was limited to the exercise of an activity as a spiritual leader or religious teacher for the period. Mr Singh's application for LTR status was refused on the basis that the exception contained in Article 3(2) of the LTRD applied as his was a 'formally limited' permit. The CJEU, however, confirmed that the phrase 'formally limited' designates an autonomous concept of EU law which must be interpreted in a uniform manner throughout the Member States.[170]

Again, the Court followed the approach taken in *Kamberaj* and *Commission v The Netherlands* in insisting that the starting point of the analysis must be that the principal objective of the LTRD is integration through facilitating the acquisition of long-term residence.[171] In light of these objectives, the Court held, Article 3(2)(e) only excludes from the scope of the Directive the residence of TCNs that does not reflect any intention on the part of such nationals to settle on a long-term basis in the Member State. The fact that a permit contains a formal restriction does not in itself give any indication as to whether the TCN might settle on a long-term basis in the Member State, notwithstanding the existence of such a condition.[172] The Dutch approach was therefore incorrect in light of EU law. Very importantly, in interpreting Article 4(1) and Recital 6, the Court found:

> It is the duration of the legal and continuous residence of 5 years which shows that the person concerned has put down roots in the country and therefore the long-term residence of that person.

The equation of 'putting down roots' with duration of residence alone (rather than, for example, with passing integration tests) is a key element of the Court's reasoning and reflects a fair and equal treatment paradigm of integration, mirroring the approach of the Court in *Forster* and *Morgan* (considered below) in respect of how the integration of EU citizens should be determined.

The CJEU's case law is thus essentially addressing the conflicts, discussed above, that exist within the text of the Directive. The unifying feature, identified by the Court, which must inform the interpretation of the LTRD, is the overriding objective which it pursues – the integration of long-term resident TCNs and the right of those persons to equal treatment. Thus, the objective of integration is used in the decisions of the CJEU to limit the discretion of states to restrict access to LTR status and the benefits which are attached to that status. Continuing the 'tug-of war' between the EU institutions and the Member States on the meaning of

169 Ibid.
170 *Singh*, at para. 43.
171 *Singh*, at para. 45.
172 *Singh*, at para. 50.

integration, the concept of integration is thus once again turned around, and used as a tool to achieve fair and equal treatment rather than as a mandatory process involving the cultural assimilation of the migrant. The limits of judicial action are clear however, with the Court's 'fair and equal treatment' paradigm of integration co-existing with, rather than displacing, the concept of integration as a condition of immigration law perpetuated by the provisions of the LTRD itself.

A Fair and Equal Treatment Paradigm of Integration for Special Categories of TCNs

Outside long-term residents, some selected categories of TCNs have been afforded certain free movement rights and the right to enjoy near equal treatment and non-discrimination with nationals of the receiving state. These are students, researchers and highly skilled workers dealt with under the Students Directive, the Researchers Directive and the Blue Card Directive respectively (of which Ireland opted into the Researchers Directive). The most significant of these is the Blue Card Directive, which aims to establish a common procedure for admission and residence of more than three months for highly skilled workers and their family members. The Directive affords Blue Card holders equal treatment with nationals of the Member State issuing the Blue Card as regards a wide range of socio-economic rights and provides for freedom of movement within the EU (for the purpose of highly qualified employment) after eighteen months of residence in the first Member State as an EU Blue Card Holder. The Researchers Directive aims to establish a common procedure for the admission of third-country researchers to the Member States for more than three months, provides for a degree of mobility of Member States and equal treatment as regards recognition of qualifications, working conditions, certain branches of social security, tax benefits and access to goods and services. The Students Directive is the least far-reaching of the three Directives. It outlines the conditions of admissions and procedural rules regarding the admission of TCNs for the purpose of their studies, pupil exchange, unremunerated training or voluntary service, again providing for a certain level of intra-EU mobility for such students and access to economic activity in the host Member State (although the situation of the labour market in the host Member State may be taken into account, and Member States can determine the maximum number of hours allowed for such an activity). Students are not, however, afforded equal treatment entitlements in the same way as researchers and Blue Card holders. In addition, while students and unremunerated trainees are required only to learn the language of the course to be followed/placement to be undertaken, volunteers, who are also covered under the Students Directive, if the host state specifically requires it, may face the condition to 'if the host Member State specifically requires it, receive a basic introduction to the language, history and social structures of that Member State'.[173]

Integration conditions and measures are not permitted as a prerequisite to access to the intra-EU mobility or equal treatment provided for by the Directives. In fact, integration does not feature as a normative concept at all in the framework of entitlements provided by the Directives. In addition, these Directives provide for free movement and equal treatment (to varying degrees) in a manner such that the status of the selected categories of TCNs is brought closer to that of EU migrant, narrowing the rights gap between the two, even though it is arguable that the limited scope of the mobility provisions and their restrictive application in the Member States constitutes a missed opportunity to generate full inclusiveness of TCNs in the internal market.[174]

Highly skilled workers, in particular, are given special treatment in comparison to other categories of TCNs in a number of key integration areas. Family reunification is made easier for holders of Blue Cards by way of derogations from certain provisions of the FRD, the most significant of which in the context of integration is the derogation from the last subparagraph of Article 4(1) and Article 7(2), whereby 'the integration conditions and measures referred to therein may only be applied after the persons concerned have been granted family reunification'.[175] This means that integration cannot be used as a barrier to access to the right to family reunification, and constitutes a tacit acknowledgement that Articles 4(1) and 7(2) permit integration to be used by Member States as a tool of migration control, and a 'push factor'. In addition to the special treatment of Blue Card Holders in relation to family reunification, holders of the status can accumulate periods spent in different EU countries for the purposes of obtaining long-term resident status, provided certain conditions are fulfilled – something which is not possible for any other category of migrant.[176]

These Directives enshrine a conception of integration of fair and equal treatment combined with access to integration-related rights, which is closer to that in use in the policy Framework on Integration than that contained in the FRD and LTRD. In fact, they represent a concept of integration which comes close to that enshrined in EU law in respect of EU citizen migrants (as examined below). The Directives enshrine a fair and equal treatment paradigm of integration along the lines set out in the Tampere Programme. This being said, however, it is clear from the preambles of these Directives that the underlying rationale for the approach

173 Article 11(d). See Moritz Jesse, 'The Value of 'Integration' in European Law – The Implications of the *Forster* case on Legal Assessment of Integration Conditions for Third-Country Nationals' (2011) 17(2) *ELJ* 172, p. 185.

174 Anja Wiesbrock, 'Free Movement of Third Country Nationals in the European Union: The Illusion of Inclusion' (2010) 35(4) *Eur L Rev* 455.

175 Article 15(3), Blue Card Directive. Article 15 deals with the position of family members and lays down a number of derogations to the Family Reunification Directive.

176 Article 16, Blue Card Directive.

taken is the economic interest of the Union rather than a concern with the rights or integration of TCNs. In addition, the personal scope of the Directives is very narrow and thus this integration discourse, which runs parallel to that contained in the FRD and LRTD, affects only a very small pool of TCNs. The concept of integration represented in the Directives is not therefore strong enough to balance out the strong paradigm of integration as a mechanism of immigration control as enshrined in the LTRD and FRD. In addition, a gap is created between highly educated, highly skilled migrants and those with those in lower-paid jobs with less education who are targeted for integration as a mandatory legal process and do not benefit from the fair and equal treatment paradigm, turning the idea of integration as a means of social inclusion on its head in the process.

Integration of Refugees and Beneficiaries of Subsidiary Protection: Access to Integration-Related Entitlements and Facilities

The effective integration of refugees and beneficiaries of subsidiary protection is perceived at EU level to be one of the key challenges facing the Common European Asylum System (CEAS), as reflected in the *Policy Plan on Asylum*, which emphasizes the point that the need to ensure high quality protection standards should extend right throughout the asylum process to the full integration of those granted protection.[177] The renewed European Agenda for Integration specifically states that a 'diversity of approaches' is called for in respect of integration, depending on the different integration challenges faced by various types of migrants, including beneficiaries of international protection. According to the Commission, the integration of beneficiaries of international protection requires particular attention and policies should be designed to minimize their isolation and restrictions to their rights and promote integration (including language learning and access to accommodation).[178] This idea of a differentiated approach to integration is supported in the recitals to the primary EU refugee law instrument, the Qualification Directive, which state that the specific needs and situation of beneficiaries of refugee and of subsidiary protection status should be taken into account, as far as possible, in the integration programmes provided to them.[179] Reflecting this at a practical level, the Migration Policy Group, together with UNHCR, has also developed a specific refugee integration tool to evaluate

177 See Communication from the Commission to the European Parliament, the Council, the European Economic and Social Committee and the Committee of the Regions, *Policy Plan on Asylum-An Integrated Approach to Protection Across the EU* (COM(2008) 360 final [SEC(2009) 2029; SEC(2008) 2030)), p. 11.

178 2011 Integration Agenda, pp. 3 and 6.

179 Recital 47 states that this includes, where appropriate, language training and the provision of information concerning individual rights and obligations relating to their protection status in the Member State concerned. Qualification Directive.

refugee integration policies. This tool comprises four sets of indicators on 'general considerations'; 'legal integration'; 'socio-economic integration'; and 'socio-cultural integration'.[180]

In the previous chapter, it was seen that refugees enjoy an unparalleled range of specific, integration-related, rights in international law. Similarly, in the EU context, refugees and beneficiaries of subsidiary protection benefit from a range of rights and entitlements attached to their status, reflecting Member States' wide-ranging obligations under the 1951 Convention. These are contained in the Qualification Directive,[181] which was amended and recast in 2011.[182] While Ireland and the UK opted in to the original 2004 Qualification Directive, they did not opt in to the amending and recasting of the Directive, meaning that they continue to be bound only by the terms of the original. The provisions of the Qualification Directive as they relate to integration will be examined, followed by an assessment of the position of refugees and beneficiaries of subsidiary protection under the provisions of general immigration law discussed in the previous section.

Integration in the Qualification Directive

The Qualification Directive constitutes the centrepiece of the Common European Asylum System, the progressive establishment of which was another of the objectives set by the Tampere Council in 1999.[183] Article 1 states the purpose of the Directive as to 'lay down minimum standards for the qualification of third-country nationals or stateless persons as refugees or as persons who otherwise need international protection and the content of the protection granted'.[184] The scope of the qualifying grounds for international protection and the provisions

180 See also the user's guide to the tool, entitled *EU support for integration: What about beneficiaries of international protection? A User's Guide to EU Standards, Funds and Cooperation* (2012).

181 Council Directive 2004/83/EC of 29 April 2004 on minimum standards for the qualification and status of third-country nationals or stateless persons as refugees or as persons who otherwise need international protection and the content of the protection granted OJ L 304/04.

182 Directive 2011/95/EU of the European Parliament and of the Council of 13 December 2011 on standards for the qualification of third-country nationals or stateless persons as beneficiaries of international protection, for a uniform status for refugees or for persons eligible for subsidiary protection, and for the content of the protection granted. See generally, Steve Peers, 'Legislative Update 2011, EU Immigration and Asylum Law: The Recast Qualification Directive' (2012) 14(2) *EJML* 199.

183 For academic commentary on various aspects of the Directive, see, for example, Hugo Storey 'EU Refugee Qualification Directive: a Brave New World?' (2008) 20(1) *IJRL* 1; Hemme Battjes *European Asylum Law and International Law* (Martinus Nijhoff, 2006).

184 'International protection' in the context of the Directive means 'refugee and subsidiary protection status' as defined in Articles 2(d) and (f) and expanded upon in articles 2(c) and (e) respectively.

contained in the Directive on exclusion, revocation and *non-refoulement* have been extensively discussed elsewhere.[185] From an integration perspective, the most relevant provisions pertain to the *content* of international protection – i.e. the rights and entitlements flowing from refugee and subsidiary protection status. This section will assess the perspective on integration embodied in the Directive and consider whether the provisions of the Directive facilitate the integration of refugees and persons with subsidiary protection.

Chapter VII of the Directive, which sets out 'The Content of International Protection', covers a range of issues impacting on integration. Article 21 provides the most fundamental of protection rights: protection from *refoulement*.[186] The Directive also lays down rules regarding travel documents;[187] access to employment on the same terms as nationals; [188] and entitlements to health care, accommodation and social welfare.[189] Refugees are, broadly speaking, granted the right to treatment equal to that of nationals with regard to these core entitlements. Articles 23, 24 and 34 are of particular importance in a discussion of integration. Article 23 deals with 'Maintaining Family Unity', providing that 'Member States shall ensure that family unity can be maintained'.[190] In contrast to the position under the FRD, there is no mention of 'conditions' or 'measures' in the context of Article 23. Member States may only refuse to provide family reunification where the family member would be excluded from refugee status or subsidiary protection,[191] or 'for reasons of national security or public order'.[192] Article 24 addresses the issue of residence permits, specifying the minimum period of time for which Member States may issue residence permits to beneficiaries of international protection. A minimum of three years for refugees and one year for beneficiaries of subsidiary protection (or two years in the case of renewal) is laid down.[193]

---

185 See, for example, Maria-Teresa Bil-Bazo, 'Refugee Status and Subsidiary Protection under EC Law: The Qualification Directive and the Right to Be Granted Asylum', in Anneliese Baldaccini, Elspeth Guild and Helen Toner, *Whose Freedom, Security and Justice? EU Immigration and Asylum Law and Policy* (Hart Publishing, 2007), 229; and Jane McAdam, 'The European Qualification Directive: The Creation of a Subsidiary Protection Regime' (2005) *IJRL* 461.

186 This protection may only be revoked where a refugee constitutes a danger to the security of the Member State or the community of that Member State. Article 21(2)(a) and (b). Gil-Bazo criticizes the scope of the circumstances in which *refoulement* is permitted (ibid., p. 252).

187 Article 25.

188 Articles 26.

189 Articles 28, 31 and 29 2004 Directive; Articles 30, 32 and 29, 2011 Directive.

190 Article 23(1).

191 Article 23(3).

192 Article 23(4).

193 This at least places refugees and beneficiaries of subsidiary protection in a relatively secure legal position within the host state for a minimum period of time. Nevertheless, this limited validity required of residence permits has led to the concern being expressed that 'the non-renewal of permits may become an easy way for Member

The only provision of the Directive which expressly refers to 'integration' is Article 34 on 'access to integration facilities', which reflects Member States' duties under Article 34 of the 1951 Refugee Convention to facilitate refugee integration. Article 34 of the amended Qualification Directive (formerly Article 33(1)) provides:

> In order to facilitate the integration of beneficiaries of international protection into society, Member States shall ensure access to integration programmes which they consider to be appropriate so as to take into account the specific needs of beneficiaries of refugee status or of subsidiary protection status, or create pre-conditions which guarantee access to such programmes.

The second paragraph of this Article, which created a more limited obligation in the case of persons granted subsidiary protection – members of this category would only be granted access to such programmes where Member States 'consider appropriate' – [194] was deleted in the recasting of the Directive in 2011. However, the UK and Ireland are still obliged only to ensure access to integration programmes for refugees under Article 33 of the original 2004 Qualification Directive.

The understanding of integration underlying Article 34 reflects the inclusive and participatory conception of integration contained in the CBPs and Framework on Integration. Whereas it was seen above that the FRD and the LTRD use integration as an instrument of exclusion and a condition of admission, Article 34 refers to integration in the sense of a process that is to be commenced once the refugee is installed in the country of asylum, in order to facilitate their participation in society on an equal footing with nationals of the Member State. Integration is thus conceptualized as an entitlement rather than an obligation. This approach fits with UNHCR's definition of refugee integration as a 'dynamic and multifaceted two-way process which requires efforts by all parties concerned, including a preparedness on the part of refugees to adapt to the host society without having to forego their own cultural identity, and a corresponding readiness on the part of host communities and public institutions to welcome refugees and meet the needs

---

States to deny protection without having to engage in a formal procedure to withdraw status'. Maria-Teresa Gil-Bazo, note 185, p. 260. This possibility is expressly adverted to in Article 21(3), whereby Member States may 'revoke, end or refuse to renew or to grant the residence permit of (or to) a "refugee"' who falls under the exceptions in Article 21(2) as discussed above.

194 According to the UNHCR's report on the implementation of the Directive, at least 16 Member States did not differentiate between refugees and beneficiaries of subsidiary protection with respect to access to integration facilities (UNHCR, *Asylum in the European Union. A Study of the Implementation of the Qualification Directive*, November 2007, para. 5.5.14).

of a diverse population'.[195] Nevertheless, the vagueness of Article 34 leaves it to Member States to determine the content and objectives of integration programmes, with UNHCR's report on the implementation of the Qualification Directive illustrating that in practice the integration programmes provided for are sometimes very limited and may cover only language training or financial loans.[196] Several Member States, including Ireland, do not even formally provide for integration programmes for beneficiaries of international protection and in some countries access to integration programmes is reported to be on a discretionary basis.[197] The impact of Article 34 on Member State law and policy appears thus far to have been quite minimal.

For the most part, the content of the status recognized to beneficiaries of international protection in the Qualification Directive mirrors that of the 1951 Refugee Convention and in relation to some rights – the rights of access to employment, education and healthcare for example – the Directive goes beyond the standards set by the 1951 Convention. Thus it can be said that (aside from the problems posed by the limited minimum period for which a residence permit must be granted) once an individual has been granted refugee status, the rights flowing from this status provide the basic conditions necessary for participation in the society of the country of asylum. One area in which there is a significant lacuna is regarding access to citizenship. Article 34 of the 1951 Convention, which requires State Parties to facilitate the naturalization of refugees, is not reflected anywhere in the Qualification Directive. While it is disappointing that this innovative provision of international law is not taken up on in the Qualification Directive, it is hardly surprising given that the allocation of national citizenship lies within national rather than EU competence.

Of greater concern in the original 2004 Qualification Directive was the limited range of rights extended to those granted subsidiary protection. The status of and standards of treatment to be afforded to beneficiaries of subsidiary protection is a contentious issue, and one which led to persistent differences of view between Member States during negotiations on the 2004 Qualification Directive.[198] Notwithstanding the arguments in favour of granting equal rights to refugees and

195 UNHCR Executive Committee, *Conclusion on Local Integration* (No. 104 (LVI) 2005), preamble and (k). See also UNHCR, Note on the Integration of Refugees in Europe (UNHCR, May 2007).

196 UNHCR, *Asylum in the European Union. A Study of the Implementation of the Qualification Directive*, November 2007, note 194, para. 5.5.14.

197 This is the case in Hungary. Ibid., para. 5.5.14.

198 Jens Vedsted-Hansen, 'Assessment of the Proposal for an EC Directive on the Notion of Refugee and Subsidiary Protection from the Perspective of International Law', in Daphne Bouteillet-Paquet (ed.), *Subsidiary Protection of Refugees in the European Union: Complementing the Geneva Convention?* (Bruylant Bruxelles, 2002) 57, p. 77.

beneficiaries of subsidiary protection,[199] the Qualification Directive took advantage of the discretion afforded by international law on this point. Chapter VII included a number of derogations whereby states were permitted, under certain conditions, to limit the access of those with subsidiary protection to – *inter alia* – healthcare,[200] employment[201] and integration facilities.[202] The denial of equal access to integration facilities in particular seemed illogical[203] and, in this sense, the limited rights granted to beneficiaries of subsidiary protection under the Qualification Directive represented a victory of state concerns relating to deterrence and restriction over the facilitation the integration of a group of legally resident vulnerable TCNs.[204] The revised Directive, however, goes some way to ameliorating these deficiencies and approximates the treatment of beneficiaries of subsidiary protection in respect of the content of protection to that of refugees, removing the possibility for states to distinguish between the two groups in the key 'functional' integration areas of housing, health, employment and education. In this way, the recast Qualification Directive provides those holding this status with a range of integration-related rights and entitlements akin to those available to refugees.

Integration of Refugees and Beneficiaries of Subsidiary Protection in General Immigration Measures

The previous section outlined the unique range of rights and entitlements attached to refugee and subsidiary protection status in EU law. This section will briefly explore the position of refugees and beneficiaries of subsidiary protection under the general provisions of EU immigration law.

In addition to the importance attached to 'maintaining family unity' by Article 23 of the Qualification Directive, refugees are also covered in the FRD.

---

199 See Katherine Rohl, 'Fleeing Violence and Poverty: *Non-Refoulement* Obligations Under the European Convention on Human Rights', New Issues in Refugee Research – Working Paper No. 111 (UNHCR, January 2005), p. 30.

200 Article 29(2) provides that 'Member States may limit health care granted to beneficiaries of subsidiary protection to core benefits which will then be provided at the same levels and under the same eligibility conditions as nationals'.

201 Article 26(3) provides that regarding beneficiaries of subsidiary protection, the 'situation of the labour market' may be taken into account in determining the extent of their access to employment.

202 Article 33(2).

203 ECRE, 'Broken Promises, Forgotten Principles: An ECRE Evaluation of the Development of EU Minimum Standards for Refugee Protection' (ECRE, 2004), p. 20.

204 That being said, UNHCR's evaluation of the implementation of the Directive shows that in practice few Member States make use of the possibility to differentiate between refugees and beneficiaries of subsidiary protection in terms of the content of the protection granted (despite difficulties with the differing level of protection granted in different Member States). UNHCR, *Asylum in the European Union. A Study of the Implementation of the Qualification Directive*, November 2007, note 194.

Chapter V sets out specific rules relating to the family reunification of refugees, creating more favourable rules in certain situations in order to take the particular circumstances of refugees into account.[205] Most importantly in the context of the present discussion, refugees are exempted from the controversial integration derogation contained in Article 4(1), meaning that integration cannot constitute a barrier to family reunification for refugees.[206] As regards the 'integration measures' which Article 7(2) allows to be imposed by Member States, refugees cannot be obliged to comply with integration measures until family reunification has been granted, meaning again that integration measures cannot be used as a barrier to admission of family migrants in the case of refugees.[207] The FRD does not apply to beneficiaries of subsidiary protection.[208]

The LTRD initially excluded beneficiaries of international protection[209] from its scope.[210] This exclusion was termed 'the largest and most disappointing omission from the scope of the Directive'.[211] In 2011, the scope of the LTRD was extended to include beneficiaries of international protection, with the recitals of the amending directive stating that 'the prospect of obtaining long-term resident status in a Member State after a certain time is an important element for the full integration of beneficiaries of international protection in the Member State of residence'.[212] However, unlike the approach taken in the FRD in the case of refugees, beneficiaries of international protection are potentially subject to the integration 'conditions' and 'measures' allowable pursuant to Article 5(2) and Article 15(3) of the LTRD, meaning that they are exposed to the conception of integration as a mandatory process in migration law.

---

205 See Article 11, Article 10(2) (definition of a 'family member'), Article 12(2) (reckonable residence).

206 Article 10 provides: 'Article 4 shall apply to the definition of family members except that the third subparagraph of paragraph 1 thereof shall not apply to the children of refugees'.

207 Article 7(2) provides: 'With regard to the refugees and/or family members of refugees referred to in Article 12 the integration measures referred to in the first subparagraph may only be applied once the persons concerned have been granted family reunification'.

208 The Commission reports that in practice, family reunification for non-Convention refugees varies across the Member States (Report from the Commission to the European Parliament and the Council on the application of Directive 2003/86/EC on the Right to Family Reunification, note 135, p. 4).

209 I.e. subsidiary and temporary protection.

210 Article 3, Long-Term Residents Directive.

211 Steve Peers, 'Implementing Equality? The Directive on Long-Term Resident Third-Country Nationals' (2004) 29(4) *ELRev* 437, p. 443.

212 Directive 2011/51/EU of the European Parliament and the Council amending Council Directive 2003/109/EC to extend its scope to beneficiaries of international protection, recital 2.

An Integration Paradigm for Refugees and Beneficiaries of International Protection?

In a similar manner to the original position under the LTRD, refugees and beneficiaries of international protection are excluded from the scope of the Students' and Blue Card Directives (although they fall within the scope of the Researchers' Directive).[213] It has been argued that these Directives embody a fair and equal treatment paradigm of integration. Overall then, refugees avoid the restrictive concept of integration as contained in FRD but seem to be subject to integration conditions and measures as set out in the LTRD, and are also excluded from the elements of the fair and equal treatment paradigm of integration contained in the Students' and Blue Card Directives. Thus, while the minimum standards of treatment provided by the Qualification Directive place refugees and beneficiaries of subsidiary protection in particular in a position of near-equality to EU nationals in certain spheres of society and in a privileged position amongst TCNs, as is becoming a common theme of the analysis in this chapter, there is no real coherent approach to the integration of refugees and beneficiaries of subsidiary protection in EU law.

Integration of EU Migrants: Progressive Realization of Equality

This chapter has concentrated on the EU law and policy framework for the integration of TCNs. 'Integration' is rarely discussed as such at EU level in the context of EU migrant citizens and Guild argues that the EU abhors the concept of integration when it comes to its own nationals.[214] Nonetheless, as pointed out in the introduction to this chapter, EU law has had a transformative effect on the way in which EU migrants are perceived in Member States and constitutes a powerful instrument for their integration. Fundamentally, the twin principles of free movement and non-discrimination, as reflected in the Treaties, secondary legislation and case law, have required Member States to treat EU migrant workers on more or less equal terms as national citizens. The provision of equal social and economic rights for EU workers and their families allows them to make a life for themselves in the host state and claim an equal place in the host society, facilitating the ultimate goal of free movement of persons. EU workers are essentially assimilated to the position of a national citizen – rendering the question of their 'integration' almost superfluous. The basic conditions for the free movement of citizens and entitlements in the host state are set out in Directive 2004/38 on the right of citizens of the Union and their family members to move and reside

213 Articles 2(a), 2(b) of the Students' and Blue Card Directives, respectively.

214 Elspeth Guild, *The Legal Elements of European Identity*, note 122, p. 124.

freely within the territory of the Member States (the 'Citizenship Directive').[215] The concept of EU citizenship has led to the strengthening of the principle of non-discrimination and facilitated access to integration-related rights for both workers and economically inactive migrants. In particular, the approach of the CJEU in citizenship cases indicates that access to social benefits must in general be extended to all EU citizens lawfully resident in the host Member State, whether or not the citizen is economically active, as will be seen from the examination of the 'students' cases below.

The Role of Integration in the Interpretation of Regulation 1612/68

'Integration' has played a significant role in the reasoning of the CJEU in cases involving the entitlements of EU migrant workers. Regulation 1612/68 provides a comprehensive array of social rights to workers and their families by guaranteeing equal treatment in respect of access to a broad range of social rights.[216] Under the Regulation, EU nationals are entitled – *inter alia* – to take up employment in another Member State on the same terms as nationals[217] and to the same social and tax advantages as nationals and to equal access to vocational training.[218] Children of a resident worker are also entitled to equal access to the state's educational courses. The CJEU has taken a broad view of what is required of Member States under the Regulation, with integration forming an express part of the rationale for this approach. In *Echternach and Moritz*, the CJEU put this in plain terms:

> The equal treatment, in relation to national workers, to which workers of a Member State who are employed in another Member State are entitled as regards the benefits granted to members of their families, contributes to their integration in the society of the host country, in accordance with the aims of freedom of movement for workers.[219]

The significance of this line of case law, which included *Eind*,[220] is illustrated in *London Borough of Harrow v Nimco Hassan Ibrahim*,[221] in which the CJEU concluded that the children of a national of a Member State who works or has worked in the host Member State, as well the parent who is their primary carer,

215 Directive 2004/38/EC of the European Parliament and of the Council of 29 April 2004 on the right of citizens of the Union and their family members to move and reside freely within the territory of the Member States OJ L 158/77.

216 Council Regulation 1612/68/EEC of 15 October 1968 on freedom of movement for workers within the Community OJ L 257/2.

217 Article 1, Regulation 1612/68.

218 Article 7.

219 Para. 20.

220 C-291/05 *Minister voor Vreemdelingenzaken en Integratie v Eind* [2007] ECR I-10719.

221 C-310/08 [2010] ECR I-7091.

can claim a right of residence in the latter state on the sole basis of Article 12 of Regulation 1612/68. That right is not conditional on their having sufficient resources and comprehensive sickness insurance cover in that state, as would be required by Article 7(1)(b) and (d) and (2) of the Citizenship Directive. This decision was based partly on the reasoning that 'a contrary conclusion would be liable to compromise the aim of integrating the migrant worker's family into the host Member State'.[222]

Building on its seminal decision in *Ibrahim* and the subsequent case of *Teixera*,[223] the Court confirmed in *Alarape*[224] that the parent of a child who has reached the age of majority and who has obtained access to education on the basis of Article 12 of Regulation 1612/68 may continue to have a derived right of residence under that article if the child remains in need of the presence and care of that parent in order to be able to continue and complete his or her education. The Court also settled another issue which had arisen as a result of the *Ibrahim* case law, finding that periods of residence completed by TCN family members solely on the basis of Article 12 of Regulation 1612/68 may not be taken into account for the purposes of their acquisition of a right of permanent residence under Directive 2004/38. Unlike in *Ibrahim*, however, the Court did not specifically refer to integration as an element of its reasoning in this case.

Integration in the 'Students Cases'

Similarly, integration is a significant element of the Court's jurisprudence on access to social benefits for EU citizen students engaged in study in a Member State other than their own. In *Bidar*,[225] the CJEU found that students who are engaged in a course of study in a host Member State are entitled to equality of treatment in relation to access to maintenance grants, if they can satisfy reasonable integration conditions which may be imposed by states. The CJEU made it clear that while no right to maintenance assistance for students (and therefore other economically inactive persons) is contained in the Citizenship Directive, such a right could be directly derived from Articles 12 and 18 EC on the basis that such assistance is to be considered a benefit within the scope of the Treaty. The host Member State may require students to demonstrate a certain degree of integration into their society and for this purpose they may demand that students are settled or have resided for a certain period in its territory.

Bidar also left some room for speculation as to what constituted a 'degree of integration' and how this could be measured by Member States. Subsequent case law has provided some clarification as to the nature of the integration requirements

222 Ibid., at para. 43.

223 Case C-480/08 [2010] ECR I-1107.

224 Case C-529/11 *Olaitan Ajoke Alarape, Olukayode Azeez Tijani v Secretary of State for the Home Department* (not yet reported, 8 May 2013).

225 Case 209/03 *Bidar v London Borough of Ealing* [2005] ECR 1-2119.

which may be imposed. In *Forster*,[226] a condition of five years' uninterrupted residence was found to be appropriate for the purpose of guaranteeing that the applicant is integrated into the society of the host Member State. The Court took a 'formalistic' approach to defining integration which relies solely on the time of legal residence: social integration, measured through the individual situation of the applicant and the genuine nature of the link between the individual and the host society, does not matter at all.[227] A similar approach is evident in *Morgan*,[228] in which the Court found that the requirement of a first stage of studies in the student's Member State of origin was disproportionate as it was not indicative of the degree of integration into the society of the said Member State at the time the grant is applied for. The requirement was found to be too general and exclusive and would 'unduly favour an element which is not necessarily representative of the degree of integration in the society of that Member State at the time where that application for assistance was made'.[229]

Member States will not, it seems, be allowed to use the integration test as a barrier to the rights of EU citizens exercising their free movement rights under EU law. In addition, it seems that integration is conceived mainly in terms of length of residence. A comparison with long-term resident TCNs is instructive in this regard. As was shown above, long-term resident TCNs are not considered to be integrated by virtue of their length of residence alone – they may also be required to pass integration tests and language tests in order to prove their integration and access long-term resident status.[230] However, Jesse argues that the judgments could have unforeseen positive effects in the context of assessing TCNs' integration, as any legal assessment of restrictive national integration conditions limiting the attainment of residence titles for TCNs cannot disregard the assumption of integration after five years of legal residence in *Forster*. Indeed, it was seen above that the approach of the Court of Justice of the EU in respect of EU nationals may have had a 'spill-over' effect into its jurisprudence on TCNs, which it has been seen takes a reasonably prescriptive approach to the concept of integration used in the immigration directives, which may in turn have the effect of neutralizing some of the fears expressed in the aftermath of the adoption of those directives.

Integration as a Barrier to Expulsion of EU Migrants

Finally, 'integration' is expressly referred to in Article 28 of the Citizenship Directive. Article 28 provides that before taking an expulsion decision on grounds of public policy or public security, the host Member State shall take account of considerations such as how long the individual concerned has resided in its

226 C-158/07 [2008] ECR I-8507

227 Moritz Jesse, note 173, p. 178.

228 Joined cases C-11/06 and C-12/06 *Morgan and Bucher* [2007] ECR I-9161.

229 Para. 46.

230 See Moritz Jesse, note 173.

territory, his/her age, state of health, family and economic situation, social and cultural integration into the host Member State and the extent of his/her links with their country of origin. This mirrors the ECHR jurisprudence examined in Chapter 5. 'Social and cultural' integration is probably specified in order to distinguish this type of integration from the integration which is generally deemed to be achieved by EU citizen migrants through length of residence alone. The function of integration in the Citizenship Directive thus contrasts with the express use of 'integration' in the FRD and LTRD. In those Directives, it is conceptualized as a potential barrier to admission for TCNs, whereas in the Citizenship Directive it is conceived as a barrier to expulsion.

Integration as Inclusion for EU migrants

Overall, EU law relating to the free movement of EU citizens enshrines a vision of integration as the progressive realization of equal rights. This mirrors the conception of integration under development by the UN human rights treaty monitoring committees, as explored in Chapter 4. In addition, integration is conceived of as primarily dependent on residence and not on assimilation into the culture or values of the host state. It would be contrary to EU law to subject EU workers or their families to integration tests or language proficiency tests, especially prior to admission to a Member State or as a pre-condition to the exercise of free movement. As Kostakopoulou observes, the exercise of the wide range of substantive rights enjoyed by EU workers does not require any transfer of loyalty to the host state.[231] She accurately points out that:

> All this suggests that the Community views the integration of the worker and his or her family into the social fabric of the host state as the end product of equalisation, and not of assimilation into the values and culture of that state.[232]

The hypothesis that the aim of integration in the context of EU migrants is not to assimilate individuals into the cultural and political values of the host society, but rather to include them in the social and economic fabric of the state, is supported by the decision of the CJEU in *Garcia-Avello*.[233] In this case, the Court refused to accept 'integration' as a justification for restricting rights of EU nationals. Mr Garcia Avello, a Spanish national, and his Belgian spouse, Ms Weber, wanted that their children's surname to be Garcia Weber, in accordance with well-established usage in Spanish law whereby the surname of children of a married couple consists of the first surname of the father followed by that of the mother. The Belgian government rejected their application to have the children's name

231 See Theodora Kostakopoulou, *Citizenship, Identity and Immigration in the European Union* (Manchester University Press, 2001), p. 71.

232 Ibid.

233 C-148/02 *Garcia-Avello v Etat Belge* [2003] ECR I-11613.

registered, stating that that type of application was habitually rejected on the ground that, in Belgium, children bear their father's surname. The government argued that this position was justified – *inter alia* – on the basis that it contributed to facilitating the integration of the children in Belgium. The Court rejected this claim outright, finding that:

> With regard to the objective of integration pursued by the practice in issue, the practice in issue is, in view of the coexistence in the Member States of different systems for the attribution of surnames applicable to those there resident, neither necessary nor even appropriate for promoting the integration of the nationals of other Member States within their State of residence.[234]

This judgment signals that arguments made to justify restriction of the rights of EU citizen migrants based on integration concerns will be given short shrift by the CJEU, in stark contrast to the position legally enshrined in the LTR and FR Directives.[235]

Difficulties in Identifying an EU Paradigm of Integration

As noted in the introduction to this chapter, understanding the legal framework constituted by European Union law is vital to understanding integration in EU Member States. EU law relating to the movement of EU citizens, in particular, conditions Member States responses to this category of migrants. In terms of the direct interplay between national and EU integration policy, of the three jurisdictions focused on in this book, Ireland most explicitly takes its lead from EU integration policy. While the development of a specific integration policy in the UK is in the very early stages, it has not, as yet, mentioned EU policy as a touchstone or reference point. French integration policy has traditionally been rooted in defending a specific national model of integration based on a particular reading of Republicanism,[236] however it was shown in Chapter 2 that recent French definitions of integration are very close to the EU definition. It has been seen that the ideas contained in the EU Framework on Integration have been diffusing throughout Europe by operation of the EU Integration Fund, the National Contact Points on Integration, the EU Integration Forum and the inter-ministerial meetings, among other EU mechanisms.

There are, however, major difficulties with modelling domestic integration policy on EU policy. The soft law EU integration framework applies to TCNs only

---

234 Para 45.

235 The *Garcia-Avello* ruling was followed in C-353/06 *Stefan Grunkin and Dorothee Regina Paul* ECR [2008] I-07639.

236 Sergio Carrera, 'The Normativity of Integration in National Law: France', in Sergio Carrera, *In Search of the Perfect Citizen?*, note 12, p. 347.

and not to EU citizens, while domestic integration policies do not generally make these distinctions and apply to all legally resident migrants, including EU citizens. Another gap is that neither Ireland nor the UK has opted in to the legally binding measures which have potentially the greatest impact in practice on TCN migrants' integration: the LTRD and the FRD. While France is bound by these directives, it has presented the FRD, in particular, as legitimizing the development of pre-departure integration strategies.[237]

Perhaps the most significant difficulty in looking to the EU for a normative model for integration, however, is the lack of an overarching paradigm embodied in EU law. Conflicting conceptions of integration prevail in relation to EU migrants on one hand and TCN immigrants on the other. For EU migrants, integration is conceptualized as a process of social insertion or inclusion, with a progressively wider range of rights being granted to EU citizen migrants as they become integrated in the host Member State. Integration is not equated with social and cultural integration or with the acceptance by the migrant of the 'values' of the host state, rather it appears to be measured by length of residence. In contrast, integration for TCNs is seen as a multi-faceted process including social and cultural integration and acceptance of national values. Integration for TCNs is also conceptualized as a potential condition precedent to legal immigration and as a mandatory process which may be imposed by states. A further element of conceptual confusion is introduced by recent case law of the CJEU which uses a fair and equal treatment paradigm of integration to constrain the discretion of Member States in their implementation of the LTRD and the FRD.

Within the broad category of TCNs, further contradictions also exist. Regarding the integration of TCNs, the (broadly speaking) inclusive concept of integration contained in the policy documentation is turned on its head in legally binding immigration measures, with the concept of integration used as an instrument of immigration control and exclusion in the FRD and LTRD. Other legally binding immigration measures (for example, the Blue Card Directive) do not expressly refer to the concept of integration but provide for integration-related rights in the form of equal treatment and free movement rights. In the case of refugees, access to integration programmes must be 'facilitated' and refugees must be afforded a range of integration-related rights which brings their position closer that of EU migrants rather than other categories of TCN. There is no consistent approach to integration across the legal categories of TCN.

All of this weakens the potential of the EU approach to integration to influence Member States in constructing coherent integration policies. Most significantly, the conflicting legal conceptions of integration employed in the contexts of TCNs and EU citizens could mean that different integration policies are required for EU citizens and other migrants. This is perhaps an inevitable consequence of the project of European integration. However, the division of migrants into EU migrants and others, with different levels of integration rights and responsibilities, introduces a

237 Ibid., p. 292.

differentiated form of integration which seriously undermines the ability of the EU approach to integration to influence Member States in the adoption of inclusive, equality-based integration strategies.

Conclusion

On the whole, despite the advances in EU citizenship law (which will be studied in Chapter 7), those with hopes for the EU as a model for an innovative paradigm of community, belonging and entitlement, detached from the nation state, will be disappointed. If one considers the basic dichotomy between EU citizens and TCNs, this becomes clear: barriers to free movement within the EU for EU nationals are increasingly being lifted whereas the legal measures relating to TCNs, even where relatively inclusive as in the case of refugees, confirm their position as outsiders. EU law on free movement and citizenship thus replicates the approach of the statist model of inclusion and exclusion on the basis of nationality. The construction of a European postnational space and identity is highly beneficial to migrants originating within the EU but legitimates the exclusion of those from third countries. Such migrants must overcome barriers to entry and integration erected by Member States but also by the EU. It thus seems that the more that is required of states as regards solidarity with their EU partners, the deeper the divide between EU migrants and other classes of migrants, ultimately undermining the social cohesion and equality aspects of integration.

PART III
Functional and Wider Perspectives on Integration and Law: Domestic Legal Regimes

Chapter 7

The Boundaries of Membership in EU Member States: Access to Citizenship

Introduction

Integration studies and commentaries have frequently underlined the important interaction between integration and citizenship. Ager and Strang, for example, identify 'rights and citizenship' as the foundational domain of their conceptual framework for understanding refugee integration.[1] In this conceptual framework, 'rights and citizenship' are characterized as the starting point for 'articulating the (potentially conflicting) assumptions and principles that shape policy and public debate' on integration.[2] In their view, notions of nationhood and citizenship shape core understandings of the rights accorded, and responsibilities expected, of refugees such that, in order to develop an effective integration policy, governments need to clearly articulate policy on nationhood and citizenship.[3] All of this supports the idea discussed in Chapter 3 that national public philosophy shapes integration principles and practice.

Citizenship framed in this way also has multiple connections with the working definition of integration outlined in Chapter 2. From the functional perspective, citizenship forms a central constituent part of fundamental rights protection. Despite the development of universal human rights norms in the twentieth century and the corresponding erosion of the nexus between citizenship and rights protection, citizenship continues to be the key to accessing the full range of fundamental rights at the domestic level. In particular, full security of residence and access to political rights still depend on the acquisition of citizenship. In terms of political participation in particular, citizenship is central to representation within the political process and may mean that political parties are less likely to take populist anti-immigrant positions. Furthermore, as Waldrauch et al. note, a state of affairs in which there is a large population of permanent or long-term residents who are subjected to the laws of a state without legislative representation

1 Alistair Ager and Alison Strang, 'Understanding Integration: A Conceptual Framework' (2008) 21(2) *JRS* 166.

2 Ibid., p. 174.

3 Ibid., p. 175. See also, Alistair Ager and Alison Strang, 'Refugee Integration: Emerging Trends and Remaining Agendas' (2010) 23(4) *JRS* 589.

constitutes a serious democratic deficit.[4] Very importantly, in EU Member States, national citizenship entails EU citizenship and the consequent valuable rights to free movement and rights protection as an EU citizen.

From the wider perspective, the potential of citizenship discourse to influence and shape issues of social inclusion, diversity and equality in turn impacts upon the integration framework. The links between citizenship and national identity in particular are an important component of the wider context in which integration takes place at the national level.[5] Nationality is the 'juridico-political expression of membership'[6] in modern societies. As Mullally observes, it provides – on a legal level at least – a preliminary answer to the question, 'who belongs?'[7] It is also the ultimate expression of sovereignty, states being more or less free to determine the criteria for entry into the national polity, in this way delineating the boundaries of national membership.

Other writers, organizations and state practices mirror the approach of Ager and Strang in linking citizenship and integration,[8] with citizenship cast in the dual role of instrument and indicator of integration. On a European level, citizenship is seen as one of the key indicators by which integration can be benchmarked, with the Migrant Integration Policy Index (MIPEX) recording the best and worst practices regarding access to nationality in 31 countries and citizenship also included as one of the EU indicators of integration.[9] The rate of citizenship acquisition as an indicator of immigrant integration is subject to debate within

4 Rainer Bauböck, Eva Ersbøll, Kees Groenendijk and Harald Waldrauch (eds), *Acquisition and Los of Nationality, Summary and Recommendations* (Institute for European Integration Research Austrian Academy of Sciences, Vienna, January 2006), p. 17.

5 Thomas Faist, *Dual Citizenship in Global Perspective: From Unitary to Multiple Citizenship* (Palgrave Macmillan, 2008), p. 15.

6 Siobhán Mullally, 'Citizenship and Family Life in Ireland: Asking the Question "Who Belongs?"' (2005) 25 *Legal Studies* 578, p. 578.

7 See Siobhán Mullally, ibid. She refers in turn to Carens, 'Who Belongs? Theoretical and Legal Questions on Birthright Citizenship in the United States' (1987) 37 *University of Toronto Law Journal* 413.

8 See, for example, Adrian Favell, 'To belong or not to belong: the postnational question', in Andrew Geddes and Adrian Favell (eds), *The Politics of Belonging: Migrants and Minorities in Contemporary Europe* (Ashgate, 1999); Immigrant Council of Ireland, 'Getting On: From Immigration to Integration' (ICI, May 2008); and Gökçe Yurdakul and Michael Bodemann (eds), *Citizenship and Immigrant Integration* (Palgrave Macmillan, 2007), in particular Chapter 3, Irene Bloemraad, 'Citizenship and Pluralism: Multiculturalism in a World of Global Migration'. See also OECD, 'Naturalisation: A Passport for the Better Integration of Immigrants?' (OECD, 2011).

9 British Council and Migration Policy Group, Migration Integration Policy Index III (2011), www.integrationindex.eu. See also, Jan Niessen and Thomas Huddlestone (eds), *Legal Frameworks for the Integration of Third Country Nationals* (Martinus Nijhoff, 2009); Eurostat, 'Indicators of Immigrant Integration, A Pilot Study' (*Methodologies and Working Papers*, 2011).

the research community,[10] and not all the Member States have a unified view on the usefulness of access to citizenship as an integration indicator. However, EU studies have found that 'longitudinal and non-longitudinal research indicates that citizenship acquisition has a positive impact on immigrants' position on the labour market, political participation and social inclusion'.[11] Despite the potential of citizenship as an integration tool, however, citizenship is also, by its nature, an exclusionary device.[12] The exclusionary elements of citizenship are reflected in the way that integration tests are being used in some countries as a barrier to accessing citizenship, which will be looked at below in the case of France, the UK and other European states. More fundamentally, formal legal citizenship is a powerful instrument of social closure,[13] and thus constitutes a key way in which 'outsiders' may become 'insiders' in a society, but also a mechanism to keep undesired outsiders as such. Approaches to nationhood and citizenship thus provide the 'normative context for understanding integration'.[14] Different national traditions of citizenship provide differing normative contexts and have given rise to different models of integration policy, as discussed in Chapter 2. The French and the German,[15] the British and German[16] and the US and Israeli citizenship traditions are often compared and contrasted, for example.[17]

This chapter will be broken into three parts, starting by looking at the ascription of birthright citizenship. Some of recent experiences and debates in Ireland in the area of citizenship, most notably the 2004 constitutional referendum which removed the automatic right to Irish citizenship of children born in Ireland (Irish-born children of migrants will be referred to in this context as 'Irish-born children'). This abolished the last pure *jus soli* regime in Europe and mirrors restrictions on *jus soli* in the UK and France, which will also be explored. The analysis will show that debates on citizenship reveal a good deal in relation to views as to membership more generally. The second part of the chapter concentrates on access to naturalization, looking in particular at naturalization procedures and the use of 'integration' as a barrier to accessing citizenship. Overall, it will be seen that legal access to citizenship, which is becoming increasingly restrictive in most European

---

10 European Website on Integration Special Feature (prepared by the Migration Policy Group), 'Access to Nationality for Third-Country Nationals' (2012), p. 6.

11 Ibid.

12 Bryan Fanning and Fidele Mustawaribo, 'Nationals/Non-Nationals: Immigration, Citizenship and Politics in the Republic of Ireland' (2007) 30(3) *Ethnic and Racial Studies* 439. See also Rogers Brubaker, *Citizenship and Nationhood in France and Germany* (Harvard University Press, 1994), p. 21.

13 Rogers Brubaker, ibid., p. 23.

14 Alistair Ager and Alson Strang, note 1, p. 176.

15 See, for example, Rogers Brubaker, note 12.

16 See, for example, Adrian Favell, *Philosophies of Integration: Immigration and the Idea of Citizenship in France and Britain* (2nd edn, Palgrave, 2001).

17 David Abraham, 'Constitutional Belonging, Citizenship and Belonging' (2009) 6(1) *ICON* 137.

countries, contrasts with the importance placed on citizenship attainment in academic literature on integration. The gradual 'thickening' of political membership and citizenship, referred to by Kostakopoulou (amongst others),[18] is illustrated by the Irish citizenship referendum, integration and language requirements for citizenship and the surrounding debates in the UK, and the increasingly stringent requirements to demonstrate 'assimilation' to obtain French nationality. The boundaries of membership are thus increasingly difficult to cross for migrants in Europe. Finally, despite the apparent stranglehold of domestic law over citizenship practice, this is an evolving area and it must be recognized that there have been significant incursions by international and EU law into the margin of discretion of states. In its final section, the chapter considers the contribution of international law relating to nationality to current debates on citizenship in Europe, as well as the emerging promise of EU law in this sphere.

Access to Citizenship at Birth: *Jus Soli* v *Jus Sanguinis* Approaches to Birthright Citizenship

The capacity of states to define their nationals is a key aspect of state sovereignty.[19] Citizenship is attributed by birth or through naturalization processes, both of which will be discussed below. Looking at whether a state employs a *jus soli* or a *jus sanguinis* approach to birthright citizenship can be seen as an outmoded way to view citizenship regimes.[20] Most countries now operate on a mixture of the two, even countries such as Germany which traditionally operated a descent-based citizenship regime (*jus sanguinis*),[21] and the UK and France which have generally ascribed citizenship to most persons born on their territory (*jus soli*). Nevertheless, the ascription of birthright citizenship remains central to understanding conceptions of membership and citizenship underlying citizenship regimes. In addition, *jus soli* is seen as desirable to integrate immigrant populations, with one of its most 'important effects' being guaranteed access to citizenship for children of immigrant origin – thereby reducing concerns about internal exclusion and insecurity of

18 Dora Kostakopoulou, 'Matters of Control: Integration Tests, Naturalisation Reform and Probationary Citizenship in the United Kingdom' (2010) 36(5) *Ethnic and Migration Studies* 829.

19 This was conclusively established as a matter of international law in the Nottebohm case (*Lichtenstein v Guatemala*) (second phase) 1955 *ICJ* 4.

20 Siobhán Mullally, 'Citizenship and Family Life in Ireland: Asking the Question 'Who Belongs'?', note 6, p. 580.

21 The German Citizenship Act of 2000 introduced a *jus soli* element into German citizenship law. See Anja Wiesbrock, *Legal Migration to the EU* (Martinus Nijhoff, 2010), p. 648.

residence.[22] Consistent with the Irish case discussed above, the trend in European states is towards imposing conditions on *jus soli*, linked to prior parental residence and other conditions ostensibly linked to integration.

Citizenship Debates in Ireland and the 2004 Referendum[23]

On foot of the Belfast Agreement, signed as a central part of the peace process in Northern Ireland in 1998, the Nineteenth Amendment to the Constitution Bill 1998 which proposed the amendment of Articles 2 and 3 of the 1937 Constitution (amongst other articles), was approved by the Irish electorate. The amended Article 2 affirmed the entitlement of every person born on the island of Ireland to be part of the Irish Nation.[24] This changed the existing position under the 1937 Constitution whereby access to citizenship was simply to be determined 'in accordance with law',[25] and in effect reinstated the constitutional imperative of birthright citizenship which had been contained in the 1922 Constitution.[26] This brought access to Irish nationality into the constitutional sphere. Irish-born children of immigrants were the unintended beneficiaries of the inclusive spirit of the Belfast Agreement and the constitutionalization of the *jus soli* principle, which coincided with a significant increase in immigration into Ireland. This coincidence was subsequently described by the Irish Supreme Court as an 'accident of history'.[27]

22 Iseult Honohan, '*Ius Soli* Citizenship', EUDO Citizenship Policy Brief No. 1 (EUI, 2010).

23 The following writings are drawn upon extensively in this section: Siobhan Mullally, 'Citizenship and Family Life in Ireland: asking the Question 'Who Belongs'?', note 6; Bryan Fanning and Fidele Mutwarasibo, note 12; Steve Garner, 'Babies, Bodies and Entitlement: Gendered Aspects of Access to Citizenship in the Republic of Ireland' (2007) 60(3) *Parliamentary Affairs* 437; Donncha O'Connell and Ciara Smyth 'The Constitution and Family Rights', in Ursula Fraser and Colin Harvey (eds), *Sanctuary in Ireland? Perspectives on Asylum Law and Policy* (IPA, 2003); Bryan Fanning and Fidele Mustawaribo, 'The Citizenship Referendum' in Bryan Fanning (ed.), *New Guests of the Irish Nation* (Irish Academic Press, 2009); Siobhán Mullally, 'Citizen children, 'impossible subjects' and the limits of migrant family rights in Ireland' (2011) 1 *EHRLR* 43.

24 The text of the amended Article 2 reads: 'It is the entitlement and birthright of every person born in the island of Ireland, which includes its islands and seas, to be part of the Irish Nation. That is also the entitlement of all persons otherwise qualified in accordance with law to be citizens of Ireland. Furthermore, the Irish nation cherishes its special affinity with people of Irish ancestry living abroad who share its cultural identity and heritage'.

25 Article 9.1.2 of the 1937 Constitution.

26 Article 3 of the 1922 Constitution provided that those domiciled in the area of the jurisdiction of the Free State at the time of its coming into force who had been born in Ireland, had parents born in Ireland or had been ordinarily resident in the area of the jurisdiction of the Free State for seven years would become citizens, however anyone who was the citizen of another state could choose not to become an Irish citizen.

27 *AO and LO v Minister for Justice, Equality and Law Reform* [2003] 1 IR 1, p. 172, *per* Fennelly J.

The amended Article 3 asserts the state's desire to recognize the 'diversity of traditions and identities on the island of Ireland'. Article 3, as amended, is in integration terms the most significant provision in the Irish Constitution, symbolically speaking, as it constitutes the only express recognition of the value of diversity in the 1937 Constitution.[28] This broad phrase was not conceived in order to address the diversity of identity and tradition created by immigration and the spirit of the provision has been undermined by subsequent events, culminating in the constitutional amendment of 2004. In the context of a sharp increase in immigration, it became clear that the wider implications for citizenship of the inclusive impulse which had driven the amendment of Articles 2 and 3 in the context of the reconciliation of communities in Northern Ireland had not been considered.[29]

In parallel to these constitutional changes the jurisprudence of the Irish courts on the residency rights of non-citizen family members of Irish citizens was evolving. The Supreme Court in *Fajujonu v Minister for Justice*[30] had determined that asylum seekers and other immigrants with Irish citizen children were entitled to reside in Ireland on the basis of their children's constitutional right to the care and company of their parents. Following this decision, applications for residency from parents on the basis of their children's citizenship were routinely granted throughout the 1990s. With the advent of significant inward migration into the state, questions surfaced in relation to the perceived 'loophole' created by the combination of automatic birthright citizenship and the administrative approach followed in relation to residence permits which had followed the *Fajujonu* decision. The *Fajujonu* approach was effectively reversed with the decision of the Supreme Court in *AO and LO v Minister for Justice, Equality and Law Reform*.[31] Nevertheless, media and public attention remained focussed on the issue of birthright citizenship.

Outside the legal sphere, there was a corresponding increase in public discussion of immigration and asylum issues between 1997 and 2004.[32] The politicization of immigration gathered momentum in the run-up to the 2002 general elections, with immigration predominantly characterized as an asylum-seeker 'crisis'.[33] Two anti-immigration independent candidates, belonging to the 'Immigration Control

---

28 Speech of Mary McAleese, President of Ireland, at 'Diverse Views on Diversity', Immigrant Council of Ireland conference, 3 November 2010.

29 Deputy Power put it as follows in the Dáil debate following the referendum: 'It was never the intention that the constitutional provisions arising from that Agreement would lead to the position in which we found ourselves through no fault of those who drafted the Agreement or the referendum subsequent to that Agreement'. Dáil Éireann – Volume 591 – 28 October 2004 – Irish Nationality and Citizenship Bill 2004: Second Stage (Resumed).

30 [1990] 2 IR 151.

31 [2003] 1 IR 1.

32 This is explored in detail by Bryan Fanning, 'The Political Currency of Irish Racism 1997–2002' (2002) 91 *Studies* 319, p. 442.

33 Also discussed in Bryan Fanning, ibid.

Platform', stood in these general elections, with neither being elected. In North Central Cork, a Fianna Fáil TD was elected on the basis of what many saw as populist exploitation of the asylum issue.[34] The conflation of the issues of illegal immigration and asylum in the public mind extended to legislative provisions, with the *Illegal Immigrants* (Trafficking) Act 2000 (italics added for emphasis) targeting trafficking of asylum seekers.

In April 2004, the Government announced that a referendum was to take place. The Twenty-Seventh Amendment of the Constitution Bill 2004 proposed that Article 9 be amended to include the following section, Article 9.2:

> 9.2.1 Notwithstanding any other provision of this Constitution, a person born in the island of Ireland, which includes its islands and its seas, who does not have, at the time of his or her birth, at least one parent who is an Irish citizen or entitled to Irish citizenship or nationality, unless otherwise provided for by law.
>
> 9.2.2 This section shall not apply to persons born before the date of the enactment of this section.

Garner distils a fourfold justification presented by the Government for holding the referendum. First, the IBC 'loophole' was threatening the 'integrity' of the immigration system; secondly, membership of the EU required in practical terms the approximation of Irish citizenship laws with those of other EU countries to avoid 'citizenship tourism';[35] thirdly, people with no real links to Ireland should not be allowed to benefit from citizenship; and finally, a crisis was being caused in the maternity system by non-national mothers seeking to give birth in Ireland in order to obtain citizenship for their child.[36] The most emotive of these claims and the one which engendered the most controversy was the essentially economic claim of 'baby tourism' perpetuated by the Minister for Justice of the time, Michael McDowell, to the effect that national maternity hospitals were being overrun by non-national pregnant mothers seeking to give birth in Ireland for the purpose of obtaining citizenship for the child and residence for the rest of the family.[37]

---

34 For a discussion of this, see the contributions of Senators Minihan and Mansergh, amongst others, in the Seanad in the run-up to the citizenship referendum. Seanad Eireann – Volume 176 – 7 April 2004 – Citizenship Rights for Non-Nationals: Motion. See also the comments of Deputy O'Flynn himself, speaking on the Bill after the citizenship: Dáil Éireann – Volume 591 – 28 October 2004 – Irish Nationality and Citizenship Bill 2004: Second Stage (Resumed).

35 This argument was direct result of the decision of the European Court of Justice in *C-200/02 Zhu and Chen v Secretary of State for the Home Department* [2004] ECR I-9925.

36 Steve Garner, note 23, p. 439.

37 See 'Proposed Citizenship Referendum' (Michael McDowell: Minister for Justice, Equality and Law Reform), *Sunday Independent*, 14 March 2004. See also the response of the Minister to a question on the citizenship referendum of Deputy Finian McGrath, Dáil Éireann – Volume 586 – 27 May 2004 – Written Answers – Citizenship Referendum.

The Minister made a number of striking observations in support of the amendment which directly related to integration. He consistently rejected the suggestion that the aim of the amendment was to deny children of the immigrant community access to citizenship, stating, for example:

> The changes we make to citizenship law must show that there is a continuing *céad míle fáilte* for those who migrate legitimately to Ireland with a view to establishing a substantial connection with the State by creating new livelihoods for themselves, contributing to the development of society, sharing in our prosperity and founding families and raising children here.[38]

This quote begs the question as to what the Minister meant by 'legitimate' migrants: does this exclude asylum seekers and refugees, for example (a refugee's time spent in the state as an asylum seeker is not reckonable for the purposes of access to citizenship), or individuals who have been smuggled into that state (who seem to be classed as illegal immigrants under the Illegal Immigrants (Trafficking) Act 2000)? From the viewpoint expressed in this statement, the situation prior to the amendment of the Constitution devalued citizenship as a tool of integration, as citizenship was too easily accessible for children born to families with no real connection to the state and therefore with questionable links to the rest of the polity and consequent lack of commitment to the state. This raises the question as to whether integration is to be based on a commitment to inclusion, openness and ensuring equal rights for all members of society, old and new, or on requiring immigrants prove their 'fidelity to the nation'.

The political discourse surrounding the referendum debates and the parliamentary debates on the Irish Nationality and Citizenship Bill 2004 following the endorsement of the constitutional amendment reveal a spectrum of views on the intersection between immigration, integration and citizenship. Fianna Fáil and the Progressive Democrats, the political parties in government at the time, focussed on the idea that Irish citizenship was something to be earned by those who had contributed to Irish society.[39] Others voiced the opinion that granting citizenship might encourage immigrants 'to contribute more to our democratic society and promote an effective integration, harmony and mutual respect'.[40] Others expressed

---

38 Dáil Éireann – Volume 591 – 27 October 2004 – Irish Nationality and Citizenship Bill 2004: Second Stage.

39 Dáil Éireann – Volume 591 – 28 October 2004 – Irish Nationality and Citizenship Bill 2004: Second Stage (Resumed), comments of Deputy Power. 'It is clear that Irish citizenship should be available to those from other shores who have lived in and contributed to Irish society and who wish to apply for citizenship' (373).

40 Dáil Éireann – Volume 593 – 24 November 2004 – Irish Nationality and Citizenship Bill 2004: Report Stage. (Comments of Deputy Breen).

frustration at the inefficiency of the asylum system at the time and the lack of a coherent immigration policy, which in their view impeded integration.[41]

In spite of the considerable controversy engendered by the proposed amendment,[42] the referendum was passed by a three to one majority, proving resoundingly popular with the Irish electorate. The position introduced only six years previously regarding constitutionally protected birthright citizenship was reversed. The Irish Nationality and Citizenship Act 2004, was adopted, and commenced on 1 January 2005.[43] The overarching theme to emerge from the lead-up and result of the referendum was the sense in which citizenship was perceived by the contributors to the debate on the 2004 referendum not just as a set of rights, but primarily as a mechanism of exclusion of immigrants who had 'not made a contribution to Irish society'.[44] The evolution described here of the use of citizenship from a symbol of inclusion and reconciliation in the context of the Belfast Agreement, to a means of exclusion due to the changing social environment, reflects the interconnectedness of law to its societal and political context and the multiplicity of factors which influence changes in citizenship policy.

The Current Birthright Citizenship Regime in Ireland

Sections 6–12 of the Irish Nationality and Citizenship Act 1956, as amended (the '1956 Act'), govern the acquisition of Irish nationality at birth, with section 6, 6A and 6B and 7 containing the most important provisions. A person is entitled to be an Irish citizen if either of their parents was an Irish citizen at the time of their birth, irrespective of their place of birth. If they were born outside Ireland to an Irish citizen who was himself or herself born in Ireland, then they are automatically an Irish citizen. Section 7(3) provides that while a person born outside Ireland to an Irish citizen who was also born outside Ireland is entitled to citizenship, they are not automatically an Irish citizen. Such a person's birth must be registered under section 27 in order to obtain citizenship, and citizenship commences only as and

41 See the comments of Deputy McGuinness, Dáil Éireann – Volume 591 – 28 October 2004 – Irish Nationality and Citizenship Bill 2004: Second Stage and Deputy Costello, Dáil Éireann – Volume 591 – 27 October 2004 – Irish Nationality and Citizenship Bill 2004: Second Stage.

42 See, for example, the proceeding of a conference hosted by Trinity College Law School, 'The Citizenship Referendum: Implications for the Constitution and Human Rights' (Trinity College Dublin, May 2004), as well as concerns of the Irish Human Rights Commission ('Commission "concerned" over citizenship referendum', *Irish Times*, 5 May 2004) and the Labour Party ('Referendum a Railroading Affair', *Irish Times*, 15 May 2004).

43 Irish Nationality and Citizenship Act 2004 (Commencement) Order 2004 (Statutory Instrument No. 873 of 2004).

44 See, for example, the remarks of the then Minister for Social and Family Affairs, Mary Coughlan, quoted in 'Amendment will Guard Citizenship from Abuse, says Government', *Irish Times*, 11 June 2004.

from the date of such registration.[45] The Irish citizenship of successive generations living outside Ireland may be maintained in this way by each generation registering in the Foreign Births Register before the birth of the next generation.

A more complex picture emerges for children born in Ireland to non-national parents. Pursuant to section 6A of the 1956 Act (as inserted by the Irish Nationality and Citizenship Act 2004 [the '2004 Act']), a person born in Ireland with neither of their parents Irish citizens or entitled to be Irish citizens is not entitled to be an Irish citizen unless one of his or her parents has, during the period of four years immediately preceding the person's birth, been resident in the island of Ireland for a period of not less than three years or periods the aggregate of which is not less than three years. Thus, citizenship for such persons born in Ireland is not automatic. Section 6B details the meaning of 'residence in the island of Ireland' for the purposes of section 6A and provides for the furnishing of a declaration that the parent resided in Ireland for the period stated in the declaration.[46] Importantly, periods spent as a student or an asylum seeker are not reckonable in calculating the period of residence.[47] In relation to asylum seekers, this controversial policy decision was based on the rationale that to provide otherwise 'would serve to encourage false claims and the protraction of the asylum process'.[48] This is an illustration of the overlapping factors shaping citizenship policy.

The legislative provisions thus enshrine a mixture of a *jus soli* (much diluted post the 2004 Act) and a *jus sanguinis* approach. The above analysis reveals the differential expectation of attachment and belonging in relation to those who obtain Irish citizenship by descent and those who obtain it due to presence in the state. The Irish diaspora can obtain Irish citizenship through successive generations without any residence in the state, but immigrants to Ireland must prove their commitment to the state through residence of a minimum of four years residence prior to the birth of the child who is obtaining citizenship on *jus soli* grounds. The method of ascription of Irish citizenship by descent reflects the country's extensive experience of emigration and diaspora, and has symbolic importance in that context. It also illustrates the foundations of citizenship laws in national identity, historical experiences of migration and public philosophy. When juxtaposed against the regime for children of relatively new migrants, however, a contradiction becomes apparent between immigrants living in the state who will be required to prove their commitment to the state through a period of residence,

---

45 This registration requirement was introduced by section 2 of the Irish Nationality and Citizenship Act 1986.

46 The Irish Nationality and Citizenship Regulations 2005 (Statutory Instrument No. 1 of 2005) provide further detail on the form of the declaration and who may witness the declaration. Section 29A of the Irish Nationality and Citizenship Act 1956 creates the offence of knowingly and recklessly making a false or misleading declaration.

47 Section 6B(4)(b) and (c).

48 Comments of Minister McDowell, Dáil Éireann – Volume 591 – 27 October 2004 – Irish Nationality and Citizenship Bill 2004: Second Stage.

and successive generations of Irish emigrants who may never have lived in Ireland and are not subject to this requirement. This diasporic conception of Irishness represents a different perception of connections or ties to the state to that contained in US citizenship law, for example, according to which persons who have acquired US citizenship by descent cannot in general transmit US citizenship to their children unless they have previously established residence in the United States.[49]

Debates in the UK and France: Restricting Jus Soli *in Reaction to Increased Immigration*

The amended Irish position in respect of birthright citizenship quite closely resembles the mixed system of attribution in operation in the UK since the abolition of pure *jus soli* in 1983, when the British Nationality Act 1981 was brought into force.[50] Section 1 of that Act provides that, in order to acquire citizenship at birth, one of the parents of the child must be either a British citizen or be settled in the UK (i.e., have permanent residence). This followed the progressive restriction of the immigration rights of British nationals born outside the UK in former British colonies.[51]

Caroline Sawyer describes the loss of *jus soli* as a fundamental cultural change in the context of the UK, even though it was not one which provoked a considerable amount of debate when it was introduced. She argues that the provisions for being born British and becoming British may now look like those of other European states, but that 'reaching that result has left the old country behind'.[52] Her observation that even though British nationality laws have become much more restrictive and exclusive than they used to be in this regard, they are still well within the 'range of normality', and have not attracted much international criticism,[53] has a resonance with debates on citizenship in the Irish context. While there has been extensive criticism of the implications of the 2004 referendum from Irish commentators, the changes have attracted little international comment and probably would not have provoked so much debate if it were not for the politically charged atmosphere surrounding the reform and the fact that an amendment to the Constitution was required. This shows that it is not the citizenship rules in themselves but the means by which they are arrived at that is relevant from an integration perspective. In both countries, the linking of immigration and nationality law and the desire to make more exclusive, or close off, membership for new immigrants, has been

49 Section 301(c)–(g) of the Immigration and Nationality Act [8 USC 1401].

50 See sections 1 and 2 of the British Nationality Act 1981 (which deal with 'acquisition by birth or adoption' and 'acquisition by descent', respectively).

51 Caroline Sawyer, 'EUDO Citizenship Observatory Country Report: United Kingdom' (EUI, 2009).

52 Ibid.

53 Ibid., at para. 15.

the driving force behind these reforms.[54] This has resulted in these two countries, former colonial master and servant with very different experiences of immigration, having a similar trajectory in terms of birthright citizenship.

Citizenship regimes are understood to be among the clearest expressions, from a legal perspective, of the public philosophy of a state, with national identity, sovereignty and historical experience shaping the legal rules for attribution of citizenship. In France, the concept of citizenship has always been the centrepiece of the Republican form of government, with French citizenship theory based on the idea of political community rather than ethnic origin.[55] Nonetheless, French birthright citizenship has since 1790 been based on various combinations of *jus soli* and *jus sanguinis*. The idea of *droit du sol* has traditionally applied in France, whereby all persons born in France were entitled to French citizenship, although this has been diluted to a certain extent in recent decades. The application of the principles of birthright citizenship was the main subject of the debates which took place in the 1990s surrounding the concept of citizenship.[56] Significant changes in the thrust of citizenship law have reflected politicized debates on integration and mirrored the swings between right and left-wing governments. In 1993, the controversial '*loi Pasqua*', introduced by Jacques Chirac's right-wing government, was 'an attempt to restrict access to French nationality from several angles'.[57] Among other controversial measures,[58] it operated to require French-born children of non-citizen parents born abroad to state their wish (*volonté*) to acquire French nationality between the ages of 16 and 21 and satisfy a number of conditions.[59] Some of the reasons offered for this 'reform' were the non-European origins of many of these children and the fact that in an economic crisis, the traditional instruments of republican 'assimilation' constituted by the army and the school were less efficient than they had been.[60] The law formed part of wider immigration

54 See generally, Iseult Honohan, 'Citizenship Attribution in a New Country of Immigration: Ireland', available at http://ucd-ie.academia.edu/IseultHonohan.

55 On the French conception of citizenship, see generally, Patrick Weil, *Qu'est-ce qu'un Francais? Histoire de la nationalité française de la Révolution* à *nos jours* (Grasset, 2002). See also Yves Lequette, '*Réflexions sur la nationalité française*' *Cahiers du Conseil constitutionnel* No. 23 (Dossier: La citoyenneté, 2008).

56 The evolution of the law in this area is traced by Sergio Carrera, *In Search of the Perfect Citizen? The Intersection between Integration, Immigration and Nationality in the EU* (Martinus Nijhoff, 2009), pp. 312–318.

57 Christophe Bertossi and Abdellali Hajjat, 'EUDO Citizenship Observatory Country Report: France (EUI, 2012), p. 12.

58 See generally, Christophe Bertossi and Abdellali Hajjat, ibid.; and Sergio Carrera, *In Search of the Perfect Citizen? The Intersection between Integration, Immigration and Nationality in the EU*, note 56.

59 Article 11 of *Loi no. 93–933 réformant le droit de la nationalité, JO 22 juillet 1993*.

60 As discussed in Patrick Weil, *Rapport au Premier ministre sur les législations de la nationalité et de l'immigration* (*La Documentation Française*, 1997).

policy with the aim of restricting access to French nationality and to limit the application of *jus soli*.[61]

Reform in 1998 by the new left-wing government in respect of this aspect of nationality law reinstated the legal position pertaining prior to 1992, whereby French-born children of non-citizens born abroad acquire French nationality automatically when they reach the age of 18.[62] The criteria for the grant of citizenship in these cases are that the individual must have been born and reside in France and have had their usual place of residence there for a period of at least five years since the age of 11.[63] This change in the law paralleled a new anti-discrimination agenda which was feeding into a new policy approach to migrant integration.[64] It also followed a report drafted by the eminent citizenship theorist, Patrick Weil, which recommended that the requirement for the 'manifestation of will' of the child be abolished.[65] One element of the 1993 law which significantly diluted *jus soli* and which was not repealed in 1998, was the removal of the right to double *jus soli* for children born in France after 1 January 1994 to at least one parent born in a French territory that had become independent.[66] In summary, today, French nationality is attributed at birth if one of the child's parents is French (regardless of place of birth) (*jus sanguinis*)[67] or if the child is born in France and also has one parent born in France (double *jus soli*).[68] In addition, a person born in France, whose parents are neither French nor born in France, will automatically become French at the age of 18 if they still reside in France and can prove they have had their residence in France for five years since the age of eleven.

Thick and Thin, Open and Closed Visions of Nationality and Belonging

It has been argued that the primary implication of the Irish 2004 referendum is that an entitlement to 'Irishness' is primarily an essence that can be transmitted genetically.[69] In terms of access to the polity, the present position certainly privileges those with Irish parents or grandparents even when they do not live in the state or may never have been in the state, over those present in the state

61 Paul Lagarde, '*La nationalité française rétrécie: commentaire critique de la loi du 22 juillet 1993 réformant le droit de la nationalité*' (1993) *Revue critique de droit international privé* 82.

62 *Loi no. 98–170 relative à la nationalité, JO 16 mars 1998.*

63 Article 21–7 of the Civil Code.

64 See, for example, Fassin, '*L'Invention Française de la Discrimination*' (2002) *Revue française de science politique* 403.

65 Patrick Weil, *Rapport au Premier ministre sur les législations de la nationalité et de l'immigration*, note 60.

66 Bertossi and Hajjat, note 57, p. 11. See Article 47 of *Loi no. 93–933 réformant le droit de la nationalité, JO 22 juillet 1993.*

67 Article 18 and 18–1 of the Civil Code.

68 Article 19–3 of the Civil Code.

69 Steve Garner, note 23, p. 443.

with non-Irish parents. Pursuant to the changes introduced by the Irish Nationality and Citizenship (Amendment) Act 2004, introduced following the referendum, children born to non-national parents may acquire citizenship by birth only if the non-national parents can show a 'genuine link' to Ireland (which is proved if one parent has been lawfully resident within the state or in Northern Ireland (or entitled to be resident) for a period of three years or more).[70] In integration terms, this means that citizenship of children born in Ireland depends on a degree of integration of their parents, measured through length of residence. The use of the concept of citizenship in the Irish context as a tool of integration is thus, in the case of Irish citizen children, dependent on a certain level of integration having already been attained by a third party – a parent. The increasingly conditional nature of *jus soli* as related to integration is also evident in the British and French nationality frameworks. In the UK, one parent must have achieved either citizenship or permanent residence in order for their child to acquire citizenship at birth, and in France one parent must be a citizen or have been born in France themselves. The children in each case can make up for the lack of integration of their parents by eventually becoming integrated themselves, with British-born children able to obtain nationality through registration at the age of 10 provided certain residence requirements are met[71] and (as discussed), French born children obtaining nationality automatically at 18.

The evolution of the Irish approach mirrors the development of the law in the UK and France, with all three countries imposing restrictions on the *jus soli* principle in response to increased immigration. Indeed, most EU Member States now operate their citizenship regimes on the basis of a similar type of approach to that enshrined in the amendment to Article 9 of the Irish Constitution. Despite this widespread acceptance of the legitimacy of this approach and the continuing openness of citizenship regimes in these countries as compared to other states, citizenship conceived in these terms is not just a set of rights but a device of exclusion. In comparative terms and despite significant differences between them, Irish, British and French citizenship laws enshrine a middle-ground between the very open birthright citizenship regime in the US,[72] where citizenship is given to nearly every person born on US soil, and the traditionally ethnically centred citizenship frameworks in Germany and Israel. It has been argued that thinner visions of citizenship, along the US model of individualistic equal protection of

70 Section 6A of the Irish Nationality and Citizenship Act 1956, as inserted by the Irish Nationality and Citizenship Act 2004.

71 Section 1(4) of the 1981 Act provides: 'A person born in the United Kingdom … shall be entitled, on an application for his registration as a British citizen made at any time after he has attained the age of ten years, to be registered as such a citizen if, as regards each of the first ten years of that person's life, the number of days on which he was absent from the United Kingdom in that year does not exceed 90'.

72 Section 301 (a) and (b) of the Immigration and Nationality Act [8 USC 1401]. See generally, Lauren Gilbert, 'National Identity and Immigration Policy in the U.S. and the European Union' (2007–2008) 14 *Columbia Journal of European Law* 99.

mostly negative rights, are better suited to integrating foreigners into the solidarity of social life by way of civic-constitutional and cultural principles than thicker citizenship foundations with sharper exclusions on ethnocultural lines and more explicit social rights and ties – such as those traditionally present in Germany and Israel.[73]

As Iseult Honohan observes, we don't have to see policy changes relating to citizenship as inherently linked to conceptions of citizenship or national identity.[74] In relation to *jus soli* citizenship regimes, she emphasizes the point that possible forces underlying changes also include declining populations, large numbers of immigrants (for reasons of justice, social cohesion and/or security), international conventions and norms of non-discrimination and states learning from, or competing with, one another.[75] Nonetheless, the importance of the citizenship dimension of public philosophy and political thought in European states is clear from the analysis in this section. The ascription of citizenship at birth is based on a presumption of membership, which reflects the fact that at birth certain persons have a high probability of developing the close attachments and loyalties to a particular society and state that are supposed to underlie citizenship.[76] While changes in citizenship law are not solely linked to national identity, the ascription of citizenship at birth is, at the very least, an indication of attitudes to membership and belonging.

Access to Citizenship through Naturalization

While the acquisition of citizenship at birth is symbolic of attitudes to political and social membership, most immigrants will acquire citizenship through naturalization, and access to citizenship through naturalization can be characterized as a key integration mechanism.[77] Dual citizenship is permitted under Irish citizenship law, as it is in France and the UK, and this common characteristic of citizenship frameworks can be seen as an indicator of an open and inclusive citizenship regime. From an integration perspective, this allows immigrants to maintain the identity of their country of origin on a legal level while adding another layer to their legal identity. This accords with the two-way conception of integration,

---

73 David Abraham, note 17. See generally, Anja Wiesbrock, *Legal Migration to the EU* (Martinus Nijhoff, 2010), p. 648; Daphne Barak-Erez, 'Israel: Citizenship and Immigration Law in the Vise of Security, Nationality an Human Rights' (2008) 6(1) *ICON* 184; Ayelet Schachar, 'Citizenship and Membership in the Israeli Polity', in T. Alexander Aleinikoff and Douglas Klusmeyer (eds), *From Migrants to Citizens: Membership in a Changing World* (Carnegie, 2000), p. 386, in particular pp. 409–410.

74 Iseult Honohan, 'The Theory and Politics of Ius Soli', EUDO Citizenship Observatory (EUI, June 2010), p. 1.

75 Ibid., p. 1.

76 Rogers Brubaker, note 12, p. 35.

77 As it is in the MIPEX study, for example. See note 9.

which does not require immigrants to relinquish their identity in order to become part of the polity of the host country. Overall, comparative EU research reveals 'a diverse and complicated picture' across the Member States regarding the laws and procedures for acquiring citizenship, and finds that '(a)ttitudes towards migration and the process of immigrant integration are among the significant factors which determine the requirements and procedures adopted'.[78] The regimes examined in this section illustrate this diversity, with the spectrum of approaches ranging from the facilitation of naturalization through improved procedures to the imposition of stringent language and integration tests.

Ireland: A Liberal Naturalization Regime Marked by Ministerial Discretion

Part III of the 1956 Act, as amended (sections 14–20) governs the acquisition of citizenship by naturalization in Ireland. Citizenship is conferred by means of a certificate of naturalization granted by the Minister (section 14) and the conditions for the issue of this certificate are set out in section 15. These are that the applicant is of full age, of good character, has had a period of one year's continuous residence in the state immediately before the application and four year's residence out of the previous eight years, intends to reside in the state after naturalization and has made an oath of fidelity to the nation and loyalty to the state. Section 15 provides for the 'absolute discretion' of the Minister in deciding whether to grant the application for naturalization on satisfaction of these conditions – one of the few instances in Irish law where a Minister is granted the sole power of deciding an outcome of an application in his absolute discretion.[79] This discretion is subject only to the requirements of constitutional justice,[80] and there is no legitimate expectation to a grant of citizenship consequent upon fulfilling all of the statutory

78 European Website on Integration Special Feature, note 10. See also OECD, 'Naturalisation: A Passport for the Better Integration of Immigrants?' (OECD, 2011); Tineke Strik, Anita Böcker, Maaike Luiten and Ricky van Oers/INTEC, 'Integration and Naturalisation tests: the new way to European Citizenship' (Synthesis Report, 2011).

79 The unusual nature of the power was pointed out by Clark J in *Abuissa v Minister for Justice, Equality and Law Reform* [2010] IEHC 366.

80 *Mishra v Minister for Justice* [1996] 1 IR 189. Kelly J found that in this case, the requirements of natural and constitutional justice had not been met and required the Minister to give fresh consideration to the application. *Mishra* was followed in *Robert and Muresan v Minister for Justice, Equality and Law Reform*, High Court, Unreported, Peart J, 11 February 2004. The judgment was also cited in the context of ministerial discretion in deportation proceedings in *Sinik v Minister for Justice, Equality and Law Reform*, High Court, Unreported, Smyth J, 19 July 2002 and in the context of ministerial discretion in awarding subsidiary protection in *Gavrylyuk v Minister for Justice, Equality and Law Reform* [2008] IEHC 321. An example of a case in which the Minister was found to have acted incorrectly was in *H(L.G.) v Minister for Justice, Equality and Law Reform* [2009] IEHC 78.

criteria.[81] The Minister is entitled in exercising this absolute discretion to take into account public policy considerations, including in relation to immigration policy, which have little or nothing to do with the facts in the individual case.[82] In *Mishra v Minister for Justice, Equality and Law Reform*,[83] Kelly J observed that the Minister was entitled to adopt a general policy not to naturalize people who would be unemployable in their chosen profession and would therefore emigrate after naturalization.

While the relevant statutory provisions do not require the Minister to give reasons for his decision to refuse a certificate of naturalization, it was confirmed by the Supreme Court in 2012 in *Mallak v Minister for Justice, Equality and Law Reform*,[84] in a departure from the previous approach of the High Court,[85] that the Minister does have such a duty to give reasons. Fennelly J stated that just because the applicant was applying for the 'privilege' of citizenship, which he has no right to compel the state to grant to him, this did not mean that he enjoyed inferior legal protection when pursuing that application,[86] and on consulting a wide range of sources such as Irish legislation, EU law (including the Charter of Fundamental Rights) and jurisprudence of the Irish and UK courts, the Court found that 'at this point, it must be unusual for a decision maker to be permitted to refuse to give reasons'.[87] This at least enhances the legal protection available to the migrant in the naturalization process, and the transparency of the process itself, although it does not displace the overall control of the Minister.

The overarching theme of ministerial discretion in the field of citizenship is evident in the Minister's power to dispense with the conditions of naturalization in certain cases as set out in section 16. These include in the case of recognized refugees or stateless persons (s. 16(1)(g)); naturalized citizens applying on the behalf of a minor child; and where the applicant is 'of Irish descent or Irish associations' (s.16(1)(a)). The concept of Irish associations is based on association through blood rather than extending to associations with the Irish State or contribution to Irish society,[88] thereby reflecting (as is the case with the birthright citizenship regime) an ethnically centred conception of citizenship. However, despite this underlying tendency, individuals applying for citizenship through naturalization in Ireland are not required to demonstrate proficiency in English (or Irish), nor

81 Ibid. See also *H(L.G.) v Minister for Justice, Equality and Law Reform* 2009 [IEHC] 78.

82 Ibid., p. 204.

83 *Mishra v Minister for Justice* [1996] 1 IR 189.

84 [2012] IESC 59. See generally, Clíodhna Murphy, 'Reconciling Sovereignty Claims with Individual Rights? Access to Citizenship After *Mallak* and *Sulaimon*' (2013) 49(1) *Irish Jurist* 193.

85 *Abuissa v Minister for Justice, Equality and Law Reform* [2010] IEHC 366; *Mallak v. Minister for Justice, Equality and Law Reform* [2011] IEHC 306.

86 *Mallak v Minister for Justice, Equality and Law Reform* [2012] IESC 59, at para. 50.

87 Ibid., at para. 74.

88 See section 16(1).

are they required to satisfy any integration requirements. This is unusual amongst wealthy Western nations, as can be seen from the analysis below. On comparison with other citizenship frameworks, and perhaps contrary to some of what has been argued in this chapter, Irish citizenship law could be said to encompass an open form of citizenship, using residence alone as the indicator of embededdness in Irish society. A more pragmatic view would seem to be that rather than being founded on inclusive integration principles or an open conception of membership, this openness is explicable by reference to the context in which the citizenship framework was developed: that of negligible inward migration. This reflects the reality that 'choices among citizenship rules are usually shaped more by historical experience, existing cultural norms, and expedient political calculations than by deduction from abstract principle or compelling reasons of logical consistency'.[89]

As already mentioned, the onset of the economic crisis in Ireland resulted in a change of government and the abolition of the Office for the Minister for Integration. Contrary to the trend across EU countries, recent reforms to the practice of naturalization in Ireland have not concentrated on erecting barriers to accessing citizenship. Rather, the focus in recent changes to the naturalization process has been on speeding up the process for those who have applied, making naturalization more financially affordable and introducing citizenship ceremonies to welcome new citizens into the Irish nation.[90] This runs counter to European trends and, revealingly, reflects a changed discourse in Ireland of lessened concerns about immigration and threats to social cohesion perceived to be posed by the creation of large migrant communities. However, proposals for the reform of other aspects of the acquisition of citizenship would bring Ireland closer to the model of access to naturalization currently in use across Europe. The more or less defunct integration strategy, Migration Nation, envisaged a formal pathway to permanent residency and citizenship for those who qualify as one of the key actions to be taken in the sphere of citizenship.[91] In January 2012, the Minister for Justice and Equality indicated that his department is working on developing a language and integration test to be imposed on applicants for naturalization, although the form of this test is as yet unclear.[92] The Minister's rationale for this move reflected the diffusion of the discourse of civic integration around EU Member States, which is explored in detail in the next section. He stated:

---

89 See T. Alexander Aleinikoff and Douglas Klusmeyer (eds), *From Migrants to Citizens: Membership in a Changing World* (Carnegie, 2000), p. 2.

90 Irish Nationality and Citizenship Regulations 2011 (S.I. No. 569/2011); Irish Nationality and Citizenship (Amendment) Regulations 2011 (S.I. No. 284/2011); Civil Law (Miscellaneous Provisions) Act 2011.

91 Office of the Minister for Integration, *Migration Nation: Statement on Integration Strategy and Diversity Management* (May 2008), p. 9.

92 Irish Naturalisation and Immigration Service, 'Immigration in Ireland 2011 – a year-end snapshot – major changes and more to follow' (INIS, 3 January 2012).

> (S)uch tests are a standard part of the naturalisation process in many countries worldwide; the ability to speak the language – even at a most basic level – together with some knowledge of the way business is conducted in Ireland is an essential part of the integration process for immigrants and must form an integral part of eligibility for naturalisation.[93]

Citizenship as a Reward for 'Successful' Integration? Integration and Language Requirements in Naturalization Procedures

In the European context, common barriers to accessing citizenship relate to language proficiency and proving a certain degree of integration or knowledge of the host country.[94] The emergence and evolution of language and integration tests as a key element of the naturalization process have been mapped in detail and analysed by legal scholars.[95] Most European states require a competency in the local language before citizenship is granted. In addition, many states are introducing tests of knowledge of life, culture and institutions in the host country as a prerequisite to obtaining citizenship. These integration tests evidence a requirement for a more active participation for those seeking citizenship who do not passively belong, territorially or ethnically. Those without citizenship by birth must prove their commitment to the state and ability to participate in social solidarity.[96] Thus prospective naturalized citizens are expected to gain a knowledge of the functioning of the society and political system that is in many cases beyond that of the majority of members of the polity by birthright. A good example of this is the Life in the UK test, which has been criticized on the basis that most Britons would not pass if given the test.[97] Carrera describes the purpose behind the normativity of integration in nationality law as:

---

93 Ibid.

94 See generally, the contributions to Ricky Van Oers, Eva Ersboll and Dora Kostakopoulou (eds), *A Re-Definition of Belonging? Language and Integration Tests in Europe* (Martinus Nijhoff Publishers, 2010), in particular Bernhard Perchinig, 'All you Need to Know to Become an Austrian: Naturalisation Policy and Citizenship Testing in Austria' (p. 25); Ricky Van Oers, 'Citizenship Tests in the Netherlands, Germany and the UK' (p. 51); and Judit Toth, 'Ethnic Citizenship: Can it be Obtained and Tested?' (p. 211). See also Gerard-René de Groot, Jan-Jaap Kuipers and Franziska Weber, 'Passing Citizenship Tests as a Requirement for Naturalisation: A Comparative Perspective', in Elspeth Guild, Sergio Carrera and Kees Groenendijk (eds), *Illiberal Liberal States: Immigration, Citizenship and Integration in the EU* (Ashgate, 2009).

95 Ibid.

96 See David Abraham, note 17.

97 In February 2012, an Ipsos MORI Poll commissioned by the UK television channel 'Channel 4' showed that seven in ten of the British citizens surveyed failed a short test based on a number of questions from the Life in the UK test. See http://www.channel4.com/info/press/news/seven-in-ten-britons-fail-citizenship-test.

> managing and safeguarding the notion of the "perfect citizen" belonging to the nation state. This notion is based on a compendium of features and characteristics composed of subjective stereotypes, traditional perceptions and visions of the past and present, principles and classical values deemed to rule the "one and only society", and conceptions of the self and the Other.[98]

The following two sections consider the interaction of integration and nationality law in France and the UK.

Citizenship and Assimilation in France

As mentioned in previous chapters, France has traditionally been perceived as enshrining an assimilationist model of integration. This model is evident in the conditions for naturalization as a French citizen, which require proof not just of 'integration' (as is required for family reunification visas, for example) but of 'assimilation' into the French conception of the political community constituted by the nation. The requirement to prove one's assimilation, in the form of sufficient knowledge of the 'rights and duties' of French citizenship, dates to 2003, prior to which only proficiency in French was required.[99] In 2011, the requirements were further toughened, when the Civil Code was amended to include reference not only to 'rights and duties' but also to 'essential principles and values of the Republic'.[100] In addition, the idea that the individual applicant must demonstrate, not just knowledge of the principles and values of the Republic, but *adherence* to these, was introduced.[101] The first paragraph of Article 21.24 of the Civil Code now provides:

> No one can be naturalised if he does not demonstrate his or her assimilation into the French community, in particular by a sufficient knowledge (according to their level), of the French language, history, culture and society, the level and the evaluation methods of which will be set by decree in the Council of State, and the rights and duties conferred by French citizenship as well as adherence to the essential principles and values of the Republic.[102]

---

98 Sergio Carrera, *In Search of the Perfect Citizen? The Intersection between Immigration, Integration and Nationality in the European Union*, note 56, p. 441.

99 *Loi no. 2003–1119 relative* à *la maitrise de l'immigration, au séjour des étrangers en France et* à *la nationalité, JO 27 novembre 2003.*

100 *Loi no. 2011–672 du 16 juin 2011 relative à l'immigration, à l'intégration et à la nationalité, JO 17 juin 2011.*

101 Ibid. See also Tineke Strik, Anita Böcker, Maaike Luiten and Ricky van Oers/ INTEC, note 78, pp. 19–20.

102 *'Nul ne peut être naturalisé s'il ne justifie de son assimilation à la communauté française, notamment par une connaissance suffisante, selon sa condition, de la langue, de l'histoire, de la culture et de la société françaises, dont le niveau et les modalités d'évaluation sont fixés par décret en Conseil d'Etat, et des droits et devoirs conférés par*

The 2011 law also introduced a requirement for the person undertaking the assessment of their assimilation to sign the 'Charter of rights and duties of the French citizen'.[103]

'Assimilation' is tested not through a formal written or set oral test, but is measured when the applicant submits their application for citizenship to the town hall and is interviewed by an official there. While this procedure lacks a degree of legal certainty and transparency, it avoids the rigidity of a formal test and allows the applicant's subjective characteristics to be taken into account. The administrative procedure to be followed has been set out in secondary legislation, which gives some indication as to what 'assimilation' entails.[104] As was seen above, until 2012, the requirements were becoming more and more stringent and difficult to satisfy, with decrees published in 2011 and 2012 imposing stricter conditions in the form of higher levels of knowledge of French language, culture and history.[105] As was seen in the context of birthright citizenship above, however, this area of the law is highly politicized, and reforms were introduced in October 2012 by the government of the newly-elected Socialist Party, abolishing the idea of specific multiple-choice questions on French history and culture (which was never actually introduced prior to the change in government) and opening up the naturalization procedure to students and immigrants with a less stable employment status.[106] A presumption of integration has also been introduced for the under 25s.[107] The relevant circular clarifies that a 'deep or encyclopaedic' knowledge of French history, culture and society is not required, and the interview should be conversational rather than in the form of a questionnaire requiring specific answers: what must be shown is that they have a grasp of the basic principles

la nationalité française ainsi que par l'adhésion aux principes et aux valeurs essentiels de la République'.

103 Article 21.24, second paragraph. '*A l'issue du contrôle de son assimilation, l'intéressé signe la charte des droits et devoirs du citoyen français. Cette charte, approuvée par décret en Conseil d'Etat, rappelle les principes, valeurs et symboles essentiels de la République française*'.

104 See, for example, *Décret n° 93–1362 du 30 décembre 1993 relatif aux demandes de naturalisation et de réintégration*; *Décret n° 2011–1265 du 11 octobre 2011 relatif au niveau de connaissance de la langue française requis des postulants à la nationalité française au titre des articles 21–2 et 21–24 du code civil et à ses modalités d›évaluation*; *Décret n° 2012–126 du 30 janvier 2012 relatif au niveau et à l›évaluation de la connaissance de l›histoire, de la culture et de la société françaises requis des postulants à la nationalité française au titre de l›article 21–24 du code civil.*

105 '*Un décret durcit les conditions de naturalisation en France*', *Le Monde*, 2 February 2012.

106 Circular No. INTK1207286C, '*Procedures d'accès à la nationalité française*', 16 October 2012.

107 Ibid.

necessary for the exercise of citizenship.[108] These reforms may signal a respite in the evolution of increasingly restrictive, integration-focussed citizenship rules.

As can be seen from the above, French naturalization policy is openly assimilationist in nature in requiring adherence to French Republican values. Reflecting the difficulties involved in delineating the boundaries of this policy, the wearing of the Muslim veil by women seeking citizenship has become a site of conflict, with the veil constructed as an indicator of the 'insufficient' assimilation of the woman in question. This is both a product of and has contributed to the construction of the Muslim veil, and particularly the *burqa* and the *niqab*, as incompatible with French egalitarian values. Thus, in 2008, the *Conseil d'Etat* confirmed that it was legal to deny a woman citizenship on the basis that her wearing the face veil during her citizenship interview was evidence of her failure to adapt to the purported French conception of gender equality.[109] The woman was living in France, married to a French man, with three French children. Citizenship ceremonies also have a significant place in the French naturalization process[110] and, in a few cases, women wearing a Muslim headscarf have not been admitted to the ceremony, on the basis that they are wearing ostentatious religious symbols.[111]

Citizenship has thus become the ultimate forum for the promotion of French values, as defined centrally by the state. Using citizenship as a barrier to access for those who are seen as not capable of filling the mould of the idealized French citizen gives rise to one of the clearest expressions of the 'clash of cultures' mentality involved in enshrining integration conditions into citizenship law, speaking volumes about the national public philosophy which ultimately underpins integration policy in France. Caught up in the theorizing about French citizenry, values and Republican principles, in the midst of the political manoeuvring, the Muslim woman becomes the fall guy, at the centre of the French state's 'policing of the intimate lives of immigrant others'.[112]

---

108 Ibid.

109 *Conseil d'Etat*, 'Refusal of French nationality to a person who shows a religious practice incompatible with the essential values of the French community' (no. 28679827, June 2008). On theories of legislative and judicial developments in France leading up to the decision in *Mme M*, see generally Patrick Weil, 'Why French *Laïcité* is Liberal' (2009) 30(6) *Cardozo Law Review* 2699. On the case itself, see Anastasia Vakulenko, 'Gender Equality as an Essential French Value: The Case of *Mme M*' (2009) 9(1) *HRLR* 143.

110 Article 21.28 and 21.29 of the Civil Code.

111 See generally, Abdellali Hajjat, *Les frontières de 'l'identité nationale': l'injonction à l'assimilation en France métropolitaine et coloniale* (La Découverte, 2012), p. 211.

112 Siobhán Mullally, 'Civic Integration, Migrant Women and the Veil: At the Limits of Rights?' (2011) 74(1) *Modern Law Review* 27, p. 40.

Testing Knowledge of 'Life in the UK'

While France can trace the requirement to assimilate back at least as far as 1927,[113] other European states which have not traditionally operated immigration and citizenship policy on the basis of conceptions of integration and assimilation have also introduced formal citizenship integration tests.[114] These include the UK, which has moved from the '*laissez faire*' attitude to citizenship encapsulated in the British Nationality Act 1981,[115] whereby those with long-term residency rights were allowed to apply for citizenship after five years in the country with a minimum of legal requirements, to requiring applicants to prove that they have sufficient knowledge of English and of life in the UK. Prior to these changes, the naturalization regime in the UK closely resembled that currently in place in Ireland, being a relatively 'low-key, private and bureaucratic process'.[116] In 2004, naturalization policy and procedure underwent a paradigm shift when the Government introduced a 'Life in the UK' test as well as requiring proficiency in English as a prerequisite to naturalization.[117] Up to 2013, these requirements could be satisfied by taking and passing a course for English for Speakers of Other Languages (ESOL) (which includes a component based on the official handbook *Life in the UK: A Journey to Citizenship*) or by passing a test on a computer which is based on the handbook.[118] From 28 October 2013, the process has become more difficult, with applicants required to prove that they possess a B1 intermediate level of conversational English, as well as passing the Life in the UK test.[119] The original test mainly comprised questions relating to everyday life and administrative processes, however, from March 2013, the questions have been based on history, values and culture.[120]

---

113 Bertossi and Hajjat, note 57, p. 15.

114 Tineke Strik, Anita Böcker, Maaike Luiten and Ricky van Oers/INTEC, note 78.

115 Sarah Spencer, *The Migration Debate* (Policy Press, 2011), p. 226.

116 Ibid., citing UK Border Agency, 'Multi-Annual Programme for the European Fund for the Integration of Third-Country nationals for the Period 2007–2013 as part of the General Programme 'Solidarity and Management of Migration Flows' (Home Office, 2008), p. 13.

117 See, in particular, paragraphs 33B and 33C of the Immigration Rules ('Knowledge of language and life in the United Kingdom').

118 See paragraph 33B of the Immigration Rules.

119 Home Office, 'Statement of Intent: Knowledge of Language and Life in the UK for Settlement and Naturalisation' (April, 2013).

120 Those who sat the test before 25 March 2013 were tested on the basis of *Life in the UK Handbook 2nd Edition: A Journey to Citizenship* (UK Government Stationery Office); those who sit the test on or after that date are tested on the basis of *Life in the UK Handbook 3rd Edition: A Guide for New Residents* (UK Government Stationery Office). See also the UK Border Agency Life in the UK Test website, at http://lifeintheuktest.ukba.homeoffice.gov.uk/htmlsite/self2_20.html.

In introducing the Life in the UK test, the UK Government of the time conceived of it as a key element in its aims to reinforce solidarity and promote the 'common bond' of British citizenship[121] as a mechanism to provide a link between diverse communities, particularly in the wake of the social disorder involving second-generation immigrant communities in Burnley, Oldham and Bradford in the summer of 2001.[122] The reforms thus formed part of the Government's broader 'community cohesion' agenda, focussed on a shared sense of a future vision for the local and national communities,[123] which gained a greater momentum in light of the terrorist attacks carried out in London in 2005 by British citizens. In line with this agenda of encouraging loyalty and shared citizenship, citizenship ceremonies were also introduced, with the idea of giving new citizens a sense of the importance of entering the British nation.[124] Reports commissioned to review the Life in the UK test admitted the shortcomings of the test, including the fact that statistics showed that it is easier for some ethnic communities to pass than others and that many British citizens by birth would not pass the test.[125] Nevertheless, the test was not modified to deal with these issues and the Advisory Board on Naturalisation and Integration, which helped the Government in the development of the tests and citizenship ceremonies, was disbanded in 2008. The scope of the group of people covered by the requirements was extended to those seeking settlement (indefinite leave to remain) through a change to the Immigration Rules in 2007.

The Labour government attempted to take citizenship reform a step further in the Borders, Citizenship and Immigration Act 2009 in adopting the idea set out in a report entitled *The Path to Citizenship* introducing the idea of 'probationary citizenship', whereby the time to access full citizenship would be lengthened in order for the individual to show their commitment to the UK and the contribution that they would make.[126] This was linked to the concept of 'active citizenship', with applicants demonstrating social contribution through volunteering, raising the bar even higher for those seeking entry to the British polity. Unsurprisingly, the reforms were very contentious; both within Parliament and among academic

---

121 On the idea of the 'common bond', see Lord Goldsmith's subsequent report, 'Citizenship: Our Common Bond' (2008).

122 See Derek McGhee 'The Paths to Citizenship: A Critical Examination of Immigration Policy in Britain since 2001' (2009) 43(1) *Patterns of Prejudice* 41. See the government document, *Secure Borders, Safe Haven: Integration with Diversity in Modern Britain* Cm5387 (Home Office, 2002).

123 Final Report of the Commission on Integration and Cohesion, *Our Shared Future* (June 2007).

124 Lord Goldsmith, note 121, p. 10.

125 Lord Goldsmith, note 121, p. 118 and 119. The suggested reforms include, for example, incorporating more of a regional element into the test.

126 UK Border Agency, 'The Path to Citizenship: Next Steps in Reforming the Immigration System' (Home Office, 2008); UK Border Agency, 'Earning the Right to Stay, A New Points Test for Citizenship' (Home Office, 2009).

commentators,[127] and the Conservative-Liberal Democrat government announced in 2010 that it would not be implementing the earned citizenship policy.[128]

Many commentators have criticized what they see as a significant restrictive turn in UK citizenship law embodied in the citizenship test and the actual and proposed reforms thereto.[129] On the other hand, Kymlicka points out that viewed in themselves, specific reforms have been 'moderate and pragmatic', if looked at separate from the broader context of anti-immigration measures and the retreat from multiculturalism in the UK, along with the trajectory of citizenship policy generally which has become progressively more assimilationist and racially biased.[130] Notwithstanding different viewpoints on the efficacy, fairness and aims of the citizenship test, both the test itself and the surrounding debates have clear implications for citizenship both as a legal category and as a normative concept in the UK.[131] In trying to create an 'inclusive civic Britishness', the integration test is a constitutive element of the concept of citizenship in the UK. The attempt to introduce the idea of 'earned citizenship', in particular, was an attempt to define (or redefine) what a good citizen should be. This ideal of citizenship is legally imposed on migrants through the naturalization process in a way that it cannot be on existing citizens in a liberal democratic state. In a sense then, as was seen in the French context above, migrants seeking citizenship are the 'collateral damage' of a country seeking an identity. Measures apparently seeking to improve their integration into a functioning and cohesive national identity and society are in fact measures to try and redefine the society itself. Unfortunately, this means that measures which are ostensibly designed to aid migrant integration can result in exclusion from a secure legal status completely, and become an attempt to make migrants prove that they fit in to a society which does not in fact exist. The fact that this can result in exclusion from legal status is ultimately unacceptable and disingenuous.

While the Conservative-Liberal Democrat government shelved the idea of earned citizenship, it has continued to focus on ways to limit access to settlement and citizenship, taking the approach of just shutting off paths to these statuses

---

127 See Arabella Thorp and Gabrielle Garton Grimwood, 'Borders, Citizenship and Immigration Bill [HL]' Research Paper 09 (House of Commons, 2009); Ann Dummet, 'Changes to Citizenship' (2008) 22(3) *Journal of Immigration Asylum and Nationality Law* 213; Bernard Ryan, 'Integration Requirements: A New Model in Migration Law' (2008) 22(4) *Journal of Immigration, Asylum and Nationality Law* 303.

128 UK Border Agency, 'Government Announcement on Settlement Reforms' (Press release, 5 November 2011).

129 Dora Kostakopoulou, 'The Anatomy of Civic Integration' (2010) 73(6) *Modern Law Review* 933; Bernard Ryan, note 127; Derek McGhee, note 122.

130 See also Randall Hansen, 'Citizenship tests: an unapologetic defense', in EUI Working Paper, 'How Liberal are Citizenship tests?' (RSCAS 2010/41, EUI 2010), p. 25.

131 On the argument that deportation is constitutive of citizenship, see Bridget Anderson, Matthew Gibney and Emanuela Paoletti, 'Citizenship, deportation and the boundaries of belonging' (2011) 15(5) *Citizenship Studies* 547.

altogether rather than increase the requirements at the application stage. The route to settlement has been cut off for most categories of migrants within the Points-Based System, as well as overseas domestic workers, with Government policy expressly aiming to 'break the link between work and staying in the UK permanently'.[132] This is in fact a much more restrictive approach and could result in many more individuals being denied citizenship in the long term. As mentioned above, in July 2012 it was also reported that the Government intended to introduce an overhaul of the citizenship test required for naturalization, and the new test has been in place from March 2013.[133] The intention of the Government is for the test to put a stronger emphasis on British history and culture, making clear the 'responsibilities' of settling in Britain – clearly reflecting the legacy of the Labour years. In discussing the new test, the Immigration Minister Mark Harper, much like his Irish counterpart, made the link to integration explicit, stating:

> The new book rightly focuses on values and principles at the heart of being British. Instead of telling people how to claim benefits it encourages participation in British life. ... This is just part of our work to help ensure migrants are ready and able to integrate into British society and forms part of our changes which have broken the automatic link between temporary and permanent migration.[134]

It is also interesting to note that, despite the significantly different historical and theoretical foundations of citizenship in France and the UK, the increasingly prescriptive requirements for naturalization in France and the UK converge at the point of linguistic assimilation. From 1 January 2012 (France) and October 2013 (UK), linguistic assimilation must be shown by applicants for naturalization in both countries by presenting a linguistic diploma that certifies the B1 level of the Common European Framework of Reference for Languages.[135] Policy, practice and legislation in this area are thus converging in a variety of ways across the EU.

Implications of the Move to an Integration-Focused Model of Naturalization

The effect of integration testing in purely numerical terms – of lowering the number of naturalizations granted – is as yet an unresolved question. Part of the stated reasons for the reforms introduced in France in 2012 was reversing the

132 Home Office, 'Statement of Intent: Changes to Tier 1, Tier 2 and Tier 5 of the Points-Based System; Overseas Domestic Workers; and Visitors' (February 2012), p. 3.

133 European Website on Integration Special Feature, note 10, p. 4.

134 BBC News, 'UK citizenship test 'to cover Britain's greats'' (28 January 2013).

135 Circular No. NORIOCN1132114C, '*Circulaire relative au niveau de connaissance de la langue française requis des postulants de la nationalité française*', 30 November 2011; Home Office, 'Statement of Intent: Family Migration' (June 2012), p. 7; Home Office, 'Statement of Intent: Knowledge of Language and Life in the UK for Settlement and Naturalisation' (April, 2013).

decline in naturalizations there, which was between 30 and 45 per cent between 2010 and 2012.[136] In the UK context, an Oxford study concluded:

> The introduction of the Life in the UK test and more stringent English language requirements in 2004 does not seem to have changed the increasing trend in naturalisations. It is possible that there would have been even more naturalisations without these new requirements (including not only the newly-required knowledge and skill tests but also the fees required to prepare for and take them). Further, the language and knowledge requirements would seem to pose a disproportionate burden on nationals of poorer, less educated and non-English-speaking countries (Ryan 2008), and may have deterred applications among nationals of such countries.[137]

Quite aside from the question of the impact on the number of individuals able to access citizenship, the well-documented convergence of European naturalization practice around the features of integration and language tests supports the argument that despite certain historical and contemporary differences, integration and citizenship regimes are converging around an exclusionary model tilting towards the assimilation model of integration. This conclusion is reinforced by UNHCR's 2009 report entitled *Mapping Integration*, which contains a comparative study of integration law and policies (including citizenship law) in a wide range of European countries. Of all the countries surveyed, only Belgium was found to include easy access to citizenship as part of a tool to improve integration.[138] The Report illustrates that states clearly do not, in general, perceive facilitating access to citizenship as a mechanism for integration. Many European states view integration testing in accessing citizenship as a mechanism of ensuring that those to whom they allow access to the polity respect the fundamental values of that polity, however, it is difficult to see how in practice this can be measured through a series of questions on history and culture which, in many cases existing citizens may have difficulty passing and which can often be learned by heart. This marks the replacement of 'naturalization as a means of integration', with naturalization as the 'crowning of a completed integration process'.[139] It also illustrates the disjuncture between the way in which citizenship is seen by NGOs and many academics as key to facilitating integration and a prerequisite to meaningful inclusion within

136 '*Manuel Valls veut faciliter l'acquisition de la nationalité française*', *Le Monde*, 18 October 2012.

137 Scott Blinder, 'Naturalisation as a British Citizen: Concepts and Trends' (The Migration Observatory at the University of Oxford, May 2012).

138 Although, Portugal provides an example of a Member State which has made the naturalization process easier and more inclusive, and sees the active promotion of citizenship acquisition as a tool to improve the conditions for social integration. European Website on Integration Special Feature, note 10, p. 5.

139 Rainer Bauböck, Eva Ersbøll, Kees Groenendijk and Harald Waldrauch (eds), note 4, p. 7.

the polity, and the reality of government approaches to citizenship which is often to use the naturalization process as a method of testing how 'integrated' (usually in a cultural sense) the individual already is. Governments test individual commitment to integration on a superficial level without connecting integration to real equality or inclusion (i.e. the governmental responsibilities regarding integration). This illustrates various conceptions of integration pulling in different directions: integration as inclusion confronts integration as a means of exclusion and assimilation.

Ryan noted that the proposed move to 'earned citizenship' in the UK was indicative of a move away from the conception of integration as the equalization of opportunity to being a blunt instrument used as a means of excluding certain migrants from security of residence and citizenship.[140] More generally, the use of integration as a 'border practice' in domestic citizenship law, to maintain the clear lines between citizens and non-citizens, illustrates the parallel evolution of international and national law in this sphere, with the UN treaty bodies setting out an increasingly well-developed conception of integration as the full realization of equality for migrants, which would not require them to relinquish their cultural identity, language or religious beliefs in order to be entitled to equal opportunities – as explored in detail in Chapter 4.

Thinking about Integration Tests in Light of International Law on Nationality

Much scholarship to date has proceeded on the basis that integration tests as a part of the naturalization process are a new development and constitute an illegitimate (and potentially discriminatory) measure used by states exercising their sovereign powers to pursue a neo-nationalist civic integration agenda.[141] Vigorous debates are taking place as to the place of citizenship tests in liberal democracies, and the legitimacy, liberality and efficacy of such tests.[142] These discussions can be highly subjective and based on differing notions of liberalism, nationalism, democracy and integration. Recent trends in citizenship testing have, however, rarely been analysed in terms of international law. Rather than focussing on the perceived

140 Bernard Ryan, note 127.

141 See, for example, Dora Kostakopoulou, note 129; Sergio Carrera and Elspeth Guild, 'Are Integration Tests Liberal? The 'Universalistic Liberal Democratic Principles as Illiberal Exceptionalism', in EUI Working Paper, 'How Liberal are Citizenship tests?', note 130, p. 29. Also, Moritz Jesse, 'Why Pre-Departure Integration Requirements in Whatever Shape, Form or Size are Illegal and Would not Serve Any Purpose If they Were', Paper delivered at Society of Legal Scholars Conference, 11 September 2012.

142 See, for example, the contributions to EUI Working Paper, 'How Liberal are Citizenship tests?', note 130, which compiles the contributions to an online academic debate on the EUDO Citizenship Forum.

'liberal' or 'illiberal' nature of such tests, this section thinks about these tests in terms of international nationality law.

Even though nationality law is one of the core areas of state sovereignty, public international law exerts a certain influence on the nationality policies of EU Member States, with Waldrauch et al. noting that 'emerging norms of international law, most importantly those codified in the 1997 European Convention on Nationality, have had a clear impact in setting minimum standards'.[143] The foundational principle of international law that states are free to determine who they will permit to be national citizens, has evolved and been modified in parallel with developments in human rights law. With the development of individual human rights through the UN treaty system, the individual right to a nationality, as recognized in the 1948 Universal Declaration of Human Rights, has been established. The 1951 UN Refugee Convention provides that contracting states should facilitate the naturalization of refugees and the 1954 UN Convention Relating to the Status of Stateless Persons[144] and the 1961 Convention on the Reduction of Statelessness address the problem of stateless persons,[145] for example.[146] Human rights treaties have also addressed specific issues of discrimination in nationality law, including gender equality.[147] Allowing dual or multiple nationality is also now the norm, and in 1993, for example, the Second Protocol amending the Convention on the Reduction of Cases of Multiple Nationality and Military Obligations in Cases of Multiple Nationality recognized that preserving the nationality of origin is an important factor in encouraging the acquisition of nationality by the large numbers of people who had settled permanently in Europe, which would in turn enhance their integration.[148]

143 Rainer Bauböck, Eva Ersbøll, Kees Groenendijk and Harald Waldrauch (eds), note 4, p. 5. See also, Lisa Pilgram, 'International Law and European Nationality Laws' (EUDO Citizenship Observatory, March 2011).

144 *Convention Relating to the Status of Stateless Persons*, 28 September 1954, United Nations, *Treaty Series*, vol. 360, p. 117.

145 *Convention on the Reduction of Statelessness*, 30 August 1961, United Nations, *Treaty Series*, vol. 989, p. 175.

146 On statelessness in Europe, see Laura Van Waas, 'Fighting Statelessness and Discriminatory Nationality Laws in Europe' (2012) 14(3) *EJML* 243.

147 See, *inter alia*, Article 9 CEDAW ('States Parties shall grant women equal rights with men to acquire, change or retain their nationality…'); Articles 7 and 8 UN *Convention on the Rights of the Child*, 20 November 1989, United Nations, *Treaty Series*, vol. 1577, p. 3.

148 *Second Protocol amending the Convention on the Reduction of Cases of Multiple Nationality and Military Obligations in Cases of Multiple Nationality*, 6 May 1963 ETS 149.

Considering the Interaction of Integration and Nationality Law: The International Legal Framework

The most significant development in international nationality law in the regional European context has been the adoption in 1997 of the European Convention on Nationality (ECN),[149] which currently binds 11 of the 28 EU Member States (excluding France, the UK and Ireland). Comparative research has shown that the ECN has helped to influence the relaxation of requirements for the acquisition of nationality in connection with tolerance of multiple nationality, avoiding statelessness and gender equality with respect to the transfer of nationality to children.[150] Article 6 deals with acquisition of nationality, with paragraph 3 stating that each State Party 'shall provide in its internal law for the possibility of naturalization of persons lawfully and habitually resident on its territory'.[151] The ECN requires that states facilitate the naturalization of certain persons, including persons who were born on the territory and reside there lawfully and habitually (Art. 6(4)(e)) and refugees and stateless persons (Art. 6(4)(g)). In elaborating on Article 6(3), the explanatory memorandum to the ECN provides clarification, stating that a State Party may fix 'justifiable conditions for naturalisation, in particular as regards integration'.[152] Article 5, however, prohibits discrimination (distinctions or other practices) within nationality law 'on the grounds of sex, religion, race, colour or national or ethnic origin', although the explanatory report clarifies that some preferential treatment is at the centre of nationality law as 'the very nature of the attribution of nationality requires states to fix certain criteria to determine their own nationals'.[153] The explanatory report notes that these criteria could result, in given cases, in more preferential treatment in the field of nationality. Common examples of justified grounds for differentiation or preferential treatment are the requirement of knowledge of the national language in order to be naturalized and the facilitated acquisition of nationality due to descent or place of birth.[154] The ECN thus seems to acknowledge the legitimacy, in principle, of language and integration testing as part of the naturalization process.

The Inter-American Court of Human Rights has also given an insight into its thinking on integration and language testing, in its advisory opinion on amendments to the Constitution of Costa Rica.[155] Costa Rica was seeking to amend the provisions of its Constitution to provide, among other things, that anyone who

---

149 *European Convention on Nationality*, 6 November 1997, ETS 166.

150 Rainer Bauböck, Eva Ersbøll, Kees Groenendijk and Harald Waldrauch (eds), p. 6.

151 *Explanatory report to the ECN*, at para. 51.

152 Ibid.

153 *Explanatory report to the ECN*, at para. 49.

154 *Explanatory report to the ECN*, at para. 40.

155 *Re Amendments to the Naturalisation Provisions of the Constitution of Costa Rica*, OC-4/84, *HRLJ* (1984), vol. 5, 161.

applied for naturalization must know how to speak, write and read the Spanish language and would be subject to a comprehensive examination on the history of the country and its values. This was in addition to its amending of the list of eligible persons for naturalization in Article 14 to include 'a foreign woman who, by marriage to a Costa Rican loses her nationality or who after two years of marriage to a Costa Rican and the same period of residence in the country, indicates her desire to take on our nationality'. In considering the legality of these provisions, the Court expressed the classical view that naturalization is 'a voluntary act aimed at establishing a relationship with a given political society, its culture, its way of life and its values'.[156] Following this line of reasoning, the Court acknowledged that the proposed language and 'history and values examination' conditions fell within the 'margin of appreciation reserved to the state as far as concerns the enactment and assessment of the requirements designed to ensure the existence of real and effective links upon which to base the acquisition of the new nationality'.[157] The conditions could not be viewed as unreasonable and unjustified in themselves. However, the Court emphasized its concerns about the potential discriminatory effect in practice of these requirements, which risked becoming 'the vehicle for subjective and arbitrary judgments as well as instruments for the effectuation of discriminatory policies which, although not directly apparent on the face of the law, could well be the consequence of its application'.[158]

Since the adoption of the ECN in 1997, the context has evolved significantly, with ever more European states using citizenship tests relating to culture, society and institutions as a key part of the naturalization process. This new 'threat' to the acquisition of citizenship was recognized in the 2002 report of the Council of Europe on acquisition and loss of nationality.[159] Responding to the changing context and use by states of citizenship tests, the report warned that requirements for knowledge regarding the language, culture and history of the state should 'exclusively be used and regarded as an element of integrating non-nationals and should not be used as a discriminatory means for a State to select its nationals'.[160] Presenting a different concept of integration to that which states appear to be imposing on migrants in the context of citizenship tests, it says:

> Elements of a State's law regarding integration should not be contrary to an individual's human rights or discriminatory, nor should "integration" be interpreted as being the same as "assimilation". "Integration" does not mean taking up living habits or religion or other such matters but means the ability to

156 Ibid., at para. 35.

157 Ibid., at para. 63.

158 Ibid.

159 'Conditions for the Acquisition and Loss of Nationality adopted by the Committee of Experts on Nationality on the basis of a draft prepared by Andrew Walsmley' (CJ-NA (2002) 1, Strasbourg, 14 January 2003).

160 Ibid., at para. 36.

> live together and requires tolerance from individuals towards others despite the fact that they are different.[161]

The report's recommendations included identifying the possibility of further rules for the acquisition and loss of nationality in addition to those already included in the ECN, specifically mentioning 'matters relating to integration and the nationality of immigrants'.[162] In this regard, the report emphasizes citizenship as a tool for further integration rather than a reward for integration, including identifying 'the need to assist the integration of foreigners in their new country of residence' and 'the degree of knowledge required of the state's language, constitution, laws, history, etc. in order to be naturalised' as potential areas for consideration for further clarificatory elaboration within the ECN.[163] Similarly, in 2010, the Fourth Council of Europe Conference on Nationality concluded that the Council of Europe should pay more attention in its future work to the relationship between integration and nationality.[164] In practice, the likelihood of the ECN being amended in the near future, however, is remote.

Difficulties with Arguing that Integration Requirements in Nationality Law are Contrary to International Law

As seen above, despite some murmurs of concern expressed by the Council of Europe in its 2002 report on the application of the ECN, international law presumes that states are permitted to require persons to demonstrate a certain amount of loyalty and knowledge of the state before affording them citizenship status. In fact, international law takes citizenship seriously, and emphasizes the significance of a person agreeing to become a party within a new political and social entity. This view was central to the seminal *Nottebohm* case, in which the International Court of Justice emphasized:

> Naturalization is not a matter to be taken lightly. To seek and to obtain it is not something that happens frequently in the life of a human being. It involves his breaking of a bond of allegiance and his establishment of a new bond of allegiance.[165]

---

161 Ibid., at para. 37.

162 Ibid., at para. 52(a).

163 Ibid.

164 'Conclusions, Fourth Council of Europe Conference on Nationality: Concepts of Nationality in a Globalised World' (CONF-NAT (2010) CONCL. E, Strasbourg (17 December 2010).

165 *Nottebohm Case* (second phase), Judgment of April 6th, 1955, I.C.J. Reports 1955, p. 24.

Once the application of the tests does not directly discriminate against certain groups (for example, by providing that integration tests need only be taken by those belonging to a specified religion, by women, or by individuals of a specific nationality), states enjoy a wide margin of appreciation in incorporating integration tests into their legislation. In respect of certain groups – for example refugees and stateless persons – the margin of appreciation is smaller, as states are required, in a general way, to facilitate their acquisition of citizenship and as such, integration tests which make acquiring citizenship unduly difficult are open to question. Citizenship tests which disproportionately affect such groups certainly undermine the spirit of the law in this regard, as well as the letter of the law in the case of the ECN's treatment of stateless persons. Even where direct discrimination occurs, the acquisition of nationality is generally considered by states to be a privilege rather than an individual right, with states refusing to recognize that their autonomy in this sphere is limited by human rights law or otherwise, meaning that 'the emergence of a "rights culture" has challenged but not (yet?) substantially altered a system that is governed by the logic of state sovereignty in nationality attribution'.[166]

On the other hand, the conception of the role of integration in the naturalization process as employed by the Council of Europe, in particular, presumes that naturalization and tests associated with it are a tool of integration. Citizenship tests designed to be a 'blunt instrument' to exclude certain migrants from security of residence and citizenship do not sit well with this conception. In particular, where such tests become a vehicle for the effectuation of discriminatory policies, they become particularly problematic in international law terms. In this regard, the decision of the European Court of Human Rights in *Genovese v Malta*[167] – in which it was found that provisions of Maltese law which stated that children born out of wedlock would only be eligible for citizenship if their mother was Maltese were in breach of Article 14 ECHR, read in conjunction with Article 8 – could form a platform for a more nuanced development of the case law relating to discrimination in nationality law. This case, while most significant for its recognition that the impact of the right to citizenship on the child's social identity was such as to bring that right within the general scope and ambit of Article 8, crucially shows that the margin of appreciation allowed to states in defining the terms of naturalization is not unlimited. However, that case involved a fairly straightforward case of discrimination (against children born out of wedlock). One of the problems with integration testing generally is that it is difficult to determine both the true motivations for and the effects of such testing, meaning that the discriminatory effect is difficult to gauge and to prove, with governments keen to justify more restrictive arrangements by reference to the benefits of the test to migrants themselves. For example, the UK Government, in its equality

166 Lisa Pilgram, note 143, p. 3.

167 Application No. 53124/09, Judgment of 11 October 2012.

impact assessment on increasing the language requirements required for access to indefinite leave to remain ('settlement'),[168] states that the policy aims as follows:

> By increasing the level of English required at settlement, the policy seeks to ensure that those intending to live permanently in the UK should have a sufficient command of English, and knowledge of life in the UK and of British values, to enable them to integrate successfully, play a full part in the wider community and have effective access to the labour market. English language skills help migrants obtain employment and help those in employment to increase their skills. The ability to communicate face-to-face assists in day-to-day interaction with shops, schools and other public services and with the community as a whole. This is of benefit both to the migrant and to wider society.[169]

In relation to the possibility of discrimination in the new requirements, the Home Office adds: 'To the extent any indirect discrimination is not mitigated by the detail of the changes, it is proportionate to achieving the policy objectives'.[170] International law's acceptance of integration and linguistic tests in principle, combined with the indeterminacy of the concept of integration itself and the wide margin of appreciation generally granted to governments in citizenship matters, leaves room for governments to side-step the issue of indirect discrimination in this way.

Overall then, citizenship tests in the form of integration requirements and language tests are not in themselves illegal in terms of international law, and proving that such tests are a disproportionate means of pursuing the legitimate aim of integration would also be very difficult. Developments in international law have thus not kept pace with the manner in which citizenship tests are being instrumentalized by states essentially as a means of limiting access to citizenship. The legal position also leads us back to Kymlicka's questioning of *why* relatively straightforward access conditions for citizenship, in the form of citizenship tests, are seen as 'bad'. As already mentioned, the answer lies with the reorientation of the concept of integration, the retreat from multiculturalism and the restrictive turn in citizenship discourse in national legal and policy regimes – context issues which would be very difficult to take account of in an international law analysis of the integration tests themselves.

---

168 Home Office, Policy Equality Statement: Family Migration (Home Office, 11 June 2012).

169 Ibid., pp. 20–21.

170 Ibid., p. 22.

EU Law and the National Attribution of Citizenship: *Rottmann* and the Opening of Possibilities

As mentioned in Chapter 6, the EU opens up a 'transnational' dimension to debates about identity and belonging, which might be expected to help to orientate integration policy at the national and EU level in a more inclusive direction. The creation of European citizenship in particular opens up possibilities for multiple spheres of belonging and multiple identities and levels of citizenship. Habermas argues that the EU structure could offer an antidote to the 'constitutional patriotism' of European states as it requires states to consider citizenship as capable of existing without the prerequisite of homogeneity.[171] In theory, the idea of European citizenship detaches the notion of citizenship and belonging from the traditional anchor of the nation state, such that:

> European developments prompt a rethinking of the connection between the state, the nation and pluralism in its various forms, and invite us to consider the possibility of transcending these connections.[172]

Some commentators have emphasized the 'constructive potential' of Union citizenship and the extent to which it will penetrate national citizenship, thereby effecting incremental, but transformative, institutional change.[173]

However, it must be said that in strictly legal terms, European citizenship has not yet posed a serious challenge to the supremacy of national citizenship. It is superimposed on and subsidiary to national citizenship and does not affect the way national citizenship is obtained.[174] As the CJEU confirmed in *obiter dicta* comments in *Micheletti*, the determination of nationality falls within the exclusive competence of the Member States, but this competence must be exercised with due regard to the requirements of Community law.[175] In *Kaur*, the Court stated that 'it is for each Member State, having due regard to Community law, to lay down the conditions for the acquisition and loss of nationality'.[176] EU citizenship has not to date involved a significant dislocation of power away from the nation state: the

171 Jurgen Habermas, 'The European Nation State: Its Achievements and its Limitations: On the Past and Future of Sovereignty and Citizenship' (1996) 9 *Ratio Juris* 125.

172 Dora Kostakopoulou, 'Integrating Non-EU Migrants in the European Union: Ambivalent Legacies and Mutating Paradigms' (2002) 8 *Colum J Eur L* 181, p. 184.

173 See, for example, Dora Kostakopoulou, 'European Union Citizenship: Writing the Future' (2007) 13(5) *European LJ* 623; Jo Shaw, 'The Interpretation of European Union Citizenship' (1998) 61(3) *Modern Law Review* 293.

174 This is clear from Article 20 TFEU itself.

175 Case C-369/90, *Micheletti and Others v Delegacion del Gobierno en Catanbria* [1992] ECR I-4329.

176 Case C-192/99, *R v Secretary of State for the Home Department ex parte Kaur* [2001] ECR I-1237, para. 19.

position in the EU 'enshrines the traditional sovereign prerogative over allocations of citizenship'.[177]

Notwithstanding the limitations of the impact of EU law on national rules for the attribution of citizenship, the influence of EU law in the domain of nationality is undoubtedly increasing, with the '*avant garde*' approach of the CJEU[178] propelled by the phrase that 'EU citizenship is destined to become the fundamental status of the citizens of the Union'.[179] The ECJ has, over the last decade, taken an 'active stance' with regard to shaping the concept of Union citizenship in cases such as *Baumbast*,[180] *Martínez-Sala*,[181] *Grzelczyk*,[182] and *Bidar*,[183] (among others).[184] However, it was not until 2010, in its decision in *Rottmann*,[185] that the Court was first required to address specific questions relating to interaction of EU and domestic law in the sphere of citizenship and the scope of Member State's discretion to lay down the conditions for the acquisition and loss of nationality.[186] Mr Rottmann was an Austrian citizen who had acquired German nationality without disclosing to the German authorities that he was the subject of criminal proceedings in Austria. Upon being naturalized in Germany, he automatically lost his Austrian citizenship. German nationality was then withdrawn on the basis that it had been obtained by fraudulent means and he thus became stateless, losing his EU citizenship in the process. The CJEU became involved when the German supreme Federal Administrative Court made a preliminary reference as to whether this was contrary to Community law. The Court found that this situation, 'by reason of its nature and consequences' (i.e., the loss of Union citizenship) came within the ambit of EU law,[187] and that the national court should use a proportionality test 'to ascertain whether the withdrawal decision at issue … observes the principle of

177 Jacqueline Bhabha, 'Identity, Citizenship, Exclusion in Europe' (1998) 20 *Hum. Rts Q.* 613.

178 Gerard René De Groot and Anja Seling, 'Court of Justice of the European Union decision of 2 March 2010, Case C-315/08 Janko Rottman v Freistaat Bayern case note 2: the consequences of the Rottmann judgment on Member State autonomy – the European Court of Justice's avant-gardism in nationality matters' (2011) 7(1) *Eur Const LR* 150.

179 See, among lots of examples, Case C-184/99 *Grzelczyk* [2001] ECR I-6193, at para. 31.

180 Case C-413/99 *Baumbast* [2002] ECR I-07091.

181 Case C-85/96 *Martinez Sala* [1998] ECR I-02691.

182 Case C-184/99 *Grzelczyk* [2001] ECR I-6193.

183 Case C-209/03 *Bidar* [2005] ECR I-2119.

184 De Groot and Seling, note 178, p. 450.

185 Case C-135/08 *Rottmann* [2010] ECR I-1449.

186 See generally, Dimitry Kochenov and Richard Plender, 'EU Citizenship: from an incipient form to an incipient substance? The discovery of the treaty text' (2012) 37(4) *ELR* 369; René De Groot and Anja Seling, note 178; EUI Working Papers/EUDO Citizenship Observatory, Jo Shaw (ed.), 'Has the European Court of Justice Challenged Member State Sovereignty in Nationality Law?' (RSCAS 2011/62).

187 Case C-135/08 *Rottmann* [2010] ECR I-1449, at para. 42.

proportionality so far as it concerns the consequences it entails for the situation of the person concerned in the light of EU law'.[188]

The decision in *Rottmann* was welcomed as a 'milestone'[189] in nationality law and hailed as 'opening the way for further incursions in the sphere of nationality sovereignty, as aspects of nationality laws are held up for scrutiny against the standards inherent in EU law'.[190] As well as proportionality, rules concerning national citizens which fall within the ambit of EU law must also respect the general principles of EU law (including the prohibition on discrimination on the grounds of race, religion, ethnicity, sex, sexuality, disability and age). Among the many questions raised by *Rottmann*, perhaps the most relevant for the purposes of this chapter is the extent of the restraint which EU law places on the scope of Member State's discretion in applying national rules on the acquisition of nationality – in particular, in the case where integration testing leads to the denial of national (and therefore EU) citizenship.

While the CJEU in *Rottmann* focussed on loss of EU citizenship, Shaw and others have argued that there should be no 'bright lines' drawn between loss and acquisition of nationality, and the principles set out in *Rottmann* should be applicable in the context of rules on acquisition.[191] Against this, the Court expressly distinguished the situation in which an applicant is deprived of Union citizenship which he had previously enjoyed, and where they had never enjoyed such rights and thus could not be deprived of them. In addition, the fact that the applicant would have been rendered stateless is an important characteristic of this case. However, if the Court accepts going forward that the *Rottmann* principle should apply equally to decisions on acquisition, then it may be possible to argue, depending on the precise circumstances of the case, that an integration test, or a specific part of it, places a disproportionate restriction on an individual's ability to acquire EU citizenship or that it is directly or indirectly discriminatory. It is unlikely that the idea of integration testing in itself would be seen to be unreasonable or arbitrary, especially given the Court's reassurance to Member States (albeit in the context of loss of nationality in circumstances of fraud) that:

> It is legitimate for a Member State to wish to protect the special relationship of solidarity and good faith between it and its nationals and also the reciprocity of rights and duties, which form the bedrock of the bond of nationality.[192]

188 Ibid., at para. 54.

189 De Groot and Seling, note 178, p. 451.

190 Jo Shaw, 'Concluding thoughts: *Rottmann* in context', in Jo Shaw (ed.), 'Has the European Court of Justice Challenged Member State Sovereignty in Nationality Law?' (RSCAS 2011/62), 33, p. 41.

191 Ibid.

192 Case C-135/08 *Rottmann* [2010] ECR I-1449, at para. 42 and para. 51.

De Groot and Seling argue that a general judicial protection against arbitrariness implies that it must be possible to argue in court that the answer given on a specific question was correct, that the question was unclear or even that the question lacks any relevance in the context of the goal of the test: measuring the degree of integration of the applicant.[193] Here, the same problems arise in relation to determining the aim and effect of integration and questions in integration tests as were seen in the case of international law. Nevertheless, the decision may have some impact on governments thinking about imposing ever more difficult-to-satisfy language and integration requirements for naturalization – such as those that have been imposed in France and the UK. In particular, the denial of citizenship on the basis of displays of religious affiliation, as is permissible in French law, could be legally problematic. In a similar vein to De Groot and Seling, Jo Shaw opines that if the procedures regarding citizenship acquisition are highly discretionary or lack a procedure for judicial review, they could be subject to challenge.[194] In this regard, we may have already seen a side-effect of the *Rottmann* decision in the judgment of the Irish Supreme Court in *Mallak*, discussed above, which drew on EU law (among other sources) to impose a duty to give reasons on the Minister considering naturalization applications. Thus, while the full impact and reach of the Court's approach in *Rottmann* remains to be seen, it certainly opens up Member State nationality laws to greater scrutiny, and a proportionality analysis. The intrusion of the 'external' influence of EU law into a domain which is perceived to be the paradigm expression of national sovereignty, and increasingly linked to a narrow form of national identity and national values which may be unreflective of multicultural societies, can only be a good thing for individual migrants seeking access points to the polities of EU states.

Conclusion

This chapter has emphasized the importance of citizenship from an integration perspective and explored the Irish, UK and French citizenship regime in a comparative perspective. However, the limitations of formal citizenship in integration terms are apparent. Formal citizenship cannot of itself ensure social inclusion, and many citizens by birth are excluded and marginalized despite their legal status. In addition, the primacy of national citizenship and its allied understandings of bounded national community and rights protection are challenged by the development of universal human rights, globalization and regionalization. Chapter 4 illustrated the point that conceptions of integration which are based on narrow conceptions of national identity and a strict dichotomy between the citizen and the non-citizen are put under significant pressure by international human rights norms. The supranationalization of core rights of individuals and duties of states

193 De Groot and Seling, note 178.

194 Jo Shaw, 'Concluding thoughts: *Rottmann* in context', note 190, p. 41.

through the medium of international human rights law has a direct impact on the form of national integration policy. Evidence from comparative research across Europe, on the other hand, indicates that integration conditions in citizenship law are not focussed on creating equal opportunities but serve to distinguish 'desirable' from 'undesirable' potential members of the citizenry on the basis of a superficial test. Thus developments at the national level run directly counter to those at the international level.

The significance of citizenship and national identity in public philosophies of integration has been illustrated in this chapter. The incoherency of national citizenship frameworks is also evident. For example, in the case of Ireland, the discourse surrounding the 2004 referendum revealed a relatively closed conception of belonging and a preoccupation with maintaining the borders of the welfare state. More generally, it is much easier for those with an ethnic Irish background who have never spent any time in the state to obtain citizenship than it is for immigrants who have lived in the state and contributed to Irish society, also providing evidence of an ethnically-centred conception of citizenship. Nevertheless, it was also shown that Irish law imposes few conditions on access to citizenship, unlike most European states (including the UK and France), which impose language and integration requirements on applicants for citizenship. Related to this point, the role of integration in the Irish citizenship framework is also unclear. While the discourse surrounding the citizenship referendum suggested that the law was devised to ensure that children of those without some degree of integration into Irish society did not obtain citizenship, this has not as yet been translated into integration conditions in the naturalization process. In addition, 'integration' in the sphere of citizenship appears to be perceived as mainly relating to length of residence rather than commitment to the state or cultural integration, with the primary example of this being that the birthright citizenship of children born to non-national parents depends on the degree of integration of their parents measured solely in terms of length of residence. Overall, the question of whether citizenship is a tool for progressive integration or a reward for completed integration is as yet unresolved in Irish law, as it is in most European states.

Despite the anchoring of citizenship regimes in national public philosophy together with the instrumentalization of citizenship by states seeking to promote a certain vision of national identity, this chapter has also pointed to the external dimensions of nationality law in the form of international and EU law. It was shown that the international law of nationality recognizes legitimate reasons why states would want to impose conditions on access to membership, including integration and language tests, however, states' discretion in the development of a citizenship regime is not unlimited. In this regard, the future development of ECHR case law on discrimination in nationality law will be crucially important. In addition, the EU presents an example of a supranational organization with its own legal form of citizenship, and the *Rottmann* decision discussed in this chapter illustrates the potential impact of the EU citizenship regime can have on national citizenship law. Overall then, while the boundaries of membership are drawn by the domestic law of EU Member States, looking to international law and the emerging promise of EU law in this regard reminds us that domestic governments do not delineate these boundaries in a normative vacuum – leaving some room for alternative legal conceptions of citizenship based on the cosmopolitan promise of international law or the heterogeneous form of citizenship enshrined in Article 20 TFEU.

Chapter 8

Religion, Education and Integration: Lessons from the Irish Experience

Introduction

In delivering his judgment in the Irish Supreme Court in the seminal case of *Campaign to Separate Church and State v Minister for Education*[1] Keane J observed:

> As in many other countries around the world, religion plays an important part in Irish life and has done so for many centuries. That unquestionable fact is reflected in the provisions of Article 44 of the Constitution. Even were such provisions absent from the Constitution, however, the Courts could not disregard, at least in a context where it becomes relevant, the fact that religious beliefs and practices are interwoven through the fabric of Irish society.[2]

Keane J supported this broad statement by giving some examples of the ways in which Irish law accommodates the practice of religion, including the way in which the Irish law of trusts continues to treat trusts established for the advancement of religion as entitled to charitable status without any proof that they are for the public benefit (since such trusts are presumed to be for the public benefit),[3] and the exemption, as of right, of ministers of religion and others from the obligation of jury service.[4] If we add to this list the prohibition on blasphemy in the Irish Constitution[5] and the constitutional requirement for the President and judges to take a religious oath,[6] a clear sense of the legal recognition of the importance of religion in Irish public life begins to emerge.[7] The Irish constitutional and legislative framework for the protection of religious liberty was developed in the context of

1 [1998] 3 IR 321.

2 Ibid., at 359.

3 This position pertains even after the modernization of the law of charities by the Charities Act 2009. See section 3(4) of the Charities Act 2009, which provides that 'It shall be presumed, unless the contrary is proved, that a gift for the advancement of religion is of public benefit'.

4 Juries Act 1976, Schedule I, Part II.

5 Article 40.6.1i.

6 Articles 12.8 and 34.5.1.

7 See also section 36 of the Defamation Act 2009, which establishes a controversial prohibition on the publishing or the utterance of blasphemous matter.

the numerical and cultural dominance of the Catholic faith (with established small minorities in the form of the Church of Ireland and Jewish faiths). It remains to be seen how this framework copes with, on the one hand, the increased secularization of Irish society and, on the other hand, the diversification of religious belief brought about by immigration. This chapter explores the connections between religion, education and integration, using Ireland as a case study. It examines the place of religion in Irish public life through an analysis of the law relating to religion and the education system, in addition to the legal regulation of the use of religious symbols in public spaces, particularly focussing on schools.

The chapter will use the two interrelated issues of the state funding of the denominational education system and the presence of religious symbols in the public sphere (in particular in state education) to address the question of how the existing legal framework copes with the diversity of religious belief now represented in Irish society. The first of these issues forms part of the broader issue of the regulation of the state's relationship with religion and has been the subject of perennial debate in Ireland as well as of a certain body of case law. The second is illustrative of the legal approach to the protection of individual religious liberty and, while it has not arisen in a controversial way in Ireland as yet, has arisen as a key legal issue in other jurisdictions. In the case of each of these subjects, the current legal position in Ireland will be analysed, with the underlying aim of assessing what kind of integration paradigm emerges from Irish law and practice in this area. The compatibility of the Irish approach with international law in light of ECHR jurisprudence and the Optional Protocol jurisprudence of the Human Rights Committee (the 'CCPR') along with the Concluding Observations of the CCPR on State Reports will also be assessed.[8] Before embarking on this substantive legal analysis, the nexus between religion, education and integration will be briefly explored and the content of and background to the relevant Irish constitutional provisions described.

The Nexus between Religion, Education and Integration

While overall, the role and position of religion in the public arena can be seen as demonstrative of how the common spaces of society are delineated, issues relating to religion can be more specifically classed as impacting on integration in two main ways, described by Doyle as 'freedoms *from* religion' and 'freedoms *of* religion'.[9] The first of these concerns the regulation of the relationship between the

8 For an interesting discussion of the relationship between international law and religion generally, see Mahshood A. Baderin, 'Religion and International Law: Friend or Foes?' (2009) 5 *EHRLR* 637.

9 Oran Doyle, 'Article 44: Privileging the Rights of the Religious', in Eoin Carolan and Oran Doyle (eds), *The Irish Constitution: Governance and Values* (Thomson Round Hall, 2008).

state and religion, which impacts on freedom *from* religion. The approach taken to this complex question throws into relief the relationship between adherents to majority and minority religions and the capacity of minority religions to survive. If the state consistently and in legal terms supports the existence of one religion and privileges it over others, this may diminish the capacity of adherents to minority religions to express and practice their religion in the public arena. Equally, if the policy of the state is to maintain a policy of not supporting religion at all or seeking to exclude religion from the public sphere, as is historically the case in France, this may cause difficulties in terms of religious practices with public manifestations. Finally, it may indicate on an institutional level the degree of openness of the institutions of the state to those who do not form part of the traditional majority.

The second way in which religion and integration interact is on the level of individual religious liberty and freedom *of* religion: to use the wording of Article 44.2.1 of the Irish Constitution, the guarantee of 'free profession and practice of religion'. The extent to which this right is protected has a direct impact on the integration paradigm embodied in states' legal practice. This links to the core question of the approach taken to cultural integration and whether individual immigrants are required to remake themselves in the mould of an idealized member of the imagined political and cultural community in the course of the integration process. States take different approaches to this question, with some following the legal approach that to allow manifestation of private beliefs in the public sphere reinforces difference, works against integration and has the potential to lead to societal conflict, while others have followed a multicultural policy of permitting individuals to visibly maintain their cultural and religious identity. France, on the one hand, and the United Kingdom, on the other, are often portrayed as occupying the opposing ends of the spectrum on this point.[10] The lack of consistency in the approach of states to the question of the manifestation of religious belief in the public sphere has been referred to by the European Court of Human Rights on numerous occasions.[11]

The two discrete issues on which this chapter will focus are illustrative of these two elements of the relationship between religion and integration but are also notable in that they both concern education, reflecting the fact that education is frequently 'the main battlefield in state-religion controversies'.[12] Education

10 See, for example, Siobhán Mullally, 'Civic Integration, Migrant Women and the Veil: at the Limits of Rights?' (2011) 74(1) *Modern Law Review* 27; Adrian Favell, *Philosophies of Integration: Immigration and the Idea of Citizenship in France and Britain* (2nd ed., Palgrave, 2001); Sebastian Poulter, 'Muslim Headscarves in Schools: Contrasting Legal Approaches in England and France' (1997) 17 *Oxford Journal of Legal Studies* 43.

11 See, for example, *Sahin v Turkey* [2005] 41 EHRR 8, at para. 109.

12 See Ahmet T. Kuru, 'Passive and Assertive Secularism: Historical Conditions, Ideological Struggles and State Policies Towards Religion' (2007) 59 *World Politics* 568, a 569.

also has a complex nexus with integration, cutting across many policy areas.[13] Education is a key element of the fundamental rights protection which is a prerequisite to integration, in its role as 'that most significant human right, ... in the absence of which many other human rights are likely to be beyond reach'.[14] As well as providing the skills and competences necessary for full societal participation and the key to attaining substantive equality, schools are also an important place of contact for immigrant and local communities.[15] The 'practical approach' advocated in the EU Handbooks on Integration, for example, considers the 'acquisition of competences' as one of two processes critical to improving immigrants' outcomes in terms of social and economic mobility, education, health, housing, social services and societal participation.[16] Educational issues such as language support are high-profile integration issues involving public funding,[17] and in Ireland the issue of admission policies to schools has recently come to the fore.[18] Thus education forms part of the functional aspects of integration identified in Chapter 2. On a more theoretical plane, states often consider state education as the medium by which to convey shared national values to young citizens.[19] Thus the Canadian Supreme Court has emphasized the idea that 'teachers are a medium for the transmission of values'[20] and has stated:

> A school is a communication centre for a whole range of values and aspirations of a society. In large part, it defines the values that transcend society through the educational medium. The school is an arena for the exchange of ideas and must,

13 Ager and Strang, for example, identify education as one of the four overall 'markers and means' of integration in their construction of a system of indicators for integration (Alistair Ager and Alison Strang, 'Understanding Integration: A Conceptual Framework' (2008) 21(2) *JRS* 166). The Migrant Integration Policy Index ('MIPEX') categorizes 'Education' as one of the seven key policy areas involved in integration (British Council and Migration Policy Group, Migration Integration Policy Index III (2011), available at www.integrationindex.eu).

14 Dympna Glendenning, *Education and the Law* (Butterworths, 1999), p. 251.

15 See Alistair Ager and Alison Strang, note 13, p. 172. It should be noted that the MIPEX index ranked Ireland among the least prepared of the 31 countries surveyed to help newcomers with specific needs to do just as well in school. British Council and Migration Policy Group, Migration Integration Policy Index III, note 13.

16 European Commission, *Handbook on Integration for Policy-makers and Practitioners* (Brussels, 2nd edn, May 2007).

17 Commission to the Council, the European Parliament, the European Economic and Social Committee and the Committee of the Regions, *Immigration, Integration and Employment* (COM(2003) 336 final), p. 20.

18 See generally, Eoin Daly and Tom Hickey, 'Religious freedom and the 'right to discriminate' in the school admissions context: a neo-republican critique' (2011) 31 *Legal Studies* 615.

19 See Jean Baubérot, 'Secularism and French Religious Liberty, A Sociological and Historical View' (2003) *Brigham Young University Law Review* 451.

20 *Ross v New Brunswick School District No 15* [1996] 1 SCR 825, at para. 42.

> therefore, be premised upon principles of tolerance and impartiality so that all persons within the school environment feel equally free to participate.[21]

This forms part of the liberal approach to education, in the tradition of John Rawls, whereby liberal values are communicated to children in school in order to educate them as good citizens of the liberal state.[22] While the approach encapsulated in the above quote is reflected to a certain degree in the Irish constitutional jurisprudence which acknowledges that the ethos of the school in question forms part of the education of the child, unlike the Canadian example, the Irish model considers the moral education of the child to rest mainly at the discretion of the parents, with the state's role limited to facilitating this education. The entanglement of religion, education and integration forms the subject-matter of this chapter.

Irish Constitutional Provisions on Religion and Education

While the extent of the influence of religion on the 1937 Constitution has been the source of considerable academic commentary since the Irish Constitution's inception, at this stage it is accurate to observe that: 'No one denies that the Constitution was influenced to some extent by Catholic teaching and doctrine'.[23] Examination of the drafting history of the Constitution reveals the Catholic influence on the drafting thereof, largely through the strong influence which John Charles McQuaid (later to become Archbishop of Dublin) had with the then Irish Prime Minister Eamon de Valera, along with the weaker input of the Irish Jesuit order.[24] This influence is clearest in the preamble, which provides:

> In the Name of the Most Holy Trinity, from Whom is all authority and to Whom, as our final end, all actions both of men and States must be referred,
>
> We, the people of Éire,
>
> Humbly acknowledging all our obligations to our Divine Lord, Jesus Christ, Who sustained our fathers through centuries of trial,

21 *R. v M. (M.R.)*, [1998] 3 SCR 393.

22 Rex Ahdar and Ian Leigh, *Religious Freedom in the Liberal State* (Oxford University Press, 2005), p. 230.

23 Gerard Hogan, 'De Valera, the Constitution and the Historians' (2005) *Irish Jurist* 293, p. 294.

24 See the only such comprehensive examination in the excellent study contained in Dermot Keogh and Andrew McCarthy, *The Making of the Irish Constitution 1937* (Mercier Press, 2007), in particular chapters 3 and 4.

> Gratefully remembering their heroic and unremitting struggle to regain the rightful independence of our Nation,
>
> And seeking to promote the common good, with due observance of Prudence, Justice and Charity, so that the dignity and freedom of the individual may be assured, true social order attained, the unity of our country restored, and concord established with other nations,
>
> Do hereby adopt, enact, and give to ourselves this Constitution.

While no decision has been solely based on the preamble; it 'has been judicially adverted to in a number of cases'.[25] The religious dimension of the preamble has been referred to in numerous cases, most notably in *Quinn's Supermarket v Attorney General*[26] in which Walsh J interpreted the preamble as acknowledging that 'we are a Christian people'.[27] In any case, from a textual perspective, this 'monolithic statement of credal faith'[28] appears to endorse the authority of a Christian, Catholic God as the ultimate source of authority in the state, and the source of validity of the Irish legal system, contradicting the notion, also contained in the Preamble, that the source of legal validity of the legal system is popular sovereignty – the will of the people.[29] The preamble, although not an operative part of the Constitution, has thus been relatively influential and has been used as a reference point for determining the underlying values of the constitution.

Of particular interest to the present discussion is the much-discussed provision on the free practice of religion, Article 44. As it originally appeared in the 1937 Constitution, the article read:

1. The State acknowledges that the homage of public worship is due to Almighty God. It shall hold His Name in reverence, and shall respect and honour religion.
2. The State recognises the special position of the Holy Catholic Apostolic and Roman Church as the guardian of the Faith professed by the great majority of the citizens.
3. The State also recognises the Church of Ireland, the Presbyterian Church in Ireland, the Methodist Church in Ireland, the Religious Society of Friends

25 Gerard Hogan and Gerry Whyte, *Kelly: The Irish Constitution* (3rd edn, Butterworths, 2003), p. 53.

26 [1972] IR 1.

27 See also *Norris v Attorney General* [1984] IR 36, p. 64 and, more recently, *Sinnott v Minister for Education* [2001] 2 IR 545.

28 Richard Barrett, 'Church and State in Light of the Report of the Irish Constitution Review Group' (1998) 5(1) *DULJ* 51.

29 The problems inherent in the natural law and the popular sovereignty accounts of legal validity are explored in Oran Doyle, 'Legal Validity: Reflections on the Constitution' (2003) 10(1) *DULJ* 56.

in Ireland, as well as the Jewish Congregations and the other religious denominations existing in Ireland at the date of the coming into operation of this Constitution.

4. Freedom of conscience and the free profession and practice of religion are, subject to public order and morality, guaranteed to every citizen.
5. The State guarantees not to endow any religion.
6. The State shall not impose any disabilities or make any discrimination on the ground of religious profession, belief or status.
7. Legislation providing State aid for schools shall not discriminate between schools under the management of different religious denominations, nor be such as to affect prejudicially the right of any child to attend a school receiving public money without attending religious instruction at that school.
8. Every religious denomination shall have the right to manage its own affairs, own, acquire and administer property, movable and immovable, and maintain institutions for religious or charitable purposes.
9. The property of any religious denomination or any educational institution shall not be diverted save for necessary works of public utility and on payment of compensation.

Article 41.1, in particular, stood in contrast to the freedom of religion guarantee contained in Article 8 of the 1922 Free State Constitution, which was secular in its terms. The position to be accorded to the Catholic Church was one of the thorniest issues faced by de Valera and his team of drafters in the drafting of the Constitution. The Catholic Church was putting de Valera under pressure to recognize the Catholic Church as the 'one true church', whereas de Valera favoured a less confessional article which would preserve equality before law for religious minorities.[30] The compromise which was eventually reached was subsequently criticized as giving offence to non-Catholics,[31] with the Committee on the Constitution of 1967 recommending that 'the deletion of this provision would, in particular, dispel any doubts and suspicions which may linger in the minds of non-Catholics, North and South of the border, and remove an unnecessary source of mischievous and specious criticism'.[32] The provisions were deleted following a referendum in 1972.[33]

Despite the criticism subsequently levelled at Article 44.2.3, it should be noted that at the time of its enactment, the provision was viewed with a certain amount of disappointment by elements in the Catholic Church, whereas the recognition of

30 For a detailed description of the process of negotiation and drafting of Article 44, see Dermot Keogh and Andrew McCarthy, note 23, pp. 150–173.

31 Committee on the Constitution (1967).

32 Ibid.

33 Fifth Amendment of the Constitution Act 1972.

the minority religions was welcomed by these groups.[34] Article 44.2.3 represented the only explicit constitutional recognition of the pluralist nature of Irish society in the 1937 Constitution. From this perspective, while the deletion of this provision was necessitated by the deletion of the 'special position' clause (which is to be welcomed from the point of view of accommodating diversity of beliefs), the Constitution has now unfortunately lost this express recognition of religious diversity,[35] even though the list of religions referred to would now be outdated, causing a different set of problems. In any event, with its most controversial elements removed, 'the underlying secular nature of the rest of Article 44 fully shone through'.[36] Article 44 now constitutes a fairly conventional freedom of religion provision, with the notable exception of Article 44.1 which states:

> The State acknowledges that the homage of public worship is due to Almighty God. It shall hold His Name in reverence, and shall respect and honour religion.

Religious belief and expression is thus positively endorsed and encouraged by Article 44.1. It may be argued that Article 44.2 (the substantive freedom of religion guarantee) must be read in light of Article 44.1, with the consequence that the courts are obliged to prefer religious to pointedly non-religious world views, the scheme of constitutional protection on balance therefore favouring religious over non-religious belief and expression.[37] This view is reinforced by the judgment in *McGee v AG*[38] in which the Supreme Court clarified that Article 44 applies to acts related to religious conscience and not more generally to non-religious based social conscience.[39] Overall, the 1937 Constitution and, most specifically, Article 44 do not enshrine an approach of state neutrality towards religion (as will be clearly seen from the discussion below on endowment of religion and state funding of denominational schooling). This has formed the starting point for judicial reasoning in the cases which will be discussed below and is key in integration terms as it has formed part of a matrix of constitutional and legislative factors which, along with the numerical and cultural dominance of the Catholic faith and the implementation of public policies that reflect broad Judaeo-Christian principles, has arguably lead to a *de facto* establishment of the Catholic Church in Ireland.[40]

---

34 Barrington J gives a potted history of the controversial provisions in his judgment in *Campaign to Separate Church & State Ltd v Minister for Education* [1998] 3 IR 321, at 355.

35 *McGee v Attorney General* [1974] 1 IR 284, at 317, *per* Walsh J.

36 Gerard Hogan, 'De Valera, the Constitution and the Historians', note 22, p. 302.

37 Oran Doyle, 'Article 44: Privileging the Rights of the Religious', note 9.

38 [1974] 1 IR 284.

39 In that case, Mrs McGee's objection on the state putting fluoride in drinking water was not religious in nature but was a form of social belief and therefore not protected under Article 44.

40 See Rex Ahdar and Ian Leigh, note 21, p. 80.

At the same time however, Article 44 does not allow for any discrimination to be made on the ground of religious profession, belief or status and this has been interpreted as encompassing both positive and negative discrimination.[41] The courts have consistently emphasized the requirement of neutrality as between the religions as the basis for the scheme of constitutional protection of religion. Keane J remarked in *Campaign to Separate Church and State v Minister for Education*:

> there is no reason in principle why the State, through its different organs, should not confer benefits on religious denominations, provided – and it is, of course, a crucial proviso – that in doing so it remains neutral and does not discriminate in favour of particular religions.[42]

The conclusions reached on a preliminary literal reading of Article 44 would therefore be that the state has a positive attitude towards religion (Article 44.1) without straying into the territory of the funding of religion ('endowment' of religion being prohibited in Article 44.2.2) whilst also maintaining a strict policy of neutrality as between religions (Article 44.2.3). On this basis, immigrants seeking to preserve their religious identity might expect that:

1. Religious belief is probably more strongly protected than non-religious belief including cultural belief;
2. Expressions of religious belief would be strongly protected; and
3. Minority religions would be legally required to be placed on a level footing as the well-established, numerically dominant religions.

The following chapter should shed some light on whether these assumptions are correct. We will see that in practice, the case law has been 'anything but neutral on the question of religion'.[43]

As mentioned above, debate throughout Europe and the world on religion and integration has focussed on the education system. Through the interaction of Articles 41 and 42 of the 1937 Constitution, in Ireland, parents are constitutionally entitled to insist on their children receiving religious formation as part of their

41 *Quinn's Supermarket v Attorney General* [1972] IR 1.

42 *Campaign to Separate Church & State Ltd v Minister for Education* [1998] 3 IR 321, at 359.

43 Oran Doyle, *Constitutional Law: Text, Cases and Materials* (Clarus Press, 2009), at 10–01.

education.[44] Article 42 places education firmly within the control of the autonomous 'moral institution' protected by Article 41 – the family.[45] Article 42.1 provides that:

> The State acknowledges that the primary and natural educator of the child is the Family and guarantees to respect the inalienable right and duty of parents to provide, according to their means, for the religious and moral, intellectual, physical and social education of their children.

The state must ensure that 'the children receive a certain minimum education, moral, intellectual and social',[46] while Article 42.3.2 excludes the possibility that the state could require parents to give their children a religious education. The state is required to 'provide for' primary education rather than to simply 'provide' such education,[47] as well as to endeavour to 'supplement and give reasonable aid to private and corporate educational initiative, and, when the public good requires it, provide other educational facilities or institutions', but with the express caveat that state provision of education must respect the rights of parents regarding religious and moral education. The minimalist nature of the state's role in the provision of education has been consistently upheld by the courts.[48] This constitutional structuring of the right to education has been interpreted as forming the basis for the state funding of a denominational education system whereby children are educated in a segregated manner along religious lines.

---

44 See Michael Farry, *Education and the Constitution* (Round Hall Sweet and Maxwell, 1996), in particular Chapter 7, 'Rights and Duties of the Family and Parents', pp. 56–74, and Chapter 8, 'Control of Education and Parents', pp. 75–101. See also, Gerry Whyte, 'Education and the Constitution: convergence of paradigm and praxis' (1994) 25–27 *Irish Jurist* 129.

45 Article 41 provides: '1° The State recognises the Family as the natural primary and fundamental unit group of Society, and as a moral institution possessing inalienable and imprescriptible rights, antecedent and superior to all positive law. 2° The State, therefore, guarantees to protect the Family in its constitution and authority, as the necessary basis of social order and as indispensable to the welfare of the Nation and the State'.

46 Article 42.3.2.

47 Article 42.4 states: 'The State shall provide for free primary education and shall endeavour to supplement and give reasonable aid to private and corporate educational initiative, and, when the public good requires it, provide other educational facilities or institutions with due regard, however, for the rights of parents, especially in the matter of religious and moral formation'.

48 *Crowley v Ireland* [1980] IR 102; *Conway v INTO* [1991] 2 IR 305. See also, *O'Keefe v Minister for Education and Science* [2006] IEHC 13; *O'Callaghan v McDonnell, Minister for Education and Science* [2006] IEHC 299; *TM v JH, JM and Minister for Education* [2006] IEHC 26.

Denominational Education and State Funding

Irish Law and Practice

The Education Act 1998 ('the 1998 Act') essentially codifies the form of the education system which has been in place since at least the foundation of the state,[49] whereby the state finances denominationally controlled education, with recognized schools receiving state funds but run by the religious 'patron' through a board of management.[50] Ninety-seven per cent of primary schools in the state are of the Roman Catholic or Church of Ireland ethos (91 per cent being Catholic and 6 per cent being Church of Ireland).[51] In recent years, the Government has recognized that the education system needs to adapt and has started various processes to explore the possible transfer of some schools run by the Catholic Church to other school patron bodies in a number of areas of the country.[52] The consultation process with parents on this move for reform is on-going[53] and, as yet, no school transfers have taken place.

The 1998 Act confirms the minimalist role of the state in the running of schools which it funds, providing only a limited amount of general guidance on the way in which the powers of the patron and of the board of management are to be exercised. The board of management is required, *inter alia*, to 'uphold, and be accountable to the patron for so upholding, the characteristic spirit of the school as determined by the cultural, educational, moral, religious, social, linguistic and spiritual values and traditions which inform and are characteristic of the objectives and conduct of the school'[54] while at the same time to 'have regard to the principles and requirements of a democratic society and have respect and promote respect for

---

49 See Michael Farry, note 43, p. 102.

50 A 'school' for the purposes of the 1998 Act is defined as an establishment which provides primary education to its students and which may also provide early childhood education, or provides post-primary education to its students and which may also provide courses in adult, continuing or vocational education or vocational training (section 2(1), Education Act 1998).

51 See Department of Education, 'Information on Areas for Possible Divesting of Patronage of Primary Schools', www.education.ie.

52 'Report of the Advisory Group on Patronage and Pluralism in the Primary Sector' (Department of Education and Skills, June 2012); 'Report on the pilot surveys regarding parental preferences on primary school patronage' (Department of Education and Skills, 2012).

53 Of 38 areas surveyed in 2013, there was sufficient parental demand supporting immediate changes in school patronage in 23 areas. Parents of children up to 12 years old could participate in the survey. See Department of Education and Skills, 'Report on the surveys regarding parental preferences on primary school patronage' (2013), available at http://www.education.ie/en/Publications/Policy-Reports/Report-on-the-surveys-regarding-parental-preferences-on-primary-school-patronage.pdf.

54 Section 2(b) of the Education Act 1998.

the diversity of values, beliefs, traditions, languages and ways of life in society'.[55] How these duties are to be reconciled in the case of a conflict is unclear and this will be discussed further in the context of the discussion below on religious dress. The functions of a school under the 1998 Act include the promotion of the 'moral, spiritual, social and personal development of students ..., in consultation with their parents, having regard to the characteristic spirit of the school'.[56] The right of schools to guard their 'characteristic spirit' (including religious ethos) is therefore protected in law. Also relevant in this regard are the Rules for National Schools, 1965, which were promulgated in 1965 and have been amended numerous times since then. While these rules do not have a legislative basis, they are adhered to by every state-funded national school in the country as a prerequisite to obtaining funding for staff and teacher salaries. Rule 68 states:

> Of all parts of a school curriculum, Religious Instruction is by far the most important, as its subject matter, God's honour and service, includes the proper use of all a man's faculties and affords the most powerful inducements to their proper use. Religious instruction is, therefore, a fundamental part of the school course, and a religious spirit should inform and vivify the whole work of a school.

Furthermore, at primary school level, the religious education element of the school curriculum is not devised or supervised by the state as is the case for other elements of the curriculum, but is determined by the relevant denomination in charge of the school.[57]

The protection of the 'ethos' of denominationally controlled schools is further supported by the Employment Equality Acts 1998 – 2008 (as amended) and the Equal Status Acts 2000–2011. These Acts allow for teachers to be selected on the basis of their religion as well as for students to be admitted (or not admitted) on the basis of their religion, in order to preserve the ethos of the school. Section 37(1) of the Employment Equality Act 1998, which it is useful to quote in full, provides for an exemption from employment equality law for religious-run institutions in the following terms:

> A religious, educational or medical institution which is under the direction or control of a body established for religious purposes or whose objectives include the provision of services in an environment which promotes certain religious values shall not be taken to discriminate against a person for the purposes of this Part or Part II if –

55 Section 2(e) of the Education Act 1998.

56 Section 9(d) of the Education Act 1998.

57 *The Primary School Curriculum* (Department of Education and Science, Dublin 1999), Introduction.

(a) it gives more favourable treatment, on the religion ground, to an employee or a prospective employee over that person where it is reasonable to do so in order to maintain the religious ethos of the institution, or

(b) it takes action which is reasonably necessary to prevent an employee or a prospective employee from undermining the religious ethos of the institution.

Similarly, section 12(4) of the Employment Equality Act 1998 allows for admissions to schools of nursing and teaching to be determined on the basis of religion, in order to allow denominationally-run hospitals and schools to maintain their religious ethos.[58] Equivalent provisions in the Employment Equality Bill 1996 (which was found to be unconstitutional for other reasons) were found by the Supreme Court to be permissible on the grounds that they were necessary to give life to the free practice and profession of religion guarantees also contained in the Constitution.[59] The Court followed earlier jurisprudence in coming to the conclusion that it is constitutionally permissible to make distinctions or discriminations on the grounds of religious profession, belief or status, but only insofar as this may be 'necessary to give life and reality to the guarantee of the free profession and practice of religion in the Constitution',[60] accepting the Attorney General's argument that it was the legislative intention to allow for positive discrimination with this aim in mind.[61]

Regarding admission policies, section 7(3) of the Equal Status Act 2000 allows primary and post-primary educational establishments to admit persons of a particular religious denomination in preference to others or refuse to admit as a student a person who is not of that denomination where the 'objective of the school is to provide education in an environment which promotes certain religious values'.[62] In the case of a refusal, it must be proved that the refusal is essential to maintain the ethos of the school but in the case of preference of one religious denomination over another this step is seemingly not required. While this would

58 For example, Employment Equality Act 1998 (Section 12) (Church of Ireland College of Education) Order 2008 (Statutory Instrument No. 251 of 2008).

59 *In re Article 26 and the Employment Equality Bill 1996* [1997] 2 IR 321. See also *McGrath and O Ruairc v Trustees of Maynooth College* [1979] ILRM 166 in which the plaintiffs argued that their dismissal from academic positions in Maynooth College following their laicisation constituted discrimination on the grounds of their religious status. In that case, the Supreme Court found that the provision was inapplicable to private institutions not in receipt of state funding.

60 *In re Article 26 and the Employment Equality Bill 1996* [1997] 2 IR 321, at 356.

61 Ibid., at 358.

62 In its concluding observations, the CERD Committee has expressed its regret that the provisions of the Equal Status Act give the power to schools to refuse to admit students to denominational schools on grounds of religion if it is deemed necessary to protect the ethos of the school. UN Doc CRC/C/IRL/CO/2 (29 September 2006), para. 26. It recommended that Ireland consider amending the legislation in this regard.

appear to conflict with the requirement set out in Article 44.2.4 that 'Legislation providing State aid for schools … shall not be such as to affect prejudicially the right of any child to attend a school receiving public money without attending religious instruction at that school', the case law (including the Supreme Court decision in *Re Article 26 and the Employment Equality Bill 2006*)[63] would suggest that the courts would uphold this provision on the basis that it is necessary in order to preserve the religious ethos of schools and thus to protect the free practice and profession of religion.[64] Whyte notes that two constitutional principles are potentially in conflict here. On the one hand, one could argue that the public funding of schools that discriminate on the grounds of religion in relation to admissions policy implicates the state in religious discrimination contrary to Article 44.2.3. On the other hand, 'the State is clearly free, under the Constitution, to finance denominationally controlled education and one could argue that the concept of denominationally controlled education necessarily assumes that schools should be free to have regard to religion in deciding which students to admit'.[65] The practical consequences of the exception from non-discrimination rules for admission policies were seen in 2007, when a number of children mainly of African origin failed to gain places in primary schools due to overcrowding and a policy of admitting Catholic children first.[66] This sparked debate over the nature of the education system and has led to the establishment of a number of multi-denominational and non-denominational schools.[67]

The preservation of religious ethos consistently trumps ordinary equality rules in Irish law with the result that freedom *of* religion is privileged over freedom *from* religion.[68] The legislative provisions ensure the preservation of the status quo whereby the public services of education and hospital care are predominantly

63 [1997] 2 IR 321.

64 Gerry Whyte, 'Religion and Education – the Irish Constitution', Paper presented by Gerry Whyte at Joint Conference of the Irish Human Rights Commission and Trinity College School of Law, 'Religion and Education: A Human Rights Perspective', 27 November 2010.

65 Ibid.

66 For commentary on this see, for example, 'Education and integration', *Irish Times*, 7 September 2007; and 'School admission policies open to equality challenge', *Irish Times*, 13 September 2007. In response to the outcry and to a letter sent to them by the Equality Authority, see *Statement by the Catholic Primary Schools Management Association (CPSMA) on Catholic Primary Schools admission policies* (27 September 2007). However, in 2009, Archbishop of Dublin Diarmuid Martin acknowledged that the present structuring of the system may be untenable: 'Catholic control of schooling not tenable, says archbishop', *Irish Times*, 17 June 2009. See also Economic and Social Research Institute, 'Adapting to Diversity: Irish Schools and Newcomer Students' (ESRI, Research Series No. 8, June 2009), pp. 58–68.

67 See Oireachtas Library and Research Service, 'Understanding the Challenges of Immigration for Education Provision' (Spotlight No. 1, 2008), pp. 22–23.

68 See generally, Gerry Whyte, 'Protecting Religious Ethos in Employment Law: A Clash of Cultures' (2005) 12(1) *DULJ* 169.

provided by religious bodies and funded by the state. This approach, taken together with the factual situation that the relevant religious denomination and 'ethos' in the majority of cases is the Catholic religion, means that the majority of children of immigrants (Catholic and non-Catholic alike) will through necessity attend schools run by Catholic entities with Catholic teachers and a legally protected Catholic ethos – if they gain access to such a school.[69]

It has been argued before the courts that the system of denominational education violates Article 44.2.2, which provides that 'The State guarantees not to endow any religion'. The courts have taken the view that the constitutional requirement to allow for the promotion of a religious ethos, particularly in the educational context where the wishes of parents in respect of religious education must be respected, informs the interpretation of the constitutional prohibition of endowment. 'Endowment' has been interpreted in a narrow sense as meaning the vesting of property or income in a religion *as such* in perpetual or quasi-perpetual form. In contrast to the narrow meaning of 'endowment', the legal concept of religious 'education' under the Irish Constitution is broad, with a distinction being drawn between religious 'instruction' in the form of formal religion classes and religious 'education' which is more nebulous and may permeate the ethos of the school. The approach taken in Irish constitutional law on questions of endowment contrasts with the treatment of the United States Constitution's Establishment Clause by the US Supreme Court for example,[70] which has been interpreted as envisaging 'a wall of separation between church and state',[71] which 'must be kept high and impregnable' (although this separation is imperfect in practice).[72] The US courts have developed a complicated and sometimes confused jurisprudence on how and under what circumstances public aid can be given to religion indirectly.[73] McMenamin J summed up the distinction between the Irish and American constitutional schemes for religion when he stated in *McNally and Reilly v Attorney General*[74] that:

69 See generally, Eoin Daly, 'Religious Freedom as a Function of Power Relations: Dubious Claims on Pluralism in the Denominational Schools Debate' (2009) 28 *Irish Educational Studies* 235.

70 The First Amendment (the Establishment Clause) states: 'Congress shall make no law respecting an establishment of religion or prohibiting the free exercise thereof; or abridging the freedom of speech, or of the press, or the right of the people peaceably to assemble, and to petition the Government for a redress of grievances'.

71 Thomas Jefferson, 'To Messrs. Nehemiah Dodge and Others, a Committee of the Danbury Baptist Association, in the State of Connecticut', January 1, 1802 (available at http://www.stephenjaygould.org/ctrl/jefferson_dba.html).

72 *Everson v Board of Education* 330 US 1 (1947), p. 18.

73 See, for example, the controversial decision in *Zelman v Simmons-Harris* 536 US 639 (2002). See generally, Christopher Eisgruber and Mariah Zeisberg, 'Religious Freedom in Canada and the United States' (2006) 4(2) *ICON* 244.

74 [2009] IEHC 573.

> where the terms of the Establishment Clause are neutral, or "blind" as to religion, the Constitution of Ireland actively recognises the existence of diverse religious denominations and guarantees them certain rights. It might be said that in United States jurisprudence there is a wall of separation; under the Constitution of Ireland there is a constitutional "domain" of religious recognition.[75]

The justification for the approach of the Irish courts in endorsing the state funding of a denominational education system has been largely based on the importance of the parental role in education. In *Campaign to Separate Church and State v Minister for Education*, Barrington J used a historical approach in considering the meaning of the relevant provisions of the Constitution. He reasoned that the Constitution foresees children receiving religious education in schools recognized by the state in accordance with their parents' wishes. He then distinguished between religious 'instruction' and religious 'education', finding that parents were 'not obliged to settle merely for 'religious instruction'.[76] He thus found that the present system, which in the instant case meant that chaplains in community schools were paid by the state, was a manifestation under modern conditions of recognized and approved principles in Articles 42 and 44 of the Constitution.[77] Under Article 44.2.4, children cannot be required to attend religious instruction in schools in receipt of public funding and this means that children are entitled to be excused from classes specifically aimed at teaching religion. In *Campaign* however it was found that this does not extend to an entitlement to religious 'education' in its broad sense. This was put in blunt terms by the Supreme Court, as follows:

> A child who attends a school run by a religious denomination different from his own may have a constitutional right not to attend religious instruction at that school but the Constitution cannot protect him from being influenced, to some degree, by the religious ethos of the school. A religious denomination is not obliged to change the general atmosphere of its school merely to accommodate a child of a different religious persuasion who wishes to attend that school.[78]

This implies that the display of religious symbols in schools in receipt of public funds and probably the integrated curriculum employed by the majority of schools – whereby religious education is not confined to a formal class but is integrated

75 *McNally and Reilly v Attorney General* [2009] IEHC 573, at para. 139.

76 *Campaign to Separate Church & State Ltd v Minister for Education* [1998] 3 IR 321, at 356.

77 In reaching these conclusions, the Supreme Court endorsed the approach previously taken in the Supreme Court in *Re Article 26 and the Employment Equality Bill 1996* [1997] 2 IR 321.

78 *Campaign to Separate Church & State Ltd v Minister for Education* [1998] 3 IR 321, at 358.

throughout the curriculum[79] – are constitutionally permissible.[80] Nevertheless, the Supreme Court gave no indication how, outside religious 'instruction' classes, schools were to balance the rights of parents to insist that their children receive a holistic religious education with the rights of parents who did not wish their children to receive such an education. Reflecting the 'parental choice' model, current attempts to open the primary school system to ensure respect for all traditions and religions (as already mentioned) have focussed on consulting parents as to what type of school they would like in their area.

The courts have also emphasized that the main pre-condition to the adoption of this approach is equality as between religions. This requirement has been emphasized since the earliest cases to address the constitutional provisions on religion. In *Re Tilson*,[81] for example, the Supreme Court hastened to clarify the point that a decision of the High Court in upholding the validity of a pre-nuptial agreement that the children of the marriage would be brought up as Catholics would apply equally in the case of any other religion.[82] In *Corway v Independent Newspapers*[83] the Supreme Court expressed doubts that the common law crime of blasphemy which had at its heart the protection of the established Church had survived the Constitution, because it did not apply equally to all religions. In the *Campaign* decision itself, the Court emphasized the importance of the constitutional requirement that if a school is in receipt of public funds then any child must be eligible to attend it and must have the right not to attend any course of religious instruction. It is difficult to reconcile this finding that any child must be eligible to attend a school which is in receipt of public funds with section 7(3) of the Equal Status Act 2000, which allows for admission policies to operate on the basis of religion. Of even greater importance in terms of equality as between religions is the point made by Laffoy J in her judgment in *O'Shiel v Minister for Education*[84] in which she observed that for parental choice of education to be

79 The integrated curriculum can be seen as resting on sections 15(2)(b) and 9(d) of the 1998 Act, as well as Rule 68 of the Rules for National Schools, 1965. See Oran Doyle, 'Egalitarianism, Religious Preferences and the Integrated Curriculum', Joint Conference of the Irish Human Rights Commission and Trinity College School of Law: 'Religion and Education: A Human Rights Perspective', 27 November 2010.

80 Gerard Hogan and Gerry Whyte, note 24, p. 318. Nevertheless, Doyle points to another strand to the courts' jurisprudence which appears to have grown stronger over the last number of years: namely, recognition of parental autonomy over their children (see *Northwestern Health Board v HW* [2001] 3 IR 622 and *N v Health Services Executive* [2006] 4 IR 374 for example). For this reason he suggests that it is difficult to predict what the courts' approach to the integrated curriculum would be. Oran Doyle, ibid., p. 8.

81 [1951] IR 1.

82 Ibid., pp. 43–44. See also *Quinn's Supermarket v Attorney General* [1972] IR 1, at 24.

83 [1999] 4 IR 485.

84 [1999] 2 IR 321.

meaningful, the state must fund a number of options.[85] The reality that there is no permanent public sector for primary education and only a very limited provision in secondary school education means that there is no alternative to denominational education (overwhelmingly Catholic in nature) for a large number of parents and their children, particularly outside the small number of urban centres in which the number of multi-denominational schools has been rapidly growing.[86]

A key question arising from these observations is whether the current status quo constitutes discrimination in favour of the longer-established religions, in violation of the obligation in Article 44.2.3 not to 'impose any disabilities or make any discrimination on the ground of religious profession, belief or status'. Does the Constitution require the State to fund alternative schools such that new minority religions are on an equal footing as the Catholic Church and the Church of Ireland? On balance, it seems that no such obligation exists under Article 44.2.3, read with the other relevant provisions of the Constitution. If the government chose to fund only Muslim schools into the future in order to facilitate the free practice of Islam in the state, such a policy would be constitutionally unassailable, as we have seen that positive discrimination in favour of a religion is permissible if necessary to permit the free practice and profession of that religion. However, it seems that the nature of the state's obligation in relation to education: namely to 'provide for' education rather than to 'provide' education, is too weak to *compel* the state to take such a course of action. In any event, in the wake of *TD v Minister for Education*[87] and *Sinnott v Minister for Education*,[88] the courts will not compel the executive branch of government to spend public funds in such cases by way of mandatory injunctive relief.[89] Finally, in practical terms, it must be acknowledged that current policy in respect of new schools is to fund the establishment of multi-denominational schools with Educate Together as the school patron, and that the Irish Government is seeking ways, as mentioned above, to widen the choice of primary schools in areas where this is required.

On balance then, the Irish framework is ill-fitted to the current reality that nearly 60 per cent of primary schools have newcomer pupils and over 90 per cent of secondary schools have newcomer pupils, many of whom do not share the religion which forms the basis of the ethos of the school.[90] The extent and impact of the changes which may be brought about through the processes of reform in relation to diversity of patronage currently underway remain to be seen. As it stands, in the current context, the difficulty posed by the legal position that '(a) religious

85 Ibid., at 348.

86 Dympna Glendenning, *Religion, Education and the Law* (Tottel Publishing, 2008), p. 294.

87 [2000] 4 IR 259.

88 [2001] 2 IR 545.

89 See generally, Conor O'Mahony, *Educational Rights in Irish Law* (Thomson Round Hall, 2006).

90 Economic and Social Research Institute, note 60, p. 45.

denomination is not obliged to change the general atmosphere of its school merely to accommodate a child of a different religious persuasion who wishes to attend that school'[91] crystallizes. This approach is predicated on the assumption that parents each of religious denomination may opt to send their children to schools run by that denomination, which is not the case in practice. The combination of the legal and the factual situation outlined in this section would thus appear to negate both the 'parental choice' theory and the equality theory underlying the constitutional framework. The case law leaves unresolved many of the questions arising in the context of a more religiously diverse society, stemming from the fact that the last major case to deal with Article 44 was decided more than a decade ago when this diversity had not yet developed. Nonetheless, it seems from the judgment of McMenamin J in the High Court in *McNally and Reilly v Attorney General*[92] that the traditional approach of the courts to religion in the Constitution will continue to be adopted by the courts in the context of increased religious diversity. Without making any reference to the changing patterns of religious belief in Ireland, he invoked the 'pluralistic Christian values' underlying Article 44, stating:

> Article 44.2.3 prohibits any disabilities or discrimination on the grounds of religious belief or status. But these provisions must be seen as being embedded within the overall constitutional framework of Article 44, informed by its pluralistic Christian values, but to be interpreted harmoniously *inter alia* by reference to the Article 44.2.5 guarantee of religious autonomy, which, far from eschewing internal disabilities and discriminations which flow from the tenets of a particular religion, may on occasion actually allow for support subject to other constitutional rights guarantees. In this way the State may on occasion justifiably "lend its weight" to the support of one denomination in autonomous affairs.[93]

An Integration Paradigm Emerging from the Legal Framework for Education?

As outlined in Chapter 2, official Irish integration policy places little emphasis on 'cultural' or religious aspects of integration and the links between the form of the education system and integration have not yet been formally acknowledged. Migration Nation simply states that 'respecting cultural differences' is important without going into detail as to how, and observes that Ireland differs from other European countries in that the issue of Muslim radicalization has not come to the fore in Ireland while in many European countries it is considered a key integration

91 *Campaign to Separate Church & State Ltd v Minister for Education* [1998] 3 IR 321, at 358, per Barrington J.

92 [2009] IEHC 573.

93 Ibid., at para. 150.

issue.[94] Nevertheless, the law and practice of the Irish education system described in this section can be analysed in integration terms, and in these terms can be viewed in three ways.

The first of these is linked to the question as to whether in practice the equality as between religions, upon which the constitutional and legislative scheme is purportedly based, actually exists. It is arguable that the system enshrines a *de facto* assimilation approach because most adherents to minority religions (along with those of no religion) will, through lack of any alternative, attend Catholic schools, where they are entitled to be excused from formal religious instruction but are unable to escape a broader religious education. Recent empirical research which suggests that in secondary-level schools at least, almost all non-Catholic newcomer students attend religion classes (even if not all of those attending participate) would appear to support this viewpoint.[95] In addition, in her study of the experiences of minority belief parents in the denominational primary system, Lodge concludes that '... differences in belief are denied in the denominational primary system and those whose beliefs are different are rendered invisible and subordinate'.[96] Tied to this point is the fact that the structure of the school system places Catholic immigrants (for example, the majority of Polish immigrants) in a better position than non-Catholic immigrants, potentially making it easier for them to integrate. This may create a differentiated form of integration whereby those resembling the host community in religious terms are permitted to maintain their identity while those from different religious backgrounds are required to relinquish their identity and fit into a Catholic school system.

Alternatively, the situation could be interpreted as protective of minority religions, as positive discrimination is clearly permitted under legislation and the Constitution in order to protect religious practice and ethos. Research has established that those schools that use 'religion' as a selection mechanism in fact have a higher proportion of newcomer students.[97] The relevant Economic and Social Research Institute (ESRI) report suggests the explanation that this may be due to the fact that 'some schools which very openly select on religion are actually minority faith schools, and these schools are more likely to have newcomer students'.[98] The Church of Ireland College of Education, for example, has used statutory instruments in order to ensure priority in allocation of places is given

94 Office of the Minister for Integration, *Migration Nation: Statement on Integration Strategy and Diversity Management* (May 2008), p. 33.

95 Economic and Social Research Institute, note 60, p. 105.

96 Alison Lodge, 'Denial, Tolerance or Recognition of Difference? The Experiences of Minority Belief Parents in the Denominational Primary System', in Deegan, Devine and Lodge (eds), *Primary Voices: Contemporary Issues in Primary Education* (IPA, 2004), p. 32.

97 Economic and Social Research Institute, note 60, p. 64.

98 Ibid.

to members of the Church of Ireland.[99] Similarly, the Protestant 'Block Grant' whereby schools are allocated a grant for qualifying pupils which is offset against fees is designed to counteract the problem that due to the geographical distribution of Protestant schools most parents seeking to have their children educated in a school with a Protestant ethos would be required to send their children to boarding schools and render this affordable for parents.[100] In 2009, the Minister for Education announced that he was considering abolishing this grant, sparking controversy.[101] In 2009, a further 'ancillary grant', provided to Protestant fee-paying schools for non-teaching costs (secretaries, caretakers, etc.), was abolished.[102] By way of further example, in 2008, members of the Jewish community were allowed to go into 'quarantine' while a state exam was sat on a Saturday and sit the exam the following day, in order to protect their observance of the Sabbath.[103]

The third perspective relates to the manner in which schooling under the current system is effectively segregated along religious lines. While the growing number of multi-denominational schools which are run by the non-denominational patron Educate Together must be acknowledged (as must the establishment of a number of state-run primary schools on a pilot basis[104] and the move to divest patronage of some Catholic schools to other bodies), the proportion of these schools in the system remains negligible. We have seen that the system of denominational education is protected in the Constitution as well as enshrined in legislation. This certainly cannot be characterized as 'interculturalism', which is often expressed as the guiding principle for Irish integration. The efficacy of the Intercultural Education Strategy 2010–2015 (which was published in September 2010 but the implementation of which has been allocated no funding) must be questioned when the fundamental philosophy underlying the education framework is that each religion or philosophy is educated with their own.[105] Desmond Clarke examined the implications of the Irish education system in a forceful manner in 1998, even before immigration increased religious diversity in Ireland, expressing the view that:

---

99 The Employment Equality Act 1998 (Section 12) (Church of Ireland College of Education) Order 2008 (Statutory Instrument No. 251 of 2008) is the most recent of these.

100 See Dympna Glendenning, *Religion, Education and the Law*, note 86, p. 75 for an explanation of the background and operation of the Protestant Block Grant.

101 See 'O'Keeffe "on collision course with Protestant faith"', *Irish Times*, 21 October 2009.

102 See generally on these grants, Eoin Daly, 'The Constitution and the Protestant School Controversy: Seeing the Woods for the Trees' (2010) 1(1) *Irish Journal of Legal Studies* 84.

103 See 'Jewish pupils face quarantine over postponed Leaving exam', *Irish Times*, 5 June 2009.

104 See 'First State-run primary schools to open today', *Irish Times*, 1 September 2008.

105 Department of Education and Skills and the Office of the Minister for Education, *Intercultural Education Strategy, 2010–2015* (16 September 2010).

> By adapting its educational policy to the theologies of competing churches, the State reinforces the divisive and sectarian theologies of the churches in the civil life of citizens. … (A)n education policy which supports, protects and finances the sectarian theological divisions of churches is inconsistent with the constitutional requirement to treat all citizens equally and to provide publicly funded services, such as healthcare or education, through institutions which treat all citizens in a non-discriminatory manner.[106]

This leads back to the broader integration debate as to whether accommodating diversity leads to separation and fragmentation within societies.[107] Ahdar and Leigh criticize the paradox whereby the religious diversity which many commentators celebrate in society as a whole is seen as a symptom of failure if it leads to fragmented worship through the withdrawal of pupils.[108]

Compatibility of the Irish Education System with International Human Rights Law

European Convention on Human Rights

The European Court of Human Rights' (ECtHR) approach to the relationship between state and religion has been characterized by the its willingness to allow states a broad discretion by way of a wide margin of appreciation and also a wide interpretation of the limitation provisions in Article 9, which provides thus:

> Everyone has the right to freedom of thought, conscience and religion; this right includes freedom to change his religion or belief and freedom, either alone or in community with others and in public or private, to manifest his religion or belief, in worship, teaching, practice and observance.
>
> Freedom to manifest one's religion or beliefs shall be subject only to such limitations as are prescribed by law and are necessary in a democratic society in the interests of public safety, for the protection of public order, health or morals, or for the protection of the rights and freedoms of others.

---

106 Desmond Clarke, 'Education, the State, and Sectarian Schools', in Tim Murphy and Patrick Twomey (eds), *Ireland's Evolving Constitution: 1937–1997* (Hart, 1999), 65, p. 75.

107 For a discussion of some of the related issues in the education context (focusing on the UK), see Laura Lundy, 'Family Values in the Classroom? Reconciling Parental Wishes and Children's Rights in State Schools' (2005) 19 *International Journal of Law, Policy and the Family* 346.

108 Rex Ahdar and Ian Leigh, note 21, p. 260.

These limitation provisions are mirrored in part in Article 44 of the Irish Constitution which makes the protection of religious freedom subject to 'public order and morality'. The substantive approach taken in cases such as *Kokkinakis v Greece,*[109] *Karaduman v Turkey,*[110] *Otto-Preminger-Institut v Austria*[111] and *Murphy v Ireland*[112] has led to criticism of the Court on the basis that it has not always acted in accordance with its own conception of the importance of the protection afforded by Article 9, as encapsulated in the often quoted passage from *Kokkinakis*:

> (a)s enshrined in Article 9 (art. 9), freedom of thought, conscience and religion is one of the foundations of a "democratic society" within the meaning of the Convention. It is, in its religious dimension, one of the most vital elements that go to make up the identity of believers and their conception of life, but it is also a precious asset for atheists, agnostics, sceptics and the unconcerned. The pluralism indissociable from a democratic society, which has been clearly won over the centuries, depends on it.[113]

Nevertheless, the limits of state support for a particular religion in pluralist societies has been the focus of a number of ECtHR judgments, with the Court placing increasing emphasis on the role of states in promoting pluralism through tolerance. This has resonance in the Irish context discussed above. The case law interpreting Article 2 of Protocol 1 to the ECHR, which provides that 'no one shall be deprived of an education' and requires the state 'to respect the rights of parents to have their children educated in accordance with their religious and philosophical convictions', is of special interest from an Irish perspective.[114] Ireland has a reservation to this provision to the effect that the right to education in the Protocol was not sufficiently explicit in protecting the parental choice of school and the right to educate in the home whether or not such schools were private schools or schools recognized or established by the state. The Court's jurisprudence interprets the rationale of the second sentence of Article 2, Protocol 1 as safeguarding the possibility of educational pluralism – which is key to a democratic society – and '(i)n view of the power of the modern State, it is above all through State teaching that this aim must be realised'.[115] The key entitlement of parents is 'to enlighten

---

109 (1994) 17 EHRR 397.

110 (1993) 74 DR 93.

111 (1994) 19 EHRR 34.

112 (2004) 38 EHRR 13.

113 *Kokkinakis v Greece* (1994) 17 EHRR 397, p. 418. See Paul M. Taylor, *Freedom of Religion: UN and European Human Rights Law and Practice* (Sweet and Maxwell, 2009), p. 347.

114 For an overview of the case law, see Carolyn Evans, 'Religious Education in Public Schools: An International Human Rights Perspective' (2008) 8 (3) *HRLR* 449.

115 *Kjeldsen, Busk Madsen and Pedersen v Denmark* (1976) 1 EHRR 737, at para. 50. Approved in *Folgerø v Norway* (2008) 46 EHRR 47, at para. 84. On *Folgerø*, see

and advise their children, to exercise with regard to their children natural parental functions as educators, or to guide their children on a path in line with the parents' own religious or philosophical convictions'.[116] While the second sentence of Article 2 of Protocol 1 does not prevent states from imparting through education information or knowledge of a directly or indirectly religious or philosophical kind, and the state enjoys a margin of appreciation in respect of decisions relating to the school curriculum, it must take care that information or knowledge included in the curriculum is conveyed in an objective, critical and pluralistic manner.[117] On the basis of this reasoning, the Court found violations of Article 2 of Protocol 1 in *Folgero v Norway*[118] and *Zengin v Turkey*,[119] finding that the syllabuses under examination in each case gave preponderant weight to one religion over all others (Christianity and the Sunni interpretation of Islam, respectively). Above all, states are prohibited from pursuing 'an aim of indoctrination that might be regarded as not respecting parents' religious and philosophical convictions. That is the limit that must not be exceeded'.[120] Importantly from the perspective of the present discussion, schools must be a meeting place for different religions and philosophical viewpoints and the state's obligation of neutrality implies that pluralism must be guaranteed.[121] The Strasbourg Court's vision of the relationship between religion and education thus clearly encompasses an emphasis on pluralism, inclusion and dialogue between religions.

The scope of states' margin of appreciation in providing education in a manner which respects pluralism and parental choice was the subject matter of the recent decision of the Grand Chamber in *Lautsi v Italy*.[122] This case concerned the display of crucifixes in state schools in Italy, which the applicant argued was contrary to the principle of secularism by which she wished to bring up her children. The school in question refused to remove the crucifixes. The applicant complained before the Court that the display of the crucifix in the state school was in breach

---

Peggy Ducoulombier, '*Folgerø v Norway*: dispensation from religious education: from the United Nations Human Rights Committee to the European Court of Human Rights' [2008] 3 *EHRLR* 391.

116 *Kjeldsen, Busk Madsen and Pedersen v Denmark*, at para. 54 (approved in *Valsamis v Greece* (1997) 24 EHRR 294, at para. 31).

117 *Kjeldsen, Busk Madsen and Pedersen v Denmark*, at para. 53 (approved in *Folgero v Norway* (2008) 46 EHRR 47, at para. 84).

118 (2008) 46 EHRR 47.

119 (2007) 46 EHRR 44.

120 *Kjeldsen, Busk Madsen and Pedersen v Denmark*, at para. 53, as cited in, *inter alia*, *Valsamis v Greece* (1997) 24 EHRR 294.

121 *Folgerø v Norway* (2008) 46 EHRR 47, at para. 84.

122 Unreported, Application No. 30814/06, Judgment of the Grand Chamber of 18 March 2011. For academic commentary, see, for example, Jessica Giles (2012) 1(1) *Oxford Journal of Law and Religion* 289; Paolo Ronchi, 'Crucifixes, Margin of Appreciation and Consensus: The Grand Chamber Ruling in *Lautsi v Italy*' (2011) 13(3) *Ecclesiastical Law Journal* 287.

of Article 9 and of Article 2 of Protocol 1. The Chamber of the Court found that there had been a violation of Article 2 of Protocol 1 together with Article 9.[123] In particular, the Chamber emphasized the point that the state was obliged to maintain religious neutrality in the context of public education and stated that the presence of Catholic religious symbols in classrooms could not be reconciled with the educational pluralism which is essential to democratic societies, as envisaged by the ECtHR. This decision was overruled by the Grand Chamber in March 2011.

In its Grand Chamber judgment, the Court found that there was no violation of Article 2 of Protocol 1 (also holding that no separate issue arose under Article 9). The Court's starting point was that there was no evidence that the display of a religious symbol on classroom walls may have an influence on pupils. The Court also seemed to accept the Italian government's argument that the presence of crucifixes in state-school classrooms was the result of Italy's historical development, a fact which gave it not only a religious connotation but also an identity-linked one, now corresponded to a tradition which they considered it important to perpetuate. The Court then emphasized the margin of appreciation enjoyed by states in reconciling the exercise of their functions in relation to education with respect for the rights of parents to ensure such education and teaching in accordance with their own religious and philosophical convictions. The Court found that, in principle, it must therefore respect states' decisions in these educational matters, including the place they accord to religion, provided that those decisions do not lead to a form of indoctrination. This margin of appreciation was considered to be particularly important in the situation under consideration as there is no European consensus on the question of the presence of religious symbols in schools. The Court assessed the question of the impact of the display of the crucifix in light of all the circumstances, noting in particular that the presence of the crucifixes was not associated with compulsory teaching about Christianity. In addition, the Court placed some weight on the fact that 'Italy opens the school environment to other religions'.[124] The evidence showed that it was not forbidden for pupils to wear Islamic headscarves or other symbols or apparel having a religious connotation, for example, and alternative arrangements were possible to help schooling fit in with non-majority religious practices. There was nothing to suggest that the authorities were intolerant of non-Christian pupils. Crucially, the Court characterized the crucifix as an 'essentially passive symbol', which could not be deemed to have an influence on pupils comparable to that of didactic speech or participation in religious activities.[125] In all the circumstances, despite the fact that the display of the crucifix granted preponderance to the majority religion in

123 Judgment of 3 November, 2009. See also the case comment of Nicholas Gibson, 'Right to Education in Conformity with Philosophical Convictions' [2010] *EHRLR* (2)208.

124 *Lautsi v Italy*, Unreported, Application No. 30814/06, Judgment of the Grand Chamber of 18 March 2011, at para. 74.

125 Ibid., at para. 72.

the classroom, it did not form part of a process of indoctrination and there was thus no violation of Article 2 of Protocol 1.

While the decisions in *Folgerø* and *Zengin* indicated a trend towards narrowing states' margin of appreciation in the sphere of religion and the provision of education, in particular in relation to the content of the school curriculum,[126] the Grand Chamber's judgment in *Lautsi* illustrates the limits of this approach, which seemingly will not be extended to all practices in schools with a religious dimension. The key finding that the presence of religious symbols in schools, in the absence of any other form of indoctrinating or proselytizing pressure, will not in itself constitute indoctrination constitutes an acknowledgement from the Court that freedom of religion can be protected in settings which are not necessarily purely secular. The Court's approach means that its requirement for state 'neutrality' in public education will not necessarily be equated with pure secularism. Thus, in her concurring opinion, Judge Power (the Irish judge) stated, in explaining where the judgment of the Chamber had gone wrong:

> The Chamber referred, correctly, to the State's duty to uphold confessional neutrality in public education (§ 56). However, it proceeded to conclude, incorrectly, that this duty required the effective preference or elevation of one ideology (or body of ideas) over all other religious and/or philosophical perspectives or world views. Neutrality requires a pluralist approach on the part of the State, not a secularist one. It encourages respect for all world views rather than a preference for one. To my mind, the Chamber Judgment was striking in its failure to recognise that secularism (which was the applicant's preferred belief or world view) was, in itself, one ideology among others. A preference for secularism over alternative world views – whether religious, philosophical or otherwise – is not a neutral option.[127]

It seems that the Court will consider whether, taking into account all the circumstances, the practice in question has a meaningful impact on religious freedom, such that it is a form of indoctrination. It will also bear in mind the historical and cultural context in which the practice of the education system of states has developed. This nuanced position is to be welcomed. However, the Court's reasoning in its very brief judgment is unsatisfactory in a number of respects. Its reference to the crucifix as a 'passive symbol' is tautologous, as symbols are by nature passive – what would constitute an 'active symbol'? Most importantly, the analysis of the Court does not provide any real guidance as to what precisely will

---

126 This point is made by Peggy Ducoulombier, note 115; see further Samantha Knights, *Freedom of Religion, Minorities and the Law* (Oxford University Press, 2009), p. 335. Knights cites *Hasan and Chaush v Bulgaria* (2002) 34(6) EHRR, para. 62; *Metropolitan Church of Bessarabia and others v Moldova* (2002) 35 EHRR 306, paras 116 and 119.

127 Concurring opinion of Judge Power.

result in a practice falling on either side of the dividing line between acceptable practice and 'indoctrination'.

The *Lautsi* decision is highly significant from an Irish perspective. On the specific issue of religious symbols, most Irish public schools under the patronage of the Catholic Church have Catholic religious symbols including crucifixes on display in classrooms and throughout the school. The small proportion of schools under the patronage of other religions may equally display religious symbols associated with their faith. This practice is probably acceptable under the Irish Constitution (as mentioned above), and it would appear from the *Lautsi* decision that this display of religious symbols in state-funded schools in itself does not violate Article 2 of Protocol 1.

However, when viewed in the context of the education system as a whole, the question as to whether the display of religious symbols in Irish schools form part of a process of indoctrination becomes more complex. McGoldrick notes that 'the degree of interference with parental rights inherent in the current Irish education system is much more severe than that upheld by the Court in *Lautsi*'.[128] The curriculum cases decided by the ECtHR indicate that states have a narrow margin of appreciation in respect of the religious content of compulsory elements of the school curriculum. Article 2 of Protocol 1, together with Article 9, requires that knowledge or information contained in the curriculum must be conveyed in an objective, critical and pluralistic manner. In the Irish setting, while children may be exempted from religious instruction, the general ethos of the school and the integrated curriculum which is in use in the majority of schools cannot be avoided – in fact, that is the whole point of the integrated curriculum. The Court's judgment in *Folgerø v Norway*[129] makes it clear that the principles derived from the ECHR case law apply not only to specific religious instruction but to education in the broad sense as referenced by Barrington J in *Campaign to Separate Church and State*. As the Court in *Folgero* stated:

> Article 2 of Protocol No. 1 does not permit a distinction to be drawn between religious instruction and other subjects. It enjoins the State to respect parents' convictions, be they religious or philosophical, throughout the entire State education programme. That duty is broad in its extent as it applies not only to the content of education and the manner of its provision but also to the performance of all the "functions" assumed by the State. The verb "respect" means more than "acknowledge" or "take into account". In addition to a primarily negative undertaking, it implies some positive obligation on the part of the State.[130]

128 Dominic McGoldrick, 'Religion in the European Public Square and in European Public Life: Crucixes in the Classroom?' (2011) 11(3) *HRLR* 451, p. 495.

129 (2008) 46 EHRR 47.

130 Ibid.

The Irish educational setting, in which religious symbols are displayed as part of an approach whereby a particular religious ethos is integrated into every aspect of school life, could be found to have an influence on pupils which falls foul of the requirement that 'the curriculum is conveyed in an objective, critical and pluralistic manner, enabling pupils to develop a critical mind particularly with regard to religion in a calm atmosphere free of any proselytism'.[131] This would place the ECHR in direct opposition to the Irish Constitution, as interpreted by the Supreme Court, under which parents are entitled to insist on their children receiving a broad religious education going beyond religious instruction to permeate the ethos of the school.

There are some weighty counter-arguments that can be made in defence of the Irish education system. Unlike Italy, Ireland's education system is denominational rather than secular.[132] As mentioned above, the role of the state in Irish public education is somewhat unique, with boards of management in charge of the direct running and decision-making in schools and the state refraining from interference in the religious education and instruction of pupils. Thus the state could argue that it cannot be accused of imposing beliefs in the classroom as it is, in both legal and practical terms, a degree removed from decision-making in this sphere and merely facilitates the education of children in accordance with parental wishes as required by the Constitution. There is no state regulation of religious symbols or religious symbols in schools (unlike the Italian model, in which the display of the crucifixes was prescribed by law). In addition, similarly to in Italy, expression of religious difference is accepted in Irish schools, with pupils allowed to wear religious dress if they choose and attempts are generally made to accommodate the practice and profession of all religions.

Moreover, it could be argued that in Ireland the state maintains religious neutrality and facilitates pluralism by following a policy of equality between the religions, in principle allowing for funding of minority religious schools and non-religious schools. This would ignore the reality that the majority of children of minority religions and no religion attend Catholic schools out of necessity through lack of choice. Overall, from the brief, poorly reasoned analysis in *Lautsi*, it is difficult to assess whether the Irish education system – with its integrated curriculum and overwhelmingly Catholic state-funded denominational schools – could be said to enshrine 'indoctrination'. However, it does seem, on the basis of the approach taken in *Lautsi*, that the ECtHR will not rush to classify school systems as contrary to Article 2 of Protocol 1. The Irish education system would be assessed, in the light of the historical and cultural context in which it developed, in terms of whether the school setting has an actual proselytizing effect on pupils.

131 Ibid., at para. 62.

132 See generally, Siobhán Mullally and Darren Donovan, 'Religion in Ireland's "Public Squares": education, the family and expanding equality claims' (2011) *Public Law* 284.

International Covenant on Civil and Political Rights

The CCPR expressed concern in its 2008 concluding observations on Ireland's state report on its implementation of the ICCPR about the fact that the vast majority of Ireland's primary schools are privately run denominational schools that have adopted a religious integrated curriculum, thus depriving many parents and children who so wish to have access to secular primary education.[133] The CCPR viewed this situation as raising issues under Articles 2 (prohibition of discrimination), 18 (freedom of religion), 24 (children's rights) and 26 (right to equality) and observed that Ireland should 'increase its efforts to ensure that non-denominational primary education is widely available in all regions … in view of the increasingly diverse and multi-ethnic composition of the population of the State party'.[134] A similar recommendation was made by the CCPR in relation to Greece, where allegations were made concerning discrimination against members of minority religions in the field of education, with individuals being required to declare their religion prior to being exempted from compulsory Greek Orthodox religious instruction classes. The CCPR encouraged Greece to hold consultations with representatives of minority religions, in order to find practical ways to permit religious instruction to be given to those desiring such opportunities.[135]

Article 18 ICCPR, which protects freedom of religion, is particularly important in this context and is striking in its similarity to Article 44 of the Irish Constitution. It provides thus:

> 1. Everyone shall have the right to freedom of thought, conscience and religion. This right shall include freedom to have or to adopt a religion or belief of his choice, and freedom, either individually or in community with others and in public or private, to manifest his religion or belief in worship, observance, practice and teaching.
>
> 2. No one shall be subject to coercion which would impair his freedom to have or to adopt a religion or belief of his choice.
>
> 3. Freedom to manifest one's religion or beliefs may be subject only to such limitations as are prescribed by law and are necessary to protect public safety, order, health, or morals or the fundamental rights and freedoms of others.
>
> 4. The States Parties to the present Covenant undertake to have respect for the liberty of parents and, when applicable, legal guardians to ensure the religious and moral education of their children in conformity with their own convictions.

133 UN Doc CCPR/C/IRL/CO/3 (30 July 2008), para. 22.

134 Ibid.

135 Greece, UN Doc CCPR/CO/83/GRC (24 May 2005), p. 14.

General Comment 22 goes some way towards clarifying the implications of Article 18(4) in terms of the relationship between the state, parents, religion and education.[136] Public school instruction in subjects such as the general history of religions and ethics is permitted under Article 18(4) if it is 'given in a neutral and objective way'. Public education that includes instruction in a particular religion or belief is inconsistent with Article 18(4) unless provision is made for non-discriminatory exemptions or alternatives that would accommodate the wishes of parents and guardians. Thus while the guarantees relating to parental choice in education in Article 44 and 42 of the Irish Constitution are interpreted by the Irish courts as justifying the funding of denominational schools, Article 18(4) of the ICCPR is interpreted in the reverse, as placing limits on instruction in a particular religion in public education.[137]

The CCPR has dealt with the issues arising in this chapter in a number of its Optional Protocol decisions, which have considered the issues in terms of articles 2, 18 and 26. Articles 18 and 26 are closely linked, as 'in general, arrangements in the field of religious education that are in compliance with Article 18 are likely to be in conformity with Article 26 as well, because non-discrimination is a fundamental component in the test under Article 18(4)'.[138] This approach mirrors that of the Irish courts, which have emphasized the importance of equality of treatment of religions by the state. The jurisprudence of the CCPR in this sphere has not been subject to the same criticism as the ECtHR as it has not allowed states as wide a margin of discretion as that Court.[139] In *Waldman v. Canada*,[140] the author claimed that providing Roman Catholic schools in Ontario with full state funding – while he was required to send his children to a private Jewish school as no funding was available for other non-secular schools – impaired in a discriminatory fashion his right to manifest his religion including to provide a religious education for his children. The CCPR found that this constituted a violation of Article 26, confirming that the ICCPR does not impose any obligation on states to fund religious schools but if it decides to do so, the funding must be made available without discrimination. Here, the traditional preferential treatment of Roman Catholic schools with the aim of protecting the Roman Catholic religion did not justify the discrimination. To apply this reasoning to the Irish context, in principle, the Irish system is non-discriminatory, as funding is in theory available without discrimination to schools of all religions as well as secular schools.

136 CCPR General Comment No. 22, 'The right to freedom of thought, conscience and religion (Art. 18)' (30 July 1993).

137 The freedom of religious minorities is also protected through Article 27 of the ICCPR.

138 *Arieh Hollis Waldman v Canada* (694/1996), CCPR/C/67/D/694/1996 (1999), concurring statement of Mr Scheinin, para. 3.

139 Paul M. Taylor, note 113, p. 178.

140 *Waldman v Canada* (694/96), CCPR/C/67/694/1996 (1999).

However, in Ireland the vast majority of schools are Catholic and therefore it is arguable that the Irish system enshrines a form of indirect discrimination.

A number of other decisions have dealt with the provision of religious education and further illustrate the problematic nature of the Irish denominational education system in the light of international human rights law. *Hartikainen v Finland*[141] dealt with the compulsory teaching of the history of religion and ethics as an alternative to religious instruction. In the view of the CCPR, the alternative classes were adequate as they were delivered in a neutral and objective way which respected the beliefs of those of all religions and none. *Leirvag et al. v Norway*[142] took place at the same time as the ECHR case *Folgero v Norway* and involved exactly the same issues. The authors claimed that the framework of the mandatory religious instruction class in Norwegian schools, from which only limited exemptions were available, violated their Article 18(4) rights. The CCPR came to the same conclusion as the ECtHR, upholding the authors' claim that the operation of the subject and in particular the partial exemption system violated Article 18(4) of the ICCPR. Of interest from an Irish point of view was the following statement:

> (T)he Committee notes that the CKREE subject combines education on religious knowledge with practising a particular religious belief, e.g. learning by heart of prayers, singing religious hymns or attendance at religious services. While it is true that in these cases parents may claim exemption from these activities by ticking a box on a form, the CKREE scheme does not ensure that education of religious knowledge and religious practice are separated in a way that makes the exemption scheme practicable.[143]

This criticism is directly applicable to the Irish education system generally. While Article 44.2.4 of the Irish Constitution specifically provides for the right of every child to attend a school in receipt of public monies without attending religious *instruction* at that school, the use of the integrated curriculum in denominational schools along with the pervasive ethos of the school means that such a child may be exposed to a religious *education*, perhaps rendering the exemption insufficient to satisfy the requirements of Article 18. Education of religious knowledge and religious practice are inseparable in the Irish context. The lack of real choice for those who do not wish to attend Catholic schools compounds the problem.

Finally, the former UN Special Rapporteur on Freedom of Religion or Belief has described the 'sectarian' approach, whereby each pupil learns only about his or her religion separated from children of other beliefs, as a 'ghetto approach'. He supported the idea of a more comprehensive scheme of religious education in which all children could participate, which would contribute to the understanding of others, to cultural and moral differences and foster a spirit of human rights and

141 (40/1978), 9 April 1981.

142 (1155/2003), CCPR/C/82/D/1155/2003 (2004).

143 Ibid., at para. 14.7.

tolerance.[144] The Irish education system enshrines this 'ghetto approach' with a ripple effect for the integration paradigm in Irish law, as discussed above. This segregated approach to education has also been criticized by the UN Committee for the Elimination for all Forms of Racial Discrimination in relation to Ireland,[145] and the UN Committee for Economic, Social and Cultural Rights in relation to Northern Ireland.[146]

Individual Expression of Religious Belief: Religious Symbols in Schools

The 'Headscarf Debate': The Transformation of the Public Sphere?

The wearing of religious clothing and symbols, most notably the Muslim headscarf, in the public sphere and in particular in public schools has been the focus of much judicial and academic discussion since the changes in world and religious politics brought about by the events of September 11, 2001. The importance of the issue has been characterized in diverse ways in terms of social cohesion,[147] gender equality,[148] children's rights, individual human rights[149] and immigrant integration.[150] In integration terms the chosen approach clearly indicates the extent to which visible difference is accepted and the extent to which immigrants are expected to relinquish their religious identity in favour of an identity modelled on that of a model member of the host community. Significantly, the presence of religious symbols, including the headscarf, is viewed by some as evidence of the 'failed' integration of immigrants, or even as a symbol of a reluctance to integrate, particularly in the case of Muslim immigrant-origin communities.[151] Accordingly, the legal position regarding religious symbols in a public space can be seen as an indication of the importance which a state places on cultural integration, and, to

144 Carolyn Evans, note 114, p. 452, citing Amon, Introductory Note to International Consultative Conference on School Education in Relation to Freedom of Religion or Belief, Tolerance and Non-Discrimination, 2002.

145 UN Doc CERD/C/IRL/CO/3–4 (10 March 2011), para. 26.

146 UN Doc E/C.12/1/Add.79 (5 June 2002), para. 23.

147 See *R (Begum) v Headteacher and Governors of Denbigh High School* [2007] 1 AC 100, per Baroness Hale, at 132.

148 Siobhan Mullally, 'Feminism and Multicultural Dilemmas in India: Revisiting the Shah Bano Case' (2004) 24 *Oxford Journal of Legal Studies* 671. See also Pascale Fournier and Gökçe Yurdakul, 'Unveiling Distribution: Muslim Women with Headscarves in France and Germany', in Michal Bodemann and Gökçe Yurdakul (eds), *Migration, Citizenship, Ethnos* (Palgrave, 2006), pp. 167–185.

149 See, for example, Tom Lewis, 'What not to Wear: Religious Rights, the European Court and the Margin of Appreciation' (2007) 56 *ICLQ* 395.

150 Dominic McGoldrick, *Human Rights and Religion: The Islamic Headscarf Debate in Europe* (Hart Publishing, 2006), p. 17.

151 Ibid., pp. 17–20.

borrow Joppke's phrase, provides a 'mirror of identity'.[152] These broad debates also encompass access to citizenship and integration requirements in naturalization procedures, as was seen in the last chapter.

The spectrum of legal approaches taken to the issue in different jurisdictions is also striking, with much academic commentary focusing on comparing and contrasting the types of legal approaches in operation across the globe.[153] It has been argued in this book that state responses to integration issues, and particularly 'cultural integration' issues, are conditioned by conceptions of national identity and membership, historical experience and organizational political principles (the 'public philosophy' of the state) and from this perspective the varying responses of states to the regulation of religious dress in public space is unsurprising. Nevertheless, European legal practice would appear to be converging to a certain degree around the restriction of the presence of religious dress in the public sphere. This trend is manifested in various forms in different countries. In 2004, France passed a law prohibiting the wearing of ostentatious religious symbols in public schools.[154] In the same year the German Supreme Court held that a teacher was prohibited from wearing a headscarf while teaching in the classroom.[155] In the UK, the House of Lords has found that it is permissible for schools to prohibit the wearing of certain religious symbols in circumstances where this is a proportionate response.[156] In 2009, one canton in Switzerland went a step further in the related sphere of places of worship, with the population voting to ban the construction of Muslim minarets.[157] In 2010, Belgium and France became the

152 Christian Joppke, *Veil: Mirror of Identity* (Polity Press, 2009).

153 Sebastian Poulter, note 11; Manisuli Ssenyonjo, 'Limits on the Freedom to Manifest One's Religion in Educational Institutions in Uganda and the United Kingdom' [2009] 7(2) *ICON* 275; Dympna Glendenning, *Religion, Education and the Law*, note 86, in which she surveys legal practice in numerous jurisdictions.

154 *Loi du 15 mars 2004 encadrant, en application du principe de laïcité, le port de signes ou de tenues manifestant une appartenance religieuse dans les écoles, collèges et lycées publics* (JO, 17 mars 2004); see also *Circulaire du 18 mai 2004 relative à la mise en oeuvre de la loi n° 2004–228 du 15 mars 2004 encadrant, en application du principe de laïcité, le port de signes ou de tenues manifestant une appartenance religieuse dans les écoles, collèges et lycées publics* (JO, 22 mai 2004). For a critical analysis of the law, see Joseph Carens, 'Démocratie, multiculturalisme et *hijab*' (2005) 1 *Esprit* 54. See also Claire de Galembert, 'Le voile en procès' (2008) 68 *Droit et Société* 11.

155 Judgment of 24 September 2003-BVerfGE 108, 282. See Cindy Skach, 'Case Comment – *Sahin v Turkey* App. No. 44774/98 / Teacher Headscarf Case; Case No. 2BvR 1436/02' (2006) 100 *American Journal of International Law* 186; and Christine Langenfeld and Sarah Mohsen, 'The Teacher Headscarf Case' (2005) 3(1) *ICON* 86.

156 *R (on the application of Begum) v Denbigh High School Governors* [2007] 1 AC 100.

157 See BBC, 'Swiss voters back ban on minarets', 29 November 2010, http://news.bbc.co.uk/2/hi/8385069.stm. Application No. 66274/09, *Association Ligue des Musulmans de Suisse and Others v Switzerland*, and Application No. 65840/09 *Ouardiri v Switzerland*, in relation to the ban, were deemed inadmissible by the ECtHR (on 28 June 2011), on the ground that the applicants could not claim to be the 'victims' of a violation

first European countries to ban the full face-covering veil in public places.[158] The Parliamentary report which preceded the adoption of the law in France essentially justified the adoption of the law on the grounds that the full veil was a symbol of Islamic fundamentalism, and that it was oppressive to women, contrary to the constitutional principle of equality.[159] At the level of international law, this trend has been endorsed and perhaps even encouraged by the jurisprudence of the European Court of Human Rights. This will be discussed in greater detail below.

These developments have been characterized (notwithstanding important differences between the approaches of states) as pointing in the direction of a structural transformation, by way of law, of public spheres in Europe with countries in Europe increasingly employing models of secularism that they hope will limit (rather than exacerbate) social conflict.[160] A significant element of this trend is that the wearing of the Islamic headscarf in public schools is frequently taken as having in and of itself an important political significance that threatens public order and individual freedom in a democracy.[161] Approaches in other jurisdictions on other continents have differed. In Canada, constitutionally enshrined values of tolerance and multiculturalism have been at the heart of the rationale not to allow restrictions on the wearing of religious symbols in as blunt a manner as many European jurisdictions.[162] The South African courts have taken a broadly similar approach, stressing that it is incumbent on schools to instil in its learners the values of cultural and religious tolerance.[163] In the US, secularism has been viewed in a primarily negative sense as prohibiting state interference with personal behaviour and this, taken with the strong emphasis on freedom of expression, has meant that religious dress has been broadly tolerated.[164]

---

of the Convention. A number of applications are still pending, *Baechler v Switzerland* (Application No. 66270/09); *Koella Naouali v Switzerland* (Application No. 1317/10); *Al-Zarka v Switzerland* (Application No. 9113/10).

158 For a report on the Belgian ban, see BBC, 'Belgian lawmakers pass burka ban', 30 April 2010, http://news.bbc.co.uk/2/hi/8652861.stm. In relation to the ban in France, see Siobhán Mullally, 'Civic Integration, Migrant Women and the Veil: at the Limits of Rights?', note 10; Myriam Hunter-Henin, 'Why the French Don't Like the Burqa: *Laïcité*, National Identity and Religious Freedom' (2012) 61(3) *ICLQ* 613. The Grand Chamber of the ECtHR will rule on an application concerning the French law: *SAS v France* (Application 43835/11).

159 *Rapport d'Information fait en l'application de l'Article 145 du Règlement au Nom de la Mission d'Information sur la Pratique du Port du Voile Intégral sur le Territoire National* (Report of the National Asssembly, 26 January 2010). The constitutional validity of the law was confirmed by the Conseil Constitutionnel (Decision no. 2010-613 DC of 07 October 2010 - *Loi interdisant la dissimulation du visage dans l'espace public*).

160 Cindy Skach, note 155.

161 Ibid.

162 *Multani v Commission Scolaire Marguerite-Bourgeoys* [2006] 4 LRC 496; 2006 SCC 6.

163 *Pillay v KwaZulu-Natal MEC of Education and Others* [2007] 1 LRC 125, para. 62.

164 *Tinker v DesMoines Independent Community School District* 393 US 503 (1969).

Irish Law and Practice

In contrast to many other European jurisdictions, the issue of the wearing of religious dress and symbols has not as yet arisen in Ireland in a legal setting and from the limited available research it does not appear to have arisen in a controversial way in schools.[165] An exception occurred in 2009 when correspondence between a school principal and the Department of Education and Science on the topic of the wearing of the hijab was published by a national newspaper.[166] In response to the public debate provoked by this publicity, the Minister for Integration carried out a consultation with key stakeholders (including the principals of every primary and secondary school in the country) to determine whether there was a need for formal guidelines to be developed. The Minister made the following recommendations, taking into account – *inter alia* – the legal position in Ireland and policy in the EU:

1. The current system, whereby schools decide their uniform policy at a local level, is reasonable, works and should be maintained.
2. In this context, no school uniform policy should act in a way that, in effect, excludes students of a particular religious background from seeking enrolment or continuing their enrolment in a school. However this statement does not recommend the wearing of clothing in the classroom which obscures a facial view and creates an artificial barrier between pupil and teacher. Such clothing hinders proper communication.
3. Schools, when drawing up uniform policy, should consult widely within the school community.
4. Schools should take note of the obligations placed on them by the Equal Status Acts before setting down a school uniform policy. They should also be mindful of the Education Act 1998. As previously mentioned, this obliges boards of management to take account of 'the principles and requirements of a democratic society and have respect and promote respect for the diversity of values, beliefs, traditions, languages and ways of life in society'.[167]

---

165 Economic and Social Research Institute, note 60. For academic commentary, see Tom Hickey, 'Domination and the *Hijab* in Irish Schools' (2009) 16(1) *DULJ* 127 and Eoin Daly, 'Restrictions on Religious Dress in French Republican Thought: Returning a Secularist Justification to a Rights-Based Rationale' (2009) 16(1) *DULJ* 154

166 See 'Principal calls for guidelines on wearing of hijab in schools', *Irish Times*, 19 May 2008; 'Groups to Lobby for Right to Wear Hijab', *Irish Times*, 2 September 2008. On this 'brief controversy' see Siobhán Mullally and Darren Donovan, note 132, pp. 211–213. See also Máiréad Enright, 'Girl Interrupted: Citizenship and the Irish Hijab Debate' (2011) 20(4) *Social & Legal Studies* 463.

167 Report on the need for a Guidance Note to Schools when reviewing their policies on School Uniforms prepared by the Minister for Integration, Conor Lenihan TD, and jointly launched by Minister for Education and Science, Batt O'Keeffe TD and Minister for Integration, Conor Lenihan TD (2008) p. 6.

Official policy therefore favours a flexible response contingent on the circumstances. If these matters came before a court however, what is the position in Irish law? The legislation affords little assistance, as boards of management are required under the Education Act 1998 to both uphold the characteristic spirit of the school and promote tolerance and diversity. The case law indicates the priority accorded to freedom to practice and profess religion in rights-balancing exercises. In *Quinn's Supermarket v AG*[168] and subsequent cases the Supreme Court has effectively elevated the free practice guarantee over the non-discrimination guarantee,[169] making it clear that discrimination – in either a negative or positive sense – on the basis of religion may be justified on the basis that the discrimination is necessary to allow free practice of religion.[170] In delivering his judgment in *Quinn's Supermarket*, Walsh J made the following, often-quoted statement, which is directly relevant to the discussion on the wearing of religious symbols and religious dress:

> It appears to me … that the primary object and aim of Article 44 … and in particular the provisions of s.2 of that article, was to secure and guarantee freedom of conscience and the free profession and practice of religion subject to public order and morality … Any law which by virtue of the generality of its application would by its effect restrict or prevent the free profession and practice of religion by any persons would be invalid having regard to the provisions of the Constitution, unless it contained provisions which saved from such restriction or prevention the practice of religion of the person or persons who would otherwise be so restricted or prevented.[171]

It thus seems almost certain that legislation along the lines of that adopted in France – a blanket ban on particular ways of manifesting religious belief in schools or in public – would be unconstitutional in Irish law. The *Quinn* decision embodies a vision of societal cohesion which involves society making exemptions from norms in certain circumstances in order to accommodate those of different religious beliefs, in contrast to the approach taken in France that religious practices must be subordinated to secularist norms in order to maintain a cohesive society. The approach in *Quinn* is encapsulated in the comments of Kenny J in stating that:

---

168 [1972] IR 1.

169 Oran Doyle, *Constitutional Law: Text, Cases and Materials*, note 42, at 10–08.

170 This approach was followed in *Mulloy v Minister for Education* and the Attorney General [1975] 1 IR 88. In that case the Supreme Court found that the discrimination on the ground of religious status by a scheme run by the Department of Education was repugnant to Article 44 of the Constitution on the basis that there was no question that the discrimination was required in order to facilitate the free practice and profession of religion. *M v An Bord Uchtála* [1975] was decided on similar grounds. See also *McGrath and O Ruairc v Trustees of Maynooth College* [1979] ILRM 166 and most recently *Re Article 26 and the Employment Equality Bill* [1997] 2 IR 321.

171 [1972] IR 1, pp. 23–24.

> We are in religion a pluralist society made up of people of people of many persuasions and beliefs and so it is likely that parts of legislation will occasionally indirectly affect the practice of some religion. If the State has to abstain from law-making on matters which indirectly affect the practice of religion by some of its citizens, the scope of legislation will be seriously reduced. Yet this will be the result if the State cannot exempt from the application of some of its legislation those whose practice of their religion will be affected by it.[172]

Nevertheless, the free practice of religion may be restricted on the grounds of public order and morality. 'Public morality' in particular is a nebulous and potentially wide restriction on religious freedom[173] and cannot be dismissed, the extent to which courts may be influenced by populist religious intolerance having been shown in *Schlegel v Corcoran*[174] in which the Irish High Court found that to refuse to give consent to the assigning of rooms to a Jewish person (in this case the rooms were used for a dental practice) was not 'unreasonable' in legal terms, basing the decision on the following reasoning:

> The plaintiff's objection has been characterised as a caprice and as mere prejudice; but caprice is not the right word for anti-Semitism, which, far from being a peculiar crochet, is notoriously shared by a number of other citizens; and, if prejudice be the right word, the antagonism between Christian and Jew has its roots in nearly 2000 years of history and is too prevalent as a habit of mind to be dismissed offhand, in a country where religion matters, as the eccentric extravagance of a bigot, without regard to the actual conditions under which the consent was withheld. I fail, by the way, to see the supposed connection between the problem before Mrs Schlegel and the constitutional veto (Art. 44.2.2) upon any discrimination by the State on the grounds of religious belief.[175]

In *DPP v Draper*,[176] the Court of Criminal Appeal also dealt with the concept of 'public order', which relied on the exception to find that freedom of conscience and free profession and practice of religion could not prevent the conviction of a man for malicious damage to religious statues. Doyle argues that while it must be accepted that the decision is not an easy one to distil general principles from, it raises the question of whether the delineation of an act as an offence by the

172 Ibid., p. 34.

173 See Oran Doyle, *Constitutional Law: Text, Cases and Materials*, note 42, at 10–06. Note also that CCPR General Comment No. 22, note 136, states that 'limitations on the right to manifest a religion or belief for the purposes of protecting morals must be based on principles not deriving exclusively from a single tradition' (para. 8).

174 [1942] 1 IR 19.

175 Ibid., *per* Gavan Duffy J at 25.

176 24 March 1988, *The Irish Times*. Gerard Hogan and Gerry Whyte, note 24, at 7.4.83.

criminal law is sufficient to determine that it offends public morality and hence cannot be protected as an exercise of religious freedom.[177] This analysis could be relevant to a legislative ban on certain types of religious expression.

The Supreme Court decision in *Murphy v IRTC*[178] provides a more concrete, recent example of the way in which competing rights may be balanced by a contemporary court, even though the judgment does not refer to the specific exception of 'public order and morality'. In *Murphy* a legislative prohibition on religious advertising on the radio was upheld. One of the fundamental elements of the reasoning of the Court was that the legislative prohibition in question was not an 'attack' on the free practice of religion, rather a limited 'restriction' on the manner in which the citizen may profess, express or practice his or her religion.[179] If the wearing of religious symbols was similarly characterized as a 'limited restriction', then the level of protection seemingly granted in *Quinn* could be significantly eroded. In considering this question, a court would likely take the *Quinn* approach of considering the importance of the practice given the tenets of the religion in question, taking a subjective perspective.[180] The Supreme Court in *Murphy* also accepted the social cohesion argument made by the High Court, in considering the proportionality of the legislative ban. This was put as follows by Geoghegan J:

> Irish people with religious beliefs tend to belong to different churches and that being so religious advertising coming from a different church can be offensive to many people and might be open to the interpretation of proselytising.[181]

If the Irish courts were to take a similar view as the European Court of Human Rights and opt to characterize the headscarf as a powerful external symbol with a potentially proselytizing effect this would have the effect of bringing into play 'public order' considerations and justifications. Finally, *Murphy* illustrates the role of the principle of proportionality in decision-making in this area, with the Court stating that once this principle is respected by the legislature the courts must not interfere with its acts. The Supreme Court's view that in this case, the limitation placed on the various constitutional rights was 'minimalist' was more or less determinative of the outcome of the case.[182]

Overall then, while it is difficult to conceive of an Irish court upholding an outright ban on religious dress or symbols in schools it is possible that, depending on the way in which the issues are framed, some lesser form of restriction might be tolerable. In particular, the structure of the education system may give rise to

177 Oran Doyle, *Constitutional Law: Text, Cases and Materials*, note 42, p. 292.
178 [1999] 1 IR 26.
179 Ibid., p. 23.
180 [1972] IR 330.
181 [1999] 1 IR 12, p. 18.
182 Ibid., p. 26.

some thorny legal questions in the Irish educational context. As regards teachers, under section 37(1) of the Employment Equality Act 1998, if a teacher was to wear religious dress which is not in keeping with the denominational ethos of the school, the school would be entitled to take action which is 'reasonably necessary' to avoid such undermining the religious ethos of the institution and thus teachers could be prevented from wearing religious garb of a denomination other than that of the school. What then of children practicing and professing their religion, in accordance with the wishes of their parents, in a denominational school which is not of their own denomination? What is the legal position if a Muslim girl wears a headscarf in a Catholic school, and Catholic parents complain that this is interfering with the Catholic ethos of the school, which they are entitled to insist upon as part of the broad religious education of their child? If a court seised of this issue were to use a social cohesion approach similar to that in *Murphy*, and opted to characterize the headscarf as a powerful external symbol with a potentially proselytizing effect, this question could become particularly problematic. The court would likely use a subjective analysis to assess the importance of the religious practice within the religion in question, and if the restriction constituted by restricting or prohibiting certain forms of dress were characterized as 'minimalist', then the claims of parents trying to maintain the 'ethos' of the school might be held to outweigh the individual right to religious freedom.

While I have attempted to use the general principles of the case law to discern how an Irish court might approach the issues raised in this chapter, it is quite difficult to predict the outcome in cases where two 'free practice' rights come head to head, as in the example above. The broad parameters of the Irish courts' approach to the potentially divisive issues involved in the wearing of religious dress and symbols in public spaces, and more specifically schools, remain to be determined. However, so far schools have managed to resolve these issues in a way which appears to have avoided serious conflict and balanced the rights of those involved. It has been argued that Muslim children in particular are better integrated in the Irish school system than elsewhere in Europe, as their religious freedom is given greater respect.[183] Perhaps this shows that despite the criticisms levelled at the Irish education system in this chapter, religious freedom may be better protected overall within the structures of the Irish system than in other countries, especially in Europe. In turn then, perhaps this also gives force to the argument that the Irish model shows that religious freedom, in terms of individual religious freedom, may be best protected in states with established religions or legal frameworks favourable to religion.[184]

183 Dympna Glendenning, *Religion, Education and the Law*, note 85, p. 360.

184 Rex Ahdar and Ian Leigh, note 86, pp. 95–96.

Religious Symbols, Education and International Law

European Convention on Human Rights

There is a significant body of literature addressing the European Court of Human Rights' approach to restrictions imposed by states on the wearing of headscarves (and other forms of religious dress), with most of this comment critical of the growing body of case law.[185] The Court has shown an apparent willingness to allow states wide discretion to impose such restrictions, through the use of the doctrine of the margin of appreciation and a broad interpretation of the limitation provisions. Although there have been some cases in which the court has protected the right to wear distinctive religious dress in public areas,[186] high priority has not been granted to the right to wear religious clothing in public establishments, which has often been outweighed by the desire of secular states to preserve a secular public sphere.[187] Thus the Court and the Commission found in *Dahlab v Switzerland* (in which the application was considered to be inadmissible),[188] *Sahin v Turkey*[189] and *Dogru v France*[190] that restrictions imposed by the state on the wearing of headscarves in educational institutions were permissible.[191] In *Mann Singh v France*,[192] which concerned a Sikh man who had held driving licenses in France for thirty years displaying a photo of himself in his turban and then was told that he must remove his turban for the photo for a new driving licence, the application was dismissed as inadmissible without a consideration of why this change in the law was necessary.[193] In a similar manner, in 2009, it was decided that five applications of Muslim and Sikh children seeking to wear items representing their religious belief to school after the adoption of the law in 2004 that prohibited symbols which conspicuously represent a religious belief were

185 See (in addition to those already cited) Mark Hill and Russell Sandbergh, 'Is Nothing Sacred? Clashing Symbols in a Secular World' [2007] *Public Law* 488; Anastasia Vakulenko 'Islamic Dress in Human Rights Jurisprudence: A Critique of Current Trends' (2007) 7 *HRL Rev* 717.

186 *Arslan v Turkey* (Unreported, App. No. 41135/98, Judgment of 23 February 2010). The Court found no evidence here that the applicants represented a threat to public order or that they were involved in proselytizing.

187 Samantha Knights, note 126.

188 Application No. 42393/98, 15 February 2001.

189 (2005) 41 EHRR 8.

190 [2009] 49 EHRR 8.

191 See also *Karaduman v Turkey* (Unreported, App. No. 16278/90, Judgment of 3 May 2003), and *Mann Singh v France* (Unreported App. No. 24479/07, Judgment of 27 November 2008).

192 Unreported App. No. 24479/07, Judgment of 27 November 2008.

193 *Mann Singh v France* (Unreported App. No. 24479/07, Judgment of 27 November 2008).

inadmissible.[194] The Court in reaching this decision relied heavily on its previous judgment in *Dogru*, which concerned the position in France prior to the adoption of the 2004 law.

The use of the notion of 'respect' for the religious feelings or beliefs of others, along with the promotion of pluralism and tolerance, has been one of the principal justifications of the ECtHR's support for state restrictions on the wearing of religious symbols.[195] This is tied to the perception of the Court of the Muslim headscarf as a threat to social cohesion and as a practice that could place pressure on and even have a proselytizing effect on other students in the educational setting. Thus in the early case of *Karaduman v Turkey*[196] it was established that institutions of higher education may impose restrictions as to the place and manner of manifestation of the rites and symbols of religion 'with the aim of ensuring peaceful coexistence between students of various faiths and thus protecting public order and the beliefs of others'. In *Dahlab*, which concerned the teacher of a class of small children, the Court stressed among other matters the 'powerful external symbol' which her wearing a headscarf represented and expressed the view that wearing the Islamic headscarf could not easily be reconciled with the message of tolerance, respect for others and, above all, equality and non-discrimination that all teachers in a democratic society should convey to their pupils.[197] Building on this logic, in *Sahin* the Court stated that:

> where the values of pluralism, respect for the rights of others and, in particular, equality before the law of men and women are being taught and applied in practice, it is understandable that the relevant authorities should wish to preserve the secular nature of the institution concerned and so consider it contrary to such values to allow religious attire, including, as in the present case, the Islamic headscarf, to be worn.[198]

The ECtHR's narrow analysis in linking the headscarf to gender inequality without a detailed exploration of the issue, together with the characterization of the headscarf as a proselytizing symbol with the potential to disrupt social cohesion,

194 *Aktas v France* (App. No. 43563/08), *Bayrak v France* (App. No. 14308/08), *Gamaleddyn v France* (App. No. 18527/08), *Ghazal v France* (App. No. 29134/08), *J. Singh v France* (App. No. 25463/08) and *R. Singh v France* (App. No. 27561/08), declared inadmissible 30 June 2009. See '*Aktas v France* (43563/08: wearing of religious items in French schools)' (2009) 6 *EHRLR* 814.

195 The Court has stated: 'In democratic societies, in which several religions coexist within one and the same population, it may be necessary to place restrictions on freedom to manifest one's religion or belief in order to reconcile the interests of the various groups and ensure that everyone's beliefs are respected' (*Sahin*, citing *Kokkinakis*, cited above, at 18, para. 33). See Paul M. Taylor, note 113.

196 (Unreported, App. No. 16278/90, Judgment of 3 May 2003).

197 *Dahlab v Switzerland* (App. No. 42393/98), 15 February 2001.

198 *Sahin v Turkey* (2005) 41 EHRR 8, para. 116.

undermines the aim of the Court in these cases to promote equality, respect for all religions and tolerance.[199] It contrasts sharply with the Court's characterization of the Christian crucifix as a 'passive symbol' in *Lautsi*. Thus, in *Eweida and Others v United Kingdom*,[200] the Court found that the British courts had failed to correctly balance the right of a British Airways employee to manifest her religion, through the wearing of a small crucifix at work, with the interests of the company in maintaining a certain corporate image. Placing great weight on the finding that the wearing of the crucifix in these circumstances did not constitute 'any real encroachment on the interests of others',[201] the domestic authorities' failure to protect the applicant's Article 9 rights constituted a breach of the state's positive obligations under Article 9.

It should be recognized, however, that the Court's willingness to find that the wearing of the headscarf could disrupt social cohesion in *Sahin* and *Dahlab* was in part tied to the context in these cases – the ardent secular approaches followed in Turkey and Switzerland. However, the different outcomes in the joined applications in *Eweida* demonstrated the importance of the specific facts of the case to the balancing act required by Article 9. While, as outlined above, the court confirmed Ms Eweida's right to wear a small crucifix as a member of check-in staff at an airport, in contrast, in the case of another of the applicants, Ms Chaplin, it was found that the necessity to protect health and safety on a hospital ward could outweigh the right of a nurse to manifest her religion by wearing a small crucifix. Of the four applications considered by the Strasbourg court, there was one violation found (in Ms Eweida's case), while three of the applications were rejected (that of Ms Chaplin, together with those of Mr McFarlane and Ms Ladele, who had both who had complained specifically about sanctions taken against them by their employers as a result of their concerns about performing services which they considered to condone homosexual union). Given the wide margin of appreciation generally allowed to States in these cases, and the importance of the overall factual and legal context, the ECtHR would surely be hesitant to find that religious symbols of any kind would disrupt social cohesion in the Irish context, taking into account Ireland's different attitude to Switzerland and Turkey in relation to religion in public space.[202]

Overall, the willingness of the Court to insist that schools encourage and promote tolerance and pluralism in the context of religious instruction and education, as discussed above, has not therefore impacted on the approach to

199 For an exposition of the 'narrowness' of the Court's approach, see Cindy Skach, note 155, pp. 190–193.

200 Applications Nos 48420/10, 59842/10, 51671/10 and 36516/10 (Judgment of 15 January 2013).

201 Ibid., at para. 95.

202 This point is made in the context of the United Kingdom in the Case Comment in the European Human Rights Law Review, '*Aktas v France* (43563/08: wearing of religious items in French schools)' (2009) 6 *EHRLR* 814.

the wearing of religious dress in the way which might have been expected. The rationale for this (as observed above) appears to be that the Court interprets the wearing of the headscarf in particular as itself a potential threat to tolerance and pluralism. The Court envisages the protection of pluralism as necessitating the suppression of visible religious symbols, a theory which is inherently contestable especially given its disproportionate effect on members of religious minorities in European societies. The Court clearly envisages the preservation of a secular public sphere as the manner in which state neutrality towards religion may be maintained.[203] This forms part of the Court's seeming preference for secular over religious world-views,[204] which can be seen as an important element of the foundations of the Court's attitude to dealing with diversity. The upshot of this is that freedoms *from* religion (e.g. religious education) are generally favoured over freedoms *of* religion (e.g. wearing religious dress), the reverse position to that pertaining in Ireland. A specific integration paradigm emerges from the case law discussed in this section which stresses that expression of religious difference may disrupt harmonious (secular) societies. This stands in contrast to the Irish model which favours individual religious expression and appears to envisage that harmony will be achieved if diversity is maintained but one religion is not imposed on other religions or convictions. This is achieved by allowing each religion or conviction their own part of the public space. In practical terms the ECtHR's paradigm along with its willingness to leave states a wide margin of appreciation in these cases may provide legitimation for national integration programmes which require 'visible' immigrants to relinquish their religious or cultural identity in favour of an idealized national identity of the state in question.[205]

On the specific question of permissible restrictions on religious expression in schools, the ECHR as interpreted by the ECtHR provides a lower standard of protection for individuals than Irish constitutional law. If the Irish courts were – due to the lack of relevant Irish jurisprudence – to look to ECHR jurisprudence for guidance, the result could be a dilution of the strong protection for the free practice of religion. This dilution has already taken place (albeit in a very different constitutional setting) in the UK, where it has been argued that the traditional principles of tolerance present in the common law are being eroded through the replication of the inadequacies of the ECtHR judgments by domestic courts.[206]

---

203 See Andrew Geddis, 'You Can't Say God on the Radio: Freedom of Expression, Religious Advertising and the Broadcast Media After *Murphy v Ireland*' (2004) 2 *EHRLR* 181.

204 See Andrew Geddis, ibid.; and Tom Lewis, note 147.

205 See Elspeth Guild, 'Cultural and Social Identity: Immigrants and the Legal Expression of National Identity', in Elspeth Guild and Joanne Van Selm (eds), *International Migration and Security: Opportunities and Challenges* (Routledge, 2005).

206 See Mark Hill and Russell Sandbergh, note 183.

International Covenant on Civil and Political Rights

In terms of the ICCPR, religious dress is specifically dealt with in General Comment No. 22 as one of a broad range of acts encompassed in the freedom to manifest religion or belief, with the CCPR stating:

> The observance and practice of religion or belief may include not only ceremonial acts but also such customs as the observance of dietary regulations, the wearing of distinctive clothing or head-coverings, participation in rituals associated with certain stages of life, and the use of a particular language customarily spoken by a group.[207]

The CCPR has specifically criticized the French legislative ban on 'conspicuous' religious symbols in schools in its 2008 concluding observations on France's State Report, stating that 'respect for a public culture of *laïcité* would not seem to require forbidding wearing such common religious symbols', and recommending:

> The State party should re-examine Act No. 2004/228 of 15 March 2004 in light of the guarantees of article 18 of the Covenant concerning freedom of conscience and religion, including the right to manifest one's religion in public as well as private, as well as the guarantee of equality under article 26.[208]

In the few Optional Protocol decisions on the issue of religious dress the CCPR has taken a similar approach, placing emphasis on the importance of respecting external manifestations of religious belief. In *Raidon Hudoyberganova v Uzbekistan*[209] the HRC found that the author's exclusion from the university in which she worked because she wore a headscarf for religious reasons and refused to remove it constituted a violation of Article 18(2) of the Convention.[210] The primary reason for the decision was that the state had failed to provide a specific justification for the restriction, simply justifying the expulsion of the author from the university by her refusal to comply with the ban. The decision is therefore of limited value as a precedent as it is something of a 'default' decision in light of the lack of argument presented by Uzbekistan.[211] Ruth Wedgwood in her individual opinion drew attention to the 'obscure' nature of the facts in this case. While on

207 General Comment No. 22, 'The right to freedom of thought, conscience and religion' (30 July 2003), para. 4.

208 UN Doc CCPR/C/FRA/CO/4 (31 July 2008), p. 23.

209 *Raihon Hudoyberganova v Uzbekistan* (931/2000) CCPR/C/82/D/931/200 (2004).

210 Article 18(2) provides: 'No one shall be subject to coercion which would impair his freedom to have or to adopt a religion or belief of his choice'.

211 Dominic McGoldrick, note 148, p. 153. Sir Nigel Rodley in his individual opinion appended to the decision drew attention to the fact that the CCPR had been unable to taken into account the specifics of the context as it did not explain on what basis it was seeking to justify the restriction imposed on the author.

the one hand criticizing the ‘problematic’ approach of the European Court of Human Rights in *Sahin v Turkey*,[212] she did not exclude the possibility that some restrictions on dress in educational institutions may be permissible under Article 18(2), opining that ‘a state may be allowed to restrict forms of dress that directly interfere with effective pedagogy, and the covering of a student’s face would present a different set of facts’.[213] This mirrors the approach taken by the Irish Ministers for Integration and for Education in devising the guidelines for school principals discussed above.

In *Boodoo v Trinidad and Tobago*,[214] the CCPR followed a similar approach outside the educational setting, finding a violation of the Article 18 rights of a Muslim prisoner who had had (amongst other things) his beard forcibly removed. Again, the state had failed to provide a justification and the reasoning of the CCPR was therefore constrained. Despite the CCPR’s protective approach in these decisions, it allowed a restriction on the wearing of Sikh turbans on the basis of safety in *Singh Bhinder v Canada*.[215] In *Singh Bhinder*, the CCPR found that the enforcement of hard hat regulations in Canada, which meant that the author (a Sikh man) was obliged to remove his turban, did not violate Article 18 or Article 26 of the ICCPR.[216] The limitation could be justified under Article 18(3); or if the issue was approached from the perspective of Article 26 the legislation was reasonable and directed towards objective purposes that are compatible with the Covenant. Thus even the protection under the ICCPR is not absolute and may in individual cases be trumped by safety or other considerations.

Conclusion

Going back to the three assumptions which it was suggested at the beginning of this chapter might be made about the Irish framework for the protection of religious freedom reveals a paradox. The first of these assumptions, that religious belief is more strongly protected within the constitutional and legislative order than non-religious belief, is undoubtedly true, given the express protection in Article 44 and the approach taken in legislation and in the case law. Similarly, broadly speaking expressions of religious belief are strongly protected – even though this protection has not been tested outside the context of the religions which were

212 [2005] 41 EHRR 8.

213 *Raihon Hudoyberganova v Uzbekistan* (931/2000) CCPR/C/82/D/931/200 (2004). Wedgwood opinion, paras 3 and 4.

214 *Boodoo v Trinidad and Tobago* (721/1997) CCPR/A/57/40 (2002).

215 *Singh Bhinder v Canada* (208/1986) CCPR/C/37/D/208/1986 (1989).

216 This outcome reflects similar jurisprudence under the ECHR; in *X and Y v United Kingdom* [1985] 8 EHRR 235, for example, where it was found that an exemption from motorcycle helmet laws could not be made for Sikh men whose religion obliges them to wear helmets at all times.

formerly expressly recognized in Article 44 and a number of ways in which a court might justify permitting restrictions on the wearing of religious symbols have been outlined. In relation to the third assumption, that minority religions would be legally required to be placed on a level footing as the numerically dominant religions, it has been seen that this is not necessarily the case. The analysis in this chapter has shown that the equality between religions, which forms the cornerstone of the constitutional framework, is in practice more superficial than real. The denominational education system is characterized by a lack of meaningful choice of school for most parents and their children not of the Catholic religion. Thus religious freedom in Ireland is protected, but in the context of the hegemony, in practical terms, of the Catholic Church, which status quo is protected by the law. A process of gradual change may have opened up due to new efforts to open the system of patronage of schools to a wider range of denominations and ethos.

While the legal framework for the education system as a whole is open to criticism on the basis that it has not kept up with increased religious diversity and that it encourages the segregation of religions, the strength of the religious freedom guarantees in the Constitution provide significant protection for members of minority religions. With regard to the ECHR, while the position of the Strasbourg Court is not altogether clear, some elements of the education framework could be characterized as forming a process of 'indoctrination', rendering the education system incompatible with the ECHR. However, overall, the Irish Constitution appears to provide greater protection for the manifestation of religious belief than the ECHR. Similarly, while some aspects of the relationship between the state, education and religion are problematic with reference to the ICCPR, overall, the protection of religious freedom in Ireland has contributed to the acceptance of new religious practices brought by immigration, in line with the requirements of Article 18. Finally, the underlying assumptions upon which the ECtHR in particular seems to operate are questionable, with its contrasting approaches to Christian and Muslim religious symbols failing to reflect the Court's stated philosophy of promoting neutrality in respect of religion.[217]

From a broader viewpoint, this chapter has shown how, in a similar manner as was seen in the context of citizenship, debates on religion in the public sphere hold up a 'mirror' to the identity of European states.[218] From an integration perspective, it has been argued that the structure of the Irish education system could be interpreted as representing a 'segregation' approach whereby children belonging to different religious denominations are educated separately in accordance with the tenets of their own religion. This model contrasts with the largely secular vision of education employed by the European Court of Human Rights and gives strong protection to expression of religious belief and parental rights in relation to education. Some commentators have concluded that this approach has led to

217 See Oran Doyle, 'Egalitarianism, Religious Preferences and the Integrated Curriculum', note 78, p. 11.

218 Christian Joppke, note 150.

the easier integration of Muslim children, for example, than in other jurisdictions, as visible expressions of religious belief are not legally stigmatized in Irish law. In practice however, the system may enshrine an assimilation approach in which children from minority religions are compelled to attend Catholic schools through lack of choice and thus in an indirect manner are absorbed into the Catholic ethos of the school.

Chapter 9
Conclusions

Summary

This book has examined the interaction between integration and law. It has sought to identify legal elements of the concept of integration, not only in the national context in Ireland, the UK and France but also in the international and EU law settings. It has shown that these legal elements of integration are fragmented and disparate but nonetheless significant. Legal rules and frameworks, particularly in domains such as religious freedom, immigration and citizenship, are inevitably part of the integration process whether or not they are recognized as such by lawmakers, and whether they form part of a broader integration policy framework or not. For these reasons, along with the direct influence of law on the status, entitlements and opportunities of immigrants, the legal framework for integration must be acknowledged and identified as such. Above all, the book has argued for a more developed paradigm of 'integration and law' which emphasizes the extent of the law's influence on the integration process whilst recognizing the limits of this influence. It has also sought to underline the importance of not only the internal legal foundations of national integration policy but also the pervasive influence of international and EU law on national integration frameworks.

This concluding chapter will first briefly summarize some of the findings of the book relating to the evolution of legal frameworks for integration in EU Member States, drawing on the analysis presented through all the chapters. It will then discuss the major thematic conclusions to emerge from the book. The first of these highlights the indeterminacy of the concept of integration and the contribution which law can make in delineating the meaning of integration. The incoherency and contradictions at the heart of the international, EU and domestic frameworks for integration studied in the book are the second major theme. Finally, the complex intersection between the frameworks of international, EU and national law, and the impact which this has on the shape of integration at the national level in EU Member States, is a key finding. Taken together, these conclusions help to broaden our understanding of the nexus between integration and law.

Building on these conclusions, a two-pronged approach to the development of a human rights-based approach to integration is suggested. This involves the use of a broad-based definition of integration which takes into account both its functional and wider dimensions, and the development of a conceptual framework for policy development which recognizes and utilizes the extent of the interaction between integration and law. On this basis, a number of basic recommendations for the development of a holistic and human-rights based integration policy in EU Member States are outlined.

The Evolution of Legal Frameworks for Integration in EU Member States

Outside the well-documented trend towards including express references to integration in immigration and citizenship law, there is little recognition in the official integration discourse of EU Member States of the interaction of integration and legal processes. The term 'integration' is rarely used *per se* in the legal sphere. EU Member States tend to perceive integration as either solely concerning immigration law, or as a matter of social policy. Nonetheless, in spite of the dearth of express references to integration in domestic legislation and jurisprudence, this book has shown that a significant mutually influencing process takes place between integration and law. The domestic legal foundations of this mutually influencing process can be located in the 'public philosophy' embodied in the domestic constitutional order. Chapter 3 provided a brief illustration of how immigration law and legal status impact on integration opportunities through a brief analysis of aspects of the family reunification regime in Ireland, the UK and France. It was shown how legal categorization creates significant boundaries between migrants and the existing population and also between different groups of migrants. The entitlements and restrictions attached to legal status constitute tools of and barriers to integration.

Part III of the book illustrated some of the aspects of the mutually influencing process between integration and law by assessing the legal position in relation to a number of functional and wider integration perspectives at the national level. In terms of citizenship and the politics of identity, it was shown in Chapter 7 how national citizenship law retains a key symbolic and practical importance for migrants seeking full access to the social, economic and constitutional structures of society. The restrictive turns in citizenship law in Ireland, the UK and France have resulted from increased immigration and a desire to shore up the boundaries of citizenship. Recent developments in all three of the selected jurisdictions thus suggest a relatively closed conception of the national community, with implications for the form of integration measures taken in those states. Integration issues arising in the field of religion and education were discussed in Chapter 8, in which Ireland was used as a case study. It was demonstrated that the legal approach in Ireland to the historically divisive issue of religious difference has combined a strong protection for religious freedoms with the endorsement of a 'segregated' education system. This segregated and overwhelmingly Catholic education system can be interpreted as enshrining a *de facto* assimilation model, in light of the diversity of religious belief brought about by immigration. On the other hand, however, the constitutionally mandated general tolerance of religious symbols and dress in schools allows pupils from outside the well-established religions to maintain their religious identity, which may in turn promote a greater acceptance of religious difference in the broader society than has been evident in other European states.

The legal structures relating to these various aspects of integration have few connections and have developed on a standalone basis. No coherent conception of integration, legal or otherwise, emerges from this discussion of integration and law. It cannot be said that any of the Irish, UK or French examples clearly fits into one of the traditional integration models of exclusion, assimilation or multiculturalism, with elements of each model present in the legal framework. The analysis therefore supports the view that the traditional framework for viewing integration in terms of models does not accommodate the reality of integration as a patchwork of multidimensional frameworks, with integration frameworks comprising a 'mixed bag' rather than representing a model of assimilation or multiculturalism. Close examination of the legal elements of integration in the context of EU Member States suggests that such legal elements are determined not by reference to models or principles but by a complex mix of normative processes involving national, EU and international law, political decision-making and existing legal rules which were not adopted with integration concerns in mind. For these reasons, this book demonstrates that it is more useful, from an analytical perspective, to gain an understanding of the influences which shape national integration frameworks rather than attempt to place the results of the analysis in limited categories or conceptualize them as representing models. It is argued that external influences, in the form of EU law and international law, should be recognized as an increasingly important influence on the shape of national integration policies.

The Indeterminacy of Integration

The concept of integration is largely indeterminate. Competing narratives of integration emerge from international bodies dealing with migrants, governments, NGOs and academics. The disjuncture between the framing of integration, by NGOs and migrants' rights advocates on the one hand, and governments on the other hand, is a pervasive theme. Radically different interpretations of the meaning of integration persist such that the various actors involved in integration are often talking at cross-purposes. As pointed out above, the limitations of the traditional theoretical models of assimilation and multiculturalism have been exposed throughout this book, and these models do not capture the complexity of integration processes. Similarly, alternative models for understanding integration such as comparing 'mainstreaming' with targeted integration measures do not capture the full spectrum of integration concerns.

The problems caused by the indeterminacy of integration extend to the legal sphere as different conceptions of integration are developed in different legal settings. Part II of the book explored the normative development of the concept of integration by the UN treaty bodies and the European Court of Human Rights (ECtHR) and within the EU. Different visions of integration are pursued by national legislation, national courts, the ECtHR, at EU level and by the UN treaty bodies, with no clear indication of how the parallel normative development of integration within these different legal frameworks hangs together. In addition, within these different legal spheres the indeterminacy of the concept persists, and the difficulty inherent in attempting to identify a comprehensive legal understanding of integration within any of these legal frameworks is a defining characteristic of the normative development of integration – illustrating the problems attached to imposing a legal structure or analysis on an underlying concept which remains indeterminate.

In spite of these difficulties, legal elements of integration are crucial to gaining an understanding of integration; as such elements are concrete and (for the most part) binding on national decision-makers. Law therefore has an important contribution to make to the integration debate. Assessing the legal elements of integration provides an escape route from the circular question of what integration *means* and presents an opportunity to observe how it operates in practice. Looking at integration through the prism of law can move the debate in different directions to that engendered by sociological definitions of the term. In order to identify the legal elements of integration, this book has traced how integration is conceptualized in a legal context in national legislation and jurisprudence in addition to at EU level and by international law bodies. It has also sought to underline how law intervenes in the key integration issues as identified in Chapter 2. It has proposed a broad conceptual framework for the understanding of the nexus between integration and law which goes beyond looking at the express use of 'integration' as a legal concept in immigration and citizenship law.

Incoherency and Contradictions within the International, EU and Domestic Frameworks for Integration

The normative development of integration by the ECtHR and the UN treaty bodies suffers from a fundamental lack of coherence. In relation to the ECtHR, the relative weight of the various factors used to assess integration is uncertain and it was shown that the inconsistencies arising in the jurisprudence take away from the important work which the Strasbourg Court is doing in delineating the meaning of integration. The precise role of integration itself in the balancing exercise undertaken by the Court in the expulsion cases is not altogether clear, and the role (if any) of the concept of integration outside the context of the Article 8 immigration cases is unclear. As for the UN bodies, the limited development of a concept of integration is in the early stages and fragmented between the different bodies. It was seen that the framing of integration by the UN bodies is different depending on the context and purpose for which it is being examined, in addition to the way in which the State Reports and shadow reports frame integration. These incoherencies reflect the indeterminacy of integration discussed above.

In addition, national frameworks for integration are riven with contradictions and paradoxes. The Irish case study provides a classic illustration of these difficulties. At a basic level, the rhetoric of interculturalism and social inclusion contained in Irish integration policy is contradicted in almost every aspect of Irish law considered in this book. The constitutional recognition of the 'diversity of traditions and identities on the island of Ireland' contrasts with the changes to citizenship law which effectively restrict the *jus soli* principle to children of Irish citizens and long-term residents. One of the cornerstones of Irish constitutional law, the protection of the family, is undermined in the case of families containing non-citizens. In the case of religion, religious expression is strongly protected while inadequate provision for education in different religious ethos settings persists, meaning that an approach which celebrates freedom of religion and difference co-exists with a *de facto* assimilation model. The strong protection of freedom of religion under the Constitution and the interculturalism espoused in the policy document are bypassed in the case of Sikh men wishing to join An Garda Síochána and wear their traditional headgear. Integration policy is supposedly directed at all migrants (aside from asylum seekers), however in practice different types of migrants are granted completely divergent integration opportunities by law. These contradictions are mirrored in the case of France and the UK. The strict logic of equality insisted upon in France is undermined by the extensive socio-economic disadvantage and discrimination experienced by many migrants and their descendants, while in the UK the idea of developing 'Common Ground' masks an integration trajectory, already in place in citizenship law, focussed on requiring adherence to a constructed model of Britishness which bears little resemblance to the diverse experience of existing British citizens.

These contradictions mirror similar difficulties in the EU framework. It has been argued that there are multiple, conflicting conceptions of integration contained in the framework for integration at EU level. For example, integration is conceptualized as a mandatory condition in the Family Reunification Directive and the Long-Term Residents Directive but as a justification for the extension of valuable social and economic rights in the case of EU citizens. The CJEU is currently pushing back against Member States' attempts to maintain control over long-term residency and family reunification by emphasizing the 'fair and equal treatment' paradigm of integration at the root of these Directives. In the case of refugees, integration programmes are conceptualized as an entitlement whereas in the case of third-country nationals (TCNs) such programmes may be mandatory. It has been argued that these multiple, conflicting, interpretations of integration may be fatal to the potential of EU law and policy to provide a new frame of analysis for national policymakers in the field of integration, one which could open the door to a more cosmopolitan conception of citizenship and the extension of equal treatment to TCNs.

External Influences

Many studies on integration have emphasized the important influence which a country's history, ideology of nationhood, and associated citizenship regime, have on the process of immigrant integration. In the case of Ireland, this influence is clearest in relation to the strong protection of religious freedom which stems from the central place of religion in the constitutional order. The UK has traditionally followed a liberal multicultural approach while France has focussed on moulding good Republican citizens. In the context of citizenship law, the influence of differing historical experiences of immigration and emigration on the part of different states on the concept of the nation was illustrated. While acknowledging the role of national public philosophy, the book has demonstrated that the approach to integration at the national level is also now shaped by international and regional legal frameworks. This is explicit in some instances – Irish integration policy is expressly informed by EU integration policy, for example. In other instances the connections are not so readily identifiable. Multiple connections between the concept of integration, domestic legal frameworks and EU and international law have been identified. The influence of international and EU norms is an evolving phenomenon and certainly constitutes the most important change to both the policy and legal frameworks for integration at the national level in past decades.

EU law has the most significant influence on the national framework, and the intersection between EU law, immigration, citizenship and national law is well-documented. EU law requires the acceptance of EU migrants into the structures of the host state on almost the same terms as national citizens. EU migrants achieve integration through economic activity and residence rather than through proof of cultural adaptation. It was also seen that the *Rottmann* decision of the CJEU represents a significant incursion of EU law into national citizenship law, despite the close links of this field of law with national sovereignty. Aside from EU law, another area of law which has a formative influence on integration is international refugee law, as conducted in recent years through the medium of EU law. The law relating to family reunification – generally seen as a central integration issue – provides a good example of the processes involved. Family reunification for EU migrants, exercising their free movement rights, with EU (and TCN) family members is automatic. Family reunification for refugees is more difficult, but is governed by legal frameworks put in place in order to comply with obligations under the 1951 Refugee Convention as well as EU law. Both these groups – and particularly EU migrants – are in a better position than non-EU migrants seeking reunification, whose family members are subject to discretionary ministerial decision-making powers (Ireland), language tests (the UK and France) and integration tests (France). It can be seen that groups which are not subject to the influence of international or EU legal processes are thus left vulnerable and subject to the wide discretion of national decision-makers. Another clear example of the influence of external normative processes on the national framework for integration is the manner in which the development of the concept of integration by the ECtHR in the context of the protection of family and private life constitutes a direct limitation on how the state uses its power to expel non-citizens. The direct effect of this jurisprudence on legislation in the UK was examined. Finally, the implications of the international human rights framework, even in domains such as citizenship and religion, have been pointed to in the final two chapters.

The importance of these parallel, overlapping and intersecting legal frameworks means that the normative development of integration taking place within those frameworks contributes to a comprehensive understanding of integration and law. In addition, looking to the international and supranational elements of integration may provide an escape route from the politics of identity inherent in considering integration solely in the context of the nation state. Current literature has identified and analysed the trend towards the conceptualization of integration as a mandatory obligation in immigration and citizenship law. In order to refocus the debate in a more human rights-oriented direction, there is a need to move beyond this framework and to develop a wider conceptual framework for discussing integration and law. One way to refocus integration policy and practice on social inclusion and equalization of opportunity is to insist on the recognition of the concepts of integration under construction by EU and international actors. Highlighting the contributions of EU and international law helps to decouple integration and national identity which is at the root of the twin national trends towards perceiving integration as primarily linked to identity and enshrining integration conditions in immigration legislation. In particular, the approach of international human rights bodies to integration is by nature human rights-based in nature and focuses on non-discrimination and equality, providing the basis for an alternative approach to integration to those based on national public philosophy.

Nevertheless, looking to EU and international law presents its own difficulties. In the EU context, Chapter 6 identified serious inconsistencies and a fundamental lack of coherence in the EU framework for integration. In the international context, in the case of the UN Human Rights Committee and the UN Committee on Economic, Social and Cultural Rights in particular, express references to integration are sparse and under-developed. The European Court of Human Rights' concept of integration is also limited in the sense that it is employed mainly in the narrow context of challenges to the deportation decisions of national authorities. Overall, neither EU nor international law provides a comprehensive legal framework for integration. In addition, to reiterate the points made above, integration is being conceptualized and interpreted in these different legal arenas in a way which is often contradictory. There is no coherence between the concepts of integration being developed in the domestic, EU, Council of Europe and UN settings. Thus, while acknowledging the impact of external influences on integration is crucial, these external influences do not necessarily resolve the issues relating to the indeterminacy of integration and the paradoxes inherent in the connections between integration and law.

Reconfiguring the Integration Debate

There is a need to broaden the integration debate and place it in a human rights context. This book has suggested two main ways in which this could be done. The first way in which integration can be reoriented in this way is by using a broad definition of integration which recognizes the complexity of the issues involved. As elaborated in Chapter 2, the following definition was proposed:

> Integration is an on-going, multidimensional, two-way process between, on the one hand, migrants and, on the other hand, existing members of the receiving society along with the receiving state itself. This process involves a series of interlinked spheres, which, for the purposes of this book, will be characterized as forming part of "functional" or "wider" perspectives on integration. "Functional" aspects of integration include first of all protecting fundamental rights and secondly providing a legal status which acts as a gateway to the core policy areas of housing, health, education, social welfare and family reunification. "Wider" aspects of integration connect to these functional themes but place integration in its broader thematic context. These are aspects of integration with wider connections to the broader themes of national identity, responses to diversity in society, social policy and equality – most importantly, approaches to citizenship and the place of culture and religion in public space.

The second means of reconfiguring the integration debate is to develop a conceptual framework for the analysis of integration and law which takes into account the point that integration is the subject of normative processes beyond its use as a mandatory immigration obligation in the legal system of an increasing number of European states. This book has identified specific dimensions of the interaction of integration and law which could potentially and usefully influence the approach to integration in a number of concrete ways. The next section contains a number of basic recommendations for the development of the approach of EU Member States to integration.

Recommendations for the Development of National Integration Laws and Policies

1. Engagement with the paradigm of integration as the progressive realization of equality

The UN human rights treaty bodies are, in their concluding observations on State Reports, developing a nascent conception of integration which centres on a two-way, non-coercive process of the progressive realization of equality for migrants. This nascent integration paradigm, in conjunction with the philosophy of equality and non-discrimination generally enshrined in human rights law, could provide the foundation for domestic approaches to integration, rather than relying on theoretical models such as multiculturalism, assimilation or interculturalism.

It was shown in Chapter 3 that Ireland is a distinctive case study, due in part the relatively recent nature of the emergence of immigration and integration issues and the resulting absence of a preconceived frame of analysis for integration issues. Integration is a policy area in which Ireland has an opportunity to move beyond minimum standards set in the EU and international law arenas. Similarly, the UK has only just begun to develop a specific integration policy and has the chance to take into account various paradigms of integration in the further elaboration of this policy. In comparison to Ireland and the UK, the French framework contains a more entrenched ideological vision of integration, however it was seen that this paradigm is increasingly contested and criticized as failing to meet its objectives. There are, therefore, strong arguments in favour of the engagement of policymakers and legislators in each of these jurisdictions with the equality-based integration paradigm evolving in the context of the UN treaty monitoring bodies in developing their own public philosophies of integration. This argument is strengthened by the fact that there are already elements of the progressive realization of equality paradigm contained in each of the national frameworks studied. It was seen that the progressive realization of equality paradigm enshrined in international human rights law is reinforced through international refugee law, as required to be implemented in domestic legislation by the Qualification Directive, which requires State Parties to grant to refugees a range of integration-related rights on an incremental basis, reflecting their progressive integration in the host state. In relation to EU migrants, EU law on the free movement of persons illustrates the transformative potential of law in the sphere of integration. It provides the model for a concept of integration based on inclusion, equality and non-discrimination, without any focus on cultural integration. The model adopted in the case of refugees and EU migrants should be adopted across the legal categories in order to create a more coherent framework which reflects best practice on the EU and international levels.

2. Use of the CERD Committee's concept of integration as a guideline for policy development

Following on from the above point but more specifically, the CERD Committee is, through its concluding observations, in the process of constructing a relatively nuanced and detailed concept of integration. The observations of the CERD Committee on the integration policies and practices of states could be used as a guideline for integration policy in order to ensure compliance with best practice in international law, and to implement the progressive realization of equality paradigm.

3. Facilitation of integration and naturalization of refugees, pursuant to international law obligations

State Parties to the 1951 Refugee Convention are required under international refugee law to 'facilitate' the integration and naturalization of refugees. Article 34 provides two examples of ways in which access to naturalization could be facilitated, which could be used as a starting point for real engagement with these innovative provisions of international law. In addition, as noted above, EU Member States already provide integration-related rights to refugees which place them on a similar footing as citizens, pursuant to its international and EU obligations in this regard.

4. The jurisprudence of the European Court of Human Rights as a guide to indicators of integration

The limited context in which the concept of integration is being developed by the ECtHR, along with the problems associated with the one-sided nature of the concept as pointed out in Chapter 5, means that overall the normative concept of integration under construction by the Strasbourg Court is less useful in a general sense than that under construction within the universal treaty regime. However, the jurisprudence provides some helpful insights on the assessment of practical indicators of integration (including language, labour market integration and acquisition of citizenship, for example), which could be drawn on in conjunction with work taking place within the EU Framework on Integration (discussed below).

5. Cautious use of the EU Framework on Integration as an aid to policy development

Despite the deficiencies in the EU approach to integration, as identified in Chapter 6, EU policy on the integration of TCNs generally seeks to outline ways to realize the goal of integration as a two-way process of mutual accommodation by migrants and the host society. Provided that the output of the EU Framework on Integration is approached with a level of caution, it could provide policymakers with a useful practical tool for learning about the development of integration policy and practice.

6. Recognition of the importance of 'integration and law' as a starting point for the development of a holistic and human rights-based integration policy

National constitutional law and international human rights law provide a minimum core of fundamental rights which apply to migrants, and which may be closely related to integration. The effective protection of these rights may be instrumental to the integration process, for example in the case of the protection of family unity, educational rights and the right to social security and public relief benefits. On a more concrete level, in domestic law a myriad of legal rules (as interpreted by the courts) directly affect the integration prospects of migrants, including those rules relating to family reunification, long-term residence, citizenship, religion and education. The recognition of the impact of these legal elements of integration by policymakers, legislators and the courts is a crucial part of a comprehensive integration policy, and the key to improving migrants' outcomes in terms of participation, social mobility and integration in the labour market.

The Need for Clarity at the Regional and International Levels

The above recommendations relate to the development of integration at the national level. However, the analysis in this book has also identified many deficiencies in the approaches of the regional and international bodies, and thus also provides some lessons for the development of integration on the regional and international levels. The deficiencies identified include the fragmentation and vagueness in the work of the universal treaty regime, the haphazard nature of the development of the concept of integration in the ECtHR, and the fundamental lack of coherence in the EU approach. In respect of the UN human rights treaty bodies, while it is unlikely that the bodies will follow a more unified approach, the elaboration of a general recommendation of the CERD Committee on integration, or an updated general recommendation on the application of the treaty to non-citizens, touching on integration, would be a welcome development. This would help to draw together the threads of the evolving integration paradigm of the CERD Committee and lend normative weight to the nascent human-rights based approach to integration emerging within the universal treaty regime. At the regional level, a better indication of the status of the integration criterion within the balancing exercise carried out by the European Court would be a significant development. Within the EU, more critical analysis of the effects of policy-sharing and the value of indicators in the sphere of integration is needed. A comprehensive study of all aspects of the approaches of the various EU institutions to integration, and the broad impact of law on the integration of both EU and non-EU migrants should be undertaken as a starting point in order to try to resolve some of the conflicts inherent in the EU approach.

Concluding Remarks

While this book has highlighted the importance of recognizing the impact of law on integration, as integration is not itself a legal concept, there are limitations on the contribution of the law to integration in the absence of a clear policy framework. There is a need for more developed, nuanced and long-term approaches to integration than those in existence in EU Member States at present. This book has argued that a wide approach which recognizes the connections between the various themes, socio-economic dimensions and legal elements involved in integration, is merited. This wide approach should reflect the external influences on integration, going beyond simply looking to the EU Common Basic Principles as a benchmark for national integration policy. Beyond the policy sphere, legislators and courts should acknowledge that integration does not exclusively concern non-justiciable social issues but also encompasses core constitutional and other legal rights and issues. Overall, on the evidence of the European examples considered in this book, the key challenge for both policymakers and legislators is how to recognize the contribution of 'integration and law' to the development of integration policy, without equating this with the introduction of integration conditions and requirements in legislation. In particular, turning to international human rights law for a normative model of integration could help to 'reclaim' the concept of integration, which is increasingly being used by states as a means of legitimizing restrictive migration rules and as a way to reinforce fragile, constructed narratives of national identity.

Index

For Product Safety Concerns and Information please contact our EU representative GPSR@taylorandfrancis.com
Taylor & Francis Verlag GmbH, Kaufingerstraße 24, 80331 München, Germany

www.ingramcontent.com/pod-product-compliance
Ingram Content Group UK Ltd.
Pitfield, Milton Keynes, MK11 3LW, UK
UKHW022010180926
475701UK00003B/298

* 9 7 8 1 1 3 8 2 6 7 2 0 6 *